# MUTUAL EXPECTATIONS

# Law and Philosophy Library

## VOLUME 56

*The titles published in this series are listed at the end of this volume.*

# MUTUAL EXPECTATIONS

## A Conventionalist Theory of Law

by

### GOVERT DEN HARTOGH

*Department of Philosophy,*
*University of Amsterdam,*
*Amsterdam, The Netherlands*

KLUWER LAW INTERNATIONAL

THE HAGUE / LONDON / NEW YORK

A C.I.P. Catalogue record for this book is available from the Library of Congress.

ISBN 90-411-1796-2

Published by Kluwer Law International,
P.O. Box 85889, 2508 CN The Hague, The Netherlands.

Sold and distributed in North, Central and South America
by Kluwer Law International,
101 Philip Drive, Norwell, MA 02061, U.S.A.
kluwerlaw@wkap.com

In all other countries, sold and distributed
by Kluwer Law International, Distribution Centre,
P.O. Box 322, 3300 AH Dordrecht, The Netherlands.

*Printed on acid-free paper*

# TABLE OF CONTENTS

# PREFACE

This book reconsiders some of the perennial themes in the philosophy of law: the nature of legal authority, the conditions under which it may rightfully claim obedience to its prescriptions to be a duty, the role of coercion in the way law influences the behaviour of those subject to it, the essential characteristics of legal reasoning, and the extent to which it possibly or even necessarily depends on moral argument. These themes are considered from a specific perspective, and I hope to show that taking this perspective provides new answers to the old questions - more satisfactory, even if hardly definitive answers.

To introduce the perspective, I take my starting point in what I believe to be the most powerful theory of law developed in the last century: the institutional theory of law, as it has been classically proposed by Herbert Hart in *The Concept of Law*, and refined afterwards by others, notably Neil MacCormick. According to this theory, law is in the final analysis a matter of social rules. However, Hart's analysis of what it means for a social rule to exist, subtle though it is, shows an important deficiency, which has been pointed out by MacCormick and others, and has been recognized by Hart in the 1994 Postscript to his *magnum opus*. The analysis does not take into account that the rule can only exist if the beliefs and attitudes of the people following it "have a reference to each other", as Hume put it.

What this means can be explained by looking at a theory of law that is often supposed to be an *alternative* to the institutional theory, because it takes the concept of a reason for action, rather than the concept of a rule, as its basic explanatory concept. The most prominent proponent of this approach is Joseph Raz, but his views have been largely embraced by Hart in his later work. However, Hart did not see this approach as an alternative to his original view, but rather as a complement to it. And rightly so, provided it is recognized that the reasons people should have, or should believe to have for following a rule, criticizing deviations of it etc., are of a specific kind. I will call reasons of this kind *interdependent* ones: reasons that only apply to someone, if they are properly recognized, and known to be recognized by others to apply to them as well. Neither Hart nor Raz ever fully appreciated this specific characteristic of the relevant reasons, though both occasionally came close to doing so. If it is appreciated, the lacuna in Hart's original account of social rules can be filled.

My proposal is to understand these rules as *conventions*. The nature of a convention has first been thoroughly analysed by David Lewis in his equally classic book *Convention*, though of course he relies on important work by predecessors, including David Hume and Thomas Schelling. Lewis situates conventions in the context of so-called coordination problems: people can only achieve their most desired outcome by mutually adjusting their actions, but they can do so in a number of equivalent ways. A convention picks out one of these equivalent ways, by establishing a pattern of nested mutual expectations: we expect each other to act in this particular way, know each other to expect this, know each other to know this etc.

Though there is a reference to coordination problems in Raz' *The Authority of Law*, the first authors to propose that legal rules must be understood as Lewis conventions were Chaim Gans and Gerald Postema in papers dating back to 1981-1982. The most thorough elaboration of the proposal until now was presented by Eerik Lagerspetz in *The Opposite Mirrors*. But although many people have acknowledged that the proposal seems promising because of the way it fills the lacuna in the institutional theory, it has not been widely accepted. There are several interconnected reasons why it does not really seem to get off the ground, reasons most forcefully put forward by Leslie Green in his criticism of conventionalist theories of law. Lewis understands his conventions as "solutions" to pure coordination problems. This may be adequate for understanding linguistic conventions, but it is obvious that only a small part of legal norms can be interpreted in this way. Both Postema and Lagerspetz have argued that the account can be extended to other "games", and this argument finds support in the most important contribution to the conventionalist theory of social rules generally since Lewis, developed by Robert Sugden in *The Economics of Rights, Cooperation and Welfare*. But, as I will show more extensively in chapter One, the extensions are not wide enough to cover the actual range of the law. Nor do they cover it in the right way, for they also fail to explain how the law can sometimes generate, or at least claim or pretend to generate, *obligations* to compliance.

My first task is to solve this problem in conventionalism. My strategy will be to take 'interdependent reasons' as the basic concept; in particular I will argue for the existence of interdependent *moral* reasons. As a result, the concept of "convention" will tend to become a purely technical one, even more so than it was in Lewis. On Lewis' understanding, convention is a choice between equivalent solutions to coordination problems, and hence retains *arbitrariness* as one of its basic connotations. Within the theory I will present, this connotation is no longer essential. (In this theory, coordination problems are the essential context for the exercise of legal *authority*, not for the existence of legal conventions as such.) I realize that as a result, it may be misleading to continue to speak of a "conventionalist" theory. It sometimes worries me to recall the comparable way in which John Locke's use of the notion of "consent" has been dramatically misleading, I would say, because the primary connotation he had in mind was not voluntariness, but "artificiality" as Hume would call it, i.e. conventionality. Indeed, in my doctoral dissertation of 1985 I refrained from using the concept of "convention" in this extended way. But I have found that this is unsatisfactory as well because I need a term for "social rules" which suggests the reference to interdependent reasons. And, after all, my concept of convention, is still a fully recognizable descendant of the concept Hume and Lewis used.

The explanation of the concept of convention in terms of interdependent reasons is provided in the first chapters. I hope the plausibility of this account will be enhanced by the following chapters, in which I discuss those perennial problems of legal philosophy and try to show that conventionalism has the resources to provide new insights, new arguments, or at least a new awareness of the force of old ones. Conventionalism in legal theory is usually associated with positivism; occasionally the concepts are even used interchangeably. However, the position I defend in this book is a moderate form of antipositivism. Leslie Green once said to me: "You must be the only antipositivistic conventicnalist in the world". I do not know whether this is true: surely Lon Fuller paved the way and I am not sure how to classify Gerald Postema at present. But perhaps it is true enough to justify my going over some very well-trodden terrain again. The basic ambition is to find a point of view from which ideas usually held to be mutually hostile - public reason and convention, game theory and virtue ethics, perhaps even discourse ethics and autopoiesis - can be integrated in a natural, unconstrained, non-eclectic way.

By situating my project in a tradition of legal theorizing I have also acknowledged a number of my intellectual debts. From all the persons I mentioned I learned most by reading their books, but from most of them I learned in discussion and conversation as well. Like almost anyone working in this area today, I learned immensely from struggling to find the intuitively felt inner coherence of Joseph Raz' work on legal, moral and political philosophy, though I am sure my attempts have not been fully successful. Discovering - at the IVR conference in Edinburgh in 1989 - in Eerik Lagerspetz' mind the opposite mirror of my own was a thoroughly enjoyable experience, especially because his mirror is always somewhat clearer than mine. Finding out that my old friend from an unforgettable year spent at Oxford, Jerry Postema, had been thinking along similar lines and struggling with similar problems, was equally stimulating, and his comments in December 1996 on the manuscript in the highly unorganized shape it had at the time, largely gave me the encouragement I needed to go on with the project. I found another congenial mind in Chaim Gans, who also provided very helpful comments on the chapters on political obligation.

Readers will probably be prone to detect some Dworkinian influences, especially in the chapters on legal argument. They are right to some extent. But these influences happened to reinforce the older and more formative influence of the views of the great Dutch legal scholar Paul Scholten on "finding the law". The chapter is really nothing but a reinterpretation in conventionalist terms of a slightly updated version of these views. Bob Brouwer's careful comments on an earlier draft of these chapters prevented me from making a number of legal mistakes, though I will have managed to make new ones afterwards.

Except for some material from my doctoral dissertation, the first still recognizable parts of the present text were written during the academic year 1987-1988, which I spent as a fellow in the stimulating environment of the Netherlands Institute for Advanced Studies in Wassenaar. During the year 2000-2001, NIAS again gave me the opportunity to devote some concentrated effort on the project, this time to the rather dull work involved in completing it. The most productive period in the intervening years was the time I spent as a guest of the Department of Philosophy at the University of Toronto, in the first three months of 1997. I profited from the lively intellectual climate of the department, the weekly meetings of the legal theory group, and the accessibility of the Robarts Library.

As so often before, Frans van Zetten carefully corrected the mistakes in my English without alienating me from my own style of writing. Because of his own work on social rules, no-one could be in a better position to do this job. Ria Beentjes and

Laura Walburg together succeeded in mastering the art of the camera-ready production of a manuscript.

During all the years I intermittently worked on the book, I had the invaluable opportunity to test my ideas in almost daily discussions with talented Ph.D. students who were working on related themes themselves: Peter Rijpkema, Gijs van Donselaar, Bruno Verbeek, Jurriaan de Haan, Dorota Mokrosinska and Jelle de Boer. Peter, Gijs and Bruno also helped me with written comments on several chapters. About several ideas in the book, I am not really sure from whose mind they originated. Every book is a cooperative achievement.

Wassenaar
June 2001

# ACKNOWLEDGEMENTS

Parts of the following publications have been incorporated into the present text, mostly in revised form:

- *Wederkerige Verwachtingen: Konventie, Norm, Verplichting*, doctoral dissertation, Amsterdam 1985.
- Politieke Verplichting: Gronden en Grenzen. *Algemeen Nederlands Tijdschrift voor Wijsbegeerte* 80 (1988), 231-258.
- Authority and the Balance of Reasons. In: Robert Alexy und Ralf Dreier, Hrsg. *Rechtssystem und Praktische Vernunft*, Band I, Proceedings 15th World Congress IVR, Göttingen 1991, *ARSP-Beiheft* 51, Franz Steiner Verlag, Stuttgart 1993, 136-144.
- Rehabilitating Legal Conventionalism. A Critical Review of: Eerik Lagerspetz, A Conventionalist Theory of Institutions. *Law and Philosophy* 12 (1993), 233-247.
- Coherence as a Legal Virtue: a Conventionalist View. In: P.W. Brouwer e.a. red., *Coherence and Conflict in Law*, Proceedings of the 3rd Benelux-Scandinavian Symposium in Legal Theory, Kluwer/Tjeenk Willink 1992, 227-254.
- Rechts- en Humorpositivisme. *Rechtsfilosofie en Rechtstheorie* 22 (1993-4), 51-3.
- A Conventionalist Theory of Obligation. *Rechtsfilosofie & Rechtstheorie* 24 (1995), 8-25.
- Soziale und Kritische Moral, oder "Wie sich 'Protestantismus' in der Moralphilosophie und der Moralerziehung vermeiden läszt". In: Karl Golser, Robert Heeger Hrsg., *Moralerziehung im neuen Europa*, Verlag A. Weger, Brixen 1996, 53-73.
- A Conventionalist Theory of Obligation. *Law and Philosophy* 17 (1998), 351-376.
- Is Gewoonte een Rechtsbron? In: P.W. Brouwer, M.M. Henket, A.M. Hol, H. Kloosterhuis, red. *Drie Dimensies van het Recht*, Boom Juridische Uitgevers, Den Haag 1999, 77-92.
- General and Particular Considerations in Applied Ethics. In: Albert W. Musschenga, Wim J. van der Steen, eds. *Reasoning in Ethics and Law: Theory, Principle and Judgement*. Ashgate, Aldershot 1999, 19-47.

# CHAPTER 1

## A CONVENTIONALIST THEORY OF SOCIAL RULES AND OBLIGATIONS

### 1.1. Rules, Reasons, Values, Virtues

All human interaction is guided and constrained by social rules. Children in school classes, patients and nurses in hospitals, directors participating in board meetings, even visitors to a party, generally know what they are supposed to do and not to do, and generally act accordingly, largely without effort. It is at least initially plausible to suggest that law is a body of social rules, whatever else it is.

But what exactly is a social rule? To approach this question, let me note some typical characteristics of interaction guided by social rules, without claiming that any of them is either a necessary or a sufficient condition.

Most basically, following a social rule is a form of intentional behaviour for which the agents can be held to be responsible, even if they have internalized it to the point where it becomes a matter of routine. If following a rule is a form of intentional action, it should be possible to explain it in terms of the reasons the agents have for conformity.

In the second place, social rules seem to be related to the *point* of the interaction. They usually make it easier for participants to achieve a common or shared aim: children being taught, patients being cured or cared for, boards making good decisions, or at least *a* decision, visitors to the party feeling at ease, or confirming their self-image of sophisticated people. Social rules facilitate the achievement of these aims by adjusting people's actions to each other. At the very least, they enable people to use their energy and resources efficiently, and not for managing mutual embarrassment. Without those rules, things would go worse than they do now, at least from the point of view of the people following the rules.[1]

In the third place, if someone violates the rule, the others will usually respond by feeling disapproval and expressing such feelings in various ways, ranging from subtle body language to molestation and imprisonment. What is conveyed by these expressions is not only that the person is doing or omitting something without good reason. Rule-conforming behaviour is something which the person "owes" the others, which they have a "right" to expect, though these expressions need not always have strong moral connotations. They think less of him for disrespecting their rights; if his behaviour cannot be justified or excused, it reflects badly on his person. He will be condemned, not so much as irrational but rather as rude or ruthless, sly or perfidious.

To summarize: interaction guided by social rules is a form of intentional behaviour, by which people coordinate their actions in order to enable themselves to

---

[1] I do not deny that following rules often has suboptimal results, see ch. 2.10.

achieve shared aims; conformity and non-conformity are interpreted in terms of personal character. If we are to understand what it means to follow a social rule, we should be able to account for those features. "Duties" should be understood by reference to "reasons", "values" and "virtues".

How are these elements related to each other? In particular, how can we understand the agents' reasons in terms of the relevant values or virtues or both? That is the question I want to consider in this introductory chapter.

## 1.2. Hart on Social Rules

The concept of a rule or norm – I will use the concepts interchangeably – can be used on either of two levels. Firstly, on the propositional level. The rule describes a possible state of affairs, but it has a peculiar "direction of fit": if its conditions of application are realized but the world fails to match the rule, this is not to be considered a defect in the rule, but rather in the world.[2] Things having this direction of fit (let us call them "blueprints") can be divided into two classes. Having compared the world to a blueprint of the first class ("values", "the good"), one judges to what extent the blueprint is realized, on a continuous scale from zero to complete realization. But in the case of blueprints of the second class ("prescriptions", "the right"), the decision one has to make is a binary one: either the prescription is realized or it is not. Of course a prescription can be vague, in which case it is, within a certain range, difficult or even impossible to decide whether it is realized or not. But the point is that the decision which it is difficult or impossible to make within this grey zone is the binary one. Prescriptions tend, directly or indirectly, to refer to actions, more so than values which refer to other states of affairs as well. A prescription may be particular, picking out a token action. Or it may be universal, describing certain conditions in general terms, and stating that whenever these are satisfied, a specific description should be satisfied as well. A rule is a universal prescription, governing acts.[3]

A rule, however, is not only an element in Popper's third world, but also in his second: it is a psychological and/or social reality. For it is used by people to guide their behaviour. It may be used in this way by one person, or by a number of (in this respect) unrelated persons. In that case, it is a private rule. Such rules may be considered as standard *plans*, which have the function of saving deliberation costs in recurrent situations requiring action.[4] A social rule, on the other hand, is used by a number of people for guiding their behaviour *together*. It is this "together" which causes problems of explanation.

One of the more ephemeral aspects of Wittgenstein's influence on philosophy was the astonishing popularity of the notion of a rule during the sixties. It was

---

[2] Anscombe 1957, 4, 56; Kenny 1963, 216-7; Searle 1983, 7-8.

[3] "A function which can take an indefinite variety of decision-types as inputs and deliver in each case one option – or set of options – as output..." Pettit 1990, 3. I do not want to suggest that we can identify the function without reference to the psychological and/or social reality of the rule being followed.

[4] Bratman 1987.

considered a decisive step in the direction of a better understanding of all kinds of human practices – playing games, promising, speaking a language generally, psychoanalysis, law, and even human action as such – to view the subject under investigation as rule-governed behaviour.[5] The crucial features of such conduct were usually considered to be the following. Firstly, the meaning of present action is explained in terms of options and directives for future conduct, just as the meaning of a chess move can be identified with the way it determines the possibilities for the rest of the game. Secondly, rules are reference points for a group of people interacting with one another. Both features were thought to be connected: the right continuation is the one which the group considers right.[6] Now it may be true that in deciding which move is required by the rule, we have no final criterion but the shared judgment of a group of people. Following a private rule thus turns into a *public* practice, but not yet into a *social* one.

This rule addiction culminated in the discovery of so-called institutional facts.[7] That Mr. Kok is the prime minister of the Netherlands, that AC Milano won the Champion's Trophy, or that I was fined yesterday for a parking offence, are surely facts, but they are only facts in virtue of the existence of a social rule. An intelligent being from another planet would not be able to observe these facts. If one tries to describe such a fact without reference to the rule, the description will only present the (relatively) brute fact; if the rule is then applied, this fact is found to have an institutional meaning. In this way, it seemed, we might even account for the binding force of promises without having to face the problems of either the volitional or the reliance theory.[8] If you solemnly utter the words: "I herewith promise to pay you, Jones, the sum of fifty guineas" (or, to give an even more brute description, if you produce the corresponding sounds), you undertake an obligation to pay Jones the sum of fifty guineas, for a (social or private?) rule exists providing that, whenever you utter these words, you undertake the obligation.[9] The problem is, of course, that the theory fails to explain what kind of fact the existence of a rule is supposed to be. As soon as we try to understand this, we may have to bring in either the concept of reliance or the concept of volitional commitment, which leads us back to the problems of the original theories.

---

[5] E.g. on speech acts: Searle 1969; Tugendhat 1976, lectures 14 and 15; Wunderlich 1978; on psychoanalysis: Mooij 1982; on law: Hart 1961; on action: Melden 1956; Winch 1958, 52. For the limitations of this approach, see Coyne 1981.

[6] Winch 1958, 24-33, interpreting Wittgenstein's "private language" argument.

[7] Anscombe 1958; Rawls 1955; Searle 1969, 50-4.

[8] According to the volitional theory, the will somehow binds itself, cf. Raz 1972, Robins 1984. This is a rather mysterious act. See ch. 2.8 at note 61. According to the reliance theory, a promise binds in virtue of the fact that it would be wrong to let down the person relying on it, cf. MacCormick 1972, Atiyah 1981, MacMahon 1989. But it seems she rather relies on it in virtue of the fact that it binds. See Den Hartogh 1998.

[9] "Some philosophers ask, 'How can making a promise create an obligation?' A similar question would be, 'How can scoring a touchdown create six points?' As they stand both questions can only be answered by citing a rule...", Searle 1969, 35, cf. Searle 1964; Hart 1961, 42.

Similar comments can be made about other institutional accounts, for instance about the so-called institutional theory of law.[10] I do not want to deny that this theory is true; indeed, I am in complete agreement with its basic thesis that legal facts are facts in virtue of the existence of legal rules. But I find the thesis completely uninformative as long as I have not been told what kind of thing a legal rule is. In the meantime, the theory strikes me as a marvellous example of explaining *obscurum per obscurius*.

It is true, however, that almost from the beginning attempts have been made, within this tradition, to explain what it means for a rule to exist. Peter Winch made a start in *The Idea of a Social Science* (1958), and the most thorough analysis has been presented by Herbert Hart in *The Concept of Law* (1961). The basic notion in Hart's theory of law is that of a secondary rule. In his view, law has developed from a more primitive system of social rules, by the introduction of "rules about rules", rules about identifying rules of the system, about making and changing them, and about establishing authoritatively what they require. His first task, therefore, is to tell us more about this more primitive system. That is how he comes up against the question what it means for a social rule to exist.

This analysis is of central importance to my concerns. For the points about legal philosophy which I wish to make in this book can be seen as so many amendments to Hart's legal theory. And these amendments follow from the need to remedy the defects of Hart's analysis of social rules.

The following inventory of conditions which determine whether a rule counts within a particular community can be elicited from the writings of Winch and Hart.[11]
(1)   Some order or regularity in the behaviour of a number of people (in any case more than one) must be ascertainable.

I begin with this condition in order to develop the contrast between rule and regularity in the subsequent ones.
(2a) Deviant or irregular behaviour occurs.
(2b) Regular conduct can be learned.

These two features characterize habitual behaviour. They are to some extent related; if so desired, habitual behaviour can be changed, given the necessary exercise and effort. (Hereditary behaviour can also sometimes be changed: breathing cannot, but thumb-sucking certainly can).

However, these conditions do not as yet suffice: for example, someone constantly using the same catch-phrase is not usually following a rule. The next characteristics should permit us to distinguish between rules and habits, the latter being merely a product of rote learning.

(3a) Those involved are capable of discerning deviant behaviour.[12]

---

[10] MacCormick & Weinberger 1986, Ruiter 1993, Morton 1998. Recently, some of these authors have moved in the direction of a conventionalist analysis of social norms, cf. e.g. MacCormick 1998. Interestingly, MacCormick has also proposed one of the most sophisticated versions of the reliance theory of promising: MacCormick 1972.

[11] Winch 1958, 28-33, 57-65; Hart 1961, 9-11, 54-56, 86-88, 96, 99-101. Cf. also the inventories by Duintjer 1977, 26-40, and Gumb 1972, 37-53.

(3b) In general, a negative attitude is adopted toward observed deviant behaviour; this attitude is expressed either verbally or non-verbally. (Positive attitudes to conforming behaviour are possible but not necessary.) There is, therefore, not only an overall convergence of behaviour, but also of judgment. People who thus harmonize in conduct and judgment, together make up the core of the community in which the rule holds.

(3c) Those who deviate, tend in general to react to negative responses by revising their behaviour (or to justify or excuse it, etc.). The required negative response need not come from others; social correction and spontaneous self-correction coexist side by side. Hence it is not necessarily the negative attitude of someone else which gives the sinner reason for changing course, it may (also) be deviance itself.

(3d) Just as awareness of transgression provides the transgressor with reason for self-criticism, so too it provides others with a reason for criticism. Their 'negative attitude" is, therefore, not only a usual and hence predictable reaction, it is also considered justified in their own eyes. (3c and 3d are Hart's particular contribution.)

In short, a habit is a convergence in behaviour caused by previously converging behaviour. It is like a tidal wave: water runs into the nooks and crannies caused by a former flood. By contrast, a rule is a pattern of conforming ways, which repeatedly sanctions those involved to pursue their conformity. It is a deliberate unanimity of conduct and judgment. We are not conditioned, we intentionally allow ourselves to be led.

If we compare this account with my phenomenological exercise in section 1, we recognize two elements: "reason" (3d) and "virtue" (3b). The element "value" is lacking, and the relations between the elements are not extensively explored. (Though (3c) makes a very important point which we will return to.) In particular, Hart carefully refrains from saying anything about the possible reasons agents may have for joining the queue. He only remarks that the reasons might be of any kind: "fear, inertia, admiration of tradition, long-sighted calculation of selfish interests as well as recognition of moral obligation".[13] He has his reasons for not wanting to be more specific. But the result is an important lacuna in his account which has been pointed out by Warnock.[14] Situations can develop which meet every proviso of the analysis proposed by Winch and Hart, while nevertheless there is absolutely no question of the existence of a social rule. Take the following case.

---

[12] For Winch 1958, 57ff this is the essential difference between rules and habits.

[13] Hart 1958, 93; see ch. 8.2, note 12.

[14] Warnock 1971, 45-47 (with an equally parochial example: going out without an umbrella in British climate conditions), cf. Dworkin 1986, 145; Postema 1987d, 99; Marmor 1998, 511-512; Shapiro 1998, 33-35. Hart actually recognizes the interdependent character of the relevant reasons at several places, cf. Hart 1961, 55, 112-113 (the rule of recognition has to be regarded by the courts "as a public, common standard of judicial decision, and not as something which each judge merely obeys for his part only"). But in Hart 1961 he did not systematically take it into account, as he acknowledges in his reply to Dworkin, Hart 1994, 255-256, cf. Green 1996.

Usually, groceries which easily spoil, are kept cool. Someone who keeps old newspapers inside his fridge, while leaving meat and milk outside it, deviates from this "norm", thereby leaving himself open to negative criticism. But if we ask for further specification of the criticism, we will reject an answer stating that it happens to be the rule that meat and milk are placed in the fridge; we will reject it not merely as insufficient, but rather as irrelevant. It is simply stupid to allow food and drink to go bad unnecessarily.

What is lacking in such counter-examples is that the actions of people following a rule have "a reference to each other".[15] It is insufficient simply to expect the same performances from everybody and to consider deviance a ground for criticism. After all, the reasons for expected conduct might count individually for everyone, irrespective of the doings of others. Talk of a rule is then out of the question. What is required for a social rule to be a social rule, is that each member of the group has reason to maintain a certain regular pattern in his conduct *if and only if* others (or enough of the others) do the same, and for the same reason. That's why, if asked for a reason to do as the rule requires, we are inclined to answer "because it is the rule", unenlightening as this reply may be. Everyone is required to take his or her place in a desired pattern of *interconnected* actions.[16]

## 1.3. Interdependent Reasons and Game Theory

So it appears that we should concentrate our attention on this idea of the *interdependence of reasons*. A rule exists when people intend to act in a certain way, only because they believe the others to intend to act in the same way as well. Our next question is: in what sorts of situations are such interdependent intentions intelligible? Here our phenomenological thumbnail sketch points the way: we must look for situations in which people's actions have to be coordinated in view of some desirable outcome. But if that is the case, the situations we are looking for are "games" in the sense of the theory of games: situations in which the outcome for each of the "players" depends on the choices made, not only by himself, but also by the others.

At this point David Lewis made intellectual history by showing how, in one particular situation of interdependent outcomes – the so-called Coordination game – the participants could have reason to make their choices in such a way that a pattern of interdependent choices emerges: a convention. My leading question will be whether this type of analysis can be extended to other "games", for instance the so-called Prisoner's Dilemma. As we will see, the problem here is this: in a Coordination game, people have reason to make their own choice fit into the pattern of interdependent decisions; in

---

[15] Hume, *Treatise*, III.ii.2.

[16] MacCormick 1981, 41, proposes to complement Hart's conception of social rules in this sense. Hart 1982, ch. 10, rather follows Raz in analysing law not in terms of social rules, but of exclusionary (peremptory) reasons to follow authoritative instructions. This conception even more clearly fails to account for the interdependence of reasons. It is also inconsistent with his own account of the defeasibility of legal norms, as I argue in ch. 11, cf. Chapman 1998b.

Prisoner's Dilemma games and others, however, they seem to have reason rather to *deviate* from the pattern – which makes it difficult to understand how the pattern can either emerge at all, or be sustained once it has emerged. At that point we will have to bring in the other element mentioned in section 1, the element of virtue.

But let me first explain what I think I am committed to by the use of this analytical apparatus, for this often gives rise to misunderstanding. In the first place, I am committed to assume intentional agency. A person's actions can normally be understood by the way in which they fit into the structure of his desires, beliefs, and intentions.[17] Needless to say, this is only a default assumption: I do not want to deny the occurrence of utterly irrational behaviour. In the second place, I am committed to ontological (rather than methodological) individualism: beliefs, desires and intentions belong to individual minds; there is no such thing as a collective mind. Social reality is to be understood by the way in which the beliefs, desires and intentions of individuals *depend upon* each other.[18] Hence we have not really explained people's behaviour by showing that it is governed by a rule; we should go on to explain why the rule is followed. In the third place, I am committed to an assumption about people's desires: that at least many of them have a maximizing structure. If a person has wants or desires, she can order states of affairs according to the extent to which they fulfil her wants; she has a use for the relational concepts 'better than' and 'as good as'. Decision theorists tend to say that she has a preference ordering; the concept of an 'ordering' implying at least that these relations are reflexive, transitive and continuous. I insist, however, that the concept of a preference ordering tells us almost nothing about the nature or content of these desires; it merely specifies some elementary structural characteristics, in particular the fact that, within the general class of "blueprints", these contents have the nature of values rather than prescriptions. That is why I said they had a maximizing structure.[19] Apart from this, nothing is specified: the desires may be egoistic, altruistic, or impersonal, they may be outcome-oriented or action-oriented, agent-neutral or agent-relative, forward-looking or backward-looking, and so on. Nor does decision theory, in introducing the concept of a preference ordering, say anything about the relation between desire and goodness: whether things are good because they are desired, or desired because they are good. It merely assumes that *quidquid appetitur, appetitur sub specie boni* (whatever is desired, is desired as good), it explains the maximizing structure of the good, and articulates formal conditions for the coherence of judgments in which those basic relational concepts are used: the axioms of decision theory.[20]

---

[17] Davidson 1980, essay 12; Dennett 1978, essays 1, 12, 14; Elster 1979, 153-156. I assume that intentions cannot be reduced to beliefs and desires, cf. Bratman 1987, ch. 2.

[18] This type of individualism should not be confused with "atomism", if this is taken to mean what Nozick (1977), 1997 refers to as Crusoe-theory: the explanation only refers to beliefs, desires and intentions a person could have if he were the only one to have such mental states. This absurd theory is, of course, inconsistent with the idea of the interdependence of reasons, and with strategic concepts generally. See Pettit 1993, chs. 3-4, for a persuasive argument in favour of individualism and holism, against collectivism and atomism.

[19] Broome 1991, ch. 1; Gauthier 1986, ch. 2.

[20] See any introduction, e.g. Kreps 1990; for dynamic decision theory McClennen 1990, in particular ch. 7. Some of these axioms are controversial, e.g. the separability or modularity axiom, see ch. 2.8.

If desires have a maximizing structure (we want to realize more of the good rather than less), and if the basic ordering relations satisfy some conditions of coherence, it is possible to construct a utility scale for each agent. Again, by introducing the concept of 'utility', whatever its historical connotations, nothing is specified about the contents of desire or the nature of the good. Goodness, and the satisfaction of the correlated type of desire, can be measured on a continuous scale; this scale measures "utilities".[21] Though it may be hard to believe, decision and game theory are equally compatible with neo-Aristotelian virtue ethics as with micro-economics.

Note that I do not claim that all desires have a maximizing structure. On the contrary, the very concept of a rule requires that at least the desire to follow a rule has a binary structure: it is either satisfied or it is not. Some of our desires make, or recognize, *requirements* on us. I also recognize that even for desires with a maximizing structure, it may not always be possible to measure their aggregated satisfaction on one continuous scale: they may be incommensurable. The only claim I make in this connection is that in many situations in which people are engaged in common enterprises governed by rules, the subset of their relevant preferences satisfies the condition of commensurability.

My use of the concept of 'utility' seems to presuppose the Humean conception of reasons being derived from beliefs and desires. But this conception misrepresents the internal point of view of the deliberating subject. It is not her belief which provides her with a reason, for if the belief is false, she may not actually have the reason she believes she has. Hence the true reason is not her belief, but the fact which she thinks she has apprehended.[22] These facts need some normative background in order to be relevant to Practical Reason. Here a similar move from the subjective to the objective seems to be required by the agent's internal point of view: it is not her desire as such which provides the necessary background for some fact to be a reason, for the desire may be criticizable. However, the court of appeal for actual desires can either be thought of as consisting of the agent's pattern of desires as a whole, or of a system of objective values, or of a mixture of both. (Alternatively, the objectivity of value can be thought of as being constituted by an ideal harmony of desire.) As I indicated already, I do not want to commit myself to any particular view on the relation between value and desire. But two points have to be recognized: on the one hand that specific desires can fail to invest some facts with the force of reasons because they are criticizable, on the other that the same fact may provide a reason for one agent but not for another because of their different motivational make-up.[23]

For the external point of view, the Humean model is adequate.[24] We explain people's intentional actions by reference to their actual beliefs and desires, even if the

---

[21] This is an interval-scale, with an arbitrary zero-point and unity, allowing for positive linear transformation of the numbers, as e.g. from Fahrenheit to Celsius. It cannot be used for making interpersonal comparisons.

[22] See ch. 7.4.

[23] To that extent, the Humean model should not be completely rejected.

[24] Some authors have argued that beliefs may motivate without the presence of desire, e.g. Nagel 1970, Platts 1980 and, most radically, Dancy 1993.

beliefs are false and the desires open to criticism.[25] Many if not most economists, if pressed, will still assert their formal adherence to the so-called revealed preference conception of utility, according to which we only ascribe beliefs and desires to people on account of the actual choices they make, in order to predict other actual choices they will make. Why people should be expected to behave as if they were informed by reasons, if as a matter of fact they need not *have* the corresponding beliefs and desires, is one of the deeper mysteries of economic science. The economists may protest that they are only interested in coherent choice, but the point is that their understanding of coherence makes no sense outside the framework of the belief/desire model of folk psychology. However that may be, if it is true that social rules must be understood in terms of interdependent reasons, we will have no use for the behaviourism of revealed preference theory in that enterprise.

It will be clear that I am prepared to permit myself a less restricted diet of motivational assumptions than is usually associated with rational-choice theory. I am certainly not postulating *homo economicus*. This may raise the suspicion that the game-theoretical framework has no useful work to do in my theory. If I am ready to ascribe additional motives to people whenever I run out of the usual motivational assumptions of rational-choice theory, my explanations may seem to smell strongly of *virtus dormitiva*: people follow norms because they have a disposition to do so. I hope to convince the reader that my explanations are more interesting than that. Indeed, it is one of my aims in this book to show that the theory I develop really makes a difference – in this case a difference to the solutions proposed for some perennial problems of legal philosophy. And if it makes a difference, it cannot be vacuous.

Although I am quite tolerant about the nature and content of the preferences which set up the interaction patterns ("games") I want to discuss, one might wonder whether my concept of rationality does not still represent the reductionism usually associated with rational-choice theory. And, indeed, the concept of rationality I will use is a purely instrumental one: the rational choice is the one which maximizes utility. But again, I do not claim that this is all there is to being rational. I have already made room for the rational criticism of desires. The only claim I make is that in so far as you have rationally acceptable preferences with a maximizing structure, it is unquestionably rational, other things being equal, to decide for the option which in the long run maximizes your utility (leaving aside the problem of time-discounts).[26] That too seems a quite harmless, indeed trivial assumption to make.

In the last analysis, however, even among these very modest assumptions there is none which I wish to treat as a foundational axiom. My contention is, rather, that none of the results I derive from them is so implausible as to force us to modify or surrender them.

---

[25] We should not express the point by saying that the beliefs and desires provide people with their motivating reasons, for the reasons which motivate are the same reasons which the actor recognizes as normatively valid, hence they are facts, not mental states. (I owe this point to Jonathan Dancy.) However, the action is causally explained by mental states, including the belief of the actor that these facts provide her with valid reasons.

[26] The ceteris paribus clause covers the case in which, besides desires with a maximizing structure, you have desires with a binary structure as well.

## 1.4. Presupposing Strategic Rationality

My use of game theoretical concepts will be extremely modest. Nowhere the argument will rely on any complex mathematical result. The point of using these concepts is only to make clear the structural differences between situations of interdependent outcomes ("games") which may help or hinder the development of patterns of interdependent choices, and, most importantly, may help to explain why in some cases particular assumptions are needed, especially motivational ones, which are not needed in others. I also want to show how in each of these situations, patterns of interdependent choices may be predicted to maintain themselves once they have somehow arisen. However, I will not be much concerned with the vexed question of the emergence of norms. One reason is that no answer to this question is necessary for addressing the problems of legal philosophy I am interested in. All I need is an account of what it means for a social rule to exist.

It is true that in the conventionalist theories which have been developed so far, the questions of the emergence and the maintenance of social rules have been treated as very closely related or even identical. But on my account these questions are to be kept apart. At this point I cannot fully explain the reasons for this insistence[27], but there is one pertinent observation I should make. The game-theoretical notions I will use are those of classical game theory. The very notion of interdependent reasons presupposes agents who are aware of each other's capacities of practical reason. Their form of reasoning is strategic: for every option they consider, they take into account that if the option is a reasonable choice, the others will anticipate it being made. This assumption is characteristic for what I call "classical" game theory: it makes a rather strong assumption of common knowledge. The players know the options each of them has, the outcomes of each combination of choices and the utilities each of them attributes to each of these outcomes: in short they know the game they are playing. They also know that the others are "perfectly" rational. Not only do they have this knowledge, they ascribe it to each other, know that the others ascribe it to them etc.

In the interest of realism I will at certain points relax these assumptions of perfect common knowledge, introducing some uncertainty concerning the game (in particular the relevant utilities of other players) and some fallibility in reasoning. But even then I will conceive of the people following any social rule as strategic agents. This is worth stressing because on the whole, the game-theoretical study of social norms in recent years has gone off in an altogether different direction, deviating from Lewis in this respect. The basic idea is that in an environment in which several "strategies" are played, and in which it is possible at any moment to try out every other possible strategy, the number of agents playing a particular strategy will reflect the success of the strategy in the recent past. This idea can be interpreted in terms of biological evolution. In that case, the measure of "success" is the survival of offspring, and the trying out of

---

[27] See ch. 2.6.

new strategies is a consequence of the recombination of genes and of random mutation. Or the idea can be interpreted in terms of social evolution. In that case, it is assumed that people are able to identify each other's strategies and to measure the utility-return of those strategies, and tend to copy the most successful ones. However, they do not anticipate that others will second-guess their learning behaviour.[28] These agents all commit the *parametric fallacy*: each of them takes himself to be the only deliberating agent around, and considers the behaviour of the others as a constant environment of his choice, a fact of nature.

This biological approach to the development of cooperative behaviour has been enormously fruitful. However, it explains at most the emergence of a convergent pattern of private rules, not the following of social rules. Now it is undeniable that human social relations are characterized by the existence of some form of common knowledge, even if this knowledge is not always perfect, i.e. completely "transparent". So for any pattern of behaviour which the evolution theories predict to emerge, we can ask: suppose the agents have common knowledge of this pattern, and suppose each of them has the capacity of reflective reasoning – would that make a difference?

Sometimes it will not. In these cases I am prepared to consider the possibility that the social norm is nothing but a *crystallization* of the underlying pattern of private-rule following behaviour. Given that pattern, common knowledge will follow naturally for people who have the capacity for it.[29] Even if the social rule emerged among strategic agents, it may be somehow significant that the behaviour it prescribes could have been produced by an evolutionary process as well. Sometimes, however, a behaviour pattern can be predicted to arise among non-strategic agents, when it cannot be predicted that it will be maintained by strategic ones, at least not if the other motivational assumptions are kept equal. It is even possible that the non-strategic agents can be exploited by the strategic agent who is aware of their non-strategic reasoning.[30] In those cases, it is clear that the evolutionary approach does not really explain the emergence of norms. This exemplifies its general weakness: it abstracts from potentially relevant information which human subjects obviously have at their disposal.[31] Even when both clever people and stupid ones exhibit the same patterns of behaviour, we cannot be sure that one explanation accounts for both patterns.

---

[28] Sugden 1986; Skyrms 1996, both building on Maynard Smith 1982. Young 1996 assumes that people choose a best reply to the behaviour of others which they expect on account of recent sample evidence, cf. Schotter 1981, Kliemt 1986. This is still a form of parametric learning behaviour. For all but the most simple behaviour patterns, it is incoherent to assume that people will be able to identify them without recognizing that they exemplify the same kind of intelligent behaviour as their own "replying" choices. This is evident in Schotter and Kliemt, who require their agents to be able to identify very complex strategies. Young's subjects, on the other hand, start by making random choices and then wrongly ascribe meaning to other people's similar random choices, cf. also Bicchieri 1993, ch. 6; Skyrms 1996, ch. 4.

[29] E.g. if a pattern of convergent private rules has emerged in an iterative Coordination game, the pattern will only be reinforced by the development of common knowledge of those private rules.

[30] One example is the agent who has adopted the unconditionally cooperative strategy in one-shot PD-games because he acts in an environment in which his chances to meet a similarly motivated agent are very high, cf. Skyrms 1996, ch. 3.

[31] Cf. Cudd 1993, 128; Sen 1998, x.

For example, population dynamics can explain the development of the signalling systems which are used by certain species of birds and insects,[32] but it is obvious that this is a far cry from the linguistic competence of human beings.[33] One option which is only available to beings capable of strategic thinking, is to make variations on established communication patterns which are immediately recognizable to others. Common knowledge introduces a flexibility to conventions which is totally lacking in its evolutionary predecessors.

What I intend to show is that, on the assumption of strategic agency, we may still be able to explain the maintenance of social rules, even if not their emergence.


### 1.5. Coordination Problems

According to David Lewis, conventions tend to emerge and to be maintained among a number of persons who recurrently face a certain *coordination problem*.

What kind of problem is this? Suppose we are parachutists dropped behind enemy lines. It is imperative that we join forces as soon as possible. So we want to go wherever we may expect the others to go. But this is true of everyone of us. No-one has any reason to go to any particular place.

More generally, people have a coordination problem if the following applies to them: person $P$ must choose from a number of alternative options $a$-1, $b$-1, $c$-1, and so on; $R$ must choose from $a$-2, $b$-2, $c$-2, etc.; $S$ must choose from $a$-3, etc., and each has a decisive reason to choose option $a$ if and only if all the others do so too, and similarly for option $b$. The same, however, need not apply to the choice of $c$: a couple of meeting points is enough to make the choice problematic. It is not even necessary that everyone has the same choice of alternatives. For the classification of options as $a$ or $b$, the only criterion is whether meeting points are generated, not whether these actions come under the same description in any other way. Of two alchemists, who think they can secretly make gold out of the ingredients $O$ and $H$, one must bring $O$ and the other $H$, and not both $O$ or both $H$. It is not uniformity that is required but collaboration.[34]

All those involved reason as follows: I must go where the others go, I've got to find out where that is. How will each of the others reason? "I must go where the others go, I've got to find out where that is. How will each of the others reason?" 'I must go, ... and so on' and so on", and so on in an unending spiral. To determine what I must do, I must already know what I will do: for that fact is needed by the others to determine what they will do, and I need that fact to determine what I will do. There is no-one who, independently of the others, can make a justified choice and thereby provide grounds for the others to choose. Everyone waits for everyone else.

Assume there is ground for the supposition that $R$ chooses $a$: then $P$ has a good reason to do the same. Everyone involved who can surmise the supposition of $P$, will

---

[32] Skyrms 1996, ch. 5.

[33] Bennett 1964, ch. 2.

[34] Lewis 1969, 12.

expect $P$ to choose $a$ and thereby borrow a reason to choose $a$ as well. (Even though they may simultaneously think $P$'s supposition unjustified). $R$ may also belong to those involved. Their patterns of thought can again be replicated by a subsequent group. And so on. Each member of a subsequent, replicating group who was already a member of a previous group, gets an extra reason to choose $a$. In this way a cumulative series of replications develops which must overcome all indecision. But this development must have an independent point of departure; otherwise everyone remains imprisoned in the reciprocal interdependency of their expectations.

Let us try to characterize games of (pure) coordination more precisely. What I have called 'meeting points' Lewis calls 'proper equilibria'. A Nash equilibrium is reached when neither chooser would have been able to achieve a better result if he had chosen differently on his own. The concept of a 'proper equilibrium' is a bit stronger. A proper equilibrium is achieved if it is true for each player that, given the other player's choice, he will not only fail to improve his outcome by making any deviant choice, but can only worsen it.[35] We initially define a Coordination game as any game with at least two proper equilibria.[36]

Suppose, however, there are two proper equilibria, but both players vastly prefer one of those. In that case the situation intuitively does not seem problematic at all: each of us will head straight for the better outcome, confident that the other will do so as well. It is difficult to explain the rationality of this choice in the usual terms of rational-choice theory.[37] It is sometimes suggested that this is a simple case of calculating the average expected utility for each choice. But this criterion cannot be used because, for example, for every alternative open to $C$, $R$ would have to guess correctly the probability of $C$ choosing that alternative. But $R$ cannot determine how probable $C$'s choices will be without an idea of the probabilities that $C$ attributes to $R$'s choices. And to know that, he would have to know what idea $C$ had of the probabilities attributed to his choices by $R$, and so on. Expected utility reasoning in this type of context commits the parametric fallacy: you treat your co-player's choices as constants and your own as variables.[38] Throughout this book, as I announced in the previous section, I will assume people's reasoning to be strategic: they know the others to be equally rational as they are themselves. Then they also know that *if* – a big if – there is a determinate solution to their problem of choice, this choice will be anticipated by their co-player, and that

---

[35] If we only require two equilibria, zero-sum games qualify as games of coordination.

[36] Lewis actually requires two proper coordination equilibria (i.e. by unilateral deviance you can neither improve your own position nor that of your partner), but this is an unnecessary restriction, Den Hartogh 1985, ch. 8.

[37] Gibbard 1965; Regan 1980, 18ff; Sugden 1993, 73 ff; Hollis & Sugden 1993. One might suggest that in such situations only the best possible and the worst possible outcome are relevant: if for all choices the worst possible outcome is the same, one should go for the option with the best possible outcome. An alternative explanation is that in such situations a basic convention exists to "think as a team". See ch. 2, note 45.

[38] Elster 1978, 106-118. For this reason the founders of game theory, Von Neumann and Morgenstern, rightly did not allow probabilities into the domain of game theory, and to that extent the attempts of e.g. Harsanyi & Selten 1988 or Skyrms 1990 to develop game theory as a part of Bayesian decision theory are misguided. Cf. Mariotti 1996 for more technical criticism. However, if the assumption of common knowledge of rationality is given up, forms of game theory can be developed which rely on inductive evidence concerning other people's behaviour, see ch. 1.4. and note 28.

should not be a reason to choose differently.[39] In other words: if any game has a solution, it must be an equilibrium. It does not follow that if any game has at least one equilibrium outcome, it must have a solution.[40]

Whatever the explanation, it is clear that in a game with at least two proper equilibria it is only difficult to choose if the players have no common preference for one of those. In such a game, therefore, a coordination *problem* only exists if there are at least two proper equilibria which are equally valued by all players, provided there is no proper equilibrium which is valued higher. The equilibria must, at the same time, be optima.[41]

### 1.6. Conventions

Coordination problems are not always "solved", but solutions *do* occur. In explaining how this works, Lewis follows Thomas Schelling.[42] The basic idea is this: of the equivalent alternative meeting-points, choose the alternative that somehow *stands out*. You may assume that your co-player will follow the same maxim, so you may expect him to make this salient choice as well. That is a further reason to make it yourself. And you can assume that he realizes both that you will make that choice and anticipate him making it, and so on and so on. In this way, all parties take turns playing into one another's thoughts until the desired goal has been harmoniously reached. Reasoning in this way, "we are windowless monads doing our best to mirror each other, mirror each other mirroring each other and so on."[43]

Lewis builds his theory of conventions on these ideas in the following way. Suppose that a certain coordination problem regularly reoccurs in a group, and assume that the first time the rendezvous succeeded – possibly because all participants identified the same salient alternative, or perhaps because by chance all made the same choice. If the problem arises again, the situation is different in one significant aspect: amongst all acceptable alternatives, one stands out because it has already been chosen once before. That precedent provides the alternative with a particular prominence. Everyone has reason to choose that alternative in the expectation that everyone else has the same expectation too, etc. The next time the problem comes up, the same reasoning can be followed, this time with even greater confidence. Choosing this alternative emerges as a regularity and this regularity itself is reason enough to repeat the choice,

---

[39] Luce & Raiffa 1957, 63-65, cf. Von Neumann & Morgenstern 1944, 48. Expected-utility reasoning does not satisfy the postulate, for if I ascribe any probability under 100% to your choice, and this leads me to a solution, you will anticipate this, and so your reaction should be predictable with 100% probability, which falsifies the assumption.

[40] See ch. 2.3 & 6.

[41] Lewis does not make this requirement. In ch. 1.7. we will find that an additional requirement should be made: there is no risk involved in doing one's part in converging on any of the meeting-points (or on minimally two of them); it is compatible with making a maximin-choice.

[42] Schelling 1960, ch. 3.

[43] Lewis 1969, 38.

again and again, so that it becomes self-confirming. A convention, Lewis concludes, is a regularity of conduct which reconfirms itself.[44]

It is characteristic of a convention that everyone (usually) has convincing reasons to uphold it but at the same time everyone would also have had equally good reasons to uphold an alternative convention if that happened to have been the prevailing one. (Which side of the road we drive, which day dustbins are emptied or markets held, which part of town the shoe shops or night-clubs are concentrated, which paper we consult for housing ads, what image – skull or what not – is used to warn against poison, etc.). All possible conventions are equally good; which one becomes established is a matter of chance. In that sense, the prevailing convention is *arbitrary*. It only has the (incomparable) advantage of being established *in fact*. (Hence it is mistaken to conclude from the fact that some norms are "merely conventional" that there can be no compelling reason to adhere to them.)[45] Now Lewis' insight is that this arbitrary character of conventions can be related to the identifying feature of coordination problems: access to more than one equivalent proper equilibrium. The pub The Saracen's Head does not distinguish itself particularly favourably from the other pubs in town; any other pub would offer an equally pleasant ambience in which to meet one's friends. Yet we all go to The Saracen's Head because we all know it is the only place where we can be sure to meet one another.

### 1.7. Conventions in Assurance games

There is an almost complete isomorphy between the philosophy of money and the philosophy of law. The first attempts to answer the question: why are people prepared to accept things without any intrinsic value, like pieces of paper, in exchange for nutritious loaves and beautiful pictures? The second asks: why do people accept legislative and judicial pronunciations as binding, whether they agree to their content or not? We find the same type of answer to both questions.

The first school of thought in monetary philosophy is the theory of Natural Money. Gold and silver (or cattle, beads, rice, salt) have their own objective and permanent value, and therefore it is reasonable to accept and to issue pieces of gold and silver as tender for goods of equal value. If the circulation were to stop suddenly, the people left behind with the gold would not be the worse for that; therefore nobody needs to be afraid to take it. How about paper money? The Nederlandsche Bank who issues it assures me in print that on request it will supply the bearer a specified amount of those objective valuables. We know the Bank is capable of making good its promise, because the total amount specified by the paper issued is "covered' by the gold and silver in its possession. Therefore we only need to trust the Bank in order to take its paper. The

---

[44] "A metastable, self-perpetuating system of preferences, expectations, and actions, capable of persisting indefinitely," Lewis 1969, 48.

[45] E.g. Aristophanes, *Clouds* 1399ff, discussed in Nussbaum 1990, 222.

value of this fiduciary money remains dependent on the objective value of the treasures stored in the Bank's vaults.

The second school is Monetary Realism. On this view, it does not matter whether shells, shingles, gold, silver, nickel, copper and paper have any objective value in themselves; what matters is only that people believe they have. For whatever people believe to be real, is real in its consequences (Thomas' axiom).[46]

Thirdly we have, of course, Monetary Positivism.[47] People accept paper currency because the state commands them do so on pain of punishment.

Each of these theories is obviously unsatisfactory. The true theory is Monetary Conventionalism.[48] Admittedly, the game that people involved in exchange are playing is not simply a Coordination game, as we have defined it. The game certainly has multiple equivalent proper equilibria (taking gold, silver, cattle, beads, rice, salt). Everybody's best outcome is achieved when everybody accepts whatever is accepted by others.[49] But even if only one proper equilibrium-cum-optimum existed, it is not at all evident that people would converge on that outcome, because it would be dangerous to do one's part. Nobody likes to be the last poor soul who takes worthless assignats in exchange for goods which really can feed and clothe real dragoons. To play it safe, one could decide to exchange without intermediary: to go to the market with one's eggs, philosophy books or grand piano's in order to return with grand piano's, philosophy books, or eggs. If everyone maximins in this way, the outcome is still an equilibrium (not necessarily a proper equilibrium), but clearly a suboptimal one. A game of this type is called a Deer Hunt[50] or Assurance game. Participants in transactions involving money are playing an n-person iterated Assurance game.[51]

Now suppose a transparent pattern of mutual expectations exists to accept, let us say, beads. Then everybody has a reason to sell his eggs for beads on the market and go to the shop to buy books or piano's for those beads later. Barring exceptional circumstances, the convention is stable, for if we may expect other people to take our money, we have reason enough to take it ourselves.[52] If trust is lacking, state

---

[46] "Though the word for the monetary unit is hollow, we think and speak as if it denoted some entities that can be counted. This is important for making talk about the unit function." Olivecrona 1971, 302.

[47] *Staatliche Theorie des Geldes* (Knapp). According to Lagerspetz 1984, this is the common theory in Roman Law and medieval political theory (e.g. Aquinas).

[48] Lewis 1969, 7-9; Lagerspetz 1984.

[49] Therefore the game is not a Prisoner's Dilemma, as Steiner 1978 suggests.

[50] "S'agissoit-il de prendre un cerf, chacun sentoit bien qu'il devoit pour cela garder fidèlement son poste; mais si un lièvre venoit à passer à la portée de l'un d'eux, il ne faut pas douter qu'il ne le poursuivît sans scrupule et qu'ayant atteint sa proie il ne souciât fort peu de manquer la leur à ses compagnons." Rousseau, *Discours sur l'Origine de l'Inégalité parmi les Hommes* (1754), the beginning of part II. The term "Assurance game" was coined by Sen 1967.

[51] Lagerspetz 1984.

[52] This is the modern form (first developed by Menger and other representatives of the Austrian economic school) of the contract-theory of money which Pufendorf and Locke already defended, analogously to their contract-theory of law. The development of this theory is an example of the way contract-theory has been refined by replacing the idea of a tacit agreement by an invisible hand mechanism, cf. Den Hartogh 1990 on Locke's theory of political obligation prefiguring Hume's account of justice as an artificial virtue. The passage from the *Treatise* mentioned in note 15 actually refers to the development of (languages and) currencies.

commands will be of no avail, as the history of the assignats shows.[53] So positivism is dead wrong. Realism is right in thinking that appropriate beliefs are indispensable, but it is wrong in not requiring those beliefs to be justified. Natural money theory (the so-called goods theory and the metallic theory) may accurately describe phases in a historic development, but it does not explain the use of fiduciary money – and even gold is largely fiduciary money. I am not giving away any secret if I tell you that the gold in the vaults of the Nederlandsche Bank is not sufficient to make good on all its promises at the same time. (And if you tried to collect even one little bar, you would not succeed.) The social rule to accept paper currency is a convention.

The convention to accept this particular form of money solves a pure coordination problem; the convention to accept any money at all solves an assurance problem. Conventions of the first type – let us call them 'Lewis conventions' – are characterized by their arbitrary character: it does not matter whether we use forins or dollars, paper currency with the image of Erasmus or of a snipe, as long as all people within a certain territory do the same. A convention of the second type is not at all arbitrary: the proper equilibrium it enables us to reach has no equivalent alternative. If it is objected that this is to stretch the conventional meaning of 'convention', I agree. I do not believe that in their daily use, concepts like 'convention' or 'norm' have any clear or theoretically interesting demarcation lines. The basic connotation in my technical use of the term 'convention' is the existence of interdependent reasons, reasons derived from a transparent pattern of mutual expectations. The pattern need not be arbitrary in any sense.

## 1.8. The Role of Virtue

Clearly, the conventions discussed so far do not amount to norms with an obligatory character. They are "hypothetical imperatives", indications of how to maximize one's utility, e.g. by realizing the net returns of a desired rendezvous. The moment the rendezvous is no longer desired, and one prefers to go it alone, the convention loses its normative force. If you want to silently drown in beer and sorrow, you avoid The Saracen's Head. So one characteristic of social rules as described in section 1 is still missing in our account of conventions: the idea that deviating conduct is open to criticism, and not only in the sense that it is instrumentally irrational (non-utility-maximizing).

Let me discuss a game which resembles the one we considered in the previous section: a combination of the Coordination and the Assurance game. We want to meet, there are multiple equivalent meeting-points, but in order to get to any of those we have to make a substantial investment of time, energy or external resources, which will be

---

[53] "The punishments are superfluous if they agree with our convention, are outweighed if they go against it, are not decisive either way." "If I expected the others to be on the left, I would be there too, highway patrol or no highway patrol." Lewis 1969, 45, 44, cf. Hayek 1973, 41-42, Sugden 1986, ch. 1. See ch. 9.2 below. Ten years ago, a Dutch minister for emancipation proposed the replacement of all gender-specific names for professions by neutral ones. None of those new names has ever been adopted.

lost if the meeting fails to take place. As we saw, a convention arising in such games will be stable: people need not worry whether their investments are safe; since they expect each other to go to the meeting-point, they all have sufficient reason to meet those expectations. But suppose this particular game is a little bit different. We have played it recurrently for a long time, but one day, due to a sudden fortuitous change in my preference rankings, I decide that doing my part of the "solution" will not maximize my utility (and hence today it will not the solution for me). My preferences have changed – but not, of course, your expectations.

In describing this case I am tampering with the usual assumptions of classical game theory: we have less than perfect mutual knowledge of each other's preferences. This is surely an assumption which makes for greater realism.

Because of your expectations, you go on spending your time, energy, and resources, all to no avail if I make what is now my rational choice: staying home. Now I might be concerned about the losses you stand to suffer, but if that is enough for me to keep on doing my part as ever, then my utility function, which does not reflect only self-regarding preferences, has not significantly changed at all. However, I might also care about your expectations as such. Because of those, I would consider it a breach of faith, a lack of fidelity, to simply let you down. That is still a kind of preference, but not a preference with a maximizing structure. It is also a kind of preference which can only be understood against the background of the existing situation as a whole: the game we are playing and the pattern of mutual expectations we have developed. For these reasons we cannot say, as we did regarding my possible altruistic concerns, that this particular preference should be simply incorporated into my utility function.

If I have such a preference, you may know it. In that case your expectations concerning my behaviour will be considerably strengthened. You not only expect me to do the usual thing because, for all you know, it is the rational thing for me to do, you also expect it because, even if it is not, you know that I know that you expect it, and that this very expectation will be my reason to do it. Such an expectation which is justified by reference to my known disposition to respond to it, is a form of trust. A pattern of mutual expectations of this kind will be as self-perpetuating as the purely "instrumental" conventions we considered so far. For given our dispositions, our expectations themselves provide the reasons for the actions which satisfy them.

Rational agents with less than perfect knowledge of each other's preferences (or rationality) might hesitate to comply with any expectations that they will do their part in converging on the proper equilibrium in an Assurance game, as long as they only expect each other to maximize their utility. They have something to lose. Under this assumption, Assurance game conventions may be unstable. However, stability may be restored if such people have mutual knowledge of each other's trustworthiness (even if this knowledge is less than perfect).[54]

I have described a possible development taking off from the starting-point of an existing "instrumental" convention. But on closer inspection that is not quite legitimate. For the participants in an instrumental convention, for instance a Lewis convention,

---

[54] Kreps & Wilson 1982 show that even very low probabilities of trustworthiness are sufficient to deflect the backwards induction argument for defection in the iterated Prisoner's Dilemma game of known length.

basically expect each other to do whatever maximizes their utility, and only for that reason expect each other to do this particular action $A$. So if doing $A$ does not maximize my utility, my partner's expectations, though understandable, are no longer justified, and she has nothing to complain if I do not conform: she expected me to maximize my utility, and I did. However, if she does not only expect me to be rational, but trusts me to be trustworthy, then she can blame me, both for betraying her trust and for the bad character I thereby show.

It has been suggested that mutual knowledge of trustworthiness changes the game: it makes it certain, or at least more certain, that what we are playing really is an Assurance game, and this makes it possible for an "instrumental" convention to be stably sustained after all. Similarly, even a one-shot Prisoner's Dilemma (or, rather, a game which on first sight looks like one), could be transformed into an Assurance game by the mutual ascription of a preference for fair dealing.[55]

This suggestion is on the right track, but it is not wholly satisfactory. It fails to recognize the fact that trustworthiness, and in many cases fairness as well, is a response, not only to a game as characterized by options of choice and preferences over outcomes, but rather to a pattern of beliefs existing in such a game. The reference to the beliefs should enter into the correct description of the preferences. A trustworthy person is a person prepared to honour his co-players' expectations of cooperation, and a fair person is a person who refuses to exploit these expectations. The exercise of these *cooperative virtues* does not simply involve making cooperative choices in situations in which rational people, in their absence, would tend to make defective ones; it presupposes that these people are *expected* to make cooperative choices. What the account correctly recognizes is that, on the other hand, those expectations are justified by the existence of the dispositions.[56]

---

[55] Lagerspetz 1995, 198-207; Postema 1989, 52-56; Hollis 1987, 39.

[56] On the circularity which the corrected account involves, see ch. 2.6. and Den Hartogh 1998.

# CHAPTER 2

## THE STRUCTURE OF OBLIGATORY NORMS

### 2.1. Themes for Discussion

In the first chapter, I presented an outline of the conventionalist theory of social norms which I intend to put to work in my reflections on law. In this chapter, I will fill in some of the details which will turn out to be particularly relevant for those reflections. In particular I want both to elucidate and to consolidate the thesis I suggested in the last section of chapter One: we cannot understand the existence of obligatory norms if we do not presuppose the existence of cooperative dispositions.

I will start by considering another game in which Lewis conventions may be necessary to enable agents to mutually adjust their choices, and in which those conventions may acquire additional stability by developing into proper social norms when an appeal to cooperative virtue can be made. The main interest of this game, the Division game, is that it shows how patterns of mutual expectations can help the agents to coordinate their choices in cases in which unaided individual rationality will be of no help at all, because the "solution" of the game is rationally underdetermined. Besides, in chapter Five I will argue that this particular game is highly significant for understanding the functioning of legal authority.

Similar or related claims will be made for the Prisoner's Dilemma game. This differs from the interaction patterns discussed so far because a Lewis convention will not be stable in at least some versions of this game; we need the supporting cooperative dispositions if we are to develop a pattern of mutual expectations at all. The relevant cooperative disposition is fairness, and in chapter Four, principles of fairness will also turn out to be specially relevant for understanding law.

The conventionalist theory of obligatory norms I propose has two main components: patterns of mutual expectations, and cooperative dispositions. The next topic to be discussed is the precise relation between these elements. I will argue that they have an internal reference to each other. Cooperative dispositions consist in being prepared to honour each other's justified expectations, and those expectations are justified by the existence of the dispositions. An important corollary of this fact is that the mutual expectations of the people participating in a social norm cannot have developed independently of any pre-existing expectations. Only if the pattern of expectations already exists in a general way, is it possible to form concrete expectations of behaviour in any particular case. I will show that the same is true of Lewis conventions. If this corollary is accepted, it follows that the conventionalist theory can only explain the maintenance of either conventions or norms, not their emergence.

Next, I will give a more detailed description of the cooperative dispositions, and discuss some questions about them, in particular whether they can be said to be "rational" themselves, and how they could have emerged.

The theory as a whole aims to analyse the nature of obligatory norms. The final section of this chapter, therefore, draws conclusions from the considerations presented so far for the concept of obligation. Chapter Three discusses an alternative understanding of obligatory norms, centered on sanctions and disapproval rather than cooperative virtue. Having shown that, on any plausible account, sanctions and disapproval presuppose cooperative dispositions, I will finally turn to the law in chapter Four, inquiring whether the law can be a source of obligation as conceived in the first three chapters.

## 2.2. Division games and Bargaining

Suppose two persons are in a position to obtain a good, provided they agree about the way to divide it; or are able to produce it, provided they agree about the distribution of the burdens and benefits of production. If they fail to agree, they get nothing. We suppose the good to be fully divisible; if it is not, the persons can agree about the allocation of probabilities to get the undivisible parts. This is a variation on the Coordination game we know: all distributions in which both get anything at all are proper equilibria. The difference is that these equilibria are differently ranked by the players. Their first priority is to meet, but their second priority is to meet at a specific place, and though they share the first interest, they conflict on the second.

Suppose the players are unable to communicate. In that case their problem of choice is really a problem of coordination only: if, for some reason or other, any of the proper equilibria is the focus of mutual expectations, for instance by being the salient one, then both players have decisive reason to make the appropriate choice, even though for one of them this particular equilibrium is the least attractive one. For this is the only equilibrium within reach.

But suppose they are able to communicate. In a game of pure coordination this immediately solves the problem: one player randomly proposes a meeting-point and the other agrees. But in a Division game the situation will now be different. Each player will try to get the other to accept his favourite meeting-point, or a point as close to it as possible. So the players will start bargaining. (Obviously, if the salient meeting-point is your favourite one, you have a reason for making communication impossible.) We can imagine the players going through a series of rounds in which each in turn makes an offer which the other accepts or rejects. To introduce a realistic sense of urgency, we also have to assume that on each round either the total amount (or utility) of the good, or the probability that it is still there to be divided, is somewhat reduced. Bargaining has its costs.

As before, each player has a dominant interest in meeting. However, each of them derives his bargaining position from the fact that she is able to prevent the other's favourite meeting-point from being reached. So the common task is to solve the conflict without sacrificing the predominant shared interest. However, neither player can, without weakening her own bargaining position, guarantee the other that this aim will be achieved. So it is essential to bargaining that there is a risk of failure. This risk may not be equally important for both players. If one of them very badly needs at least part of the good, and this is common knowledge to both, this weakens her bargaining position. The other player will then get the lion's share.

Making, accepting and rejecting offers frequently are not the only moves the players can make. They can also make threats. "This is my final offer, if you do not accept it, I will accept no other offer." Occasionally, more radical threats are possible: a player may announce that, if his offer is not accepted, he will not only abandon the good, but also cause his co-player some additional harm. If one of the players has a greater capacity for causing such harm than the other ("threat advantage"), he may expect a greater part of the good. However, not all threats are equally credible. For the execution of threats usually has its costs as well, so causing harm to the other also causes harm to oneself. A credible threat conveys the message: this is going to hurt you much more than me. Or, to generalize the point: the better the ratio between harm to you and harm to me, the more credible my threat.

Bargaining theory aims at identifying the unique division which rational players will agree to. The classical theory, as it was developed by Nash in 1950, basically consists of three steps.

(1)  The solution must be Pareto optimal: it will not be possible for any player to improve his position without the position of the other being worsened. That seems a reasonable requirement: if I can meet your offer with a counteroffer which gives you the same pay-off and me a higher one, you can have no reason not to accept my offer. Besides, if there is a unique solution, rational players will be able to identify it straightaway, and so be able to avoid the costs of bargaining. I offer you the solution and you accept it, that's all.

(2)  For the second step we start from the equally plausible idea that agreement will be mutually profitable. This means that for each player there is a minimum such that each offer below it will not be worth any serious consideration, for the simple reason that the player can guarantee this result by himself. So the question is: at what point will the players end up if they fail to agree? This is the so-called status quo point (or the state of nature), from which we can delineate the negotiation area: the set of all possible agreements (better than the status quo for at least one player, and no worse than that for either).

As I originally described the Division game, the status quo is the point at which there is nothing to be divided, and the negotiation area consists of all possible divisions of the good, or part of it (e.g. what remains after deducting the costs of bargaining). However, if we take the threat options of the parties into account, we have to redefine the game by identifying the status quo point in a way which reflects the impact of the possible threats on the solution. If we failed to do so, we would not take those threats seriously. The problem is, how to take them seriously without taking them *too* seriously? The identification of the status quo point should take into account the differences in credibility between threats; it should operationalize the criterion I suggested (the ratio between the harm I can do to you and the harm I will thereby do myself).[1]

(3) Given the status quo point and the Pareto frontier, the solution of the Division game is a way of projecting a point on the Pareto frontier from the status quo point. Several such identifications have been proposed. They all satisfy the so-called symmetry requirement: if the players get a different share, there must be a difference between them, either in status quo position, or in possible outcome (somehow there is a maximum or minimum share for one player but not for the other) or in "need" (the shape of the marginal utility curve). The proposals differ in the additional requirements they make. Nash, for instance, thought that feasibility of outcomes was largely irrelevant: if the difference between two bargaining problems is only that some outcomes are within the negotiation set in one but not in the other, the solution will be the same, as long as it is in the negotiation set in both problems. ("Independence of irrelevant outcomes.") The Nash solution is the point at which the product of the distances of both players from the status quo point is maximal. The game theoreticians Kalai and Smorodinsky rejected the independence requirement, as did the philosopher David Gauthier.[2] Accordingly, they proposed a revised solution.

## 2.3. Underdetermination by Reason

Bargaining is a fact of life. Obviously, actual people do not succeed in avoiding the costs of bargaining and in proceeding to the solution straightaway. Even Nash and Gauthier might have a problem if they met. One might suppose that this is to be explained by lack of rationality or lack of information, or both. In particular, people's actual preferences are usually not very well known, and in Division games they have good reason to keep it that way. And if either Nash or Gauthier is right, the other one is lacking in rationality, and hence in meeting they could not have mutual knowledge of perfect rationality. I want to suggest, however, that there is a more basic explanation: for all we know, there is no such thing as *the* solution to bargaining problems. All three steps of the identification procedure are problematical.

Let me start with the possible impact of threats on the outcome. In real life, this is primarily a function of the psychology of the players. Some people are more readily impressed than others, and the use of threats can also invoke emotional reactions of anger, frustration and resentment. It might be objected that, even if we abstract from all psychology, there are objective differences in credibility along the lines I suggested. But my point is that these differences are equally rooted in psychology. With the very same ratio between harm to the other and harm to oneself, one player will execute his threats and the other will not.

---

[1] The so-called Nash point is usually considered to be the best realization of this program.

[2] Kalai & Smorodinsky 1975; Gauthier 1986, ch. 5 (the principle of minimax relative concession).

On the other hand, if we had rational players without any such psychological traits, all threats would lose their credibility. For if the threat failed to bring the other player to accept your offer, executing it will not serve any useful purpose. If you are a perfect utility-maximizing machine, you have no reason to harm the other; this holds in particular if you thereby harm yourself as well, even to the slightest extent, but it holds also if inflicting harm just does not do you any good. However, if your partner knows that you are a rational player, he will also know that you will not execute your threats, and so will not be impressed by them at all.[3] (Though he will wonder why you make them.)

As a rational player you know all that, and so you will have at least one reason to execute your threats: to get yourself a reputation of someone who does. It could even be useful to be known as the "irrational" person who always executes his threats, irrespective of any costs to himself. So rational players will adopt a general strategy concerning the execution of threats in Division games, at least as long as such behaviour goes on record. However, we cannot decide which strategy is the optimal one in the abstract, it depends on the ensemble of the strategies of the players you meet. For example, if everyone always executes his threats, but no-one ever gives in to them, it is imprudent to use them at all. There is no general formula for the "optimal way of using threats".

The other steps in finding the solution are equally problematic. As a matter of fact, they are all question-begging.[4] They start by describing, in an axiomatic way, the properties which the solution will have, and then go on to prove that only one solution concept satisfies the requirements. But all these axioms are only plausible if they have the form: "If there is a solution, it will have the following property..." For example, if there is a solution, it will be a Pareto optimum, but it involves a petitio principii to conclude that rational players will eventually end at some place on the Pareto frontier. Bargaining theory can only identify a uniquely rational solution because it starts by assuming that there is one.[5]

The point is particularly telling in relation to the symmetry postulate. If the players are fully symmetrically placed, i.e. might change places without any difference to the game, it seems plausible to suggest that their outcomes should be equal. Each player will realize that he cannot ask his rational co-player to make any greater concession than he is prepared to make himself. But what the axiom actually tells us, is only that *if* reason specifies exactly what concessions to make, then equally rational and symmetrically situated players will make the same concessions. Whether or not the magnitude of concessions is rationally underdetermined remains an open question.

---

[3] The conclusion can only be avoided by maintaining that if it is rational to intend to do *A* (for the "autonomous" effects of the intention, see note 60 below), it is rational to do *A*, Gauthier 1984, but cf. Gauthier 1994; Robins 1996. See ch.2.8.

[4] Den Hartogh 1985.14; Sugden 1990; 1991.

[5] The assumption is made explicitly by Nash 1953, 137 (the principle of rational determinacy) and by Gauthier 1986, 143 ("Each person must suppose that there is a feasible concession point that every rational person is willing to entertain"); see comments Sugden 1990, 773-775.

In recent years the axiomatic approach to bargaining has been supplemented by a more purely game-theoretical one. The game is explicitly modelled as a series of rounds in which players claim certain shares and accept or reject such claims. It is also explicitly assumed that it is costly for both players not to reach agreement in any round, though it need not be equally costly for both. It turns out that this game has one unique equilibrium outcome which, if the costs of delay are equal for both players, is identical to the Nash solution.[6] But this result does not prove that bargaining games have uniquely rational solutions either.

The general argument for equilibrium as a solution concept is derived from the idea of strategic rationality. Suppose that as a rational player I identify the solution to any game we are playing. Then I should realize that you, being no less rational, will anticipate my identification and make your optimal response to it, and realizing this should give me no reason to reconsider my choice.[7] However, it is clear that this argument is question-begging in the same way as the axiomatic approach. It shows that, *if* there are uniquely rational strategies, they will be best replies to each other, and hence in equilibrium. It does not follow that there *are* uniquely rational strategies for any particular game.[8]

The mistake which both approaches share is not just simply to *assume* the existence of a solution without argument. Rather, they use the assumption in identifying the solution.[9] This procedure relies on a perverse interpretation of the assumption of common knowledge of rationality. We mutually know that we have a capacity for making rational choices, but that does not mean that I can give any probability-value to my own choice on this occasion being the rational one, *before* I have actually exercised that capacity, and use this probability as a premise in my reasoning. Suppose you are an expert detective: given any crime, the probability that you will discover the criminal is very high. The case of murder you are currently investigating can only be solved if A is identified as the murderer, because there simply are no other suspects. Are you allowed to reason from the premise of your special expertise to the conclusion that A did it?[10]

Anyway, however it is used, the assumption is unfounded. It is of course plausible to assume that the players will tend to become more ready to accept an offer, as the concessions it requires them to make are less. Therefore it is true that, the more we move away from the boundaries of the negotiation area, the greater the likelihood of

---

[6] Rubinstein 1982; cf. Osborne and Rubinstein, ch. 3.

[7] Von Neumann & Morgenstern (1944) 1967, 147-148; Luce & Raiffa 1957, 63-65; cf. ch. 1, note 39.

[8] There is an additional problem with so-called mixed equilibria (in which each player allows his choice of strategy to depend on some randomizing device): if the other player plays his mixed equilibrium strategy, there is no reason why I should do so as well, because I can expect the same pay-off, whatever I do.

[9] Bacharach 1989; Sugden 1991, 301. An argument of that type may be used to derive the conclusion that it is rational to make the cooperative choice in a one-shot PD-game, Hofstadter 1985, 767-780; Davis 1977; cf. Aumann 1987 on correlated equilibria. Fully rational players will know that the only possible outcomes are that both cooperate or both defect, and they prefer the first outcome. This symmetry argument is commonly, and rightly, considered to be quite suspect.

[10] The mistake is similar to that of evidential decision theory, e.g. in Newcomb's Problem, cf. Lewis 1981. "The possibility of unpredictability is a necessary postulate of practical reason", Lagerspetz 1985, 38.

agreement. But it does not follow that there is one particular point at which the movement will stop.

Indeed, there is no guarantee that it will stop at all. In actual bargaining there is always the risk that no agreement can be reached, and players cope with this risk in different ways which determine their results. It cannot be predicted that any particular strategy (within a spectrum of possible strategies with very vague boundaries) will have the best overall result, for this, as with threatening strategies, depends for each strategy on the other strategies in the population which it meets. A tough negotiatior will more often fail to reach agreement than a more conciliatory type, but in the agreements he achieves the average results will be better. This is true even if all parties are fully and transparently informed about each other's preferences. Each of the parties fears failure, and therefore has reasons of two opposed types: a reason to make concessions, and a reason to use the other's fear in order to get more concessions. But without begging the question, there is no way to decide whether these reasons can be finely balanced or not. If they are not, strategies may fail to lead to agreement, or lead to an agreement violating the symmetry postulate, without any of them being irrational. The basic point is that there may be an internal relation between these two possibilities.

### 2.4. The Role of Conventions and Norms in Bargaining

If reason cannot determine the solution, real bargaining may be needed to find one. But real bargaining is both costly and risky.[11] We have to invest in it, and, even so, cannot be sure that the investment will pay. If we finally reach agreement, even the party who gets the better deal may regret not having accepted more compliant conditions at an earlier stage. So both players have an interest in reducing the degree of underdetermination of the solution, even if pure game-theoretical reason is unable to deliver the good.

Where reason fails, convention may succeed. If we regularly confront each other in Division games of the same type, a pattern of mutual expectations to agree at a specific division will be self-perpetuating. If I offer you the conventional solution, I may expect you to agree, but if I require more, I should expect you to be very reluctant; therefore both of us have reason to conform to the entrenched pattern of expectations, and thereby to confirm it. What counts is not only that I expect you to agree, but that I know that you know that I expect this.[12] Salience has an important role to play here as well. Even if our situations are not fully symmetrical, I can expect you to accept the offer to divide the spoils in equal halves, but if I go for more, I may find that there is no other natural place to stop.[13] Another way in which we can solve our problem is by

---

[11] For example, it is rational for a player to make it impossible for herself to deviate from her offer (e.g. by buying the tickets to her favourite holiday resort), but if both players pre-commit themselves in this way simultaneously, they can no longer reach an agreement.

[12] The higher-order belief justifies the lower-order one, see ch.2.6.

[13] Schelling 1961, 61ff.

accepting arbitration. This solution also fundamentally depends on convention.[14] For both of us mutually and transparently expect each other to put up with the arbiter's decision. Similarly, an agreement once reached has a gravity of its own, even if renegotiation would be technically possible.[15]

Still, the solution is not as stable as the solution of a pure Coordination game, and as in the Assurance game, uncertainty about each other's actual preferences may introduce more instability. At any point one of the parties may still be tempted to reopen negotiations, insisting on more than his conventional share. In such cases, the stability of the pattern will be enhanced if the parties do not only conform to each other's expectations for prudential reasons, but also, or primarily, because they believe that the conventional division is a just or fair one. The sense of justice in this interpretation – giving each his due, in which one's due is, within limits, a matter of convention – is one of the cooperative virtues on which a pattern of mutual expectations may be based. People mutually expect each other to accept reasonable compromises, and in so far as the sense of justice is widespread, they will actually do so, thereby confirming each other's expectations.

The sense of justice reintroduces symmetry. If people are completely symmetrically placed, it offends our sense of justice if they do not get equal shares.[16]

Take property norms as a characteristic example of Division game rules which require respect with an appeal to the sense of justice. In their absence, people will appropriate whatever they feel they need, and more. As Hobbes classically argued, that will be a source of conflict containing all the elements of infinite escalation. (I want more than I need now, in anticipation of my future needs; you do so as well. But because of the possible conflict this creates between us, I am particularly interested in the means for strengthening my position in that conflict. And as it is not my power in absolute terms which counts against you, but the balance of power between us, I even have a reason to weaken you, if it does me no other good.) It is also, as Hume argued, a disincentive in investment. (You consider reclaiming and sowing an area of fertile land, but you know that at harvest time, others will come and take the grain, so you abandon the plan.) Everybody's position will be improved by the introduction of a scheme of rules for exclusive appropriation. But which scheme? Nobody will be indifferent about that issue.

Not any compromise will do, if an appeal to the sense of justice is to succeed. To begin with, threat potential cannot have anything to do with it; as Rawls says somewhere, "to everyone according to his threat advantage is not a conception of justice". If a compromise depends on threat potential, people will not feel morally

---

[14] A formal convention, see ch. 6.1.

[15] For experimental evidence on the role of conventions in bargaining, see Roth 1987, Binmore 1991, Young 1996, 116ff. According to Young, the conventional solution "becomes a norm that the subjects rationalize as 'fair', even though it may be idiosyncratic to the particular history of the play..." This common way of social scientists to epiphenomenalize the moral element is actually incoherent: why would people take the trouble of rationalizing actions in moral terms if they had no independent interest in their moral properties?

[16] Skyrms 1996, ch. 1, shows that 'justice' in this sense (50/50 division) is, in most conditions, the outcome to be expected from an evolutionary process if the game is one of dividing a good and the players get nothing if their claims sum to more than 100%.

bound to it; as soon as the other's capacity for doing harm is reduced, they will start pressing for better conditions. In a similar way, people will not feel bound to go on making concessions which they have been compelled to make because of urgent needs; on the contrary, they will tend to feel that need is a basis for entitlement. Similarly, people can only be required to respect any proposed scheme of distribution if they substantially profit from it. They need not profit equally. But if the parties are symmetrically situated, they will perhaps only accept an equal division as a fair one. In that case, equality may not be rationally but morally compelling.

Here we come across an idea that will be my guiding thought in much of this book. If people expect each other to act in certain ways because of a disposition to honour such expectations, the expectations as such are open to moral assessment. They may be criticizable on either of two accounts. In the first place, it may turn out that mutual adjustment of actions does not really create any surplus value at all. Secondly, even if it does, it may turn out that the benefits and/or burdens are distributed in a manner that does not satisfy the requirement of reciprocity to a degree sufficient to warrant any appeal to fidelity, or fairness, or the sense of justice.

## 2.5. Prisoner's Dilemma

From the last sections of the first chapter onwards, I discussed games in which a pattern of mutual expectations can to some extent be predicted to be self-maintaining because people have prudential reasons to conform to each other's expectations, but in which the pattern may still be rather unstable – and this for several reasons, including, most prominently, insufficient or insufficiently transparent information about each other's preferences. I argued that in these cases the stability of the pattern will be enhanced if people generally conform to each other's expectations for moral reasons. Such reasons derive from attitudes concerning the pattern of mutual expectations as such, attitudes of fidelity and justice.

This claim is not a matter of pure speculation. In the first place, I expect the reader to recognize the description from his own experience, and in the second place some corroborating findings from social psychology could be adduced.[17]

In this section we will find a similar pattern in yet another game; moreover, in variants of the same game we will find a pattern in which cooperative virtues do more than simply bolster instrumental conventions, conventions which might also exist, albeit somewhat less stably, in virtue of sheer instrumental rationality. For in these new cases, such rational considerations would advise *not* to conform to people's expectations. In cases of that kind, therefore, patterns of mutual expectation can only exist if these are expectations to behave in a cooperatively virtuous way.

The game I refer to is, of course, the Prisoner's Dilemma (PD). In PD games there is only one Nash equilibrium. However, there is another non-equilibrium outcome which is preferable to both players, though it is not the best possible outcome for either.

---

[17] Surveyed by Verbeek 1998, ch. 3; see also Fehr and Gächter 1998.

For obvious reasons, the choice which, if paired with the other player's similar choice, leads to the equilibrium, is usually called Defection (*D*), the alternative choice Cooperation (*C*).

In a one-shot PD instrumental rationality counsels Defection. This is not only because mutual defection is a Nash equilibrium. Rather, Defection is the dominant choice, it is the best thing to do whatever the other player does. If he chooses *C*, you will get your best possible outcome by choosing *D* yourself, and if he chooses *D*, you will at least avoid getting your worst possible outcome by making the same choice yourself. Suppose, however, that a pattern of mutual expectations exists to choose *C* in a certain type of one-shot Prisoner's Dilemma game. In such a game I may expect the other player to choose *C*, and I know him to expect me to choose *C* as well. In that case I would *exploit* his expectation by choosing *D* myself, and I may feel reluctant to do so, because I think such exploitation would be *unfair*. This attitude is an example of a cooperative virtue in the sense discussed: I would feel myself constrained by the expectations of the other player, and precisely that motivation, if widespread, would make the pattern of expectations self-maintaining. But in order for an appeal to a motive of fairness to be justified, some conditions must be fulfilled, partly similar to the ones identified in the previous section. Firstly, it should be true that we both prefer the outcome of mutual cooperation (*CC*) to the outcome of mutual defection (*DD*): there has to be a "cooperative surplus". The second condition is given with the existence of a pattern of *mutual* expectations, but it is worth stressing. The pattern should give me a reason to expect the other player to choose *C*, and to expect him to expect me to do so as well. I am under no obligation to dupe myself, and, on the other hand, if he is resolved to choose *C* anyway, I will not exploit his expectations, even if I may be disappointing him, by choosing *D* myself.[18]

Such a pattern may have a rather fragile existence, because people are aware that they will occasionally meet free-riders. Social psychology has made it abundantly clear that the main reason why people choose *D* in one-shot PD-games is not the hope for exploitative gains, but the fear of being duped. So they will welcome any support the convention might get from a scheme of punishment for parasites. On any particular occasion, they will try to learn a bit more about the other guy, using their general knowledge of human nature to "sniff out" a parasite.[19] And they will of course make use of any specific information about their partner they can find.

However, to the extent that such knowledge is available, either from previous meetings with the same person, or from a collective recording system within the community, the game is no longer a one-shot PD. In an iterated PD, defection is no longer necessarily the obvious choice to make from a purely prudential point of view. For people playing an iterated PD may develop conditional strategies, in which they make their choice in one round dependent on the record of their partner in previous

---

[18] For a fuller list of such conditions, see ch. 4.8. (on the principle of fairness).

[19] Cf. Dawes, Van De Kragt & Orbell 1988 on the effects of communication in experimental PD games: even if no explicit promises are allowed, discussion of the strategy to be adopted leads to an increase of cooperative choices by some 40 %.

rounds. There is no one particular conditional strategy which is always the best to follow, it depends on the other strategies within the population.

Nevertheless, it can be argued that in an environment of intelligent players conditional strategies will do well if they have the following properties.

(1)   If your co-player is making unconditionally cooperative choices (i.e. chooses to play *C* whatever you do), you should not hesitate to exploit him. For in that case, you will get the best possible outcome in each round.

(2)   Any time your co-player attempts to exploit you, you should respond by defecting. For by doing so you will at least avoid getting the worst possible outcome.[20]

(3)   If your co-player is making conditionally cooperative choices, i.e. chooses to play *C* if he may expect you to do the same, you should make cooperative choices yourself. For if you fail to do so, he may be expected to follow guideline (2) and respond by defecting, which will reduce your own pay-off.

A strategy which satisfies the second and third of these criteria is Tit for Tat: open the game with a cooperative choice, and in each following round copy the choice your partner made in the previous one. In some environments it will be possible to improve on this strategy. For example, one might satisfy the first criterion as well by occasionally trying whether one get away with a *D*-choice, or even by doing so in the first round. Or in a series of successive *D*-moves one might occasionally make a *C*-choice again, in order to prevent a "deadlock" arising from an earlier mistaken *D*-choice of your partner, or from his proper response to your attempt at exploitation. But all successful conditional strategies are close relatives to Tit for Tat, they should not be seen as rivals. In an evolutionary process, geared by any mechanism (reproductive success, copying successful strategies) to the survival of the fittest, they will generate a family of winners, making *C* the universally successful choice.[21] After a while it seems wrong to see people as following different strategies, which, after all, are private rules. People simply expect each other to react with defection to defection, they know each other to have these expectations, know each other to know this etc., and this pattern of expectations itself is always a sufficient reason not to defect. So we get an autonomous convention of conditional cooperation. There is room for expectations, but no room at all for moral motives. Or so it would seem.

And yet, that is not what happens in real life. Even experimental games, however long they run, never result in such stable patterns of universal cooperation, and we all know from experience that free-riding occurs even in long-standing relationships. Lacunas in mutual information, in particular about each other's preferences, may be part

---

[20] This should not be interpreted as "punishing", see ch. 3.1.

[21] A complication arises from the fact that being a conditional cooperator brings along special costs of gathering information: you have to invest in detecting unconditional cooperators and parasites. It follows that an evolutionary process may occasionally have niches for unconditional cooperators and parasites, cf. Frank 1988, 63; Lomborg 1996. If everyone cooperates, it is "cheaper" to do so unconditionally, but then eventually parasites will appear, feeding on the unconditional cooperators until they have wiped out both them and, as a result, themselves.

of the explanation.[22] Lack of rationality surely is another. In particular, problems are caused by people's tendency to prefer short-term to long-term gains. The attractiveness of a benefit which can be acquired at a certain date is perhaps inversely proportional to the distance of that date. The result is that people who are only strategically honest tend to betray themselves by their shortsightedness: for the gratifications of dishonesty are often close at hand, while the benefits of a pure record are far away.[23] This being the case, people may be expected to deviate from the convention, perhaps up to the point of undermining it. But if they are also motivated by a desire to be loyal and fair, they will perhaps resist the temptation. The moral motive at least contributes to the stability of the convention. Hence, even in protacted interaction with a PD-structure the resource of cooperative virtue is hardly ever redundant.

Of particular interest, finally, is the iterated $n$-person PD. In this context conditional strategies do not work.[24] If your trade union is losing members, it is hardly a good idea to publicly announce that, if any other member leaves, you will leave as well. In $n$-person PD-interaction therefore, defection is the prudential choice, and a pattern of mutual expectations of cooperation can only persist if people are motivated by a sense of fairness not to exploit each other's expectations.

This is of particular interest, because the production of so-called public goods is, at least often, an $n$-person PD. The relevant characteristic of a public good in this context is that, for some reason or other, it is not feasible to exclude people from its consumption who have not contributed to its production. Suppose for instance that the public good of national defence is to benefit one million people. If I do not contribute to its upkeep by paying my taxes dutifully, I will reduce the value of the good by a percentage of 0.00001 (or somewhat more, if I am paying more than the average), which I will hardly notice. Each person has to pay the costs of his contribution all by herself, but the benefits she thereby produces are spread evenly over the population. Yet everyone would gladly spend the required amount for having an army to defend her.

The order of my preferences will be as follows. The best outcome is everyone paying his taxes except me, the next-best everyone paying his taxes, including me. Considerably worse is the situation in which no-one pays any taxes, but it would be even worse, of course, if I were the only one to do so. This is the characteristic ordering of the PD.[25]

---

[22] For instance, some people do not play for a maximum pay-off in absolute terms, but for "winning" with a maximally differential pay-off, cf. McClintock & Liebrand 1988.

[23] Den Hartogh 1985, 242; Frank 1988, 76-91. On inconsistent time-preferences see Elster 1979, 65-76 and in particular Ainslie 1992; cf. Buchanan 1975, ch. 8, arguing that retribution tends to be underproduced.

[24] As I argue in Den Hartogh 1993, 118-120, against M. Taylor 1987, ch. 4 in particular, cf. also Edel 1979, R. Hardin 1982, ch. 11. One problem is that in large groups it is impossible to satisfy the informational requirements for common knowledge of everybody's preferences and rationality, and to adequately monitor individual contributions.

[25] R. Hardin 1971. So-called step goods are sometimes supposed to require a different analysis, Taylor and Ward 1982; R. Hardin 1982, 55-61; Hampton 1987. For an even wider conception see Verbeek 1998, 13-17: the optimal outcome can be described as a public good in all those cases in which rational choices of individuals may lead to suboptimal outcomes for all, even if this is only because the rational choice is underdetermined (prolonged bargaining, risk-avoiding choices in Assurance games etc.).

This is the "logic of collective action", first given a fully general analysis by Mancur Olson. It applies mutatis mutandis in all cases in which the individual's access to the enjoyment of the good does not depend on his own contribution. We may think of keeping clean common rooms or public spaces, free donation of blood or organs, restricting pay claims or catches or production goals or the number of one's children, maintaining quality standards (abstaining from diluting the wine with anti-freeze), paying for public transport, interfering in the public execution of crimes. These cases do not only include the production of so-called non-excludable goods, if any exist (the light of lighthouses, sea-walls, deterrence, scientific knowledge, being governed by a queen?), for there may be reasons of expediency or justice not to exclude non-paying people from consumption, even if it is somehow feasible to do so. We would not want to let an ill person die on the streets, even if he never paid the insurance premium, not from lack of funds but from lack of prudence, or of inhibitions against free-riding. It is not the intrinsic nature of the good which is relevant, but the actual mode of its production.

The conventional wisdom has it that we need the state for solving this problem, and I agree. But the conventional wisdom also has it that it is the state's task to provide me with the prudential incentive to pay which I so far lacked. I will argue in chapter Three that it is neither feasible, nor desirable, nor necessary to give the state that task. Obviously, collective action occurs, even in the absence of state coercion: people donate blood, vote, strike, participate in demonstrations, protest actions and revolutions, do fatigue-duty, pay for trade union membership, contribute to good causes, form cartels, do their share of work in kibbutzim, kolkhozes and university departments. They are able to maintain academic standards, even in perverse systems like the Dutch one, in which the security of the examinators' job depends on the number of candidates passing.[26] On the whole, people are prepared to pay their fair share of fiscal burdens, if only they remain convinced that everyone else will do so as well.[27] The law-enforcing task of the state is mostly to provide that assurance.[28]

## 2.6. The Structure of a Pattern of Expectations

Let us return for a moment to the original Lewis convention, which has emerged within an iterated game of pure coordination. Why exactly do we expect each other to converge on a particular proper equilibrium *A*? According to Lewis, if I want to reconstruct my reasons explicitly, I have to think along the following lines. In the first

---

[26] Additional explanations may refer to selective incentives (additional rewards which are only available for contributors, like legal aid to trade union members), Olson 1965, 51, and to the internal value of participation in the cooperative enterprise as such.

[27] Tyler 1990.

[28] "Niemand will allein gut sein. Unter lauter gütigen, ehrlichen Leuten würde der Bösewicht seine Bosheit ablegen, sobald er überzeugt wäre, dass er von anderer gutem Willen sich lauter Gutes versprechen kann. Hier liegt nun die Schwierigkeit, dass das Gute einzeln nur vom Allgemeinen erzeugt werden kann, das Gute aber nicht allgemein werden kann ohne das Einzelne... Es scheint alles darauf anzukommen, dass man von dem, was allgemeinen Einfluss hat, d.i. von der Regierung anfange." Kant 1984, 1407 (1773-8?)

place, there is something which "indicates to me" that you will go to A. On the very first occasion, this something will be the fact that A is salient, but the next time it will be the fact that we have met at A before (precedent), and as soon as the convention is established, it will be the fact that we meet at A regularly. If you go to A, I have a decisive reason to go to A as well. I will also realize that you will know that precisely this fact indicated to me that you will go there, and therefore have reason to go there as well, and this will give you an additional reason to go. Furthermore, I will realize that the very same fact will "indicate to you" that I will go to A, and that this will give you a further reason to go there. And so on and so forth. Within such reasoning, "we are windowless monads doing our best to mirror each other, mirror each other mirroring each other and so on."[29]

At the end of the exercise we have mutual beliefs about mutual beliefs about mutual beliefs... about our both going to A, up to some indefinite order, and these higher-order beliefs all derive from the very same "indicating" fact. There is a question whether we can stop at any particular level, without the risk that at the next higher one our beliefs will fail to harmonize. But if there is no particular reason to suspect that the relevant evidence we have at our command does not fully overlap, we may trust the whole pattern of our mutual beliefs of lower and higher order to be "transparent": our beliefs match each other, up to the highest level we are able to reach, and they would go on matching if we went up even higher. (Hence, in a virtual sense we may be said to go to infinitely high levels: we simply go on pressing the iteration button.)[30]

It seems to me that this conception of the structure of the pattern is basically misguided. The quotation from Lewis with its reference to monads is very revealing in that respect: he still has not taken seriously enough the idea of *interdependent* reasons. The idea of an independent basis of expectation is really a rudimentary form of parametric reasoning in a strategic context: it presupposes that it is always possible to assign independent probabilities to the choices of each of the players. Of course it is *possible* that one of them has an independent reason to choose one of his alternatives, but in that case it cannot really be a game of pure coordination they are playing.[31]

Consider this first "indicating" fact. If I can with any degree of confidence conclude from it that you will go to A, I have a decisive reason to go there myself. You, obviously, need no other reason, and neither do I. The whole superstructure of higher-order beliefs is completely redundant. So it turns out that we have no coordination *problem* after all: you have an independent reason to opt for one of the alternatives, and I can take that fact as a starting-point for the identification of my own rational choice. The solution is individually accessible. If, on the other hand, the "indicating" fact is insufficient for me to conclude with sufficient confidence that you will go to A, it will also be insufficient for me to conclude that you will have realized that I have a reason to go there. In this case, the superstructure of higher-order expectations cannot get off the

---

[29] Lewis 1969, 38.

[30] Cf. Schiffer 1972, 32-36; Clark & Carlson 1982; Tuomela 1984, 210; Morris & Shin 1997.

[31] Common access to an independent factual basis should therefore not be built into the definition of common knowledge as a necessary condition, as in Lewis 1969, 52-56, Schiffer 1972, 30ff, Heal 1978, 125ff.

ground. If, in any pure coordination problem, I make my choice on account of some fact which "indicates to me" what you are going to choose, the indicating force of this fact must therefore be common knowledge already, i.e. it must be a convention.[32] Otherwise our problem could not be a real coordination problem after all.

Or consider the basic idea of salience. Why would the fact that a meeting-point is salient give you any reason to go there? The answer is that it gives you a reason because you will realize that I will go there. Salience is relevant because we already mutually expect each other to converge on the salient. This is confirmed if we look at the relevant sense of 'salience'. I may know, for example, that a meeting-point has a very special meaning for you, on account of a particular fact of your biography. But if that is my reason for expecting you to go there, then, indeed, we have no coordination problem, because the solution is, again, individually accessible. Rather, the sense of salience relevant to the solution of a coordination problem is: what we mutually know will be salient to each of us.[33] For that reason it is no coincidence that the very same fact has the same "indicating" meaning for both of us: the point is that it indicates *transparently*.

It is time we gave up the idea that it should be possible for a pattern of mutual expectations to be justified on an independent basis. The order of justification within the pattern seems to be precisely the other way round: I expect you to go to *A*, because I know that you expect me to go there, and so have a reason to go there as well. How do I know? Because I know that you know that I expect you to go there and you will go there as well.[34] We know that other road-users expect us to keep to the right; we have no reason to change this belief as long as they keep to the right themselves. We do not need to know any independent reasons for their expectations. But if we do know their expectations, we know what to decide ourselves. Their expectations are a sufficient ground for our decision. And hence for *their* expectations! Everyone has reason to do what the other, for whatever reason, expects him to do. And precisely that fact is sufficient ground for everybody to continue in their expectations. Nobody needs more grounds. When a pattern of expectations has been established, on whatever basis, then it is self-perpetuating without our ever having to return to that basis again.

This structure shows what it means to say that your lowest-order expectation that I will choose *A* is *justified*. It is justified by reference to the pattern of expectations as a whole, and in particular the higher-order ones, in combination with the ascription to me of either utility-maximizing rationality or a cooperative disposition (or both). And it is

---

[32] The same point has been made by Miller 1987; Cudd 1990; and Gilbert 1989, 332-333, but on less than fully convincing grounds. For example, Gilbert objects that Lewis appeals to psychological propensities lying outside the conceptual map of game theory. He does indeed, and knowingly, cf. Lewis 1972. But that is not a problem unless the appeal is inconsistent with game theory, which it is only on the revealed preference theory of utility.

[33] This is easily confirmed by giving any audience two successive tasks: first, to note the first number that comes to mind; secondly, to write down the same number as everyone else in this room. The first task gives you a large variety of numbers (with the number 7 being more prominent for English-speaking audiences than for Dutch ones), the second task the number 1 predominantly. Cf. Mehta, Starmer & Sugden 1994. Note that there is a difference between interdependent salience and higher-order salience (what I have reason to think you have reason to believe to be salient for me); higher-order salience still reflects independent salience. Schelling 1960, 94; Sugden 1993, 81-82.

[34] Cf. Den Hartogh 1998.

therefore open to challenge from the conditions under which it makes sense to appeal to such motives anyhow. As I indicated before, this corollary is most important for the problems I hope to deal with in this book.

"Conventions are like fires: under favourable conditions a sufficient concentration of heat spreads and perpetuates itself. The nature of the heat does not depend on the original source of heat. Matches may be our best fire starters, but that is no reason to think of fires started otherwise as any the less fires."[35] The original source Lewis has in mind is agreement; but habit, precedent and first-order salience are, at best, no more than matches either.[36]

If this is the correct account of the structure of a pattern of expectations, we should identify the convention not, as Lewis does, with the regularity of behaviour, but rather with the transparent pattern of self-fulfilling mutual expectations.[37]

That no independent basis is needed, is particularly clear in the case of linguistic communication. If I say to you:"That no independent basis is needed, is particularly clear in the case of linguistic communication", you do not believe that I want you to believe that it is particularly clear etc., because you have observed that this is what people regularly want when they utter this sentence, from which you go on to conclude that I will assume you to have this belief as well. We already know each other to know (to know etc.) how to construct the meaning and force of the utterance, and that is why you know what I want you to believe.

But the power of patterns of expectation in chaining people to a particular choice independently of any independent reasons is most evident when an option is no longer equivalent to rival alternatives, and therefore would not be chosen for independent reasons at all. Suppose the equilibrium $A$ to be inferior to equilibrium $B$ on the preferential scale of all players. Confronted with the choice between $A$ and $B$ for the first time, all would choose $B$ without any hesitation. Yet a convention may exist for choosing $A$.[38] In the Netherlands, priority is given to traffic approaching a roundabout, although everyone can see that it would be more sensible for traffic on the roundabout to have priority. In such cases the conventional choice cannot be based on replicated practical reasonings based on independent "signifiers" for the anticipated behaviour, for such signifiers point unambiguously to the $B$-choice which is not made.[39]

---

[35] Lewis 1969, 88.

[36] And orders: the prudent player sticks to the strategy of his team *etsi Beckenbauer non daretur*. This is the basic mistake in overestimating the role of legislative authority in law.

[37] Shwayder 1965, 252ff. In these extraordinary pages, the first attempt is made to analyse the concept of a social rule in terms of higher-order expectations justifying lower-order ones. "I act from the knowledge that others know that I will act from the knowledge that they expect me so to behave," o.c., 256. The only element missing in his account is a context (like the coordination problem) explaining the justifying force of higher-order expectations.

[38] Lewis concludes that for a coordination problem to arise, "different coordination equilibria do not have to be equally good – only good enough so that everyone is ready to do his part if the others do", Lewis 1969, 50. But without a convention there would be no coordination problem at all!

[39] On the assumption that there is no problem to coordinate on the equilibrium which is best for all, see ch. 1.5. at note 37 and below at note 42 An inferior convention can establish itself because it has a temporal headstart on superior ones. A similar process can be observed in the diffusion of technologies with network

Nothing other than the pattern of mutual expectations binds the players to the $A$-choice: any suggestion of a dilemma is created by the convention itself. "These people are trapped."[40]

Reversing the order of justification is essential for my account of obligating norms. For the fact that I have a disposition of fidelity or fairness is not an independent reason for me to make the cooperative choice in an Assurance game or PD, nor is it part of any fact that will "indicate to you" that I will make this choice. Rather, I will feel constrained by fidelity or fairness to make that choice, because you already expect me to do so. But this does not mean that you already expect it on account of any other fact. Your only reason for expecting me to make the cooperative choice is that you know I will not let you down. The cooperative virtue and the pattern of expectations have an internal reference to each other. There is no independent basis.

If this is true, we can understand how a pattern of expectations, once established, can be self-maintaining. The expectations invoke the wish to honour them, and are thereby confirmed. But from the very same data alone (the relevant utility functions of the players and their cooperative dispositions), we cannot explain how the convention has emerged.[41] We have saved ontological individualism, but we fail to satisfy the program of methodological individualism.

To some this will be disappointing. Let me therefore point out that it is not a predicament specific to my account, but only an example of a tendency recurring in many areas of rational-choice theory. We have come across other examples. The first is the Coordination game in which one of the proper equilibria is also unambiguously the best possible outcome for all players. Intuitively, we feel they will have no problem to converge on it, but there seems to be no account in terms of plausible maxims of individual rational choice to explain that.[42] Secondly, we saw that the concept of a Nash equilibrium – expressing a requirement of strategic thinking – gives a necessary, but not a sufficient condition for an individually accessible solution. And indeed, in many games, even if there is just one equilibrium, it is not obvious that it presents the solution. However, in some games, it *is* obvious, even if we seem unable to explain this in terms of other plausible maxims of rational choice.[43] Obviously, in such a case we have matching expectations, but we cannot explain in strategic terms how unmatching

---

externalities (p.c.'s, videocassette recorders etc.). Philips has a reputation for always being too late with its technically superior products.

[40] Lewis 1969, 98. Cf. the quotation from Fontane in footnote 80. As the story of the Emperor's Clothes reminds us, such conventions tend to be rather unstable, cf. Kuran 1995 on the sudden collapse of communism in Eastern Europe.

[41] Lewis seems to recognize this when he says: "An action may be rational... even though that action was done by habit... If that habit ever ceased to serve the agent's desires according to his beliefs, it would at once be overridden and corrected by conscious reasoning." Lewis 1983, 181. But on his view, that reasoning would still start from an independent basis.

[42] But see ch. 1, note 37 for my own conjecture.

[43] E.g. iterated deletion of strongly dominated strategies.

expectations change into matching ones.[44] Interdependent reasons cannot be analyzed into independent ones.[45]

All this does not mean that my conception of either prudential or, in particular, of moral (obligatory) conventions has no dynamic aspect at all. On the contrary: we will see that it can very well account for the way in which particular norms change, or even emerge, within a system of norms as a whole.[46] The only event it cannot account for is the emergence of norms from a state of nature, i.e. a pattern of strategic interaction in which as yet there are no norms at all. So it is only a desideratum of pure theory that cannot be met.

Moreover, there is no reason to believe that there is no natural transition from the world of parametric into the world of strategic reasoning. It is entirely probable that in recurring coordination problems parametric agents, or even genes, develop matched habits of choice which secure coordination. This can easily be shown by simple models of replicator dynamics.[47] In this process first-order salience may have a role to play, if the agents are sufficiently similar in other respects. For in that case, they will tend to focus on the same focal points. What makes pure coordination problems difficult is the perfect symmetry of the game; any mechanism that can break the symmetry will get rooted once it happens to develop (e.g. by mutation). If such forms of coordination have been established, they will persist when the subjects acquire the ability of strategic reasoning, taking the form of transparent patterns of mutual expectations. In that case conventions will be *crystallizations* of convergent patterns of private habits.[48]

## 2.7. Cooperative Virtue

I have shown that the existence of norms, and especially obligating norms, can make the optimal outcome stable or even accessible in Assurance games, in particular with less than perfect mutual knowledge of preferences, in Division games, and in PD-games, in particular, but not exclusively, of the one-shot and the *n*-person variety. The analysis

---

[44] A last example: the fact that social choices are path-dependent does not really create the problems for collective decision makers that social choice theory predicts, because somehow some paths seem mutually acceptable or "natural" to them, while others do not; Chapman 1998.

[45] Recently, a number of authors have tried to account for mutually adjusted action in terms of some strong concept of collective intention, e.g. Sen 1985, 1987, 85ff; Gilbert 1989 and later work; Searle 1990; 1995 ch.1; Sugden 1993; Postema 1995; Baier 1996. I share the idea that acting as a team cannot be analysed into invidual intentions plus common knowledge, on the usual understanding of common knowledge as built from an independent basis. But in my view, this problem must be overcome by assuming "we-beliefs", rather than "we-intentions". These strong conceptions of we-intentions presuppose a volitional theory of commitment, see e.g. Gilbert (1993) 1996, 289-290; 2000, 3, 5, 24.

[46] See in particular ch. 12.

[47] Sugden 1986, ch. 3, Skyrms 1996, ch. 5. Sugden 1998, however, rightly points out that if the model is exemplified by social learning, there is still a problem to be solved concerning the way agents identify the strategy to be adopted, cf. ch. 1, note 28.

[48] A similar point can be made about the emergence of the cooperative virtues, see the next section.

could be extended to other games, for example the so-called Hawk/Dove or Chicken game.[49]

Suppose there is no need to make choices simultaneously and you start by choosing $C$. This is a clear act of trust, for you bring me into the position in which the realization of my first preference only depends on my own choice. Obviously, you are appealing to me to renounce this opportunity if my use of it would harm you. That can only be sensible if you ascribe to me a moral preference that does not surface in the matrix. This preference is not an altruistic one. For your part, you have not taken the opportunity to bring yourself out of danger in a way that would have jeopardized your interest. So what you are asking is not a favour, but a reciprocal service.

In a purely consequentialist, outcome-oriented perspective we would not be able to make this distinction.[50] For in that perspective, your choice has been made irrevocably, and hence it has become irrelevant for deciding between my options on the basis of their outcomes. Because the road to my most preferred alternative is open, abandoning it can only be a sacrifice. I can only interpret your decision as a reciprocal service if, in evaluating my options, I am not only interested in their outcomes, but also in the way my choice "responds" to yours. The point of reference is in the past. So the moral preference you have to ascribe to me in order to justify your trust, is not forward-looking or consequentialist but rather backward-looking or antecedentialist.[51]

In some cases it is to be expected that I will maximize my own utility by conforming to your expectations. I will only fail to do so if I have non-standard preferences. But this possibility may be real enough and it might lead you to prefer a safety-first choice. Unless you have reason to believe that the very fact that you show you trust me will give me a reason to honour your trust. I will then act from a disposition of reliability or trustworthiness.

In other cases it is not to be expected that I will maximize my own utility, given your action, by conforming to your expectations. But again I may act from a moral preference, this time a moral preference for dealing fairly. To be fair is different from being trustworthy, because it is only because of your act of trust that I can still realize my most preferred outcome. Doing so would not only betray, but also exploit your trust.

What is trust?[52] The answer is implied in the story just told. Common to all forms of trust is risk-taking: you act in such a way that, in comparison with your maximin choice, you get a better result if I do one thing, and a worse one if I do the other. It is possible that you expect me to make the desirable choice because you know this to be to my own advantage, but even if it is not improper to call this "trust", it is only trust in a diminished sense. You will only trust me in the full sense if you expect me not to act to your disadvantage, even if by doing so I do not further my own

---

[49] Cf. Sugden 1986, ch. 4; Skyrms 1996, ch. 4, both arguing (within their parametric framework) that "conventions" of exclusive access or property will emerge in this game.

[50] Except by abandoning the principle of "separability", McClennen 1990, see the next section.

[51] Sher 1983. I do not deny that you can have a preference for your outcome to reflect some past event as well (e.g. a desire to reward or to punish).

[52] Cf. Den Hartogh 1985, ch. 27; Baier 1986; Govier 1992; Pettit 1996. A different account is given by Lagerspetz 1998.

advantage. I may do so for different reasons. One possible reason is that I am interested in your interest: I am an altruist. Another possible reason is that I feel constrained by the very fact of your expectations.

When choices must be made synchronously, the resources of fairness and trustworthiness can only be used if a pattern of mutual expectations of cooperative behaviour already exists. Participating in this pattern is still a form of trust. Neither trustworthiness nor fairness is a purely forward-looking motive, either of an aggregative or a distributive character. To be fair, for example, means to refuse to take advantage, but not because that would lead to a less than optimal collective result, nor because it would create inequality.

Given the PD-matrix, showing the preference-orderings of the players over the possible outcomes of their game, we can only interpret the cooperative choice of rational player You as an expression of trust, and therefore the defecting choice of rational player Me as a form of parasitism. Given those interpretations, the players may develop "new" preferences concerning those choices: a preparedness to cooperate with people who show themselves to be prepared to cooperate, an aversion to parasitism.

The standard objection of game theorists to this procedure is that it is illegitimate, because in order to characterize a game as a PD we have to take into account all relevant preferences.[53] But by complying to that requirement, we would rob ourselves of the very possibility of correctly describing those cooperative dispositions and of explaining their significance for the stability or even the existence of obligating norms. That is one other reason why revealed preference theory is theoretically impoverished: it does not allow us to recognize any structure within our preference-orderings.[54] In particular, it does not allow us to describe any preferences as having an internal relation to certain types of interaction, and to patterns of mutual expectations arising in them. But you can only understand what it means to be fair, if you are allowed the concept of 'exploiting expectations', and you can only understand that concept if you are allowed to identify some games as PD-games to begin with. But if someone claims to be morally concerned about the negative externalities her choices produce for other people, revealed preference theory will not even permit her to talk about externalities: the externalities are supposed to evaporate in the concern.

Conventional game theory makes a basic distinction between utilities and beliefs. Utilities are simply given; beliefs, in particular higher-order beliefs, are to be accounted for. That excludes the possibility that utilities are in some way derived from (higher-order) beliefs. But that is precisely the possibility which is realized in the case of cooperative dispositions.

---

[53] "Such an argument is inadmissible since the numerical utility values are supposed to reflect all such 'ethical' considerations." Luce & Raiffa 1957, 96; cf. Schelling 1968, 42; Braybrooke 1976, 7, 20; Harsanyi 1977, 441; Riker 1980; Hollis 1981, 173-174, cf. 1987, 173ff; M. Taylor 1987, 29-30; Bicchieri 1993, 180; Binmore 1994, 95-117. Decomposition must be allowed anyway for analysing iterated play. Otherwise, how could people choose different strategies in a symmetric game?

[54] Cf. Sen 1977, 231. It would not allow the appeal to salience either, or even to convention itself: if we succeed in coordinating in any non-accidental way, that shows we had no coordination problem.

So we have to proceed in stages. In the first stage, we take into account all preferences with a maximizing structure. This stage results in the identification of the strategic situation as, e.g., an Assurance game or PD. In the second stage, we take into account the relevant preferences concerning such situations and concerning the legitimate mutual expectations of the people involved in them.

These second-stage preferences have several interesting characteristics. They are essentially concerned with the agents' intentional actions, or their intentions, not with any outcomes which can be described independently of the actions. They are backward-looking because they require those actions to respond appropriately to patterns of expectations which already exist. They have a binary rather than a maximizing structure, they do not conform to the model of goodness but to the model of rightness. You are required to be trustworthy and fair, and you either are or you are not – even if it may be difficult to establish whether you are.

However, I do not want to suggest in a Kantian way that such preferences are totally independent of every outcome-oriented, forward-looking and maximizing concern. For you can only require yourself to be fair if you understand the game you play as e.g. a PD, and this means that you are able to differentiate between the equilibrium and the optimum outcome. You are prepared to do your part in a collective enterprise aiming at the optimum. Cooperative virtue is only called for in cooperation. But the point is this: even if you have to be interested in the goodness of some outcomes in order to be interested in satisfying requirements of fairness and trustworthiness as well, the second interest is not instrumental to the first. You do not want your actions to satisfy the requirements *in order* to ensure the outcomes.[55]

On second thought, it turns out that Kant himself thought of the relation between goodness and rightness in a similar way. As Marx was not a Marxist, Kant may not have been a Kantian. For look at his conception of the highest good (*summum bonum*), which consists of two parts: all good things being realized and all right actions being done. (Or rather: the good things being realized for each person *in proportion to* the rightness of the actions he has done.) And the point he goes on to make is that even if you are not supposed to do the right action *in order to* achieve the good things, it would not be reasonable to do the right actions if you despaired of the possibility of the good things coming true.[56] That is why, according to Kant, you have to believe in the existence of an omnipotent Being who will match the good and the right in the end. Even if the interests are not related as means to an end, they must be seen as the factors of an algebraic product $x.y$: if one of the factors amounts to zero, the product will amount to zero as well.

The point can also be expressed in terms of the possible justifications for non-compliance. If you deviate from an existing pattern of mutual expectations, there will be two forms of defence that are at least of the right kind. Either you can say: if I conform

---

[55] "Fidelity is not an instrumental value, but it has its value only in service of other values... Its value is intrinsic, but not self-sufficient." Postema 1994, 175.

[56] *Kritik der Praktischen Vernunft*, Zweites Buch, Zweites Hauptstück, Introduction/I/II. "Dass man auch wohl ein Dupe (Geck) der Tugend sein könne... ist ein unausstehlicher und ungereimter Gedanke", Kant 1984, nr. 7059 (1776/8).

to your expectations, the result will not be advantageous to either of us. Or you can say: some (other) initial conditions for invoking a principle of fairness or a principle of good faith are not satisfied. For example: the other people do not really rely on my contribution, or the contribution I am supposed to make is disproportional to the benefit I will be allowed to enjoy from the cooperative enterprise.[57]

Finally, let me consider the objection that my account has no real explanatory power because I explain social norms in terms of other normative concepts. The answer is that I explain a class of social facts in terms of motivational assumptions. I agree that these assumptions are not ethically neutral, but I see no reason why they should be. Ethics has to be rooted in psychological and social reality somewhere. What my account intends to make available, to both the study of social fact and to normative theory, is the concept of interdependent reasons. If I am right, one important class of interdependent reasons derives from desires which do not have a maximizing structure.[58]

## 2.8. Some Questions about Cooperative Virtue

It is true that further questions can be asked about these desires. One question is: suppose you lack them, would you have instrumental reasons to develop them? If so, would you perhaps even have such reasons to act *as if* you have them, even if you do not?[59] If that could be argued, one might insist that cooperative dispositions do not involve any "new" preferences at all, but only an unusually keen awareness of the requirements of utility-maximizing rationality. Of course, as a rational agent, being aware of what reason requires you will desire to do what it requires. But that is only a "consequent", not an "antecedent" desire: you have the desire because you have the reason, not the other way around.

To make this kind of argument, we have to suppose that the fact of your cooperative disposition is itself relevant to your partner's choice, for example because she is able to identify your disposition and is herself disposed to cooperate with cooperatively disposed people. The problem is, however, that it does not depend on your actual choice whether or not these positive effects of your disposition will be realized. So why should you make any sacrifice of utility, if there is nothing to be gained from the sacrifice itself?

In this context it will be illuminating to interpret the ("binary") requirement which a cooperatively disposed person makes on himself, as a form of *commitment* to a private rule or plan. At the moment of choice you only act with reference to the rule or plan, without considering which of the options then available will maximize your utility

---

[57] See for these conditions ch. 4.8. on the principle of fairness.

[58] Or from the desire-independent requirements recognized in such desires. As I explained in ch. 1.3. I do not want to commit myself to any particular conception of the relation between "value" and desire.

[59] Sen 1974; Gauthier 1986 ch. 6 and later work; McClennen 1990, ch. 9/12; 1997. It is not always clear which of these arguments these authors wish to make, partly because they do not distinguish between antecedent and consequent desire. Another interpretation they are sometimes tempted to is that the act of commitment causally makes a deviant action unfeasible. But a moral preference is not an addiction.

(at least up to a certain threshold), or at least without acting upon such considerations. In my view, this is an adequate description of what it takes to be cooperatively disposed. The question is only whether it is possible to go all the way on nothing but rationality and consequent desires: you make the commitment because you know that making it has positive ("autonomous") effects,[60] and, having made it, as a rational person you act accordingly, because you have made the commitment.[61] This procedure is inconsistent with a property usually attributed to utility-maximizing rationality: its separability or modularity.[62] In order to realize a plan, an agent often has to make successive choices. At each of these "nodes", it is possible to identify a subplan, consisting of the choice to be made at that moment and the following ones. Separability means that the plan can only be rational if each of the subplans is rational *on its own terms*. The rationality of the plan derives from the rationality of its subplans (considered in backwards temporal ordering), not the other way around.

I cannot enter into a full discussion of separability.[63] Let me just note that, if we reject it, what used to be considered a form of robust subplanning rationality will then appear as a form of weakness of will. Either way, we should suspect actual human beings to be particularly prone to it.[64] For that reason it would not be redundant, even for agents capable of non-modular rationality, to develop antecedent desires to make cooperative choices as well.[65]

The next question is: is it possible to give an account of the emergence of these antecedent desires? Though the dispositions themselves are such that only strategic agents can exhibit them – responding, as they do, to patterns of mutual expectations of higher and lower orders -, they might have evolved from more primitive forms which can be explained by social learning theory, or even by evolution theory. At this point, the population dynamical accounts of the evolution of cooperative behaviour which have been so popular recently, may have something important to tell us.[66] For instance, if people often play asynchronous Assurance games[67] without perfect knowledge of each other's preferences, they may develop matched dispositions to coordinate on the supposedly optimal equilibrium. If you see your fellows deer-hunting, you allow the hares to run, even if today you would like hare better than deer. It may be that in doing so you only react to the others' observed behaviour, not to any expectations you ascribe

---

[60] The term "autonomous effects" has been introduced by Kavka 1987, 21, 46.

[61] The commitment then functions as an "exclusionary reason", see ch. 7.3ff. That discussion is relevant to the present question as well.

[62] McClennen 1990, 120ff.

[63] See Den Hartogh unpubl.

[64] Cf. the kidnapper who has collected his ransom, and now would prefer to let his victim go, but knows his victim will be able to identify him. The victim promises not to do so. Will the promise have any credibility? See Ellsberg 1975, referred to by Binmore 1994, 35-36.

[65] There is evidence for the existence of antecedent desires supporting conventions. For example: ownership increases the valuation of a good with more than 100%. Kahnemann, Knetsch & Thaler 1991.

[66] Gibbard 1982; 1990, 64-80; Frank 1987; Skyrms 1996, ch. 2.

[67] An asynchronous game is a game in which the players have to make their decisions successively rather than synchronously. So the second player can observe the choice made by the first.

to them; or only to first-order expectations you ascribe to them, not to any transparent pattern of higher-order ones.[68] At first sight it seems that these matched choices of starting to "rely" and to "be reliable" do not constitute what the biologists call an "evolutionary stable state', i.e. a Nash equilibrium which cannot be invaded by a few mutants (because it is a better reply to the mutant strategy than the mutant strategy is to itself). For if the "convention" is both to rely and to be reliable, you obviously do better by relying but not being reliable. However, it may be the case that such interactions mostly occur between subjects who are similarly programmed. Or it may be the case that the agents can *sniff* lack of reliability.[69] (Note that the argument in this last form is isomorphic to the argument we considered for the rationality of acting on commitments made for autonomous reasons.) In such cases, it is possible for the relevant dispositions to develop.

I have stressed at several places that some initial conditions must be satisfied before a succesful appeal can be made to the cooperative virtues. Evolutionary replicator dynamics may help us understand why these conditions are a necessary element of the program. It explains, for example, why the sense of justice insists on equal sharing between symmetrically placed agents.[70] Or why, in the so-called Ultimatum game – we have to divide fl. 100 between us, I have to make you an offer, you take it or both of us get nothing – ideas of fair dealing move people not to accept low offers, even if utility-maximizing reason prescribes them to accept any offer whatsoever.[71]

The task remains to give a plausible detailed description of the transition from the world of parametric learning to the world of full strategic rationality.

## 2.9. A Conventionalist Theory of Obligation

The existence of obligatory norms presupposes the widespread existence of a pattern of matched dispositions. A Lewis convention does not create any obligations, it is a "hypothetical imperative" only. The person who fails to follow it meets nothing but "natural" sanctions: if your linguistic mistake is severe enough you will be misunderstood. Your behaviour may be open to criticism, but only as lacking in intelligence and/or prudence. The underlying form of all patterns of expectations of this type is: I expect you to do whatever maximizes your utility. The underlying form of an obligatory norm, on the other hand, is this: I expect you to cooperate in the production of a common good, because I trust you and it would be untrustworthy or unfair to betray my trust. As I explained in section 6, (lowest-order) expectation is *justified* by appeal to the relevant higher-order expectations and the principles of fidelity, justice and fairness, which must be understood as expressing the conditions under which it makes sense to

---

[68] Cf. ch. 3.4.

[69] Frank 1987, ch. 5/6.

[70] Skyrms 1996, ch. 2.

[71] Skyrms 1996, ch. 3.

expect people to act from cooperative dispositions. Such justified expectations, I suggest, are obligations and/or duties. If they are not met, people may be expected to criticize you as lacking in virtue, and to have the appropriate motivating feelings, e.g. of disapproval or indignation.[72]

This is a rather naturalistic view of obligation and duty. Its naturalism follows from the fact that the reasons you have for meeting your obligation or duty are interdependent reasons: they presuppose a pattern of mutual expectations as a contingent social fact. That does not mean, however, that existing expectations are immune against moral criticism. For the system of our mutual expectations as a whole is structured by its underlying form: you expect me to contribute to the common good because it would be untrustworthy or unfair to betray your trust. So if I fail to meet your expectations, it is always a relevant defence for me to say either: the good I am supposed to contribute to is not valuable at all, or I am only getting an unfair share of it; or to say: it is not really untrustworthy or unfair not to honour your expectations, because, for example, you do not really intend to do your share either, or the burdens of production are unfairly distributed.[73]

From the fact that the system of our expectations as a whole is structured by an implicit appeal to underlying values and principles, it also follows that we can often establish what we may legitimately expect each other to do in conditions not explicitly covered by the manifest content of our existing expectations. We can expect the other to mirror our own reasoning if it starts from analogy and/or the relevant values and principles directly. In these cases, the implicit or latent content of our expectations can be made explicit or manifest by argument. When we criticize the manifest content of expectations, we use the same type of argument, playing out, so to speak, the latent against the manifest content.[74]

So if obligation is a kind of social fact, it is a kind of fact which often can only be established by moral argument. It is from this point of view that I intend to criticize positivism as a theory of law.

The basic point to insist on is that the cooperative dispositions and the pattern of mutual expectations have an internal reference to each other. In chapter One, I considered institutional theories of social practices, including law. It is often conceded that the existence of such practices is a morally relevant fact. The practice is described in terms of its "constitutive" rules, and then one adds: and a valid moral principle (fidelity, fairness, or whatever) exists, requiring you to conform to those rules.[75] In this

---

[72] This is an externalist account of obligation and duty: recognizing the existence of an obligation does not imply that you are motivated to meet it. But it is presupposed that most people most of the time will be so motivated. Otherwise, the corresponding expectations could not survive.

[73] For a more extended discussion see chapter 8.6. on positive and critical morality.

[74] Cf. ch. 12. 3.

[75] Cf. Rawls 1971, 344-350; Fried 1981, 16-17; Nieuwenhuis 1979. It is this order of description which may account for the lingering positivism of institutionalists: it allows them to discuss matters of legal validity in the lawyer's heaven of concepts, and only afterwards attend to matters of moral import and social importance. The very notion of a "constitutive rule" fosters this illusion. However, the constitutive rule is supposed to assert that "*x* counts for *y* in context *C*", but, outside of the special context of parlour games, the *y* refers to

way, one fails to observe that the practice could not exist unless we could count on each other generally to honour this principle. We cannot describe the "institution" in a morally neutral way, and then leave it to the autonomous individual to make up his moral mind; for the mutual ascription of a moral motive is the foundation of the institution.

This invites an obvious objection: it seems to follow that only a person who is trustworthy, or even known to be trustworthy, can assume an obligation.

The idea is not quite as absurd as it might seem. Suppose you live in a very small community, all members of which know each other from frequent interaction. In such a community the person who lies habitually will in the end be unable to do so, i.e. to make any deceiving statements whatsoever. For people will simply stop believing him. In the same way, the unreliable person will be unable to execute an intention to have other people rely on him.

But in larger communities there will be many transactions in which no sufficient evidence concerning the individual parties is available. In these cases we cannot trust them on account of their personal characteristics, but only on account of the general trustworthiness of the people in this community. Therefore the obligation does not rest on the promisor as the particular individual she is, but only as a member of a particular community. It is this anonymous pattern of mutual expectations which I propose as the proper analysans of the concept of a social norm.

The climax of this process of anonymization – the stage of the legal contract – is reached when a person, personally known to be unreliable, succeeds in making use of the anonymous norm to make himself responsible for his future conduct nevertheless. Significantly, this may require him to proceed in a more formal way than a more reliable person would have to.

Social norms are relatively autonomous patterns of mutual expectations of behaviour and behavioural dispositions, entertained by a certain number of persons who, on account of that very fact, make up a social group. These patterns can be relatively autonomous, because the lower-order expectations are justified by the higher-order ones and not vice versa: given the higher-order expectations, every member of the group has some reason to conform to the lower-order ones. This explains the persistence of the rule.

Within the class of such patterns of expectations, I have made two distinctions. The first distinction is between social norms proper, which are characterized by anonymity, and patterns of expectations directed at known persons. The second distinction is between proper conventions and obligatory rules.

We have seen how these clusters of expectations can emerge, or at least persist in different "games", types of social interaction as characterized by interdependence of outcomes. The common characteristic of situations in which Lewis conventions are liable to exist is that, in the absence of patterns of expectation, independent rational choice is underdetermined. If they had a decisive reason to make one particular choice, people would make it; they would even mutually expect each other to do so, but these

---

some normative force, and hence relies on a "regulative" convention identifying interdependent reasons for action. MacCormick 1998 recognizes this.

expectations would not generate additional reasons for action, and the pattern of expectations would not be autonomous.

This characteristic is not shared by situations in which we find that obligatory rules do exist. It has often been suggested[76] that such rules tend to arise in situations in which the independent rational choices of the individual agents would lead to a suboptimal equilibrium outcome; the "function" of the rule is to make an optimal outcome – whether or not it is also an equilibrium – accessible. But this is a dangerous way of speaking, for it makes it quite mysterious how it is possible for these rules to emerge, or at least to persist, by the rational choices of individuals. In this type of theory, a stable pattern of expectations cannot fail to point at an equilibrium.

So far, my analysis has proceeded by differentiating between motivational levels. At the level of preferences over outcomes (the utility level), the obligatory rule may not identify an equilibrium, at the level of cooperative dispositions it does.

## 2.10. Social Norms and the Common Good

A more basic question, however, is whether an obligatory rule necessarily identifies a social optimum (defined over utilities).

Jon Elster has forcefully argued that existing social norms need not be optimizing, and that, if a social optimum is identifiable, the norms enabling a group to reach it may be lacking.[77] He takes these points to be sufficient to refute a rational-choice approach towards the emergence of norms. It is puzzling why he believes this. Rational-choice theory in any form predicts that equilibria will be reached, not optima. Whether or not a theory of social norms is committed to assert that norms tend to bridge gaps between equilibria and optima, depends on the additional motivational assumptions the theory makes.

One point should be absolutely clear. From the fact that an unambiguous social optimum outcome can be determined, it does not follow in the least that a social norm will exist requiring behaviour which makes it accessible. Elster is perfectly right in saying this, but one can hardly imagine any form of rational-choice theory predicting the contrary. In an $n$-person iterated PD, for example a global environmental issue like the influence of human productive activities on the ozon layer, on climate, on deforestation, everybody can see that the equilibrium outcome of actual choices is disastrous. It does not follow that a pattern of mutual expectations of constrained behaviour will necessarily arise. The emergence of social norms is a contingent phenomenon.

Will the emergence of obligatory norms necessarily be a step towards the Pareto frontier? Within the theory of social norms I have sketched, two theses are particularly relevant to this question. The first concerns the existence of cooperative dispositions,

---

[76] Ullmann-Margalit 1977; Mackie 1977a; Musschenga 1980; Ellickson 1991.

[77] Elster 1989, ch. 3; 1990a; 1990b; critical review by Van Zetten 1997.

the second the autonomous character of patterns of mutual expectations. These ideas point in diverging directions.

Take for instance norms of trustfulness. When a pattern of mutual expectations has emerged in a siuation with the profile of an Assurance game, people are to some extent disposed not to shame one another's expectations. Within certain limits, this disposition can be said to be "content-independent"; it tends to make norms persistent, even if they have survived their usefulness.[78] This persistence is reinforced by several other mechanisms tending to strengthen the autonomous nature of the norm. In the first place, a person's adherence to the norm is an important aspect of her reputation and hence her status within a community.[79] Even if you are personally convinced that following the norm does nobody any good, you may feel obliged to go on complying because non-compliance would be socially disastrous for you.[80] (And, in order to reduce cognitive dissonance, this will tend to make you believe that the norm is useful as well.) In the second place, people tend to disapprove of actions which deviate from the norm, and they will express their resentment in all kinds of ways, from minor rebukes to social ostracism. Agents usually are motivated to avoid these forms of disapproval.[81] Thirdly, defecting from a collective enterprise for mutual advantage is a form of free-riding. If people believe, however mistakenly, that some important good is at stake requiring contributions from all, they will tend to distrust your motivation if you claim to deviate because you do not agree with their valuation. They will think you are a free-rider masquerading as a conscientious objector. Of course, all these mechanisms also reinforce each other: the defector will not only be known as someone you cannot trust to cooperate, but as a hypocrite or a coward as well (think of codes of honour), and social pressure will accordingly not only take the form of a refusal to deal with you, but also of explicit punishment.

Nevertheless, some conditions have to be fulfilled if an appeal to cooperative dispositions is to succeed. In the present context the following condition is pertinent. If obligations are to be sustained within a group, the members of the group should at least mutually *believe*, mistakenly or not, that by conforming to each other's expectations they are, in the long run, moving towards a Pareto superior outcome. People cannot be expected to cooperate if they believe that by doing so, they will only create losses, either to themselves, or to the others, or both. (The base line being defined by the

---

[78] On content-independence see ch. 6.1.

[79] It does not follow that a prudential concern for your reputation can take the place of a genuine cooperative virtue, see ch. 3.4.

[80] "Aber im Zusammenleben mit den Menschen hat sich ein Etwas ausgebildet, das nun einmal da ist und nach dessen Paragraphen wir uns gewöhnt haben, alles zu beurteilen, die andern und uns selbst. Und dagegen zu verstossen geht nicht; die Gesellschaft verachtet uns, und zuletzt tun wir es selbst und können es nicht aushalten und jagen uns die Kugel durch den Kopf... Also noch einmal, nichts von Hass oder dergleichen, und um eines Glückes willen, das mir genommen wurde, mag ich nicht Blut an den Händen haben; aber jenes, wenn Sie wollen, uns tyrannisierende Gesellschaft-Etwas, das fragt nicht nach Charme und nicht nach Liebe und nicht nach Verjährung. Ich habe keine Wahl. Ich muss." Theodor Fontane, *Effi Briest*, Von Innstetten in his dialogue with Wüllersdorf in ch. 27, discussing the unavoidability of challenging the former lover of his wife.

[81] As I argue in ch. 3.4. this mechanism presupposes the existence of an obligatory norm and does not explain it.

equilibrium outcome of independent rational choices.) In a reign of pure terror, in which everybody obeys the order of the tyrant out of fear that everybody will also, out of the same fear, obey his orders to execute punishments for disobedience, nobody will feel that she has any *obligation* to obey. It is part of the content of the mutual beliefs constituting a social norm that doing your duty is doing some good. It follows that the effects of the rule in utility terms are relevant to deciding whether or not one has an obligation to conform to it, and, even more importantly, to interpreting what exactly it is the others are entitled to expect one to do. It will be seen that this implication has far-reaching consequences for legal theory.

A characteristic conflict between the content-independent character of cooperative dispositions and the consciousness of their basic rationale has been artificially created in Milgram's notorious experiments.[82] Subjects participating in an experiment were required to send electric currents through other person's bodies – as they were led to believe – even if, obviously, this had very painful and possibly harmful effects. Most of them obeyed, albeit with obvious feelings of uneasiness. They were taking part in a cooperative enterprise governed by a norm of cooperativeness that required submittance to the experimenter's authority. The content-independent character of this norm had rather horrible consequences. Yet even these subjects showed by their uneasiness that it was relevant for them to ask: what good is my cooperative action doing, and: can I really be expected to do such things? Those questions would not have been the expression of an external morality they contingently happened to have; they follow from the nature of the cooperative disposition itself.[83]

I accept Elster's thesis that the existence of social norms can make things worse. But recognizing this cannot be part of the mutual beliefs which constitute the norm. Hence such norms are inherently criticisable. And I do not agree either that following social norms as such is irrational. For Elster, this follows from the fact that the motive for complying with a norm is backward-looking, but in my view it is an indefensible stipulation to require rationality to be the slave of purely forward-looking passions only.[84] Backward-looking desires like a preference for being fair and trustworthy would only be irrational if having them would systematically thwart the fulfilment of other desires. But that is true of forward-looking desires as well, and there is no reason to suppose that the category of backward-looking desires as such stands condemned.

---

[82] Milgram 1974, 35; cf. the discussion in Sabini and Silver 1982, 37-39, ch. 4.

[83] Strawson 1974, ch. 2.

[84] Van Zetten 1997.5.

# CHAPTER 3

## THE ROLE OF SANCTIONS

### 3.1. The Sanctioning Approach, an Alternative?

The approach of the first two chapters goes against the grain of most explanations of rule-following behaviour. In economics in particular it is almost routinely assumed that compliance can only be explained by the fear of sanctions. It is true that one of the most influential aspects of Hart's critique of the Austinian theory of law concerned the idea of laws as orders backed by threats,[1] but this view of the law is nevertheless still very common, again especially in economic theories of law. Besides, as my aim is to reformulate Hartian theory in terms of a theory of interdependent reasons, it is necessary to show that no plausible theory of interdependent reasons can be built on Austinian foundations. Last but not least, as sanctions undeniably are important to the functioning of law, we should try to understand in general terms how the existence of social norms, in particular obligatory ones, tends to be accompanied by the provision of punishments and rewards. These are the aims of the present chapter.

It is often supposed that the emergence of sanctioning tendencies is explained by the theory of conditional strategies in iterated games. Consider for instance Tit for Tat in 2-person iterated PD-games. It is commonly said that by switching from $C$ to $D$ in response to a $D$-choice of my co-player, I am "punishing" him.[2] This is a confusion. It is true that my switch conveys a message: attempts at exploitation will not be rewarded. But at the same time, defection is a fully rational strategy against a player who tries to exploit you. It would simply be stupid to go on cooperating. Therefore, what the message conveys is not a threat, but only a warning: I am no fool, so this is what you should expect.[3] Of course, defecting makes a difference to the expected pay-off of your co-player, but so do almost all possible choices of co-players in strategic games, hence this is not enough to identify sanctioning strategies. It is characteristic for the use of sanctions that you do not only accept with equanimity that your rational choice creates costs for your partner, but that you are prepared intentionally to create additional costs, even at the expense of incurring additional costs yourself.

The point of a sanction is not realized in its application at all, but only in the threat of its application. If the threat has to be executed, it has obviously failed as a threat. This brings us straight away to the basic question of the sanctioning approach: under what conditions, if any, would it be rational to incur these additional costs?

---

[1] Cf. the summary of his arguments given by MacCormick 1982, ch. 12.

[2] E.g. Sugden 1986, 114; Schotter 1981, 11; Kliemt 1986, 222ff.; Ellickson 1991, ch. 7; Bicchieri 1993, 185; and many discussions of the so-called "folk theorem(s) of game theory".

[3] For the distinction, see Schelling 1960, 123 note.

Of course, as we saw in discussing bargaining games[4], executing a threat one has uttered may be the best way to enhance the general credibility of one's threats and hence to secure future compliance. But even this does not take away the difference from conditional strategies: executing the present threat is still just a way of enhancing the effectivity of the next one. Moreover, the sanctioning approach to social rules assumes a more general use of the sanctioning mechanism. It assumes that if a social rule exists within a certain group of people, identifying and "punishing" deviations will not only be a task for the victims of those deviations, anxious to prevent future harm to themselves from further deviations, but for the population in general, or its agents. So in discussing the sanctioning approach we should concentrate on its ability to explain cooperation in n-person games. As it turns out, the approach has been developed in three different ways which we have to discuss separately.

## 3.2. The Production of Punishment as a Public Good

The first type of theory is exemplified in a paper by Robert Axelrod, using his famous "tournament" method. A norm exists, according to Axelrod, "in a given social setting to the extent that individuals usually act in a certain way and are often punished when seen not to be acting in that way."[5] To show how norms could emerge, an n-person PD game is devised in which each person has a certain chance of being seen defecting, and each person's strategy is determined along two dimensions: boldness and vengefulness. The extent of the probability of being seen defecting which you are prepared to accept, determines your level of boldness, and the probability with which you will punish a defection when you see one, determines your level of vengefulness. Pay-offs are established for defection (positive), being punished (negative), hurt as a result of other people's defection (negative) and enforcing punishment (negative). Eight strategies, differing in their levels of boldness and vengefulness, are selected at random. Then the game begins. For each opportunity to defect, a chance of being seen by each of the others is determined at random. For each player there are four opportunities to defect, after which the number of players following a certain strategy (the "offspring") is determined by its success in the recent series. This is repeated a hundred times. Three different mechanisms, Axelrod believes, can be modelled in this way: natural selection, learning by trial and error, and learning by imitation of more successful performance. The whole simulation procedure is run five times, with different randomly chosen strategies playing in the first round of each series. Only once the results showed the significant level of vengefulness and the low level of boldness that were taken to characterize the existence of a norm.

What went wrong? If we start from a moderate level of boldness and vengefulness, then the boldness level will start to fall (for defection is punished), but the vengefulness level will fall as well. For punishing has its costs, which are not met by

---

[4] Ch. 2.3.

[5] Axelrod 1986, 1097.

direct returns to the punisher himself. Punishment, in other words, is a public good. So norms (as defined) cannot help to solve $n$-person PD games, for the enforcement of sanctions is itself a $n$-person PD-game.[6]

Axelrod, however, did not despair. He devised a new game in which the players are given one additional option: to punish those who failed to punish. And indeed, this time he found that, once one starts with a sufficiently high level of vengefulness, all boldness will vanish. The entire system is self-policing in that case. However, this result depends crucially on one assumption: that the level of higher-order vengefulness (being prepared to punish non-punishers) is exactly the same as the level of lower-order vengefulness (being prepared to punish defectors). This, of course, is just dodging the problem. The problem in the first tournament was that, for each agent, punishing had significant costs and insignificant benefits. In the new tournament, this is rectified by the production of additional costs for not-punishing. But of course, this move transmits the problem to the production of these additional costs. So the same solution will be required all over again: the levels of higher-order and lower-order vengefulness can only be the same if not punishing defectors and not punishing not-punishers are *both* threatened by the same punishment (and have the same probability of being detected). This obviously starts a *regressus ad infinitum*.

This problem plagues all the usual economic treatments of social norms and institutions. It could be mitigated, albeit not fully solved, by assuming a law of diminishing costs for each higher sanction-producing level. But this assumption is not very plausible on *a priori* grounds. There is no reason to suppose that effectively sanctioning the non-sanctioners successively requires less effort on each higher level. And it can only get more, not less, difficult to detect failures of sanctioning at higher levels, for if at any level there is some positive possibility of failure, this will be multiplied at each higher level. Failures of sanctioning at level $n$ can often be excused by saying that you were not quite sure that what seemed to be a failure of sanctioning at level $n$-1 really was one, perhaps because it was not quite clear either that what seemed to be a failure at level $n$-2 really was one, etc. If punishment is a public good at the lowest level, it surely is one at all higher levels as well.

## 3.3. Leviathan as a Solution

People often assume that the problem can be avoided by a second basic form the sanctioning approach can take. Its leading idea is to entrust the task of monitoring for compliance and punishing non-compliers to a specialized agency ("Leviathan").[7] This can be seen as one way of using the device of precommitment. The problem is that, on the one hand, we are *ex ante* prepared to bring each other to cooperative behaviour by threatening to use sanctions, but on the other hand, we know that *ex post* we will not be prepared to execute the threat once it has failed to ensure cooperation. The solution is to make it *ex ante* impossible or too costly not to execute the threat *ex post*. This is done

---

[6] Buchanan 1975, 132-133; Heath 1976, 156-158; Taylor 1987, 30; Elster 1989, 132-133; Sober and Wilson 1998, 156ff.

by making an enforceable contract to pay for the execution of the threat, and to entrust Leviathan with enforcing the contract.[8]

Leviathan, on this view, is there to promote cooperative behaviour for the common good. The first point to make about this solution, however, is that it is far from maximally efficient itself. An efficient threat is needed for each act of complying to the norm which is not explained directly by self-interest. Of course this does not mean that each deviation has to be punished: a punishing rate lower than 100% may well produce sufficient deterrence. And maybe there is an inverse ratio between the risk of being caught and the severity of punishment, if caught. However, both the identification and the punishment of sinners still create costs, such as the financing of police and prison cells, but also losses of liberty, privacy and dignity.

Some of the costs are less obvious. Universities used to have academic freedom, which meant, among other things, that ensuring productivity was left to internal motivation and the desire to be of good standing among one's colleagues. More recently, however, government officials, firm believers as they are in the economic theory of norm-compliance, have lost trust in these mechanisms, and increasingly rely upon the use of external sanctions. This means, however, that results of scientific output must be identified and measured. Enormous amounts of time and energy are spent in order to achieve this aim. Even so, identification and measurement can only use crude proxy-targets for productivity (pages published, ranking of journals, etc.). The result tends to be that the first priority of university staff is to achieve the proxy-targets, disregarding the real intellectual merit of their work. It is a problem well known from planning economies.[9]

What the example also shows is that spending for detection and punishing has decreasing marginal returns. We reach the zero-level far below the threshold of full compliance. "Only I can see everywhere I litter."[10] In some contexts one may wonder whether the whole system creates any "cooperative surplus" at all. As a means to counteract suboptimal outcomes of individual rational behaviour it is of dubious efficiency.

But, as I conceded to Elster in the previous chapter, there is no *a priori* reason to suppose that the existence of social norms will have optimal results. This first point of criticism, therefore, seems only to warrant the conclusion that we should not be too optimistic about the possible efficiency of coercive agencies. It does not follow that they are not essential to the maintenance of social norms. The second point of criticism, however, is far more threatening to the approach as a whole. It also gives a new bite to the first point.

This second point of criticism can be put in the form of a dilemma. *Either* the agency still relies for its activities on the voluntary contributions of the general population, e.g. in the form of chore-duties or of payments for its services which can be

---

[7] This view is of course commonly ascribed to Hobbes. It depends on identifying the game played in the State of Nature as a PD. Both interpretations are mistaken, Hampton 1987, ch. 2; Den Hartogh unpubl. (b)

[8] J. Buchanan 1975; Levin 1982.

[9] Hirsch 1976, 132.

[10] Hirsch 1976, 139; cf. Sen 1982, 68, 97ff; Riker & Ordeshook 1973, 301.

withheld in case of bad performance. Then we have returned to the regressus problem of the first approach. *Or* the agency only makes use of its own resources for coercion. The first thing its agents do on their daily rounds is to distribute distress-warrants for arrears of contribution among the population at large. If you fail to pay up, you are fined or imprisoned. But in that case, it makes no sense to speak of "entrusting" the agency with a task, or, indeed, of a task at all. For we have to assume that the agency consists of individuals who want to maximize their personal utility, no less than anyone else. So if they have the power to coerce the others, irrespective of any evaluation of their performance by the others, they will maximize their utility in any way they see fit, and if this happens to be by coercing the others to do their part in any collective effort, that is quite accidental. They will make people pay up for anything they want to be done. The idea that they will fulfil a task which needs to be done, simply *because* it needs to be done, is guilty of all the fallacies of functionalism in social theory.[11]

In short, the basic reason to doubt the efficiency of the coercive agency is this: to the extent that it can do without the voluntary contribution it was set up to avoid, there is no reason why it should necessarily be interested in "efficiency" at all.

If you have some power to begin with, how do you acquire more? Clearly not by starting to coerce everyone around you. You rather form a band consisting of some people who agree to obey you voluntarily in exchange for part of the spoils of coercing the others. That this way of proceeding will in some way optimize the outcome of all is hard to believe. (This point also answers the Macchiavellian objection that the interests of the Prince and of the people tend to coincide.)

Fans of Leviathan, e.g. in welfare economics, usually opt for the second horn of this dilemma. At least implicitly they consider the behaviour of governments to be exogenous to the game, for they address their policy recommendations to these governments from a purely instrumental point of view.[12] The state, in their view, is obviously free to change people's pay-offs in whatever way it deems necessary for promoting the collective welfare.[13] In particular, it is free from any constraints imposed by the need to attract willing compliance. But if state personnel really is in that position, there is no reason at all to expect it to aim at promoting the collective welfare, so the

---

[11] A related problem undermines the theory of legitimate political authority that conceives of it as the justification-right to use coercive power, a right which does not correspond to any duty to obey or at least to refrain from resistance. Cf. Ladenson 1980; Sartorius 1981; Wellman 1996; Buchanan 1999; commented on by Raz 1986, 23-27; Edmundson 1998, 55. There is no point of view from which it matters whether or not the coercive agency has this "right". Cf. ch. 5, note 60.

[12] Sugden 1986, 7 calls this the 'US Cavalry model" of state action.

[13] It is the executive to which this freedom has to be ascribed. Social contract theory, on the contrary, concentrates on the efficiency of *legislative* actions, requiring Wicksell's unanimity rule, at least for the most basic, "constitutional" decisions. This is the model of "mutual coercion mutually agreed upon", a form of conditional cooperation in an *n*-persons PD, cf. ch. 2.5. at note 24. It is a plausible interpretation of Rousseau's *volonté générale*, Rousseau *Contrat Social* (1762), Book I. Ch. vi/vii; cf. Runciman & Sen 1965; and can also be found in Kafoglis 1962, 47; Buchanan & Tullock 1962; G. Hardin 1968; J. Buchanan 1975; Van den Doell 1978, 86ff; Griffiths 1978, 22 etc. But it fails to solve the problem of domesticating the executive. Disregarding that problem, the question: what would perfectly rational people unanimously decide to coerce each other to do, becomes analytically equivalent to the question: what would people with perfect cooperative dispositions unanimously decide to do voluntarily? The reference to coercion in the formula only suggests a non-moral mechanism, but does not show it to be possible.

policy recommendations are futile. If people aim at maximizing their individual utility, the state which is made up of people cannot be expected to maximize collective utility. So this is no form of precommitment at all. It is like Ulysses tying himself up, and then giving the end of the rope into the hands of the Sirens.

Leviathan cannot deliver us from the exigencies of the state of nature. "This is to think that men are so foolish that they take care to avoid what mischiefs may be done them by polecats of foxes, but are content, nay think it safety, to be devoured by lions."[14]

Is it possible to find a way out of this dilemma? Consider Hobbes' famous argument for the impossibility to bind the sovereign to any restrictions whatsoever. It makes no sense, Hobbes argued, to stipulate such restrictions unless there is some power able to compel the "sovereign" to respect them. But in that case this power is the real sovereign himself. The highest power in the chain of coercion is therefore necessarily unlimited.[15] This argument involves a fallacy of composition. It may be true that no individual is powerful enough to resist the state, but it does not follow that no coalition of individuals is powerful enough. Suppose, therefore, that the social contract takes the following form. If the state uses its power only to fulfil its duty, compelling negligent and defying individuals to do their part in the cooperative enterprise for the common good, the people promise not to collude. However, as soon as the sovereign starts acting as a tyrant, they will join forces to resist and replace him.

This is an attractive idea, but it is not available to the defendants of the sanctioning approach. They will be confronted by the original dilemma in the following form. To comply with the contract in those cases where the state systematically acts beyond its powers, is a form of collective action. Hence, either the people have to rely on cooperative dispositions to be able to unite (they can hardly ask the sovereign to coerce them to do so); or they will be unable to unite at all, hence the state retains the uncontrolled freedom of the Hobbesian sovereign. In the first case we should expect the people to participate in other forms of collective action on a voluntary basis as well, in the second case there is once more no reason to expect the sovereign to act on trust.

This argument is vulnerable at one spot only, leaving a theoretical way out of the dilemma. There is one case in which collective action really is possible for purely utility-maximizing agents. This is when the benefits of the individual contributions of each are so large that even the part of it which flows back to himself exceeds his individual costs. If we presuppose a group of $n$ people, all making the same contributions and deriving the same benefits, this will be the case when the total beneficial product of each individual contribution can be divided by $n$, and still exceeds the costs the individual is to make. It is perhaps too easily assumed that this can never be the case in groups of millions of people. But if you are to be freed from a state of permanent fear and misery, it may be individually worthwhile to support the resistance movement, even at quite substantial risks.

---

[14] Locke 1690, II.7, par. 93; cf. II.2, par. 13; II.11, par. 137; apparently against Hobbes, cf. Den Hartogh 1989/90, 205

[15] Hobbes, most clearly in *De Cive* VI.18, see also *Leviathan* ch. 18, 20. Cf. ch. 9.3. on Raz' argument that the state necessarily *claims* unlimited authority.

Nevertheless, this is obviously a very strong condition. The condition still allows tyrants an almost umlimited margin for abuse of power, which they can even enlarge by selective favouritism. My theoretical way out also depends crucially on perfect knowledge of each other's utilities and rationality, for if such ideal conditions are not satisfied, no citizen will have reason "to start the ball rolling by dashing through the city streets with gun in hand".[16] Rather, each would have reason to wait until he sees the others dashing. If we cannot appeal to any form of cooperative virtue, there is no feasible middle way "between anarchy and Leviathan".[17]

It should be added, and conceded, that to a lesser extent, these problems will occur in any situation in which people need a state to counteract "the inconveniences of the state of nature". There will always be a concentration of power which cannot be checked with full efficiency. For if it could be checked with full efficiency, there would have been no need to concentrate power to begin with. "A human being is an animal who, when it lives with others of his species, needs a master... But this master is also an animal which needs a master." And this consideration leads Kant to his famous lament: "Out of such crooked timber you can never hammer something straight."[18]

### 3.4. Spontaneous disapproval

The third form of the sanctioning approach can also be seen as a reply to the problems of the first one. The root of those problems is the fact that punishment is costly. The third form of sanctioning theory simply denies this. It is not necessary intentionally to invest in punishing activities, it is enough spontaneously to feel and to express disapproval. Human beings have two matching natural tendencies. The first is to disapprove of behaviour which is harmful to them. If someone is seen defecting in an $n$-person PD-game, even the casual observer will know he is thereby harmed, and hence will start disapproving. But the other tendency people have is to care about the approval of their fellows. Hence defectors will be punished by the attitudes their fellows cannot fail to take. Human beings are "automatically programmed enforcers".[19]

How about detection costs? It is not necessary, Philip Pettit alleges, that everyone is always busy searching actively for defectors. As long as there are enough people around to make it likely that violators will be noticed. This answer will hardly do. Even if every defection is likely to be observed by some-one, this in itself will only generate the negative pay-off of one person disapproving. It is highly implausible that

---

[16] Narveson 1976, 192; cf. Regan 1980, 43-52; Den Hartogh 1986, 117-120.

[17] J. Buchanan 1975. As his title shows, Buchanan is very much aware of the problem which, however, he nowhere tackles directly.

[18] Kant *Ueber den Gemeinspruch* (1784), sixth proposition.

[19] Pettit 1990, 741, quoting Buchanan 1975, 131; cf. MacCormick 1978, 288 on the "internal point of view"; Elster 1990, ch. 12; Gibbard 1990; Fershtman and Weiss 1998. Because Pettit builds the expectations on the attitude, and not the other way around, his account is compatible with the ascription of strategic rationality. Pettit 1996 recognizes that the others' good opinion which is sought is the opinion of being trustworthy, and is therefore expectation-dependent. See note 27.

this will often be sufficient to deter would-be defectors. But in order to produce larger negative pay-offs from nothing but spontaneous disapproval, the observer will have to incur communication costs. Why would he?

But let us forget about detection costs and consider the basic idea of the matching tendencies of disapproval and the wish to avoid it. What exactly is it that people are supposed to "disapprove" of? The simplest answer is: not getting what they want. Then the proposition is this. A pattern of mutual expectations, however it emerged, can persist because it consists of the expectations of actions which are in other people's interest, so that deviation from the pattern will tend to elicit "disapproval". A norm is a pattern of mutual expectations not to be displeased. However, in mosts contexts this is an incoherent idea. For there is no combination of choices which gives everyone the best possible outcome, so there is bound to be someone who is not completely satisfied. In a Division game, for example, the whole point of the exercise is to fix upon a particular combination of "disappointments". Hence we cannot define "harm" in the abstract, and assume that people will mutually expect each other not to cause harm. We can only identify harm in the relevant sense by reference to expectations people already have, and on which they rely to their detriment.

Suppose you are disappointed by my actions. I ask you why, and you answer that you expected me to do $A$. My next question is of course: why did you expect me to do $A$? Three possible answers could be given to that question.

The first answer is given by Lewis.[20] As we saw, Lewis assumes full strategic rationality in his agents, including the ability to mirror each other's thought processes. The full answer to the question why you expected me to do $A$ would then be: we all regularly do $A$, we mutually expect each other to do $A$, each of us maximizes his utility by conforming to these expectations, and that is precisely why we go on confidently to expect each other to do $A$. But then my reply to your complaint could be: in this case it did not maximize my utility to conform to your expectations, you knew that or could have known it, so it was irrational of you to expect me to conform.

It is, of course, logically possible that all people are systematically irrational at precisely this point, but in a framework of full rationality that is an entirely *ad hoc* assumption. Put in a general way: the first possible answer to the question why you expect me to do $A$, points to reasons I have for doing so which are themselves independent of our expectations. But in that case the mechanism of resentment cannot explain conformity which is not already explainable in some other way, or can do so only marginally.[21]

The second possible answer to the question why we expect each other to do the things which we then deplore not being done, does not presuppose strategic agents. People take each other's behaviour as a fact of nature and adapt to it. Why do you expect me to do $A$? Because we all habitually do so. If we asked the further question why we all do so, the eventual answer would point to the fact that we want to avoid disapproval, so the explanation would be circular in the end. But that is not an

---

[20] Lewis 1969, 99-100.

[21] Perhaps it can explain why I conform if it is not in my interest to do so, but suspect that you cannot possibly know that.

objection, because this account assumes that people do not inquire why the others all habitually do $A$, they simply observe that they do.[22]

I have registered my basic uneasiness with this parametric approach. It abstracts from reasoning powers which human beings obviously have and which make a difference in many contexts. As a result, it fails to explain the persistence of *a norm*. On this theory, everybody has a basically *independent* reason for doing what she knows the other wants and expects her to do, while truly mutual expectations, even if they do arise, generate no additional reasons for action.

This uneasiness is confirmed by the present account of the sanctioning mechanism. It represents the phenomena we know by the names of "disapproval", "resentment" and "punishment" in a way which makes them totally unrecognizable. For these phenomena presuppose interdependent reasons for action.[23]

We are told that Immanuel Kant used to take a daily walk through Königsberg, always exactly at the same hour.[24] Suppose that one day he is ill and does not go out. Would people resent that? Perhaps they would. For the story also goes that people used his passing by as a standard for setting their watches. So here we have the local grocer wondering what time it is, discovering that his watch fails to tell him, but realizing that he just has to wait a few minutes and then he will know for sure. This time, however, he is disappointed. He might even feel some resentment. But that would be an inappropriate feeling, and he would know that. The feeling would only be proper if the grocer presupposed that Kant himself *knew* that all the good people of Königsberg relied on his punctuality.

Feelings of disapproval are identified by their cognitive component. Disapproval does not only imply judging that your justified expectations have been disappointed, but also that the other person should not have betrayed your expectations because he knew they were justified.[25]

A proponent of the parametric account might concede this point. But, he might argue, the full sanctioning mechanism which includes such phenomena must have developed from a more primitive form, which still makes up its core. So forget about disapproval, resentment and similar feelings which may presuppose common knowledge. All we have to postulate, fundamentally, is that people have a desire not to harm each other by deviating from each other's expectations. These expectations must be understood as first-order ones only, they result from induction.

---

[22] Sugden 1986, ch. 8.

[23] Cf. Bicchieri 1993, ch. 6.

[24] The example is borrowed from someone, but I am unable to figure out from whom (Martin Hollis?). Simmons 1996, 258, is not prepared to grant that Kant has any obligation if he is aware of people's reliance, not even if he knowingly induced it.

[25] Cf. Foot 1978. Similarly, the idea of punishment implies the judgment that the inflictor of harm is justified by preceding wrong, not just the execution of a threat to deter it, Hart 1967, ch. 1. Gibbard 1990, 151, cf. 148, objects that "I can feel angry at you and yet think it makes no sense to do so..." But this objection really concedes what it objects to: if I know the required judgment to be false, I also know that I have no business to feel the emotion. Moreover, the case is necessarily atypical: people cannot feel angry all the time and think it makes no sense to do so.

If this is just part of a speculative account of the genesis of cooperative virtue, I have no problem with it.[26] But if it is meant to tell us something essential about social norms as we know them, I disagree. It is implausible that people who intentionally act in accordance with a social norm, are motivated by any such desire as the account suggests. Why do you feel constrained to tip a waiter in a restaurant in a foreign country, to which you know you will never return? In an unpublished paper, Robert Sugden suggests that it is the fact that the waiter expects to receive such tips. Why does he expect this? Because he regularly does receive them.[27] My suggestion is that, if you know that this is all there is to his expectations, you will *not* feel any unease, let alone embarassment in failing to conform to them. There is more to it: you anticipate his look if he fails to get the tip. What this look will convey to you is this message: look here, you *know* you are expected to tip, don't you? He is not only expecting you to tip in the way you expect a hare to flee if it sniffs you. His expectations amount to a kind of appeal to you or call on you, and you feel constrained in response to that appeal. For it would reflect on your character not to respond in the right way.

What all this points to, of course, is a third account of the sanctioning mechanism. If you feel constrained to do what you are expected to do, this is only because the other person relies on your doing it, and knows that you know that he relies on you. But then it is obviously presupposed that your knowledge of his reliance normally motivates you not to let him down. In other words: disapproval and resentment as expressed by sanctions *depend* on the pattern of mutual expectations as supported by cooperative dispositions. Sanctions cannot replace cooperative dispositions in the theory of social norms, because sanctions presuppose cooperative dispositions. It is not simply status which matters, but status *as...*; the categorization is relevant.

Within the sanctioning approach, the point is often implicitly recognized by extending the notion of sanctions to include so-called internal ones. The agent is supposed to be motivated by his wish to avoid a feeling of guilt. But why should he feel guilty if he deviates from the norm? Feeling guilty about an action implies a judgment of the action. The action is not deemed wrong because it elicits a feeling of guilt, but the feeling it elicits can only be identified as a feeling of guilt because the action is considered wrong. So there must be an independent reason for considering it to be wrong: it shows a lack of cooperative virtue.

Let it be conceded that the relevant form of disapproval is disapproval for lack of virtue. Could it not still be the case that people are by and large motivated to display virtue because they are basically concerned about having a virtuous reputation? I think not: whatever it is one displays in that case, it cannot be the genuine article. In this respect virtues differ from abilities: if your only concern in displaying your proficiency

---

[26] Cf. ch. 2.8.

[27] Cf. Sugden 1989, note on p. 95. Sugden 1998 argues that to a naturalistic science it cannot matter whether any of people's motives satisfies moral constraints. But why shouldn't it matter whether people believe their motives to satisfy moral constraints. Sugden's stricture would condemn Hume to be an anti-naturalist. Moreover, Sugden is forced to recognize that not all deviations from people's inductively based expectations are hold to be discreditable, e.g. people claiming less than their due.

on the violin is to earn the reputation of a Paganini, your performance may still show real talent. (It is true that we tend to believe that even the summit in artistic performance can only be reached by people who are basically interested in art for its own sake, but that is just a falsifiable belief.)

I am not at all denying the importance of the concern for reputation as a motive. Not even Kant said in that notorious passage in the *Groundworks* that a shopkeeper who is interested in maintaining a reputation for honesty cannot really be an honest man. He only said that we cannot be certain that his virtue is genuine, because his dutiful behaviour is overdetermined. We cannot be sure that respect for the Law is a sufficient motive if respect for the opinion of his neighbours has great weight as well. On this point Kant may have been unduly pessimistic: to some extent we seem to be able to recognize a person's virtue even if her virtue is not her only concern. My point is only that you cannot sustain your reputation for virtue if people know you to be motivated by a desire for regard *only*. To that extent the reputation for virtue is an essential by-product. Hence the interest in esteem, however important, cannot be the single or basic motive sustaining mutual expectations of cooperative behaviour.[28]

## 3.5. Law and sanctions

It will be obvious how these considerations relate to the law. As I said before, in spite of Hart's efforts it is still very common, especially among economists, to understand the law as a means of directing behaviour by means of sanctions. The upshot of my discussion, however, is that sanctions can only get into the picture in either of two ways. The first possibility is that they are a means in the hands of some powerful agency to make people do what the agency, for its own reasons, wants them to do. In that case, it will be sheer coincidence if this overlaps with what those people themselves, in the absence of coercion, would have reason to do or even to want each other to do. Hence the usual format of discussions in Law and Economics – establishing some indeterminacy or externality in people's spontaneous behaviour, and letting the state provide the solution to the problem – is radically incoherent.[29] If state personnel is to solve anyone else's problem, they must be the agents of those people. In that case it cannot be true that those people only contribute to the solution because they are coerced to do so.

---

[28] Cf. Honoré 1987, 66. This is admitted by Pettit 1996. He still claims that, to a significant extent, trust is generated or maintained by people's wish to be well-regarded by their fellow men, but concedes that this mechanism is parasitic on trust being justified by reasons of loyalty and virtue, or by reasons of prudence (in iterated games). This parasitic character of the regard-mechanism, however, really defeats some of the claims Pettit makes for it. He argues, for example, that *only* this mechanism explains why people's motivation for being reliable is self-reinforcing: it is a pleasure to find oneself trusted, for it is a pleasure to find oneself highly thought of. However, if people know the resilience of your motive to depend on such feelings, they will still tend to think less highly of you.

[29] See e.g. Baird, Gertner & Picker 1994.

Of course I am not denying that a fully coercive regime can exist.[30] But the directives it uses to make people do what it wants them to do, will be completely different from the rules which will develop spontaneously among the same people for regulating their mutual interaction. This is a basic divide in social arrangements, and my suggestion is that law belongs on one side of this divide. Again, I am not denying that a basically coercive regime may have reason to dress its directives in legal forms. And there is no point in trying to decide on the exact boundary between law and a system of mainly coercive directives: we will find all kinds of combinations. But if a serious attempt is made to use legal forms, some conditions for the existence of social rules must also be satisfied.[31] That is part of what Hart expressed in his thesis that law is to be characterized from the "internal point of view", for he did not refer to the point of view of subjects whose pay-offs have been intentionally changed in order to make them behave.[32] On this point he was right, even if he did not fully realize the consequences of his position.

For if sanctions cannot be the basic instruments by which people are to be directed who are supposed to take an internal point of view as regards this direction, the only alternative is to assume that the conventions themselves provide this direction.[33] That is the second way sanctions can get into the picture. People expect each other to behave in certain ways, and they expect each other to disapprove of and punish deviations from the expected behaviour. The production of punishment is itself a cooperative enterprise, whether or not it is centralized and formalized. The main point for which I have argued in this chapter, however, is that mutual expectations of behaviour cannot be derived from mutual expectations of disapproval and punishment. It is the other way around: people expect each other to disapprove of and to punish certain actions, because, on independent grounds, they already expect each other to behave in a certain way. If you disapprove of my deviation, or go on to punish me for it, you implicitly judge that I *should* have conformed, for other reasons than the fear of your disapproval or your punishment. And I have proposed the following analysis of this "should": given our system of mutual expectations, a person of normal cooperative virtue would have conformed.

Disapproval and punishment presuppose cooperative dispositions. Indeed, I am prepared to count the tendency to disapprove and to punish among the cooperative dispositions. They share all the characteristics of those dispositions as described in section 7 of the previous chapter. Even if they do not constitute the stability of norms, they certainly contribute to it. If a pattern of expectations is built on people's (other)

---

[30] See Kavka 1983 on the possibility of a "pure tyranny", cf. Den Hartogh 1998, 365-366.

[31] Cf. ch. 10.2. on law under Apartheid.

[32] See ch. 8.5.

[33] "In most cases, the law can only work as a supplement (and not a replacement) for informal enforcement of the norm." Axelrod 1986, 1106. In his defence of Austin against Hart's criticism, R. Hardin 1985 suggests that customary law, customary interpretation of law, and the customary identification of legitimate authorities – all lacunas in Austin's account which Hart pointed out – depend on conventions. That is not a defence, but a capitulation. For in that case, the basic reason for compliance with "the commands of the sovereign" cannot be the independent reason of fear for his sanctioning power; it must be the interdependent reason – whatever it is – for participating in the convention of obedience.

cooperative dispositions, people who are relatively lacking in that respect get additional, and perhaps on occasion definitive, reasons to conform. And this very fact may give the others the assurance they need that their cooperative behaviour will not be exploited.[34] At the same time, people do not simply act in accordance with their retributive dispositions in order to achieve the common good of deterrence. These dispositions are backward-looking rather than forward-looking: they are enacted in response to deviations of patterns of mutual expectations. This implies that, like the other cooperative dispositions, they presuppose the existence of those very expectations which they help to stabilize. Finally, they surely have an evolutionary prehistory or archaeology, having developed from tendencies recognizable in other species.[35]

In short, I do not want to deny the importance of sanctions. My point is only that to the extent that they can be vindicated "from the internal point of view", sanctions are themselves the expression of a cooperative disposition, one which presupposes the existence of other cooperative dispositions.[36]

In chapters Four and Five I will consider the question whether there can be any obligation to obey the law. It will turn out that a plausible answer to this question can be formulated in terms of the conventionalist theory of social norms and obligations sketched in the first chapters: reasons to comply with the law are typically interdependent reasons, and some of those reasons depend on the principles of trustworthiness, fairness and justice, and therefore involve obligations. This result will corroborate the theory of these chapters. It will also be used in the rest of the book, in which I consider the nature of law, the relation between moral argument and law, and the nature of legal argument. I will contend that it is the essential technique of the law to produce such interdependent reasons and obligations, and that, even though the actual use of this technique may be rationally and morally defective in any number of ways, this thesis implies that some forms of moral argument are necessarily relevant to establishing legal validity.

---

[34] McNeilly 1968 cf. ch. 8.4.

[35] De Waal 1996, 157-162; Gibbard 1990.

[36] This account suggests that the interest of the criminal law in retribution and in deterrence presuppose each other in the same way (see ch. 2.7.) that cooperative virtues generally and the interest in the results of cooperation presuppose each other. That would be the core of a conventionalist theory of penal law.

# CHAPTER 4

# POLITICAL OBLIGATION: ITS GROUNDS AND LIMITS

## 4.1. Crito's Problem

In Plato's dialogue *Crito* we find Socrates in jail. He has been condemned to death on charges of corrupting youth and introducing new gods. Both crimes he obviously perpetrated by his infuriating way of undermining people's conventional beliefs: requiring them to argue for these beliefs and probing the arguments. He could have prevented his trial by leaving Athens in time, but this he refused. He could have resorted to the usual methods for securing his acquittal – "pitifully appealing to the jury with floods of tears and having his infant children produced in court"[1] – but instead he claimed to defend himself not for his own sake, but only to prevent the Athenians from committing a judicial murder. After having been found guilty by a small margin of votes, he could have made a judicious use of his right to propose an alternative penalty. Instead, he added insult to injury by proposing that he should be freed and maintained at the state's expense, as he deserved this honour more than any victor in the races at Olympia. So now he will have to drink the poison-cup when the ship from Delos arrives. His friend Crito comes to see him early in the morning, and implores him not to waste this final opportunity as he did the others. For if he does, his friends will be blamed. An escape from jail will be easy to arrange. Why wait any longer? Moral scruples would be altogether out of place, for the sentence was clearly unjust, the product of nothing but suspicion and resentment.

So Socrates starts inquiring whether it would really be right for him to accept this kind offer, and he concludes that it would not. He advances two arguments for his obligation to obey an unjust law; or rather he puts them into the mouth of the personified Laws and Constitution of Athens. The first argument appeals to the necessity of having government; it interprets the obligation as an involuntary or "natural" one. The second argument appeals to a putative agreement to obey, hence it interprets the obligation as a voluntary one. Every secular argument used in the following twenty-four centuries of political thinking will on inspection turn out to be a close relative to either of these two arguments. For that reason they provide a convenient starting-point for my discussion.

In this chapter and the next, I will develop the account of political obligation I consider defensible. At the same time, I try to provide a *tour d'horizon* of the contemporary debate. The usual treatment of the issue takes the form of a contest of rival principles: either consent, or necessity, or gratitude, or fairness. But these principles do not necessarily exclude each other; rather, they are complementary,

---

[1] *Apology* 34 c.

sometimes in the sense of providing answers to different questions. Each of the principles gains in plausibility if its limited scope is recognized. For this reason, the investigation of nearly every separate proposal will result in a necessary building block of the theory as a whole.

It will turn out that the speech of the Laws recognizes this complementarity of relevant principles; in so far, it is more sophisticated than many later discussions.[2] This is a second reason for the otherwise rather conventional choice to follow Socrates' lead.

The account of political obligation to be developed here will be conventionalist in the sense explained in the previous chapters. The conventionalist framework will be especially helpful in showing how the relevant considerations we come across can be integrated into a coherent whole. But one essential part of the full account will be left out, or sketched in only the vaguest outline. This part concerns the nature of the authority to make and apply laws. The present chapter will show that the citizens of a state have some "political" obligations towards each other, in particular obligations of fairness. It will be left open whether or not these obligations include obligations to obey legal authority. Chapter Five will address that question, but a full account of the nature of legal authority will only be given in chapters Six and Seven, in which I will begin to develop a conventionalist theory of the law. Chapters Four and Five set the stage for that discussion by describing the context in which legal authority can be legitimately exercized and rationally complied with.

## 4.2. Consent

The Socrates of the *Crito* seems to hold a very rigoristic conception of political obligation: one should obey every law, however unjust. In the *Apology*, however, Socrates relates how the thirty Tyrants – the recently expelled oligarchic rulers of Athens – ordered him and four other persons to go and fetch Leon of Salamis from his home to be executed. The other four did as they were told, but Socrates went home: when political authority commands you to do an unjust thing, you should disobey. For the same reason, he assures the jury that they need not take the trouble to try and save his life by ordering him never again to bother people with his embarrassing interrogations. He announces that he will not comply with such an order. For he considers the attempt to find out the truth in this way to be a mandate given him by the gods. And on closer inspection, we find that Socrates in the *Crito* gives the loyal citizen at least a choice of reactions to a law he does consider to be unjust: to obey or to persuade. You are allowed to disobey the law, as long as you are prepared to justify your actions in public, in particular in court, and to take the judicial consequences, especially to undergo any punishment deemed appropriate.[3]

---

[2] For this reason, I agree with the favourable judgment on the philosophical quality of the dialogue expressed by Kraut 1984, 7.

[3] Kraut 1984, 87, even believes that Socrates would have judged it right to evade the sentence if only during his trial he had announced that he would do so, and had explained why he thought it right to do so.

Disregarding the exact limits of his obligations – what are the reasons Socrates gives for his belief that he has them? At one point in their speech, the Laws proclaim the principle "that any Athenian, on attaining to manhood and seeing for himself the political organization of the state and us its laws, is permitted, if he is not satisfied with us, to take his property and go away wherever he likes. If any of you chooses to go to one of our colonies, supposing that he should not be satisfied with us and the state, or to emigrate to any other country, not one of us laws hinders or prevents him from going wherever he likes, without any loss of property. On the other hand, if any one of you stands his ground when he can see how we administer justice and the rest of our public organization, we hold that by so doing, he has in fact undertaken to do anything that we tell him."[4] Socrates is under an obligation to obey the law because he voluntarily, knowingly, indeed enthousiastically, accepted this obligation by staying in Athens all his adult life.

The kind of consent invoked here is what John Locke would call "tacit consent".[5] According to Locke, this kind of consent does not entitle one to the status of full citizenship; only express consent does. Consent is a particular kind of promise; it concerns the actions of another person. By consenting to the act of another person, I convey that I undertake an obligation not to interfere in this action, not to attempt to undo its results, and sometimes to allow the person to act on my authority or responsibility. I give express consent when I do something willingly and knowingly which conventionally has this meaning and no other one. Hence it should be an act which could have no other possible attraction for me than expressing my consent; there should be no hardship involved in choosing to omit the action.[6] Some Locke interpreters suppose that tacit consent is given when the conventional meaning of undertaking an obligation is given to an omission to act.[7] If on entering the living-room you find your children watching television again, and you do not remark on the fact, you obviously agree. Consent by omission to act is a form of tacit consent indeed, but it is not the only form. As Locke's examples make clear, I give my tacit consent if I do something which primarily has another point, but which is conventionally taken to express the intention to assume an obligation as well. By taking a glass of wine I may tacitly consent to pay for the bottle. It is not an act of express consent, for nobody would want to deny that I might take the wine in the first place because I like it. There is hardship involved in choosing the alternative to consent (as there may be hardship involved in starting once again the endless debate on habits of television watching and the quality of life). So silence is not essential to tacit consent; it would be more appropriate to call it "implied consent".[8]

---

[4] *Crito* 51 d, translation Hugh Tredennick.

[5] *Second Treatise of Government*.119.

[6] Cf. Prichard 1968, 177 on promissory obligation: "There is no hardship in abstaining from making a certain noise".

[7] For example Simmons 1979, 80.

[8] On tacit and implied consent see Simmons 1993, 80ff, and the literature quoted in note 7 on page 83 and note 3 on page 213.

In every state existing today, express consent can be said to be a source of political obligations for at most a very small part of the population, comprised mainly of some immigrants and some state officials. So much the worse for existing states, the consent theorist could reply[9] – and a case can be made for saying that Locke would agree with her. For the passage on express and tacit consent can be most readily understood as reflecting his left-wing Whig position in the debate about the oath of allegiance to William and Mary in 1689: the oath should have recognized their legitimacy, not only their de facto possession of power, and it should have been required from all adult males.[10]

A common objection against consent theory appeals to the fact that most people believe they have political obligations, while not being aware that, as individuals, they have ever knowingly undertaken them[11] Whatever the force of this appeal, however, there is a more fundamental objection. Founding political obligation on express consent makes it possible for the inhabitants of the same area to give their allegiance to different rulers – or to none at all – and under different conditions. But in that case, there is no state as such but a free market occupied by agencies offering state-type services like protection. It is a form of anarchism to believe that such market provision should be preferred to state provision.

Political obligation, if it exists, will be a form of mutual adjustment of interdependent choices, hence it cannot be a bilateral relation between a state and each of its individual citizens separately. The basic deficiency of consent theory is its monadological conception of possible reasons for obedience. If there are such reasons, they can only be interdependent ones.[12]

Perhaps there is no need to require consent "all the way down". Perhaps we can take the existence of a state for granted, for example as the result of a natural tendency for a market in state-type services to develop monopolies.[13] Though we still need a justification for this slackening of the requirement of consent, we can see that it would not necessarily destroy the voluntary character of the obligation. After all, two people in marriage clearly have incurred their duties voluntarily, even if they had no choice concerning the forms and legal consequences involved in the institution of marriage.[14] Suppose that, taking the identity of the monopolist for granted in a similar way, we assure its legitimacy in the following way: we ask every citizen on reaching the age of political adulthood either to accept or to refuse to accept the obligation to obey the law. And suppose we do not attach any negative consequences to refusal, except of course that the excludable benefits of living in a society regulated by law will be withheld. Then nobody could be bound who did not want to be.

---

[9] Simmons 1993, 248ff ("Lockean anarchism").

[10] Den Hartogh 1990a.

[11] See already Hume, *Essays Moral Political and Literary*, II 12, 'Of the Original Contract'; *A Treatise of Human Nature*, III, ii, viii, 'Of the Source of Allegiance.'

[12] Could we not ask each citizen to accept obligations on condition all other citizens accept them as well? Unfortunately, conditional strategies are not feasible in *n*-person PD-games, see ch. 2.5. at note 24.

[13] Nozick 1974, part I.

[14] Cf. below, note 28 on Green.

The same consequences follow if political obligation is founded on forms of implied consent from which one could abstain without any important hardship. It is often suggested that taking part in elections (even by voting for the eternal opposition, or voting *blanco*) could be interpreted as an act of consent.[15] The government could even make the point explicit when summoning you to the ballot box. "If you stay at home, you will henceforward have full discretion to disobey any laws we pronounce, as you think fit – excepting only the laws which recognize pre-existing natural rights and obligations."

The suggestion is absurd. The whole of this chapter and the next one will spell out why, but it is useful at this point to give a preliminary explanation. I assume that a state is an organization of people inhabiting a certain territory for coordinating their actions in schemes of mutually advantageous cooperation according to common rules.[16] What exactly would be the moral relation between this political community and the independents it allowed to stay in its midst? Clearly the community could not allow the independents to have no duties at all towards its members, or only the duties the independents are prepared to recognize themselves. That would be tantamount to a permit to free-riding, and would put the more conscientious, even of the independents, at a disadvantage in their dealing with the unscrupulous. A Lockean suggestion would be to concede that the independents have enforceable duties, but to insist that both the duties themselves and the acceptable ways of enforcing them should be identifiable by "natural law" only. It is of course true that some crimes are identifiable as such without any recourse to conventions: murder, rape, perhaps even some forms of theft. But even for these crimes there are many borderline cases which can only be securely classified by appeal to conventions, and this is certainly true for the acceptable means of enforcement. The natural law is in need of interpretation and of specification, and interpreting and specifying it is exactly what the law sets out to do. So if the community is allowed to deal with the independents according to natural law, it will deal with them according to its own interpretation and specification of it, i.e. according to its laws, and surely the independents are in no position to complain about that, for they are claiming the right to do the same.

The upshot is that we cannot expect any political community to grant the independents other terms of interaction than its own members grant each other. The independents may have reasons to complain, of course, but only if members have the same reasons as well. Otherwise we will want to say to these people who are not ready to give their consent on fair conditions, that they *should* be ready to do so. In Kant's words: "When you cannot avoid living side by side with others, you ought to leave the state of nature and proceed with them into a rightful condition..."[17] But in that case, of

---

[15] Plamenatz 1963, Vol. I, 220-241; Raphaell 1970, ch. 4 (renounced in the sec. ed., 1976); Downie 1971, 85-86, 102-103; Gewirth 1962; Singer 1973, 45-59 ("quasi-consent"); Lemos 1978, 100; Weale 1978, 71-72. One must insist that it should be *mutual knowledge* for the participants that their act has this meaning. This convention is surely lacking in actually existing states – pace Singer and Weale. And for good reasons. For further criticism see Simmons 1993, 220ff and the literature quoted there, in particular in notes 9 and 13.

[16] On the tension between consent theory and the territorial form of political organization which characterizes the present state system, cf. Wellman 1996, 217-218, 232; Morris 1998, 37; Copp 1999, 15. Cf. ch. 5, note 31.

[17] *The Metaphysicial Elements of Justice*, sec. 42, transl. Mary Gregorr.

course, the actual consent does not matter, only the reasons for consenting, which are at the same time reasons for accepting the burdens of political community without having consented at all. It can be argued that this shift away from the requirement of actual consent occurs in every contract theory of the legitimacy of the state: I am not excused for disobedience if I withdraw my consent, but only if I have good reasons for withdrawing it, i.e. for refusing to obey. We have to attend to the reasons directly.[18]

## 4.3. Consent and Hardship

It is incompatible with the whole point of instituting state authority to allow people withholding their consent to be exempt without further consequences. For that would mean allowing them to free-ride on the rule-following of the consenters. On the other hand, when refusal to consent is followed by state actions aimed at making free-riding impossible, e.g. expulsion from the state territory, it seems that consent is not freely given, but the result of coercion and therefore void. This is the standard objection to the "membership" conception of consent theory.[19]

If we assume the population to consist of representatives of the species *homo economicus*, who make their decisions by comparing their alternatives by the appropriate utility calculations, we could easily prove the following theorem: the very fact that a person consents to obey the law, proves that his consent was not given freely. For if the arrangement of the options were not coercive, the logic of the $n$-person Prisoner's Dilemma would cause everyone to refuse his consent.

If this argument is sound, it is sufficient to deal with implied consent as well. For requiring express consent and connecting adverse consequences to its refusal, is equivalent to interpreting the act of "voluntarily" avoiding the adverse consequences as implied consent, if a convention to that effect exists.[20] If refusal to give express consent is followed by expulsion, we might as well count the person who does not emigrate as

---

[18] See for Hobbes: Hampton 1986, 187, 266-279; Kavka 1986, chs. 5 & 10; for Locke: Pitkin 1972, 56, and many other authors, discussed by Den Hartogh 1990b, see also Simmons 1993, 205-206. For Kant of course the social contract is nothing but an "a priori Idea of pure practical reason". The appeal to hypothetical consent is not a form of consent theory at all, it is a way of specifying the application of other principles, e.g. fairness.

[19] Represented by Socrates; Locke; Rousseau, *Contrat Social* Book IV, ch. 2; Ross 1930, 27; Tussman 1960; Walzer 1970; Beran 1987; Green 1988, ch. 6 & 7 (political stations given, but to be occupied only by consent). Tussman recognizes that most people do not consider the issue of staying or leaving as involving the acceptance of political obligations. These "political childbrides" will be legitimately coerced for paternalistic reasons. Pitkin 1972, 60, rightly comments that on this view consent does not really matter: we are obligated anyway, either as consenting members or as non-consenting children. Walzer 1970 interprets not-emigrating as Locke does: as a basis for the limited obligations of resident aliens (to help combatting fire but not to fight in the army); he believes that, lacking more extended means of political participation, people in western democratic states usually have these obligations and no others. Pateman 1979 develops this idea into an argument for participatory democracy.

[20] It is hard to believe that such a convention exists, cf. Simmons 1984, 807-809. How would we recognize it to begin with? Perhaps people are generally prepared to accept the argument that you should obey because you did not leave. But even that would not show the existence of a convention of implied consent, but rather the recognition of a ground of obligation applying to all who stay.

giving his consent implicitly. And if the express consent is void because of coercion, the implied consent is so as well.

It is precisely the point of having a state that many of its rules apply to all persons within a certain territory; to take this into account, consent theory should severely restrict the options of the people who are asked to consent. This is done either by threatening to expel those who refuse, or by considering staying as tacit consent. In both cases the "political adult" is given two options and no more: to obey or to leave. So clearly, there is hardship involved in choosing the alternative: tearing to pieces the whole fabric of your life, your familial, personal and professional relations. If this is not coercion, then the highwayman who offers you the choice between your money and your life is not coercing you either.[21]

This standard objection seems very powerful but is nevertheless mistaken, as Harry Beran has shown.[22] The highwayman is restricting the alternatives in order to manipulate you into a position in which you will prefer to part with your money. But suppose I enter a hospital in order to be cured of a disease which would kill me if left uncured. This particular hospital is the only one offering an efficient therapy. By entering I am taken to consent to obey the hospital regulations. (Or I am required to give my consent explicitly as a condition of entrance.) My options therefore have been restricted to either giving this consent or facing death. Nevertheless, this is not a case of coercion, for the options are not restricted in order to bring me to submission to another person's will, but because the hospital cannot do its job – which I particularly want it to do! – without requiring some uniformity of behaviour. There is hardship involved in choosing the alternative, but it is not unreasonable – not a matter of coercion or exploitation – to impose it. It is for similar reasons that we do not allow people to pick and choose their own marriage "institution".[23]

This defence of the theory of implied consent, however, is almost as damaging to the theory as the objection it so ingeniously refutes. Beran has succeeded in showing that if the alternative to consent is exile, this need not be a case of duress, voiding any consent. But he has also shown that this form of consent is only valid if it is at the same time redundant as a source of obligation. Yes, consent can be a moral reason to obey. But only if no such reason is needed.

Suppose I have collected some potatoes at the grocer's shop, when I discover that I left my money at home. The grocer is prepared to allow me to take the potatoes home, if only I promise to pay for them tomorrow. I protest that he is coercing me by restricting my options to either promising to pay or leaving without any potatoes. He

---

[21] The locus classicus for this criticism is Hume, "Of the original contract". Gans 1992, 55-56, rightly observes that it is not the amount of hardship which undermines the voluntary character of the choice made, but the unjustified restriction of the available alternatives as such.

[22] Beran 1987, 105.

[23] Klosko 1991, 680-682 argues that the analogy fails because the hospital has had no role in causing the patient's illness and allows her to stay in this "state of nature" if she wishes. But neither does the state cause one's need for protection. And it will be unable to provide for this need if it will allow anyone within its territory to stay in the state of nature. There is a difference between the two cases, but it is an open question whether the difference has moral significance. Still, Klosko is right in pointing out that consent theory itself does not have the resources to provide the answer.

replies that he does not take away my option of having the potatoes for free in order to coerce me into promising. I did not have this option to begin with: he runs a shop, not a charity. In other words, the reason why tomorrow he will have the right to demand payment, is not that I promised to pay, but that I took the potatoes.[24] The promise is only needed to secure the manner in which I will meet my obligations. That my options are restricted is justified on a ground which is independent of my promise.

A similar point applies to the hospital. I receive visitors outside of the visiting hours and am reminded of the relevant rules. I object that my recognition of the rules has no validity because I was not given the option to be cured without going through the motions of recognizing them. The hospital will point out that there is nothing extravagant in demanding conformity to the rules, because this is a contribution every patient has to make towards realizing its organizational aims. The basic argument uses two premises: that the patient has an interest in the hospital functioning well, and that functioning well requires general conformity to the rules. It is only added as an afterthought that, after all, the patient is free to leave if he wishes. If the rules required him to wear purple pyjamas only, because of the medical superintendent's particular affection for the color, this argument would be quite insufficient on its own. If I really were threatened with dismissal if I failed to comply with that requirement, it would be true that I had been coerced into compliance.

Similarly with my obligation to obey the law: my consent is either void or redundant. If the "sovereign" could give me no independent moral reason for my obedience – if the law would be nothing but an expression of her will – then by giving me no alternative but to emigrate, she would coerce me, and I could not be said to give my free consent by not taking that alternative. (If she wishes to have only obedient people in her neighbourhood, why should she not leave the country with her loyal subjects? If my neighbour wishes to play the trumpet all night, why should I be the one who has to move to another apartment?) But if she *can* give me a reason why all the people within the territory should obey her, then indeed I could be said to agree to obey her when I stay within the territory – but my "consent" would only be an additional and derivative ground.[25]

---

[24] Atiyah 1981, 3, 34-35.

[25] The basic principle is fairness. This shines through when Beran 1987, 29, writes: "Associations are justified in insisting that those who become members of an association agree to obey its rules. It is only fair that those who obtain the benefits of membership also accept its burdens." He even accepts (39-40) that you may be bound to follow a majority decision without having consented to abide by the outcome of the vote beforehand, when you belong to a group from which it is impossible to withdraw and which is in need of uniform regulations, the majority-rule being a salient procedure for deciding. But it is never impossible to withdraw, not even from a life-boat. If there is a principle obligating you in this situation, you do not *exchange* it for a principle of consent when you enlarge the possibilities of withdrawal, you merely add necessary conditions for the continuing application of the original principle. A similar observation can be made concerning Walzer's theory of tacit consent, cf. Walzer 1970, 100-101, as well as concerning Locke's, cf. note 31.

With every form of implied consent, there is some hardship involved in choosing the alternative. "But it is not unreasonable to impose it." So please tell me what principle justifies imposing the hardship. I did not consent to it, did I?[26]

One of the conditions for making membership voluntary, according to Beran, is the right to secession. But the state is justified, he concedes, in allowing secession only under certain conditions: that the seceding group is large enough to take the responsibilities of an independent state, that it does not occupy an area which is essentially or disproportionally important to the mother-state in an economic or military sense, that the new territory does not form an enclave or a series of dispersed enclaves within the old one.[27] But with what right does the state make these requirements?

The question is: how is it possible that the state is justified in closing down a path which I would have been morally allowed to go otherwise? The answer seemed to be: you consented to give the state this power. But now it turns out that before offering me the choice to consent or not, the state had already closed down that path! For I am not given the option to refuse my consent and nevertheless to continue to take that path. So my original question has not been answered at all.

Every form of implied consent involves some principle of involuntary obligation. Why is the imposition of any hardship justified? Why am I not allowed to drink my wine and pay for my own consumption only? The same point is true for all forms of explicit consent which are not allowed to go "all the way down". Why does my golf club not allow me to negotiate different terms of membership from those granted to the other members? Why does my insurance company offer me only a limited menu of standardized insurance packages? Why cannot I enter into holy matrimony with my gay friend, or with my two gay friends simultaneously? Such obligations are partially voluntary and partially involuntary. If we had an arithmetic for counting and weighing options, we could determine degrees of voluntariness. (As it is, we can only make rough distinctions.) If it is conceded that there may exist such obligations that are only partially voluntary, no a priori reason can be given why the degree of voluntariness may not approach zero. If the only exit-option on offer is death, the obligation is wholly involuntary; if it is emigration, almost wholly.

It may be true that it is essential to the moral nature of some arrangement or relationship that its partially voluntary character is recognized and maintained.[28] We

[26] Simmons 1993, 241, agrees that states could offer "reasonable" terms to residents and, as part of such terms, require the refusers to leave. Though his standards for reasonableness do not seem to recognize the need for arbitration and therefore are unreasonably high (e.g. requiring the state to share his view of just taxation), this concession already compromises his voluntarism, cf. ch. 4.7. at note 82.

[27] Beran 1987, 37-42. The result of these requirements is that the option of secession is not given to any individual; and therefore its existence cannot contribute to creating the option of implied consent.

[28] This is a major theme in Green's defence of consent theory, see e.g. Green 1988, chs. 6 & 7; 1989a, 809-812; 1989b, 109-114. He concedes that consent theory in its usual form is too individualistic: "it is wrong to think of our most important duties as being consequences of our own will", Green 1988, 205, cf. 201. But even if the social role of citizenship is fixed, exercising its duties has no value unless the role is accepted voluntarily. It is unclear, however, what kind of valuable relation is entered into in accepting this role. It is unattractive to interpret it as a relation to the authorities, for reasons I discuss in ch. 5.3. at note 27. But if it is a relation to one's co-citizens, the exercise of authority has still to be justified on functional grounds, which Green is generally sceptical about.

would not like to be members of any club which did not allow us to be non-members. But it may also be true for some valuable arrangement or relationship that its value would be undermined by allowing it to be voluntary in any significant degree. It may not matter much for your own relation to your partner whether everyone in your neighbourhood is married or not: the decision not to marry need have no external effects, or only limited ones. This is not true of a decision to accept or to refuse the duties of being a patient in Beran's hospital, or the duties of membership.

Consent theory has only this kernel of truth. Governments should offer their citizens all the exit-options compatible with the functioning of the state, with its realizing its proper organizational aims.[29] They should not erect any obstacles to emigration or change of nationality, and they should permit secession on reasonable conditions. If they fail to do so, people who would make use of these options if they were on offer, may be discharged from some obligations to obedience, depending on their reasons for opting out. If, for instance, they would rather emigrate than pay a particular tax, they have the moral right to evade that tax. But it does not follow that people who would not emigrate even if given the chance, are under any obligation to obey for that reason alone.[30] They should be given independent reasons.

## 4.4. Necessity

Interestingly, both Socrates and Locke show clear signs of awareness of this limited and derivative role of consent theory. As I suggested, Locke argues that in a particular political constellation, express consent is needed to complete the moral relation between government and citizen. His more basic argument for obedience is what he calls "tacit consent", but this he clearly describes as the enjoyment of benefits which justifies some reciprocal imposition of burdens.[31] Socrates, on the other hand, starts by arguing that the Laws have every reason to require obedience as parents and educators, and goes on to say that "nevertheless" they are also pleased to open the exit-option of emigration.

So let us look more closely at this basic Socratic argument. The Laws introduce it by putting to Socrates the rhetorical question: "Can you deny that by this act which you are contemplating you intend, so far as you have the power, to destroy us, the laws, and the whole state as well? Do you imagine that a city can continue to exist and not be turned upside down, if the legal judgments which are pronounced in it have no force but are nullified and destroyed by private persons?"[32] The question seems not to be quite fair, for what Crito expects of Socrates is not any intention to destroy the laws, but

---

[29] A similar point can be made about voice-options.

[30] Beran 1987, 107. As we will see, the principle of fairness primarily applies to non-excludable goods, and should therefore count as a principle of involuntary obligation. But almost no good is non-excludable in the sense that you could not opt out of receiving it by emigrating.

[31] *Second Treatise.* 20, 122, 130, cf. Den Hartogh 1990a, 108. Neither does Locke ask for each individual what exactly she has consented to: she is supposed to have consented to what she has reason to consent to, ibid., 203 ff.

[32] *Crito* 50 ab, translation Hugh Tredennick.

simply to save his life.[33] So we shall take the laws to mean that, by trying to evade the sentence, Socrates would, "so far as he had the power", destroy the laws and the state as a matter of fact, even if he does not intend to do so.

But this claim is hardly less puzzling. What kind of harm would Socrates be doing the laws? The premiss of the whole argument appears to be that, if all private persons act at their own discretion, i.e. do whatever they find it best to do on the whole, the existence of laws would have no point, and the state would disintegrate. Let us grant this for the moment. Does it follow that no citizen should ever act at his own discretion instead of obeying the law? Clearly not. If some persons sometimes refuse to obey, the state would hardly come to any great harm. Could it be true that the example of Socrates would have worse consequences than the disobedient acts of any other Athenian, because of the moral respect conferred on him by a considerable following?[34] As a matter of fact, Socrates argues explicitly that this respect would not survive an attempt to escape, ignominious as it would be. And in any case, whatever moral influence Socrates has could hardly be sufficient to destroy the laws or the state. "So far as he has the power" introduces a counterfactual, for he has no such power at all.

Socrates therefore cannot be referring to any actual consequences which would follow from his particular act of disobedience; he refers to the hypothetical consequences that would follow from the general practice of the nullification of judicial judgments by private persons. Therefore he is said "for his part" to attempt to destroy the law. Socrates uses the generalization argument: "What if everybody did the same? Harmful consequences would follow."[35] When this argument is used, it is obviously improper to reply: "Don't worry, they won't do it, and if they did, you would not be to blame."

One problem with the generalization argument in any form is to provide the relevant description of "the same act". It makes quite a difference whether one imagines everybody acting on the maxim of disregarding the law as soon as its requirements are inconvenient, or on the maxim of obeying the law except when it orders one's execution in clear violation of justice. This point is fatal to Socrates' case; there is no reason to make any requirement of obedience as stringent as he wants to make it. A well-known example of the same fallacy is Kant's notorious argument against "an alleged right to lie". Even when a would-be murderer comes to your door requiring to know the hiding-place of his victim which happens to be your attic, you are not allowed to deceive him, for the universal acceptance of a maxim of deception – Kant says – would destroy the very possibilities of transferring information (and hence of deceiving).[36] Of course, the

---

[33] There certainly is no reason at all to ascribe to him any desire or expectation that other people will join in the destructive enterprise, as Kraut 1984, 129-137, suggests.

[34] Cf. Woozley 1979, 113.

[35] Contra Woozley 1979, 116ff; Kraut 1984, 134-136. But I agree with both (cf. Woozley, 135-140) that the argument does not appeal to considerations of fairness; as Kraut recognizes, it is not a complete argument at all.

[36] "Ich mache, so viel an mir ist, dass Aussagen (Deklarationen) überhaupt keinen Glauben finden...", *Über ein vermeintes Recht aus Menschenliebe zu lügen* (1797). The Kantian generalization argument does not say, "harmful consequences would follow", but "it would be impossible for you to realize the end of your own maxim" (or of another maxim you cannot fail to have), cf. Hoerster 1974; Nell 1975, ch. 5. Nell shows that

universal acceptance of the maxim of deceiving would-be murderers closely on the track of their victims, would have no such consequences at all.[37]

We should set our aims somewhat lower. It has been recognized[38] that the generalization argument is at home in one particular context: that of interdependent decision. If everybody does his part, together we will produce a fine result. You consider not to contribute? "What if everybody did the same?"

But at this point we realize that the argument is incomplete. "The fine result would not be realized. So what?" We have only made it clear that the action we require is a contribution to a cooperative effort aimed at a worthy goal. But we know that it is not an indispensable or even a very significant contribution. So why should any particular individual make it his special responsibility to care?

The involuntary obligation to obey the law is sometimes compared to the obligations which arise in a life-boat, let down from a sinking ship in the midst of the ocean.[39] The passengers realize they should cooperate to have any hope of attaining land. Decisions have to be made concerning the distribution of seats, of rowing efforts, of rations. Someone, a 'natural leader", starts giving instructions which the others recognize as making sense. Obviously, everyone should do his part to reach the common goal, and this implies following the directions given.

What is the moral principle involved? "There may be a necessity for an individual, a thing, or an institution to be cared for or managed." In that case the person or persons best placed to render that care acquire a special involuntary duty to do so.[40] If a child is drowning in the pond, and you are the only person passing by, the fact that your intervention is needed to secure the child's basic interest makes such intervention obligatory, whether or not you are prepared to "consent" to being obligated. In the same way, it is suggested, the "natural leader" in the life-boat has a duty to use his special talents in the collective interest of all; he is "best placed" to fulfil the pressing need for management. But to do this job, he in turn needs the support of the others, including their willing compliance with his instructions.[41]

The two cases − the child in the pond, and the life-boat − are not completely analogous. The passengers in the life-boat have a collective task: all should cooperate if they are to survive. It follows that everybody has already got the best possible

---

Kant's theory with its subjective conception of 'maxim' has the resources largely to solve the problem of relevant description.

[37] Socrates' fallacious argument has retained a wide currency, especially in legal circles. Cf. the arguments against legal impunity of civil disobedience quoted in Den Hartogh 1989, note 63. They all suggest that a state which allows its citizens to disregard any element of the law for whatever reason, loses its *raison d'être*. See ch. 5.4. for further discussion of this argument.

[38] Already by Harrod 1936, 14 (the pioneer of "utilitarian generalization"); cf. Jacobs 1985, ch. 3.

[39] Veldhuis 1983; Soper 1984, 79-80.

[40] Honoré 1987, 128.

[41] As Greenawalt 1987b, 169, observes, this argument is "intimated" by Honoré 1987, ch. 6. Honoré actually states that such duties "necessarily go beyond the natural duty of helping others when they are in need". The additional element seems to concern the position of being best placed to provide the necessary care. But Lyons 1981 rightly comments (a) that it is often a matter of convention who is "best placed", (b) that this is also true for the "natural duty to help others in need".

prudential reason to contribute to the cooperative effort. But everybody has a duty to the others as well, and this duty seems to be well accounted for by the principle of necessity. Everybody is "locked" by fate into his responsibility for the others.

But if we are trying to use this model to explain the obligation to obey the law, two problems must be overcome. The first is the specification of the goal. It may be true that without government human life in our world would be impossible, or at least nasty, brutish and short. But governments do not restrict themselves to goals which are recognized by all to be pressing needs requiring care or management, such as internal and external security, the irrigation of the desert, the containment of flooding, or the prevention of the destruction of the natural environment. They do all kinds of things which large groups of their subjects consider second-best, indifferent, or even positively harmful or evil. Often these subjects may believe, and believe correctly, that it would be most useful to have a particular law revoked, or to let it fall into oblivion. But even when government activity is aimed at objectives universally and correctly recognized as worthwhile, they are often not as urgent as the principle of necessity requires. In that case, why would an individual have any positive obligation to contribute? With the exception of the odd act-utilitarian, people do not normally recognize an obligation to contribute to other people's non-necessary goods, even if they are "best placed" to provide them. Non-maleficence is an area of duty, beneficence largely an area of supererogation.

At this point we should remember the difference between the case of the child in the pond and that of the life-boat. By doing my share in the life-boat, I contribute to my own survival; I am not only exercising a duty of care for others. Perhaps it could be argued that in such cases my responsibility is not restricted to meeting the pressing needs of others, but extends to less urgent collective tasks as well. What seems to be decisive is that, even if I take my full share of the costs, the enterprise as a whole creates a clear net benefit for me. This does not mean that I have a decisive prudential reason to take my share; perhaps I could have invested my energy in even more profitable ways. Nevertheless, I may be morally required to contribute to the common good of a community of which I am a member.[42]

But many government activities apparently do not meet even this relaxed condition. So the question remains whether it is ever justifiable to require people to contribute to a cooperative good which they do not, or should not, recognize as a proper goal. However, I will set aside this problem for the moment, and return to it in the next chapter.

The second problem is the one we came across when trying to apply the generalization argument. There is only one person passing by the pond; and in the life-boat, the first person who refuses to be instructed may endanger the life of all (including his own). But in a state it is hardly ever true that the collective task will only be executed if literally everybody contributes. If I decline to make any contribution, the consequences to any single person will normally be almost imperceptible. If I fail to pay my taxes, no other Dutch citizen will feel the difference. The problem is therefore to

---

[42] Cf. Finnis 1980, 245-252, 314-320, 351-366: the duty of obedience derives from the duty to promote the common good.

find a principle of distribution of the collective task.[43] We agree that as a collective, we should produce order, justice and welfare, because these things are either pressing needs or at least part of our common good, but why should I shoulder any part of the burden? I am not "better placed" than anybody else.

In discussing the first problem, I proposed the principle that everybody should contribute to the common good of a group of which she is a member. Does this principle also provide the answer to the problem of distribution? It does not. For I did not yet explain the necessary and/or sufficient conditions of "membership", and this is the same problem. Of course it is possible, and perhaps praiseworthy, that a person mentally identifies with the community,[44] but this cannot be a condition of membership: all the problems of consent theory would return. The only alternative we came across so far was provided by the idea of necessity: being uniquely well situated to provide for someone's good. In political society normally no-one answers to this description.

I do not claim, by the way, that every individual contribution is virtually nil, so that nobody can have a consequentialist reason for doing anything at all. If everyone's contribution is zero, the collective outcome is zero, that is a truth of arithmetic, and arguments which try to convince us otherwise are all instances of the Sorites fallacy.[45] If we were all act-utilitarians and appreciated the usefulness of the common goal, we would all happily do our part. But our common morality is not act-utilitarianism: we do not require each other to invest our resources in the service of the most urgent need that can be identified impersonally. Even if care and management are really needed, no individual can be said to be "best situated" to render that care. This can be said only of the community as a whole. Hence our need for an individuation principle.

## 4.5. Gratitude

The interesting thing is that Socrates, unlike some contemporary advocates of the principle of necessity, clearly recognizes that the idea of a collective task needs to be supplemented by a distributive criterion. The Laws argue that by disobeying them,

---

[43] Many theories which claim a "natural duty to obedience" are incomplete at this point, for example Anscombe 1978 (when she extends the authority of the state from the protection against violence to other tasks), Veldhuis 1983, Honoré 1987. Both Wellman 1996 and Copp 1999 first reject the principle of fairness as a possible ground for political obligation and then go on to argue for a version of the principle of necessity, without recognizing that this principle needs to be supplemented by a distributive principle like the principle of fairness. Other theories at least implicitly refer to considerations of fairness, cf. note 64.
My point is related to the one Simmons 1999 makes by distinguishing between the justification of a state and its legitimacy. I agree with Simmons that in discussing the question of the state's justification we address issues (the importance of the tasks of the state and its performance) which, though relevant to the question of the state's legitimacy, do not decide it. But we have to address the issue of legitimacy as well: even if the state has an important task and does it excellently, it cannot be justified if it executes the task by exercising an authority it does not possess.

[44] Raz 1986, 97-99. Cf. ch. 5.3.

[45] Den Hartogh 1985.17. The mistake is arguably made by Smith 1973, 958; Soper 1984, 60-62; Klosko 1992, appendix 1.

Socrates "for his part" would do violence to them, but they also show why as an individual he should make it his responsibility that for his part no violence is done. The reason is that the existence of the laws and the state has conferred large benefits on him, which he should not fail to reciprocate. Because marriage is an institution regulated by law, Socrates owes his life to the laws. And he should also be grateful to them for requiring his father to give him a cultural and physical education. Violence, even in the form of returning evil for evil, is a sin against your parents, but if the laws and the state are the real sources of parental benefits, violence against them is a far greater sin. Retaliation is not a valid excuse; even disregarding the fact that, after all, he is not a victim of a wrong done by the laws, but only by his fellow citizens.

The individuation principle proposed by Socrates seems to be the principle of gratitude. The rights of parents over their adult sons are taken to be the proper analogy of the rights of the city over its citizens, and those rights derive not from their greater wisdom, but from the benefits they have conferred.

The use of the personification figure causes problems here. The existence of the laws may produce benefits, as the existence of the Gulf Stream does, but we cannot be grateful to the laws, any more than to the Gulf Stream. To reciprocate any benefits, we must identify the people who intentionally bestowed them on us. (If they did so only accidentally, we have no duty of gratitude.) But Socrates does not specify who he takes to be responsible for the benefits of law. As he disonerates the laws from the wrong done to him, it seems clear that he is not thinking of his fellow citizens. But in the context of the Athenian democracy it is not possible to make a sharp distinction between fellow citizens and state officials. (He was condemned by a jury of 500 citizens.) Perhaps he is thinking of the original lawmaker, Solon. Or perhaps the personification of the Laws and the Constitution is more than a figure of speech to him.

That we should obey the law as a way of paying off a debt of gratitude, is a way of thinking quite alien to the modern mind, at least in countries like the Netherlands. For we believe that the benefits bestowed on us are ours by right: if people fail to confer them, we claim them as our due. (But compare: it was customary in Eastern Germany to complain of sporting people and artists who stayed in the West that they were "ungrateful" to the "people" who had given them their professional education etc.) Are we right in believing this? Again, it depends on the persons we are supposed to be grateful to.

I know of only one contemporary author who believes that something like gratitude to state officials is one good reason for obeying the law.[46] When the enterprise of law is something worthwhile to undertake, and those in charge of government are doing their level best to make a success of the enterprise, then we, the subjects, have a moral obligation – a defeasible moral reason of at least some minimal force – to obey them in reciprocation of their sincere efforts on our behalf, even if some particular effort is misguided. A ruler who performs a necessary job with good faith and

---

[46] Soper 1984, 77-87. But his favourite concept is 'respect' rather than 'gratitude', for the latter would invite the "matching" of benefits. See, however, Smith 1973; Simmons 1979, 185-186: as debts of gratitude are very unspecific, perhaps *some* obedience would be enough to pay them, or even some other activity that would serve the system.

some success deserves the respect of his subjects; and this respect gives them a moral reason to go along and not oppose him.

This position is hardly attractive.[47] Why should our respect, our approval of good intention and minimally efficient execution, have to express itself in obedience even to mistaken commands? The answer seems to be that you should not frustrate and upset people who are doing their best. But if our rulers were really dedicated to their task, would they not have reason to welcome opposition if they made mistakes?[48] The question shows that the whole idea of obedience as a reciprocal benefit to rulers is mistaken. If you want to show your respect or gratitude to a person, you should indeed do something which she personally would like you to do. (She may want you to help her to perform well, but even then you will help her to perform well because she wants it.) But it would be embarrassing to state officials to obey them for that reason; for what they require you to do is not supposed to benefit *them*, but the citizens.[49]

And how are they supposed to do this – what is their job? Answer: they exercise authority, i.e. they make, apply and execute laws, and as the same author urges, these laws pretend to be obligatory. But then we should already have an obligation to obey their laws before we can judge that they are doing their job, and appreciate the fact by being either respectful or grateful. If their laws do not succeed in obligating us on some other principle, they are false pretenders and should be resisted, even if as a matter of fact their false pretentions serve us well. Self-respecting persons need not be grateful for the benefits of unjustified paternalism. Deriving the obligation to obey the law from respect owed to authority is therefore arguing in a circle.

State officials are creatures of the law, hence the obligation to obey the law cannot be a debt of gratitude owed to them. We have a right to expect them to do their job.[50] But the fact that the law exists at all is not something to which we have a "natural" (pre-legal) right, even if we have natural rights to life, liberty and bodily integrity. We cannot "naturally" – but only conventionally – expect each other to comply with traffic laws. A necessary condition for the existence of these conventions is that most of our fellow citizens comply with them most of the time. Does this fact impose on us a debt of gratitude to our fellow citizens? The idea correctly identifies the persons we have political obligations to – if we have any. It also recognizes the important fact that political obligations are not simply obligations of care for persons in need, but are connected with the reception of benefits.

---

[47] Cf. the critical comments of Raz 1984a, 744-749; Lyons 1987; Greenawalt 1987a; Gans 1992, 43ff.

[48] Raz 1984a, 748: let us not encourage these people to feel frustrated too soon.

[49] Concerning the life-boat Soper 1984, 80, says that "what is relevant is not the impact of my decision on the venture but the impact on the person who stands in front of me trying to do his best to accomplish ends thought to advance the interests of the group, as a whole, including myself". If this correctly describes what he is trying to do, why should *I* be interested in the impact of my decision on *him* ?

[50] Simmons 1979, 179 objects that we may owe a debt of gratitude to a person who did no more than his duty in helping us. This is possible indeed, but only if his duty was one of beneficence purely, not if helping belonged to the normal tasks of a job he voluntarily accepted and is handsomely paid for. Cf. Gans 1992, 44.

It has been suggested by Walker that we owe gratitude to the state rather than to our fellow citizens.[51] Is it possible to be grateful, if not to the rules of an institution, to the institution itself? If we understand the institution to be an association of people organized in a certain way for doing a certain job cooperatively, this seems indeed possible.[52] It is even possible, as Walker insists, that you are grateful to the institution without being grateful to any of the people organized by it in particular; in that case your gratitude cannot be distributed. It is not even necessarily directed to any particular collection of people as such. As long as they do their job, they may all be replaceable. Hence you may offer a donation to your *Alma Mater* out of gratitude, even though the last professor who taught you has long since retired. Still it is essential that the institution you are grateful to is an organization of people. So, if your obligation of gratitude is an obligation to the state, it is still an obligation to your fellow-citizens, whoever they are, as an organized body.

Gratitude is a proper response to the reception of benefits, intentionally bestowed on you. But the question is whether this central notion of the reciprocation of benefit is given the right interpretation. The idea is not as obviously absurd as our contemporaries are prone to think. If you have the good fortune to start life in a country in which a tolerably just and efficient system of law is in force, vigorously supported by the whole population, is there not every possible reason to feel grateful? It is not an absurd suggestion, but it has its problems as an account of political obligation.

A first problem is the following. Suppose that you have reason to be grateful to your fellow citizens.[53] Assume, furthermore, that you do not *feel* grateful. Then, it seems, you cannot compensate for this lack of proper feelings by pretending to have them.[54] But even in this case you surely have reason to reciprocate the benefits you have received from the proper functioning of the state; the reason must therefore derive from another motive.

This argument seems to derive its force from the fact that acts of gratitude are supposed to communicate the attitude of gratitude to others, in particular to the benefactor. But it is hypocritical to express a feeling you do not have. Walker, however, has argued that some obligations of gratitude do not have this symbolic character. In particular, you have an obligation not to act in ways which are incompatible with

---

[51] Walker 1988. Perhaps this is the proper reading of Socrates' puzzling idea that we should repay the Laws for the benefits they confer on us.

[52] Some states (according to some: all states) should rather be seen as organizations of a ruling élite. Then we are back at Soper's position, at best.

[53] I agree with Kavka 1983 against Simmons that the payment of debts of gratitude is without value, perhaps even injurious or insulting, if the proper feeling is lacking. (And surely the lack of such feelings can be blameworthy.) Simmons rightly recognizes the fact that children have no moral reasons to be grateful to their parents for benefits which were not accompanied by warm parental feelings. But why would the benefiting acts be valueless without proper feeling, and not the reciprocating acts? (It follows that the obligation to pay compensation for costs incurred in the course of the helpful acts is not really an obligation of gratitude. For this obligation does not depend on having the proper feelings. Not all duties of reciprocation are properly described as duties of gratitude, cf. note 55.)

[54] Cf. Sher 1987, 113. (It may be a matter of polite behaviour to pretend, even if it is obvious to all that you are only pretending.) Griffin 1986, 260, puts the point even stronger: "It may destroy your motive as one of gratitude to inject considerations of duty into it."

gratitude, and in this case it does not matter whether your benefactor even knows you are easing his way.[55] One could still wonder, however, what the action is worth without the attitude: even if it is not a communicative, it should be an expressive act. One could also wonder – and this is really the same point – whether obligations of gratitude can be enforceable ones. A lack of gratitude is only something to be deplored.

A second problem is that your co-citizens did not give their support intentionally so as to benefit you. Their motivation need not have been egoistic, but it was not primarily other-oriented either: they were contributing to a common good. Debts of gratitude, however, are only owed to people whose acts had the primary intention of creating benefits to you, or at least to a class of people including you but not including themselves.[56] And why did they make their contributions? If they did so from a motive of gratitude to their fellow-citizens themselves, as the proponent of gratitude as a basis for political obligation requires them to do, this class either excludes or includes you. If it excludes you, obviously the benefits flowing to you are only the unintended by-products of their gratitude to others, and you have no reason to be grateful at all. If it includes you, you have no such reason either: they are simply paying their own debts.[57]

This argument points to the basic weakness of the appeal to gratitude. Being grateful is to be at one end of an asymmetrical relationship: even if you know that the person you are grateful to has equal reason to be grateful to you, your "debt" does not depend on her recognizing and paying hers. (Suppose each of you, on different occasions, has saved the other one's life, without either of you knowing at the time that the other had done so or would do so.) Therefore, within a cooperative enterprise in which the good results of anyone's contribution depend on the efforts of the others, it is out of place to take gratitude as the source for the mutual obligations of the participants to each other.[58] These obligations may exist from the very beginning of the enterprise, when nothing has yet been done which deserves gratitude. But debts of gratitude only begin when you have collected enough benefits.

Gratitude, we may conclude, may be an important contributing factor to our willingness to recognize political obligations, but it cannot be the factor which grounds those obligations to begin with.[59]

So we should look for a principle which is similar to the principle of gratitude in that it recognizes the relevance of benefits we derive from the efforts of our fellow citizens, but different in that it looks to the present, not to the past, and recognizes

---

[55] Feinberg 1995, 127 and Walzer 1988 argue that duties to repay services should not be interpreted as duties of gratitude. Following Aquinas, Feinberg quotes Seneca saying that "a person who wants to repay a gift too quickly... is an unwilling debtor and an ungrateful person". It is true that in a society, conventions of reciprocation may exist that have nothing to do with gratitude. But it is quite usual for a failure to reciprocate to be interpreted as a sign of a blameworthy lack of gratitude.

[56] Simmons 1979, 170-175; Gans 1992, 44.

[57] "So the fact that we are partially 'social products' in that we benefit from current patterns and forms created by the multitudinous actions of a long string of long-forgotten people, forms which include institutions, ways of doing things, and language... does not create in us a general floating debt which the current society can collect and use at will." Nozick 1974, 95.

[58] To suppose so is a kind of parametric fallacy, cf. ch. 1.4. at note 28.

[59] Cf. Tamir 1993, 133.

mutuality of obligations. This symmetrical variation on the theme of reciprocation is the principle of fairness.

Let us take stock. The starting point of every theory of political obligation should be that some good things – the enforcement of liberty-rights, the care of the environment – can only be realized by the cooperative efforts of all the inhabitants of a certain territory, acting through a common agency which requires the contribution of everybody choosing to stay permanently within the territory. The idea of a common good is fundamental. But it must be supplemented by the answers to several other questions. These questions will require our attention for the remainder of this chapter and the next one. The first question is: why should any particular individual contribute? Gratitude to the others is the right type of answer, but not quite the right answer. The answer, whichever it is, should also explain why implied consent has its limited role to play. (You cannot withdraw from a debt of gratitude by simply going away. To that extent, the authorities of the GDR were at least consistent.) The second question is: why should the common agency have any authority, why should our obligation to contribute imply an obligation to obey? And the third question is: suppose some part of the activities of the agency is directed towards objectives that are neither necessary or desirable, is it possible that even so, I still have a moral reason to contribute to these activities? The following sections will discuss these questions, but the answer to the second and third question will only be fully elaborated in the next chapter.

## 4.6. Obligations of Fairness

Suppose a group of farmers reclaim a fertile salt marsh by enclosing it with a dyke. They divide the land and agree that everyone of them will maintain part of the dyke, according to the size of the piece of land allotted to him. Everyone of them builds his farmhouse in this polder and, in time, leaves it (I assume: without any conditions attached) to his successor. After a while, a whole new generation is living and working in the polder. Yet, every farmer still expects the others to continue their contributions to the maintenance of the dyke. Although none of the actual landholders has participated in the original agreement, they are all undeniably subject to an obligation. Maintenance of the dyke as a whole is of vital importance to all of them, and it would be unfair to saddle the others with the burdens of it. Since it is so important that everyone fulfills his obligation, the others have the right to demand or, if necessary, compel compliance.

Consequently, in this kind of situation, obligations can be created without the consent of the people involved. What are the general features of such situations? I mention the following.

(1)    A group of people is able to produce a generally desired good if everyone makes a proper contribution. If only a few people perform duly, little or nothing is brought about. The undertaking will only be profitable when enough people join in. The interdependent result can only be realized through cooperation.

(2)   To every member of the group, the benefits outweigh the burdens. (Another possible situation is that a collective duty has to be fulfilled, for example towards needy insiders or outsiders, or towards future generations.)[60]

(3)   Nevertheless, each of the participants would also be able to enjoy the benefits of the cooperative activity without making any sacrifice, as long as there are enough people who do their share. One's benefit may be somewhat less when the duty is neglected, but the difference does not compensate for the demanded performance.[61] It is easy to recognize in this kind of situation the $n$-person Prisoner's Dilemma discussed in chapter Two.

(4)   Each of the participants expects the others to make their contribution, and knows the others to expect the same from her, and knows the others to know her expectations, and so on. After all, it is not unfair to refuse to contribute when you know that nobody else is going to (or that the others do not count on a contribution from your side[62]). Usually, this characteristic is not mentioned explicitly,[63] but it is obviously essential. For if in a situation characterized by the first three conditions, you start "cooperating" without being assured of the cooperation of others, you may not contribute to the common good at all. And even if you are fully sensitive to considerations of fairness, if the others fail to contribute themselves they will not be justified to expect a contribution from you.

Under those circumstances, the principle of fairness demands a contribution from all.[64] Anyone who shirks, betrays and usually also abuses the others' confidence. (This

---

[60] Such collective duties are rightly stressed by Wellman 1996, who fails to notice, however, that "samaritanism" does not by itself cover individual duties of obedience, cf. note 43. Note also that the good to be produced need not be individually accessible: the achievement of a good which can only be enjoyed if it is enjoyed by many is also to be counted a benefit. The principle of fairness does not presuppose an individualistic conception of advantage.

[61] I agree with Simmons 1979, 106-107 note, that the principle condemns free-riding as well as parasitic behaviour: it does not matter whether by omitting to contribute I am actually causing harm to the others.

[62] Soper 1984, 70-73, correctly argues that you are not obliged to pay for benefits which are nothing but the positive external effects of other people's independent activities, not even if you cannot be excluded from enjoying these benefits.

[63] And hence indirect benefits (cf. previous note) are taken to be a problem for the defenders of the principle, Simmons 1979, 121-122. Hart, though, limits his principle to "any joint enterprise according to rules", and Rawls speaks of a "scheme of social cooperation" which must be already in force (otherwise it is impossible to accept the benefits of it). Cf. also Reiman 1972, 57; Arneson 1982, 622-623; Den Hartogh 1985, 162 ff., 272 ff. A fifth condition concerns the fair distribution of benefits and burdens, but this will be discussed in ch. 5.1.

[64] Hart 1955, 185-186; Rawls 1958, 178-179; id. 1964, 9-11; id. 1971, 111-114, 342 ff. Cf. also Broad (1916), 1971, 53; Gouldner 1973. Discussion: Wasserstrom (1963) 1975, 379-382; Lyons 1965, 161-177; Murphy 1970, 42-44; Henry 1970, 271 note; Richards 1971, 155; Smith 1973, 954-959; Nozick 1974, 90-95; Bell 1978; Miller & Sartorius 1979, 165-167; Simmons 1979, ch. 5 (thorough and detailed); Woozley 1979, 135-140; Pateman 1979, 121-129; Mackie 1981, 147-149; Arneson 1982 (important); Veldhuis 1983, 12-13; Kavka 1983; Morris 1983; Soper 1984, 70-73; Robins 1984, 127-132; Sugden 1984; Jacobs 1985, 94 ff.; Hardin 1985, 413-416; Dworkin 1986, 193-195; Becker 1986, 252-263; Regan 1986, 17-18; Simmons 1986; Van der Burg 1986, 45-47; Greenawalt 1987a, 168-178; Greenawalt 1987b, 121-158; Beran 1987, 77-84; Simmons 1987, 270-275; Wolff 1990/1, 164-167; Hurd 1991, 1649-1653; Gans 1992, 57-66; Horton 1992, 89-98; Simmons 1993, 249-260; Schmidtz 1991, 81-85; Menlowe 1993, 182-190; Feinberg (1979) 1995, 130-

is one reason, though not the only one, why it is legitimate to punish any such person: the punishment takes away the profits of his exploitative actions.) In the terminology of the first chapter: if a pattern of mutual expectations exists of contributing to a cooperative enterprise for mutual advantage, each participant to the convention has a reason of fairness to honour the expectations of the others. And that explains why the pattern is self-maintaining.

Requirements of fairness can only be made, if everyone may trust the others, or enough of the others, to be motivated by them, by another cooperative disposition, e.g. loyalty, or, exceptionally, by the fear of sanctions which it is part of the cooperative task of the political community to institute and execute. It follows that the principle of fairness only applies when sufficient people are willing to contribute. This fact explains part of the eternal attraction of consent theory: it is true that the existence of a state in which the government rules by law and not by coercion, depends on the willingness of its citizens to shoulder the burdens needed for the fulfilment of its tasks.[65] This does not rehabilitate consent theory however. Not only or primarily because the psychological state of willingness need not express itself in any action which can be plausibly interpreted as an act of consent. But mainly because, for all we have said sofar, it need not be true for anyone individually that she is willing to contribute in order for her to be under an obligation to do so. The "consent of the governed" as a collective body may be a condition for the legitimacy of a government, but it is not a principle of political obligation, for what we are looking for is a *distributive* principle.[66]

### 4.7. A Principle of Involuntary Obligation

But perhaps the principle of fairness as a distributive principle should be understood as a principle of voluntary obligation after all. In that case we have to add another condition to the four I mentioned. Such a condition has been proposed by Rawls. In his view, you are obligated to contribute only if you have decided voluntarily to share in the benefits of the cooperative activity. If you are unable to refuse, if the benefit is forced upon you, you need not acknowledge the right to demand a service in return.[67]

---

132; Wolff 1995; Cohen 1995, ch. 10; Wellman 1996, 213; White 1997; Copp 1999, 12, 32-33. Klosko 1992 is a comprehensive treatment, close to the present one in its defence of the principle for the case of non-excludable goods. Some natural duty theories contain or imply considerations of fairness, as Greenawalt 1987b, 175-176, notes. This is true of Rawls 1971 (see note 68) and Finnis 1980, cf. Finnis 1984, 119; 1989, 102; Veldhuis 1983 and Greenawalt 1985 (see note 73); cf. also Raz 1984a, 745-747, on Soper.

[65] Cf. ch. 6.4. at note 31. This is a major concern of some consent theories, e.g. Walzer 1970; 1977, 54; Herzog 1989; and arguably of Locke as well. However, obligations deriving from consent require individual consenting acts, not general consenting attitudes, cf. Simmonss 1993, 214, with references.

[66] John Locke comes close to making this distinction, Den Hartogh 1990a, 210ff; 1990b.

[67] In Rawls 1971, 111-114, the principle of fairness is counted among the principles for individual decision making that would be chosen in the Original Position, as soon as the principles for the basic structure are fixed. Obligations are based on voluntary acts, unlike natural duties. (Rawls believes that all obligations, even promissory ones, originate from the principle of fairness.)

Rawls, then, claims that a voluntary act is a prerequisite for an obligation of fairness to arise.[68] This still does not mean that he takes the obligation to derive from consent: the intention of the voluntary act need not be to accept an obligation. It is not even an act of implied consent: for even if you may be expected to know in advance that by doing it you will assume an obligation, the obligation is attached to the act on account of the principle of fairness, and not on the basis of a conventional interpretation of the meaning of the act. (In a similar way, you may know that by damaging your neighbour's garden, you assume an obligation to compensate him for the loss. That is not an act of implied consent either.)

But Rawls' additional condition must be rejected.[69] Interdependent products like a polder dyke have the character of a public good: once it has been produced, nobody can be excluded from enjoying the benefits. It is impossible to accept the benefits voluntarily, for it is not even possible to refuse them. (You could "refuse" them by leaving your farm in the polder. But if this is the only alternative, your options are restricted artificially: it is not open to you to stay without paying. As we saw in section 3 is precisely the closing of this option which needs to be justified, and its justification is the principle of fairness.)

The production of public goods necessarily takes the form of a cooperative enterprise as decribed by our four features. Hence the logic of the Prisoner's Dilemma applies: it is a dominant choice not to contribute. Given that the ratio between costs and burdens is the same for everyone, I would have reason to contribute only if the benefits of the cooperative scheme to me outweigh the costs by a factor equal to the number of the possible participants. And therefore, barring exceptional circumstances, public goods will not be provided by rational people, unless they could be moved to participate in cooperation on moral grounds.[70]

Suppose the producers of a good could easily ask a fee for the use of their product, but do not. Then they have no right at all to appeal to the principle of fairness and compel a service in return afterwards.[71] On the contrary, the situation in which an appeal to the principle of fairness makes sense, occurs precisely when it is not feasible (or morally undesirable) to demand payment (immediate or postponed) as a condition for use.[72] When Rawls' condition is relevant, however, an appeal to the principle of fairness is seldom justified.[73] I do not mean to say that it would never be unfair to take

---

[68] Because of this, in Rawls 1971 (not yet in Rawls 1964), the principle of fairness is only of minor importance to the problem of the moral reasons to obey political authority; he argues that precisely the production of public goods (among other collective activities) the principle does not work, Rawls 1971, 336. This is a reason for the parties in the original position to agree to a natural, non-voluntary duty to support (and comply with) just institutions. This natural duty, however, remains a duty of fairness, because it is agreed to in the original position which has been constructed in order to translate intuitions of fairness into articulate principles!

[69] Klosko 1994, 265-266, argues convincingly that it would be rejected in the Original Position.

[70] See ch. 2 at note 81 and ch. 3.3.

[71] Cf. Soper 1984, 70, on the "officious intermeddler".

[72] Arneson 1982; Klosko 1992; Greenawalt 1987b.

[73] Veldhuis 1983 and Greenawalt 1985 accept Rawls's prerequisite, but they believe that people might have involuntary obligations towards each other as well (like people in a life-boat). "What is crucial is that the

an excludable advantage for free. But it would be unfair only if the advantage is worth its price (second necessary feature), and this is most easily verified by asking the price, i.e. by requiring its full payment as a condition for enjoyment. If this is omitted without any good reason,[74] an appeal to the principle of fairness is otiose: the appeal is pre-empted by the applicability of the principle of consent.[75]

This can be shown by pursuing an example from Simmons. The inhabitants of a village decide on a scheme of subscription for digging a well. After the well has been dug, Jones starts drawing water from it, though he had voted against the scheme. Simmons develops his example in two versions. In the first one, Jones steals to the well at night so as to get his water without being noticed. This of course is the typical behaviour of the self-conscious parasite: Jones knows that, if he would draw water openly, his neighbours would require him to pay his share after the fact. So his act of drawing water is an act of implied consent.[76] In the second version, Jones goes to the well with his bucket yelling that he persists in his opposition against the whole scheme, and that he is not prepared to pay anything for the water. If he is not denied access for all that, then he has no obligation to pay: the other inhabitants clearly consent to his taking the water freely. So either the voluntary acceptance of benefits is an act of implied consent (having taken our meal in the restaurant, we cannot really protest that we did not undertake an obligation to pay), or it does not create an obligation.

Dropping the condition of voluntary acceptance is often thought to have unacceptable consequences: all sorts of unasked-for services would create obligations. Someone who washes my car without my knowing it, would be allowed to send me a bill. But in examples like this, there is no question whatsoever of cooperative activities, for the profit of the service and the profit of the return service are independent. All persons involved can attach conditions to their choice without difficulty and may not complain if an unconditional choice is "exploited".

Probably, most writers who defend Rawls' additional condition are still to some extent under the spell of the consent model of political obligation. Though they see that acts of consent, whether explicit or tacit, are too exceptional to be a ground for political obligation, they still look for something similar.[77] Some of them – Rawls, incidentally,

---

demand is being placed on us under a necessary scheme in which we are fairly involved and whose aim in part is to benefit us." Greenawalt 1985, 26, cf. Honoré 1987, 63, 125. Greenawalt rightly observes that the principle we need in these situations, very much resembles the principle of fair play; the latter, however, cannot be applied because it demands voluntary acceptance of benefits.... Greenawalt 1987a understands that there is always reason for a fair division of a common task, whether it is voluntarily acquired or not.

[74] I do not wish to deny that moral reasons may exist for producing excludable goods by way of cooperative schemes, distributing payments by taxing, not by pricing. For example, we may believe that access to the good should not depend on purchasing power. If the principle of fairness is rejected as a principle of involuntary obligation, no scope whatsoever can be given to these good reasons. If they are acceptable, it follows that we cannot agree with Nozick and Simmons that everyone has to pay only in proportion to his (expected) benefit.

[75] Unless you have led the others to expect you to contribute, e.g. by contributing before.

[76] He does not consent to the scheme, as Simmons rightly says, but he does consent to be obligated to contribute.

[77] Plamenatz 1968, 168-171, and Walzer 1970, 100, consider – just like Locke – the acceptance of benefits itself to be a form of tacit consent, and thus they reduce the principle of fairness to that of consent. There is

is not under suspicion – may be influenced by Hobbes' axiom: "There being no obligation on any man, which ariseth not from some act of his own".[78] This axiom was decisively dealt with by Hume, however:[79] the fact that a promise is binding calls for explanation as much as the fact that the law is binding, and in either case the answer must refer to the pattern of mutual expectations making possible an interdependent result. A promise is binding because it is unfair to let someone down who relies on it.[80]

Simmons recognizes that it is impossible to take the non-refusing of a public good as a condition of obligation. But even so, he believes an attitude is necessary that he calls "acceptance" and still holds to be sufficient for classifying obligations of fairness as voluntary ones.[81] On his view, the correct distinction to make is not that between reception and refusal of the benefits of cooperation, but rather that between willing and unwilling reception. The attitude of willing reception involves: (1) the belief that the benefits flow from a cooperative scheme and do not fall as mannah from heaven; (2) a counterfactual choice: we believe we would take them, even if we had the option of refusing. He goes on to specify both elements of the attitude. As for the first, he submits that a person's ignorance releases her from the obligation, unless it results from culpable negligence. And he observes that in modern states many citizens barely notice the benefits of government, do not deem them worth the price, and believe they are free for the taking, or are purchased from the government rather than produced by common efforts. As for the second element of the attitude of willing reception, Simmons rules out of court the disposition of the free-rider: the counterfactual choice he requires, is made by anyone who in the $n$-person Prisoner's Dilemma game of the production of a particular public good, prefers the outcome of general cooperation to the outcome of general defection. For if we allowed people to opt for free-riding, public goods would not be produced, or only be underproduced, even by people prepared to honour their obligations.[82]

The consequence of this last specification, however, is that the obligation is no longer a voluntary one at all. To begin with, it is essential for voluntarism that

---

better reason to regard Locke's tacit consent as a misinterpretation of the enjoyment of a cooperative undertaking's benefits! Cf. note 31.

[78] *Leviathan,* ch. 21. "The wish for a wholly contractual world reflects a failure to accept our social nature, the fact that an important component of our ethical identity is shaped by the social arrangements into which we are born." Hardimon 1994, 353, cf. Green quoted note 28. Voluntarism is understandably attractive as long as you conceive of political obligation as a duty owed to state officials.

[79] "You find yourself embarrassed when it is asked: Why are we bound to keep our word? Nor can you give any answer but what would immediately, without any circuit, have accounted for our obligation to allegiance." *Essays Moral Political and Literary,* II 12, "Of the Original Contract". Cf. *A Treatise of Human Nature,* III, ii, viii, "Of the Source of Allegiance." For another refutation of Hobbes' axiom see Cohen 1995, ch.10.

[80] Cf. ch. 1, note 8, on the reliance theory of promising.

[81] Cf. the attitudinal conditions for the application of the principle of gratitude, note 54. Simmons claims that these attitudinal conditions are not satisfied, an empirical claim disputed by Kavka 1986, 411; Gans 1992, 61-62; and in particular Klosko 1987, 358-362. Klosko quotes results from social psychology showing that people generally do not interpret the taxes they pay as a quid pro quo for benefits received, but rather as a fair contribution to a common enterprise. See also Strümpel 1969.

[82] Simmons 1979, 128-136; 1993, 253-255.

obligations are undertaken by voluntary acts, but a counterfactual choice is not an act, but just a redescription of preferences. Moreover, we do not even allow people their real preferences, for in that case the counterfactual choice in the $n$-person PD could easily be to defect. It is only by restricting the set of allowable preferences that we get the obligation from "choice", but such a choice is not just a counterfactual but a hypothetical choice. Simmons' move is the classical one: from actual to hypothetical consent.

I have no objections to this second part of Simmons' "acceptance" condition as such: the principle of fairness requires that for everyone involved, the benefits of cooperation exceed the burdens.[83] But it seems to me that he cannot consistently insist on the first part of the condition as well. When benefits are exchanged for payment, the willingness to pay is a clear sign that the benefits are worth the price. But with a public good we obviously cannot take the expressed willingness to pay as such a clear sign: people will be tempted to refuse payment if their enjoyment of the benefits does not depend on it. But even if we had a reliable way of recognizing people's actual state of mind, we could not require them to be actually "willing to pay". For people will not only be tempted to dissimulate their real preferences, but, if only to avoid the need for dissimulation, to adapt their preferences (or beliefs) as well. They will tend to underrate the value of public goods, or to mould their beliefs concerning the actual or desirable modes of their production into convenient patterns. Hence, if we allow the production of public goods to depend on willingness to contribute, chances are that even quite essential public goods will still not be produced at all, or in quantities far below what is needed. But this is the argument which moved Simmons to disregard the free-rider to begin with. Consistency requires him to disregard the ignorant as well. So we should take our lead from people's considered preferences as they may be ascribed to them on well-founded general psychological knowledge (with, perhaps, a margin of error on the safe side), not from preferences and beliefs as they may be assumed to be strategically expressed, or even strategically held. People's mistaken representations of their preferences do not count, not even their mistaken representations to themselves.[84] Because important interests of other people are at stake, we should consider any form of ignorance which leads a person to free-riding to be negligent or reckless.

Because we have no failure-proof means of identifying people's actual, let alone their considered preferences, it is indeed possible that the principle of fairness will lead us to require contributions from people who do not think their expected benefits to be worth the price.[85] But the alternative is to tolerate all free-riding as the bona fide use of exit-options. Fortunately, it is precisely at this point that considerations of fairness can

---

[83] But I will argue in the next chapter that this requirement should not be made for each alleged public good produced by the state, but rather for the total package of such goods.

[84] If we considered subjective standards to be decisive, "we allow people's ignorance (or their natural tendencies to underestimate personal benefits and overestimate personal burdens) to release them from obligations of reciprocation." Kavka 1983, 228. On the other hand, it is not enough that we have reasons to believe that a cooperative enterprise *would* benefit people; people should as a matter of fact mutually expect each other to contribute.

[85] This expression (cf. Simmons 1993, 256-257) is ambiguous: it may either mean "the benefits exceeding the costs", or "the best value for money on offer".

be supplemented by other considerations.[86] Suppose there is one person on board of the life-boat who prefers drowning to taking commands from anyone, or from this particular captain. It will be hard to tell whether this is a strategic move aimed at getting another captain (him?) appointed. But anyway, even if it is a real sacrifice the others ask him to make, they are justified in asking it, from loyalty and solidarity if not from fairness. This is the basic reason why Kant is right in the words I quoted before against consent theory: whatever your personal state of mind, if you are in the same boat with others, you have reason to enter with them "into a rightful condition".

To conclude this particular discussion with Simmons, it is interesting to note how paradoxical the position is he finally takes. People may generally believe that they commonly have an obligation to obey the law, but, given the actual facts of modern political society, they are mistaken: no voluntaristic account of such an obligation can plausibly be given, neither in terms of consent nor in terms of fairness, and only a voluntaristic account will do. But why does an account in terms of fairness fail? Mainly because people are largely ignorant concerning the nature of political society as a cooperative enterprise for mutual advantage... If they are, why do they think they have obligations? Even if the actual account they give is somewhat confused, referring as it probably does to "the consent of the governed", should we not charitably interpret it as at least a dim awareness of the nature of political society? After all, we found lots of philosophers talking fairness in terms of consent, and even Simmons himself mistaking his version of the principle of fairness for a voluntaristic one.

## 4.8. The Principle of Fairness: Validity and Scope

Where does all this leave us with regard to the question whether voluntary acceptance of benefits should be required as a fifth necessary condition of success for the appeal to the principle of fairness? So far I have made two points: (a) if voluntary acceptance is possible, the principle does not normally apply; (b) if voluntary acceptance is necessary, non-excludable goods will not be provided to rational agents. That may be a pity, and we have seen that for consistency's sake Simmons should be convinced by that consideration. But should everyone else? Is it enough to show that there really is a non-voluntary obligation to take part in the cooperative production of those non-excludable goods?

This has been fiercely disputed by Nozick.[87] (Since his criticism consisted of counterexamples which in some cases did not meet Rawls' condition, and even did not

---

[86] See ch. 5.1. 5.2. & 5.3 on the duty to comply with arbitration, the duty to honor legitimate expectations and associative duties respectively.

[87] Nozick 1974, 90-95. Nozick accepts Hobbes' axiom as far as positive duties are concerned; indeed, this is the foundation of his whole theory. But though he rejects thrusting benefits upon someone and then asking for payment, he inconsistently accepts taking someone's property and then paying "full" compensation. Arneson 1982, 297-298, notes a similar inconsistency between Nozick's theory of legitimate appropriation and his rejection of the principle of fairness.

concern cooperative activities at all, it was, in fact, rather "unfair".[88]) Nozick constructs a few examples of situations (cleaning the streets, mowing your front lawn) in which a public good is produced. In all cases it is, in his view, "intuitively" improbable that obligations have been created. The most detailed example is that of a Public Address System: loudspeakers blaring out news and jokes all around the neighbourhood. Nozick asks himself the rhetorical question whether it would be admissible to obligate all local residents to operate the sound source one day every year according to a schedule. The example contains certain elements which make it difficult to judge.

Some of the local residents will not mind to do their microphone duty, they may even like it; so not everyone has to make a sacrifice.

It strikes me as not improbable (although most owners of shops in shopping areas do not seem to think so) that some local residents might consider the whole operation an irritable form of noise pollution. Then the case does not concern a general benefit. (Will not one such resident have the right to veto the entire plan?[89])

By virtue of the conditions mentioned, an appeal may be made only to those people who have reason to believe that their benefit outweighs their burdens. But how can we identify those people? Is anyone to be trusted who says that, to him, a year's enjoyment of local noise does not compensate for one day's fatigue duty? How can we distinguish, under such a system, between parasites and people who are indeed not sufficiently interested?

Suppose all these complicating elements are absent: nobody really likes to do his share but everyone appreciates the interdependent result so much that its benefit is considered to be more than just compensation for the effort – there can be no serious doubt about this. And suppose the local residents really count on each other. Under these circumstances (no matter how improbable they are)[90] it is not so implausible, after all, to suggest that shirking is unfair. Nozick's counter-example appears to be totally convincing at first sight because he does postulate that the conditions for the application of the principle of fairness have been fulfilled, but it is very hard to imagine that this is really true.

However, there is one basic problem left, which his example illustrates and which my refutation of Nozick's argument has left untouched. It may be argued that it is not sufficient for everyone to derive a net benefit from his fair contribution to the cooperative scheme; it should also be the case that nobody believes (or is right in believing?) that the investment he is required to make could yield better returns (either for him or even for all) when alternatively employed. If this condition is omitted, we

---

[88] Cf. Simmons 1979, 173: they are rather counter-examples to a principle of "gratitude to the group".

[89] Could we not appeal to considerations of fidelity or loyalty to bring this stubborn resident into line? That does not seem to be the case. I suspect that we would have to inquire into the nature of the good to explain this.

[90] People probably will not develop mutual expectations of contribution if the good involved is not really important. We cannot be bothered to put our mind to it, even if the contribution required is so small as to be worthwhile.

can imagine that cooperative schemes will proliferate to such an extent that nobody has any time or resources left to spend in accordance with his own decisions.

I will return to this problem in the next chapter. For the moment, it is sufficient to establish the conclusion that the principle of fairness has at least a limited validity. For if we wanted to reject it completely for the reasons Nozick presents, we should be prepared to look at the underproduction of all non-excludable goods with moral equanimity. At this point, we can use the reversal of Nozick's argumentative strategy by confronting this attitude of equanimity with examples in which the intended aim of the cooperative enterprise is a fundamental and uncontroversial good: the polder dyke, national defence in a country surrounded by enemies, irrigation of the desert as the only means of survival for an agricultural tribe, the prevention of life-threatening forms of pollution.[91] To give the argument a general form, let us start with any situation (e.g. the life-boat) in which the efforts of every single member of a group are needed in order to achieve a result which is of overriding importance to each. In this case everyone obviously has a decisive reason to contribute. Next, we introduce one small difference: the efforts are needed of all but one. If only one person refuses to cooperate, the group will be able to achieve its common goal, but the enterprise cannot bear more than one free-rider. It would then be a dominant strategy not to contribute. But it is hard to believe, as Nozick would have us, that such a choice would be morally unexceptionable. If the people in the life-boat do not survive because nobody did his job as he should have done, we do not excuse them by saying: after all they did not consent to do those jobs. For of course they should have consented to do them, and the moral reasons for consenting are equally strong as reasons for acting without prior consent.

I conclude that the principle of fairness clearly applies in some cases as a principle of involuntary obligation. Looking for the relevant features of those cases, we will find at least the four necessary features already specified. I have left open whether or not the principle should be restricted to cases of cooperation for necessary goods. There is at least no a priori reason to assume that it should. For it is not a principle of altruistic behaviour – which could be so restricted -, but of reciprocity.

Every public good can be produced within a corresponding organization (district water board, guild, citizens' militia), whereas these organizations remain separate: there is no reason to expect that the different groups of beneficiaries will coincide. Detection, trial and punishment of parasitical or otherwise criminal behaviour are not necessarily public goods,[92] but it is defensible that they should not be produced commercially, to ensure that they remain available independently of market forces. So for this purpose as well, it is necessary that a public production body is established on a regional basis: the nucleus of a state.

However, the modern state as it actually exists, makes requirements on its citizens which cannot easily be justified by the principle of fairness. For it produces not just necessary and merely beneficial goods, but also goods which at least some

---

[91] Klosko 1992, 39 ff.

[92] Cf. Rothbard 1977, ch. 1, on the possibility of producing these goods commercially. (Deterrence, however, is an almost purely public good.)

categories of citizens do not find desirable at all, or even find positively abhorrent. According to the principle of fairness, parasites may be forced; this is not true, however, of people who are not interested or have conscientious objections. (Therefore the principle can only be applied if these categories can be distinguished from each other.) Moreover, it is not possible for citizens to itemize tax assessments and to contribute only to the effectuation of interdependent results they consider worthwile. If the principle of fairness were the only relevant principle, citizens would be entitled to withhold their contributions until they can be earmarked.

An even more important lacuna in the theory developed so far is the following. We have found that the principle of fairness can support a typically political obligation, e.g. the duty of citizens toward each other to maintain a system of law and order. But complying with this obligation does not necessarily imply obedience to authoritative decisions.[93] After all, you can see clearly what the principle of fairness demands from you; any exhortations from your fellow citizens only remind you of this. We may conclude that authority and political obligation are not necessarily connected: you can have duties towards your fellow citizens without assigning them authority (though you do assign them rights). Anarchists need not deny the moral force of the principle of fairness; they could even allow citizens the right to coerce would-be parasites to contribute to the production of clear public goods.[94] The question remains whether political obligation can ever imply the obligation to obey.

This has been denied by a surprisingly large number of recent scholars. The majority of these sceptics confine themselves to proving the inadequacy of traditional arguments.[95] The more ambitious strategy, however, is to argue that it can never be rational to submit to authority. We will consider this argument in detail in chapter Seven. The next chapter will argue in a provisional way why political obligations of fairness generate obligations – obligations of citizens owed to citizens – to obedience to political authority as well.

---

[93] Smith 1973, 956-957.

[94] On the role of coercion and obligation in an anarchist society, see Taylor 1982, 80-94; Ritter 1980, 65-71 (what he calls "anarchist authority" is only the authoritative power of obligating norms); Miller 1984, 55-57, 173-179. The thesis that the production of public goods as such calls for the state, depends on the assumption that people can only be motivated to abstain from free-riding in $n$-person PD games by coercion. I have rejected this assumption in chapter 3. Harriott 1996 presents an argument for anarchism along similar lines, appealing to evidence from social psychology.

[95] See especially Simmons 1979. Cf. ch. 5.4.

# CHAPTER 5

# THE OBLIGATION TO OBEY THE LAW

## 5.1. Arbitration

I have argued that the principle of fairness generates political obligations in the context of at least some cooperative activities for the production of non-excludable goods. But so far, I have described cooperative activities in an oversimplified way. I have assumed that no problems would occur as to the distribution of benefits and burdens. The required contribution could be either made or withheld, not reduced or augmented, whereas the interdependent result was characterized as a public good: everyone could make unlimited use of its benefits.

It will be clear that in reality the costs are mostly variable. But the profits can cause distribution problems as well. This is the case, firstly, for goods from which we would not want to exclude anybody even if we could, because for moral reasons we do not want to produce them on a quid pro quo basis:[1] legal aid, education, health care, but also punishment, the enforcement of enforceable duties and the exaction of compensation for harm. Secondly, even if the good is robustly non-excludable as well as uncontroversially necessary, there may be different options as regards the exact mode of production and the quality to be attained. It is obvious that there should be no holes in a dyke, but its slope, height and solidity, and the materials to be used, are all open to discussion. (Here the boundary between a necessary and a non-necessary good turns out to be very vague indeed: should a dyke be good enough to allow flooding only once in ten or a thousand or a hundred thousand years?) Hence all sorts of controversial decisions concerning the production of the "common good" must be made: what exactly should be produced and how much of it; how much of it should be produced on a basis of exchange, and so on. Thirdly, problems increase because it is not efficient to organize every cooperative activity separately. When a water district board is already in charge of controlling the water level, it would raise costs unnecessarily if another body were established to control water quality. So it may be advantageous for every member of the group to make a non-itemized contribution to a package deal.[2] But the packaging, even of uncontroversially necessary goods, may be controversial. Finally, it is easy to see that the scope and intensity of controversy will be very much enlarged if we allow the

---

[1] Cf. the list of "blocked exchanges" of Walzer 1983, 100-103; and comments on this list by Andre 1992; Den Hartogh 1999, 498-499.

[2] There must be good reasons for the composition of such a package, otherwise earmarked contributions are to be preferred. According to Hofstra 1986, 182, note 213, such earmarked impositions (district water board levies, road tax, radio and television licence) encounter less opposition than general taxation. Even so, we cannot give the district water board full unchecked authority to decide on the level of its levies.

production of merely beneficial goods to enter the application range of the principle of fairness, as advocated in the next section.

As we saw, it is in the interest of all to come to an agreement about the total production plan, the contribution everyone should make and – as far as this can be regulated – the distribution of the benefits. The difficulty is, however, that the individual members of the group have different preferences as to the various possible arrangements, quite apart from the fact that all of them could personally benefit from evading their duties, whatever arrangement has been chosen. The situation has the character of a $n$-person Prisoner's Dilemma to begin with; but those who are willing to cooperate fairly are also confronted with a Division game.[3] That is to say, everyone wishes, above all, to come to a general agreement, but at the same time there is a difference of preference as regards the terms of the agreement.

(A day out with the kids; everybody prefers to spend the day together, but there is no agreement whatsoever about the destination. Negotiations between more than two persons will soon become an extremely complicated matter, and by the time a compromise has been reached, the day is nearly over.)

As we saw, in a bargaining problem there is no predictable, unique result which rational negotiators will reach.[4] (If there were, it would be rational to save the negotiation costs and head straight for this result.) This underdetermined character is common to bargaining problems and pure coordination problems, and it is eliminated by the development of converging expectations. If all players expect each other to accept a certain result, know each other to expect this, and so on, then the negotiator who still refuses to accept this result takes a tremendous risk. Therefore, the negotiators have prudential reasons to accept a conventional choice among the options on the bargaining table: after all, you know what you've got by an accommodating attitude, but what you might gain by being obstinate is uncertain at best. However, the stability of the convention is strongly enhanced if it also appeals to a moral motive: if everyone is prepared to give everyone his due share, instead of trying to take maximum personal advantage. Thus, in addition to the principle of fairness, another basic principle of cooperative activity comes into play: the principle of accepting an equitable compromise.[5] The same clause that we added to the principle of fairness should be added to this principle: "provided you have reason to expect that the others will do the same". Otherwise, willingness to accept a compromise would mean nothing but a loss of ground to the hard-boiled negotiator.

If this principle is followed, the danger of soaring negotiating costs is reduced, and the risk of a deadlock – which always exists, even though everyone wishes to reach an agreement – is diminished, though by no means fully neutralized.[6] Because of the

---

[3] On "divisible PD games" (or a bargaining problem within a PD problem) cf. Coleman 1992, ch. 1 § 5.

[4] Ch. 2.3. Therefore it hardly makes sense, as Luce and Raiffa do (1957, ch. 6), to interpret the concept of a 'solution' to the bargaining game in terms of arbitration schemes: if any of the proposed solutions were the correct one, rational players could dispense with arbitration.

[5] Cf. Lucas 1966, 11 ff.; Singer 1973, 32 ff; MacMahon 1987; Waldron 1996b, 2201.

[6] Cf. the political theory of the Public Choice school, for example the classic work of Buchanan and Tullock 1962: the translation of individual preferences into collective decision making should ideally take place under

conditional character of the principle, it only applies if there actually exists a pattern of mutual expectations providing a solution to the bargaining problem which everyone can focus on. On the other hand, no existing pattern of mutual expectations can appeal to a moral motive – a sense of justice – for complying with the principles, unless certain minimum conditions of just distribution are satisfied, or at least believed to be satisfied. In most situations in which a decision must be made on the planning and execution of a cooperative undertaking, these conditions of minimal justice will not by themselves lay down a unique division of benefits and burdens. At the very least, we need fully developed conventions of justice.[7]

Remember that my use of the concept of 'conventions' implies no arbitrariness. There may exist a correct theory of justice, at least for a certain society, which fully specifies optimal conventions, though I doubt it. However, these optimal conventions still need to be commonly accepted to have moral force in actual cases. Law is situated somewhere between minimum and ideal justice.

When a bargaining problem concerns the modes of production of a public good, a refusal to observe the conventional decision might clash with the principle of fairness as well. True, if you do not want to submit to it, your behaviour is not necessarily parasitical or free-riding; after all, you yourself have to bear part of the increased negotiating costs (including the risk that no agreement is reached). If, however, the conventional decision paves the way for the cooperative production of a public good, it is at least possible that refusal to accept the decision really is a form of parasitical behaviour. Thus political obligation – the obligation to honour mutual expectations concerning cooperation in the production of public goods – depends on a combination of principles: the requirement to make fair contributions and the requirement to accept an equitable compromise.

Even existing patterns of expectations will often be insufficiently specific to solve concrete negotiation problems. That is where authority comes in: it arises from a need for arbitration.[8] It might be agreed that the eventual decision will be taken – within

---

the rule of unanimity, if only negotiation costs would not become too high; with other procedures it is possible to save on these costs. Buchanan & Tullock confine their perspective to prudential reasons to obey; stability has to be guaranteed, then, merely by (voluntarily accepted) coercion. See ch. 3.3.

[7] The conditions of minimal justice can be explored by means of a hypothetical contract theory, cf. Kavka 1986, ch. 10. If you are not prepared to accept the obligations identified by the hypothetical contract, you are either lacking in knowledge, or rationality, or cooperative virtue, for these are the values embodied in the contract. In Kavka's Hobbesian theory (rule-egoism) the base line is identified with the state of nature, which means that the theory does not identify any requirements concerning a fair distribution of benefits and burdens. Whether or not it is possible to derive fairness from prudence – I do not think it is –, surely one must insist on something like Gauthier's Lockean proviso, Gauthier 1986, ch. 7. On the other hand, the conditions for the application of both the principle of fairness and the principle of accepting a fair compromise may be fulfilled under an unjust and illegitimate regime, e.g. in a satellite state, if no feasible alternative to it is within reach of its citizenry. For the case of communist Poland, this has been argued by Dorota Mokrosinska in unpublished work. So in contrast to a presently popular view (cf. note 63, ch. 2, note 75) I believe that it is possible for a government to have authority but not legitimacy, rather than vice versa, or in other words, for the citizens to owe each other (selective) obedience to the government's commands without recognizing the right of the government to command.

[8] Cf. John Locke, *Second Treatise* § 87: "the community comes to be umpire" (a task which it can only perform by taking decisions by a majority of votes). In my view, the role of arbitration is much more

the range of norms of justice shared by everyone – by a particular person or group of persons. Or the negotiators might agree to follow a certain procedure which guarantees, or at least promises, a unique and timely decision, for example: making decisions by a majority of votes. In a large-scale long-term institutional framework, the legitimacy of authority – its ability to invoke moral reasons for complying with the decisions – will depend, not so much on the qualities of the actual person invested with authority, but on the way she is selected for the job.

It is still not immediately clear that the form of political obligation described so far is such that an anarchist could not unreservedly subscribe to it. He will not have any objections against conventional solutions of bargaining problems. Pointing to the need for arbitrating authority as such is not a decisive step beyond anarchism either, for it is not always necessary or desirable to provide arbitration in the form of a public good, that is to say on the basis of exactable capitation. In many cases, it may be desirable to let market forces do their work. Disputes in the domain of disciplinary, contract and labour law could be settled in that manner. An anarchist need not have objections to this form of authority either. However, if we are talking about enforceable obligations to contribute to the production of non-excludable goods, it is hard to see how arbitration concerning those obligations can itself be provided in any other form than as a public good. Some anarchists accept even this step. All they object to is the enforceable obligation to obey centralized authority. However, it is precisely on the boundaries between productive schemes, for instance about questions of packaging, that division problems are most likely to arise. If we have a plurality of arbitrational agencies on the same level, there may be no natural way of isolating their jurisdictions against each other. In the final analysis, all bargaining problems concerning the production of public goods are related to each other, because all of them can be paired or combined in possible compromise solutions. That is why there seems to be a need for one unified scheme of authority. For every possible division problem the scheme would identify the arbitrating authority authorized to solve it and empowered to enforce it solution. This would include possible conflicts between the arbitrating authorities concerning the boundaries of their jurisdiction.[9]

---

emphasized by Locke than the principle of consent, Den Hartogh 1990b. According to Locke, a government's authority is legitimate if it performs its arbitral function properly, not if it obtains actual consent. Cf. ch. 4, note 31. On the other hand, the scope of arbitration for Locke is much more limited than it is in my argument: it mainly concerns conflicts concerning the interpretation and execution of the Law of Nature. The need for arbitration is central to the whole social contract tradition from Hobbes to Kant. Kavka 1995 lists some additional reasons why even the morally perfect would need an authoritative procedure for settling disputes: factual disagreements owing to cognitive limitations, differences in moral views. Strangely, he omits conflicts of legitimate interests which surely could exist even among the morally perfect. Cf. note 12.

[9] Cf. Finnis 1980, 233 (with reference to the principle of subsidiarity in *Quadragesimo Anno*): it is the duty of the political community to harmonize all productive activities taking place in a subsidiary context. The state is, as Althusius would say, the "inclusive political order". But I have two objections to Finnis' view. On the one hand, as many critics have noted, his list of seven "basic goods" is far from self-evident, even to the wise, both in what it includes and in what it excludes. So we cannot assume law to be instrumental in realizing the conditions for participating in these goods. In explaining the nature of the law, we must refer to the common good it is meant to serve, but at this stage we cannot specify this good. The other point is almost the opposite of the first one: because Finnis believes his basic goods to be incommensurable, he deprives practical reason

Such a scheme can only exist if it is organized on a territorial basis. The world has known other types of legal system in which relevant jurisdictions were identified on a personal rather than a territorial basis. But in such systems it is impossible to realize the ideal of a unified scheme of authority to any extent.

The ideal can only be fully realized on a global scale. But even if it is conceded that existing state boundaries are arbitrary from a moral point of view, and that it would be desirable to install a world government, that would not mean, as Kant insisted, that we have to wait for this installation before submitting to any arbitration scheme.[10] We can never require our conventions to be optimal as a condition of recognizing reasons to comply to them.

As a matter of fact, ever since Bodin and Hobbes the ideal of a unified scheme of arbitration has been applied to a plurality of states, each of them supposed to implement the ideal for its own territory. It is important to be clear about the fact that even in this limited form the ideal has never been completely realized: in every existing state there is some rivalry between legal authorities about the extent of their jurisdiction.[11] This is true for every dimension of differentiation of authority: territory (central versus regional), domain (e.g. departments) or function (legislative, executive or adjudicative). Compromise is often reached by informal bargaining, rather than by formal arbitration. So instead of a clear boundary between anarchy and sovereignty, we actually find a continuous spectrum of possible legal worlds. On the one end of the spectrum the world in which no authority exists, and division problems are only solved –to the extent that they are solved at all – by appeal to convention. This is by now nothing more than a theoretical possibility. At the other end of the spectrum the world of Hobbesian sovereignty, which has never been more than a theoretical possibility.

I have identified the (selective) obligation to obey the authority of governments with a convention, a pattern of mutual expectations of obedience. For the pattern to have any stability at all, we should be able to count on the cooperative virtue – fairness, trustworthiness and reasonableness – of our fellow citizens. If this is possible to a sufficient extent, we are also justified in punishing people who violate our trust, and the threat of punishment will be effective, because we will on the whole be sufficiently motivated to contribute to its costs. This threat will be an additional source of assurance, and hence of stability to the pattern. States, therefore, are built on the mutual reinforcement of the appeal to cooperative virtue and the threat of sanctions.[12] Without virtue, enforcement would be impossible, or would be nothing but the submission of the

---

of the resources to specify the common good at all: it becomes a matter of decision rather than debate and design. See Westerman 1998, ch. 10.

[10] Waldron 1993, 15, with reference to Kant.

[11] Morris 1998, ch. 7.

[12] This is Hobbes' view as well, even if this is rarely recognized, see Hampton 1986, ch. 3. Kavka 1995, 15-16, cf. note 8, argues that even the morally perfect would occasionally prefer not to surrender their strong moral convictions to peaceful arbitration, and hence need the government's coercive power to assure peace. But even if this were true, they could hardly be expected to recognize this need or to consider the use of coercion legitimate.

weak to the interests of the strong. Without enforcement, on the other hand, virtue would be too fragile to sustain a viable political order.[13]


## 5.2 Merely Beneficial Public Goods

In chapter Four, I established the validity of the principle of fairness for the production of at least some public goods. But my discussion of counter-arguments to this thesis, Nozick's in particular, was insufficient to determine the scope of the principle. What I have called necessary goods clearly invoke it. But it seemed doubtful whether merely beneficial goods invoke it as well, for that would seem to leave individual agents with too little room for exercising autonomous choice concerning their own investments.

This problem has been considered in detail by George Klosko.[14] His own solution is to start from the category of necessary goods – public goods which are indispensable to any acceptable life – and then to point out that the production of merely beneficial goods is often instrumental to the production of necessary ones. Because controversial decisions have to be made about the optimal level and form of the production of the necessary goods, we have to entrust these decisions to a procedure of fair arbitration, committing ourselves to its outcomes, whatever they are – within certain limits. The limits are determined by the requirement that the umpire should base his decisions at least on reasonable, not necessarily correct or optimal, considerations.[15] It follows that it belongs to the discretion of the arbitrator to decide on the optimal level and form of the production of merely beneficial public goods as well, because this is part and parcel of the corresponding decision concerning the production of necessary goods that he is required to make. For instance, it is necessary to have a road network if one wants to employ an army. In the end, the whole resulting package is covered by the principle of fairness.

Klosko believes that this argument "saves the phenomena", both of government's practices and of people's beliefs concerning them. But that is obviously mistaken; his argument, if valid, has revolutionary consequences. For what he really proposes is a rigorous restriction on the range of acceptable considerations for initiating government policy – a restriction even stronger than the well-known neutrality principle, which requires that government policy should not be based on any controversial conception of the good life.[16] According to Klosko's principle, the state can only make any requirements on its subjects, if it considers in good faith that those requirements are efficiently conducive to the production of necessary goods. It follows

---

[13] The theory of political obligation developed in this section is a two-tiered one, and as such reminiscent of the classical double contract theories (e.g. Althusius, Pufendorf). The so-called social contract which establishes the political community rests on the principle of fairness, the political contract which establishes political authority rests on on the principle of accepting arbitration.

[14] Klosko 1992, ch. 4.

[15] Cf. Hart's scorer's discretion argument, discussed in ch. 10.5.

[16] It is even stronger because it also excludes the production of uncontroversially beneficial goods for their own sake, e.g. goods which may help one in every project whatsoever but are not strictly necessary for its meaningful pursuit.

that any time a government initiates the production of a merely beneficial good for its own sake, it forfeits the legitimacy of its decision, for it does not base this on "reasonable considerations". It may only build public roads which are required for transporting the army. (That would mean that the Dutch government could not build any public roads at all, for any conceivable situation in which the Dutch army could come to be employed, will require it to act outside of the Dutch borders.) In restricting the justified production of merely beneficial goods to whatever is instrumental to the production of necessary ones, Klosko has not at all "extended" the principle of fairness to merely beneficial goods, for from the point of view of policymaking it should not even matter whether these instrumental goods are also beneficial ones.

Perhaps we cannot avoid such drastic conclusions, but before we resign ourselves to that fate, let us reconsider another argument for extending the scope of the principle of fairness, an argument Klosko discusses as well, but gives short shrift.[17] The first problem with a merely beneficial good was the likelihood that at least some people, though they will benefit substantially from the good, will benefit even more from a situation in which this particular good is lacking but another good is present which they can procure by expending the same costs. The second, related, problem was that it seemed unreasonable to take the decision about alternative forms of expenditure out of the domain of the agent's sovereignty. Otherwise the cumulative effect of the initiation of "cooperative schemes' could be to destroy this sovereignty altogether.

The proposal which Klosko rejects, is not to consider the applicability of the principle of fairness for each scheme of merely beneficial goods separately, but for possible packages of such goods, to be decided upon by a fair procedure of arbitration. The reason why he rejects it is that it only multiplies the force of the original objections. If it is a doubtful invasion of a person's autonomy to require him to contribute to one cooperative scheme, it is sheer tyranny to require him to contribute to a whole package of such schemes. But this objection rests on a fallacy of composition.

This becomes clear if we consider the alternatives at both the level of the individual scheme and of the package. For each individual scheme, initiating it implies the risk of redirecting some people's efforts from more profitable expenditures, and it implies restricting people's autonomy with possible cumulative effects of unknown magnitude. Omitting to initiate the scheme means that a substantial and generally beneficial good will not be produced. At least on non-utilitarian conceptions, it may always seem reasonable to sacrifice the good, which, after all, is merely beneficial. But on the level of the whole package, the disadvantage of initiating it is not a simple sum of the disadvantages of initiating the individual schemes composing it. For, firstly, if for each individual participant there is at least one component scheme which is relatively unattractive, this may be compensated for everyone by adding the component scheme which is relatively most attractive to him, making the total scheme more or less equally attractive to, and sufficiently worthwhile for all. Secondly, this possibility is greatly enhanced by economies of scale that will make each individual scheme more attractive for all on average. Finally, by making the composition of the package an object of

---

[17] Klosko 1992, 85-86.

conscious decision, the risk of unwanted cumulative effects is at least controlled, even if this control is not necessarily exercised optimally. In arbitration it is not only the attractiveness of the component schemes which can and should be taken into account, but also the effects on the autonomy of the agent of initiating all of them together.

On the other hand, the disadvantage of rejecting cooperative schemes on a package level does not just result from disadvantages of rejecting them on the component level, by a process of simple addition. In this case, the whole is not less than the sum of its parts, but more. For the outcome is that no non-necessary public goods will be produced at all.[18] But a society in which only necessary public goods are produced, while for everything else people are left to private pursuits, surely will be a poor and brutish one; in particular, it will not be a society with a great deal of scope for individual autonomy. Even if people have plenty of time to do their own thing in this society, the "menu of options" from which they can choose those things will be exceedingly narrow in scope. For presumably, among the merely beneficial public goods are to be counted: education, at least beyond a certain level, the promotion of cultural and scientific activities, the maintenance of the cultural heritage and of natural values – beyond the survival value of a clean environment –, the prevention of monopolies in the area of public opinion, and social security, at least as long as the poor are not a menace to the fabric of society.[19]

So for the disadvantages, the utility curve declines with packaging, for the advantages it climbs. At a certain point the threshold will be reached at which the principle of fairness can be invoked without qualms. The production of some package of merely beneficial goods is a necessary good.[20]

This argument supports a conclusion already suggested on intuitive grounds in section 4 of the previous chapter. We may only have enforceable obligations of beneficence to provide for other people's pressing needs, but we also have enforceable obligations – of fairness, as it turns out – to contribute to elements of the common good which cannot strictly be considered pressing needs. The fact that we are involved as benefiting parties justifies enlarging the scope of the obligations.

Any remaining hesitations on this point can be met by summoning support from the other basic principle of obligation, the principle of fidelity or trustworthiness.[21] When a political community endeavours to initiate cooperation for the common good, and a pattern of mutual expectations arises, not unreasonably, that all will contribute, it would be a breach of faith to insist that one is absolved from participation simply because one's private pursuits promise a somewhat larger return in terms of one's own well-being.[22] One may defend this refusal, for instance by invoking the cumulative

---

[18] Or only to the extent that "large actors" happen to be present, cf. ch. 3.3.

[19] Cf. Dworkin 1986, ch. 11; Raz 1986, 198-203; 1994, 37-40; Postema 1987c; Kymlicka 1989, 164; Den Hartogh 2000, 21-24.

[20] This argument implies the rejection of the neutrality thesis, see Den Hartogh 2000, 26.

[21] Which is clearly needed to account for some political obligations anyway, for example to explain why officials of one country should not conspire to frustrate justice in another: that is a matter of fidelity to international law and its principles. Cf. Waldron 1993, 10.

[22] See ch. 1.8,

effects of such claims, but it should be left to a fair arbitration procedure to consider those arguments on their merits.

It is obvious that if political society has the task to provide a package of merely beneficial public goods, the need for arbitration will be greatly enlarged. For each of the possible components of such packages will be differently valued by the members of the political society, possibly to the extent of being disvalued by some of them. So the choice of the components cannot be based on a unanimous order of preferences.

The problem which on my view is solved by the joined forces of the principles of fairness and of respecting a reasonable compromise, I declared to be a matter of distribution. Do these principles offer an adequate solution to this problem, in particular in respect of the class of people they apply to? Ever since John Simmons developed his so-called particularity requirement,[23] theories of political obligation have been tested on the way they satisfy it. According to Simmons, a theory of political obligation should explain why Dutchmen have a special moral status vis-à-vis Dutch law. According to the principles of fairness and of reasonableness, the duty of obedience descends on those people who belong to a group of people who mutually expect each other to obey, and who benefit in the right way from each other's obedience. Expectations and benefits are both necessary: Belgians may receive external benefits from the proper functioning of the Dutch state, but this does not give them duties of obedience to Dutch law, though it may give them a duty not to interfere with its functioning.

However, it seems that resident aliens in the Netherlands have obligations of fairness and reasonableness towards all other residents, and even tourists have some such obligations. By "barely travelling on the highway", to quote John Locke, you acquire an obligation not to dodge paying toll (if native drivers do not dodge either). So my theory does not satisfy the particularity requirement as Simmons stated it.

But this seems to me to be a merit of the theory. Tourists and resident aliens indeed do have obligations, and those of the latter class largely coincide with the obligations of proper citizens. To the extent these obligations differ, this can be explained by the fact that the principle of fairness requires a rough balance between benefits and burdens. It follows that some countries – not necessarily identified by formal citizenship – may make larger requirements on you than others. It is obviously illegitimate for a state to press foreign tourists to join its army. If resident aliens are liable to be evicted at the outbreak of hostilities, the state does not guarantee to attempt to secure their safety, and hence is not allowed to press them into its army either. (I do not suggest that it is always legitimate for it to press its own citizens.)[24]

---

[23] Simmons 1979, 31-35; Dworkin 1986, 193; Kavka 1986, 407-415; Green 1988, 227-230; Klosko 1992, 23-26.

[24] Cf. Waldron 1993. See however, ch. 6, note 36, for another speculation: citizens are obligated to obey the law, tourists to honour the expectations of citizens. I consider my account to be an explication rather than a rejection of Rawls' "natural duty to support just institutions when they exist and apply to us", Rawls 1971, 334. The explication stresses that the duty "applies" when fairness and/or fidelity require it, and the institution exists because we are in need of arbitration. Klosko objects that natural duties are duties of everyone to everyone, whereas political duties are owed by participants in a cooperative enterprise to other participants. But the Original Position is set up to identify precisely such duties.

But many people will feel intuitively that they have a special responsibility to obey the laws of the country of which they are citizens, even if the benefits they receive from citizenship do not substantially differ from those of other residents. This special responsibility has still not been accounted for.

## 5.3. The Value of Community

It is sometimes alleged that the whole approach to the problem of political obligation taken here is fundamentally misguided. For it starts by asking what political society is for, and, having identified its possible benefits, looks for a criterion for the distribution of its burdens. But, it is argued, this is to mistake the nature of political society: it is *not* a cooperative enterprise for mutual advantage, in which the question of the distribution of benefits and burdens can be sensibly raised. Rather, it is a community of fate, and membership is a basic element of the moral identity of each of its members. The goods it provides cannot, logically, be enjoyed independently of its existence, and hence the obligations which one non-voluntarily incurs as a member do not depend on the enjoyment of such external goods either.[25] Such associative duties are "not grounded on consent, reciprocity or gratitude, but rather on a feeling of belonging and connectedness".[26]

I do not doubt that this communitarian view is the correct one for a possible legal, or, if you wish, proto-legal world. A community may indeed have the character described by the communitarians, and this community will depend for its existence on each member honouring the mutual expectations of all. But as regards the legal world as we know it, I believe the communitarian view to be fundamentally mistaken. However, like consent-theory, it contains a kernel of truth.

To begin with the basic flaws. What exactly, on the communitarian view, is the form of life which has no external justification? To answer "living in deference to political authority" is both unintelligible and objectionable. Why should you do what someone else tells you to do, no matter what he tells you to do (within certain limits)? If the reply is that this question has no answer, because the question itself is mistaken, we

---

[25] MacIntyre 1981, 56; 1984; cf. Oakeshott's distinction between civil association and enterprise association, Oakeshott 1975, part II. (He mistakenly suggests that enterprise association only requires self-interested motivation.) Recent communitarians include Dworkin 1986, 206-215; Charvet 1990; Horton 1992; Gilbert 1993, repr. 1996 ch. 12; Tamir 1993, 99-102, 130-139; Hardimon 1994 (but his central concept of "reflectively acceptable role obligations" may have a functional connotation); Gilbert 1999. Criticism: Green 1989; Simmons 1996a. Dworkin's communitarianism is hard to reconcile with (a) his "Protestant" monadological view of legal obligations, and (b) his "Kelsenian" view of the law as instructing officials how to use their coercive power. Both points are noted by Green 1989, resp. 108 (cf. Postema 1987c), 115-116. Gilbert's view is different from the other communitarian views because of its voluntarism: a "plural subject" is constituted by each member showing his willingness to be part of it. She agrees that common knowledge of this willingness is necessary, but on her view this does not require any mutual attribution of reasons for willingness. Hence the non-functional character of the theory.

[26] Tamir 1993, 137.

will surely be at a loss to understand what is meant.[27] Why obey this person, and not any other one taken at random? Why is what she says authoritative within these limits rather than other ones, perhaps more restricted or more extended? Why limits at all? Surely such questions are in need of an answer, but no answer can be provided, unless we have been informed about the point of having an authority to begin with. And, indeed, it is characteristic of all claims to authority, including parental authority, to appeal to such external justifications. The obligation to obey authority cannot belong to the rock bottom of moral duty. States are not ends in themselves.

The communitarian could reply: it is true that the claims of authority are justified by the necessity of its services to the political community, but this is a service to the existence of the community as such, not to the provision of any external goods. However, take any political society, leave out the functional exercise of authority, and leave out any form of cooperation for external goods. What is left? Nothing at all, it seems. It cannot be that the whole life of a political community consists in its being a community. A political community must be about something.[28]

It could be suggested that what is left, at least sometimes, is a nation. And indeed, a nation seems to answer the communitarian description: it is something valued by each because it is valued by all – it is a good of interdependent valuation –, not necessarily because of any other good to which it has an instrumental relation. The good essentially consists in sharing it. But this suggestion only seemingly fits the communitarian bill. The reason is that the concept of a nation, for all its notorious elusiveness, has one clear element: it straddles the division between the political and the non-political. The non-political elements, e.g. the sharing of culture, and in particular of a language, may with some plausibility be considered as proper objects of interdependent valuation.[29] And surely, they may require the political elements, but that is precisely because they are public goods of a kind, and their provision is burdened with coordination problems. So the political obligation to contribute to the production of these goods is fully accounted for by my "functional" theory. On the other hand, if any nation is only to be identified as

---

[27] MacDonald 1963, 184; McPherson 1967, 64; Pitkin 1972a, 75, revoked Pitkin 1972b, 199ff; Winch 1967, 105; revoked Winch 1967, 110; cf. discussion by Pateman 1979, 27-30; Green 1988, 193-197; 1990, 93-95; Horton 1992, 137-145. Ever since John Searle introduced the idea of a constitutive rule, attempts have been made to understand legal rules, or at least rules of recognition, as the constitutive rules of a practice comparable to the rules of a game. (Cf. recently Marmor 1996.) But on the one hand, the rules of games that can be played by only one player are not essentially different from the rules of 2-person or n-person games, hence such theories fail to account for the distinctive nature of social rules. On the other hand, in playing a game one strives for an aim (e.g. making more points than one's opponent) which can only be understood in terms of the rules of the game, but there is no such "internal" point to "playing by legal rules" as such. Both points are connected: in a 2-person or n-person game the players may mutually expect each other to comply with the rules, but these mutual expectations can only be understood by reference to the "external" aims of playing. Cf. ch. 2, note 75.

[28] For the same reason, republicanism cannot be a free-standing political ideal. Perhaps it is an essential part of the good life to participate in running the affairs of one's society, but then those affairs must have an importance independent of the importance of running them.

[29] But in the final analysis, even those elements may have this character only because they have a functional meaning as well: e.g. providing the "menu of options" for the meaningful exercise of autonomy, cf. Kymlicka 1989, ch. 8; Raz 1994, ch. 7.

the community supporting a particular state, then the whole function of this state cannot be to protect the existence of *that* nation.

As a matter of fact, of course, there hardly exists any political community with a one-to-one relation to a national community in the broader sense.[30] If the duties we have as citizens are to be identified with (part of) the associative duties we have as members of national communities, then the members of national minorities and the citizens of genuinely multinational states will have no duties at all to the larger political community they live in. Of course, people may have multi-layered loyalties: nothing prevents one from having "feelings of belonging and connectedness" to Kampen, Zeeland, the Netherlands, Europe and the world all at once. But we can hardly expect all the inhabitants of the world, of Europe, the Netherlands, Zeeland and Kampen, to harbour those feelings to the same extent, or to the extent sufficient to motivate them to accept substantial duties and to agree to their enforcement.[31]

Supporters of a communitarian view sometimes argue that political society is the one indispensable community in which men can realize their social nature. If the political community disintegrates, people will no longer be in a position to develop strong moral relations to each other, to learn how to respect the rights of others. But this argument trades on the unclarity of the notion of political society used here: whether or not this includes the relation to authority. It may be true that in the absence of political authority, moral relations between people would fade. (Though the contrary speculation that they would flourish seems to me at least as plausible.)[32] But that argument, whatever its merit, again points to an instrumental value of authority only. There is no intrinsic reason why a basic community, the environment for people's moral socialization, should be a community held together by political authority. The existence of stateless societies proves as much. There is no intrinsic reason either, why such a basic community should not be a functional one, held together by the shared aim of producing "external" public goods.

This brings me to the kernel of truth. When people are involved in a cooperative enterprise for mutual advantage, tied to each other by obligations of fairness and fidelity, the total framework may also provide them with an object of intrinsic valuation and identification. This is true for an official who finds her life's fulfilment in the exercise of role-bound duties geared to the realization of the common good or the administration of impartial justice. But it may also be true for the private citizen who cherishes being a member of such a society. A paradigm case is the situation in which the political dimension of nationhood gets a meaning of its own, when the nation state not only exists in order to protect the non-political aspects of nationhood against possibly hostile neighbours, but is also the expression of the full recognition of this

---

[30] Lagerspetz 1999 suggests that in Europe Iceland is the only example, but there may be a few others, including the Netherlands.

[31] The point can also be expressed by saying that communitarianism, like consent theory (see ch. 4.2. at note 16) cannot justify the territorial scope of the state's claim to authority. So much the worse for these claims, the communitarian could argue, as present-day consent theorists tend to do. (To my knowledge no one defends such "communitarian anarchism".) The reply is that the functional arguments for the state's authority require the territorial form, at least under present conditions, cf. Waldron 1993, 15, 22.

[32] P. Kropotkin 1910; M. Taylor 1976, ch. 7; 1982, 57.

nation among the nations of the world. Even citizens of pluralistic liberal democracies may strongly identify with this character of their polity.[33]

The question is whether this aspect of membership in a political society can generate additional, even if only complementary grounds for political obligation.[34] One could argue that when the members of an intrinsically valuable society mutually recognize each others' equal membership, the recognition implies the acknowledgement of mutual obligations.[35] This argument has a weakness similar to that of the argument from gratitude: the obligations are only acquired by a person who shares the requisite attitude, and in particular recognizes the community as a proper object of intrinsic valuation. A person who does not share that attitude, or who lacks any sense of belonging, may be defective in moral cognition, but we cannot legitimately expect him to acknowledge any obligation, at least not on this ground. Nor are we justified in enforcing any such obligation. That would be similar to forcing someone to the outward forms of worship of a god in which she does not believe.[36]

Another possible argument points to the fact that the relevant value of community is itself a public good: you cannot selectively allocate the benefits to people willing to pay its fair price. So there would be obligations, not obligations sui generis, but obligations of fairness, fidelity and justice, to take a fair share in the burdens of producing this good. The weakness of this argument is that the production of this good, being an essential by-product of the production of other goods, does not require anything beyond taking a fair share in the production of those other goods. If these subvenient cooperative schemes fail to satisfy the conditions for invoking the principles of fairness, trustworthiness, and respecting a reasonable compromise, we cannot fill the lacuna by claiming: but in any case you can be legitimately expected to contribute to the good of community. For the relevant community is the society of those who honour their non-voluntary obligations to participate in these subvenient cooperative schemes. So if there is a communitarian obligation of this kind, it depends essentially on the existence of obligation on other grounds. The most we can say is that the appeal to the value of community may tip the balance in a case of doubt, of the type we considered in the last section, in which a person claims to be released from obligations of fairness to contribute to a package of merely beneficial goods, on the ground that he stands to profit more from alternative ways of spending.

Some well-known communitarian arguments suggest that the appeal to the value of community could be given a more significant scope in the following way.[37] Suppose it is true that people will only fulfil their obligations under the principle of fairness, even when they are involved in the production of necessary goods, if they identify with their

---

[33] Feinberg 1988, 108-113; Dworkin 1989; Habermas 1993.

[34] As Gans 1992, 83-89 suggests.

[35] Dworkin 1986, 195ff.

[36] Cf. Murphy's critical comments on Waldron's account of the "natural duty to support just institutions" independently of any benefits those institutions confer on us, Waldron 1993; Murphy 1994.

[37] Cf. Taylor 1989; Tamir 1993, 103. If this argument were to succeed, it would rehabilitate Klosko's attempt, discussed in ch. 5.2., to bring merely beneficial goods under the aegis of the principle of fairness as attachments to necessary goods.

political community to a sufficient extent; suppose, further, that they will only come to identify themselves to that extent, if they are involved in cooperative schemes which go beyond those necessary goods to the provision of a substantial package of other goods. (They need not even be seen as beneficial ones from the beginning, as long as they come to be seen that way as a result of contributing.) Then the good of community is itself a necessary good, but it requires those other goods which in themselves are merely beneficial at best. The problem with this argument is that it treats the good of community as an instrumentally necessary good, while the people to whom the argument appeals must see it as an intrinsic good. For that reason, the argument cannot possibly be used in a public justification of political obligation. ("Look here, you'd better believe that you have an obligation to contribute to $x$, for if you don't believe that, you will be insufficiently motivated to fulfil your obligation to contribute to $y$.")

We should recognize, however, that there is more to membership than strict obligation, as there is more to morality than mere duty. The communitarian theory is a helpful reminder of that important truth. It identifies significant moral reasons for obedience. But the existence of these reasons will only in exceptional cases contribute to the justification of enforceable expectations of obedient behaviour by others.

Recognizing both points also goes a long way to defuse the objection we met at the end of the previous section: that my account of political obligation fails to satisfy the particularity requirement in the right way. People generally have a strong intuitive conviction, as Socrates had, that their relation to the laws of their own country is a special one. This special relation cannot be accounted for by the principles of fairness and of accepting fair arbitration. My reply is that this special relation of responsibility exists, but it should not be seen as a matter of enforceable obligations.

### 5.4. The Selectivity of the Obligation to Obey the Law

The contemporary discussion of the obligation to obey the law is marred by a pervading confusion concerning its central issue. Authors tend to align themselves to either of two rival camps. On the one hand we find the believers, who accept a general (universal) duty to obey the law, on the strength of one or more of the principles on offer – consent, fairness, necessity, gratitude, the natural duty to support just institutions or to contribute to the common good. The very fact that a law is given (or perhaps that it is given by a government meeting certain minimum conditions of legitimacy and efficiency) creates a morally relevant consideration, possibly of minimal strength, sometimes easily overridden by other considerations, but always a consideration that has to be overridden, or else will tip the balance. On the other hand we have the non-believers, who deny the existence of obligations to obey the law as such. Most of them accept that it is not impossible for such obligations to be founded on consent, necessity or fairness; they do not confess to (a priori) "philosophical anarchism". They only believe that these possibly relevant principles never, or almost never, apply, given the actual facts of contemporary society. Governments largely produce goods and services which are non-excludable, hence (they hold) outside the range of the principles of consent and of fairness, but at the same time 'discretionary' and controversial, hence equally outside the range of the principle of necessity.

These positions obviously do not exhaust the possibilities. What I have defended in this chapter is the existence, not of a general, but of a selective obligation to obey the law. If both the principle of the fair distribution of benefits and burdens, and the principle of accepting an equitable compromise apply, the very fact that something is required by law makes it obligatory to do it. But this thesis implies that, if neither of these principles, or only the first one, applies, this same fact has no moral relevance, at least not on those principles. No legal system, as distinct from a system of pure coercion, will fail to create any obligation at any time. But in every legal system we should expect to find some requirements which, in the circumstances where they apply, will fail to obligate some or all of its subjects sometimes or even always.[38]

As I argued in the previous section, the existence of obligations to authority does not belong to the rock-bottom of moral fact.[39] Obedience has to be justified as a means to promote some good or to meet some duty. It follows that the obligation to comply is always conditional. One who is looking for a ground cannot be surprised to find a limit. And, indeed, the arguments of the believers do not actually satisfy their ambition to found more than a selective obligation.

Consent theory might seem the most promising on this account, for it is often held that consenting to do $x$ creates an obligation to do $x$, irrespective of further characteristics of doing $x$.[40] But consent theory fails to provide a proper foundation for a general duty in at least four ways. (1) No duty exists when no consent has actually been given. (2) As Locke argued,[41] some forms of consent may be void *ab initio*. If that is true, the principle *Volenti non fit injuria* does not hold without exceptions. (That it does not, is indeed assumed by all legal systems, and by common and professional morality.[42]} If a number of patients have willingly and knowingly agreed to participate in a medical experiment, that does not justify the experiment if it is useless or dangerous. (3) Consent may have been given – by explicit stipulation, or by conventional understanding – on conditions which the authoritative command does not respect. Then the normative situation may be unclear. The idea that it is always clear what a promise commits one to, is of course falsified by the daily practice of contract law. (4) One such condition applies universally: a promise does not bind when it has lost its point, for instance when the promisee fails to rely on it because he has lost interest in

---

[38] A similar position is taken by Gans 1992. Simmons 1996c mistakenly ascribes to Gans a commitment to a general duty to obey and then goes on to complain that his defence of this duty is "cobbled together" from different justifications which all apply under different conditions, none of them generally.

[39] Although Mackie 1981 argues that the obligation cannot be derived from any more basic "principle", he justifies its "invention" by appealing to the utility of the corresponding convention in avoiding suboptimal outcomes – which of course is a limiting consideration.

[40] Beran 1987, 81-83.

[41] "No Man can, by agreement, pass over to another that which he hath not in himself, a Power over his own Life." *Second Treatise*.24, cf. 23, 135, 149, 168, 172, 179.

[42] Den Hartogh 2000b.

the good he expected from fulfilling the promise, or expects to receive it anyway. Even consent does not obligate someone to fulfil a pointless law.[43]

An act of consent is never like writing out a blank cheque.[44] For the point of a voluntary obligation is really very similar to that of a non-voluntary one: to create a relation of trust in a context in which independent choices might produce suboptimal outcomes. Therefore the binding force of both types of obligation is equally context-dependent.

Obviously, the principle of necessity only binds to acts providing relief in a situation of dire need. Such a situation has to exist in the first place, and even within it the scope of the obligation is limited.[45] "The Serjeant, that could command a Souldier to march up to the mouth of a Cannon, or stand in a Breach, where he is almost sure to perish, can (not) command that Soldier to give him one penny of his Money..."[46] In the same way, the "captain" of the life-boat has no authority to command you to take off your clothes or to hand him your golden snuffbox. And similarly, if obedience is required to coordinate our efforts to achieve a common good, acts which are clearly irrelevant to its achievement cannot properly be commanded. Even if gratitude to officials is a proper consideration, it would seem that a certain degree of obedience will be enough to say "thank you"; and if the disobedient act will escape the officials' notice, or is something which they personally do not care about, no harm would be done by it at all.[47]

Having argued why a certain principle creates obligations to obey political authority, believers owe us a *separate* argument why this should be understood as a general obligation, for we should expect that the principle will not always apply whenever political authority requires us to obey. This separate argument is seldom presented. There are two serious contenders.

The first argument, already propounded by Socrates,[48] is that it is part of the nature of obligation to authority that it excludes discretion.[49] We can now articulate this

---

[43] Cf. note 55 on Honoré.

[44] Powerfully argued by Raz 1986, 81-94.

[45] Lyons 1981, 69. This might be the reason (Lyons ibid., 74) why Honoré tries to strengthen his argument from necessity in various ways (see also ch. 4, note 41), in particular by appealing to implied consent.

[46] Locke, *Second Treatise* .139.

[47] Simmons 1979, 185-186, cf. ch. 4, note 46; Raz 1984a, 748.

[48] Recently, R.P. Wolff propounded the same argument, cf. ch. 7.1.

[49] Soper 1984; Finnis 1980, ch. 11; 1989; 1984, 120: "The law presents itself as a seamless web. Its subjects are not permitted to pick and choose among (its) prescriptions." Raz 1984b, 150, agrees that this is the claim of the law, cf. Raz 1979, 30-33, 117, 235-236; Raz 1986, 76-78, but sees no reason to grant the claim. On the claims of the law see ch. 9.3., cf. Greenawalt 1987b, 18-20. Finnis' main argument for accepting the claim seems to be that the scope of the government's coordinating activity is the widest possible one, because it aims at harmonizing the productive activities of lower-order agencies within one single scheme called "the common good". It does not follow, however, that there are no issues left which clearly do not call for arbitration, or that no forms of "arbitration" on the issues which do call for it, can be rejected in good faith. It is, ironically, Joseph Raz who points to a possible further argument: the government may have epistemic authority concerning the identification of coordination problems, or of possible solutions to it. Raz 1989, 1192-1194; 1990, 195, see ch. 7, note 41. As Raz stresses, however, it is implausible to suggest that citizens are never in an equally good position to identify the game they are playing.

argument more clearly by pointing out that, if we are in need of arbitration, we should accept its outcome whatever it is. The decision of the arbiter replaces our own judgment as our guide to action. For if people only accept the arbiter's judgment when it fits their own, the benefits of arbitration will be lost.

We will consider this argument in detail in chapter Seven. Anticipating this discussion, I want to point out that the idea of "replacement" is misleading for several reasons. (1) The alternative to coordinated action along the lines set out by the arbiter is not coordinated action on your own preferred scenario, but non-coordinated action. You may have both prudential and moral reasons to avoid that alternative, and correctly judge that you have. (2) However, it is equally possible that your decision turns out the other way. Arbitrational judgments are binding in a "content-independent" way, but not without limits.[50] On the contrary, the area within which they are binding is restricted, in the first place to the issues which are at stake in negotiation, i.e. the possible outcomes of the Coordination game, and in the second place to the negotiation zone, or the subset of outcomes constituted by the game's equilibria. (3) The area may be further restricted to ensure that an appeal to cooperative virtue can succeed. True, the boundaries of the range will be vague, and hence it requires private judgment to decide where they lie. But that does not mean that there are no clear cases falling either within the range or outside it. For example, the boundary between matters of public and of private concern may be in dispute, and therefore we may have reason to respect political decisions concerning this point. But it does not follow that there is any reason to obey the state if it proscribes any form of communal religious worship. If my government tries to forbid me reading John Finnis' writings on euthanasia, I will have one good reason to read them. The argument of the seamless web suggests – by the fallacious logic of the slippery slope[51] - that there is no halting place between blind obedience and no obedience. That position cannot consistently be taken by people who accept the legitimacy of conscientious refusal when the government commands something evil, as all the advocates of a general duty do. For it requires private (and fallible) judgment to decide whether what the government requires really *is* something evil.

According to Honoré, it is one thing to recognize a general obligation to keep your promises which may be either defeated or overridden, and another thing to recognize a conditional obligation. If you are prepared to keep your promises only when you have adequate reasons for doing so, you are not a reliable person, but an opportunist.[52] I suspect that Honoré here overlooks the reasons deriving from the very fact that a promise has been made. These reasons, however, are only valid within a certain context, and therefore conditional upon the presence of that context.[53] In any case, a person who only makes conditional promises may be a paragon of reliability if he always keeps them; nevertheless, his obligations surely are as conditional as his promises.

---

[50] On content-independence see ch. 6.1.

[51] Den Hartogh 1998. The fallacy involved is Sorites again. Cf. ch. 4.4. at note 37.

[52] Honoré 1987, 124.

[53] Honoré 1987, 126, accepts that pointless laws do not create obligations.

It is not true that private judgment concerning the limits of authority logically destroys authority. It is also very doubtful whether such judgment has the tendency to destroy authority as a matter of fact. This is suggested by the second argument for extending the duty of obedience into a general one. This argument points out that disobedience may have negative external effects of its own: the undermining of authority.[54] This is a slippery slope argument as well, but of the causal, not the logical variety. It relies on a very dubious moral psychology.[55] According to this conception, people are better able to follow a simple rule like "do what the authority tells you to do" without any exceptions (irrespective of the question whether following the rule in the particular case can be seen to be justified or not), than to follow the rule when it applies, and to make an exception when it is clearly warranted. If we allow people to follow the latter strategy, they will identify too many exceptions, more and more every day, until the exceptions overwhelm the rule. But perhaps it is more likely that people will lose their respect for the rule, if they are regularly expected to comply with it when there is no direct reason whatsoever for doing so.

Even if the moral psychology of the argument were basically sound, we should not only weigh the danger it points out, but also the danger of people blindly following authority when it prescribes horrible things, as well as the temptation this behaviour represents for people in authority to abuse their power. It seems to me that the old positivist adage "the existence of an authoritative decision does not decide its moral status" is much to be preferred. (It does not follow that the content of the authoritative decision can be identified without regard to its possible moral status!) But in any case, this adage cannot consistently be denied by anybody who assigns to the duty to obey no more than a prima facie status, as most of the believers do. If people are enjoined to balance an authoritative decision against possibly conflicting considerations about their real weight, how can we prevent them from concluding that the weight of the decision is zero, if that happens to be the case? If private judgment can be trusted to decide that a prima facie obligation is overridden, why cannot it be trusted to decide that no prima facie obligation exists?[56]

I conclude that it is very hard to find a principle logically fit to justify a perfectly general obligation to obey the law. Perhaps the whole idea only makes sense within a providentialist framework, in which every ruler with *de facto* ruling power is supposed to be ordained to rule by divine right. But even then, active obedience is sometimes forbidden by the same divine law, so that the exercise of private moral judgment is not completely excluded.

---

[54] Soper 1984, 42ff; Boardman 1987, 555; Klosko 1992, 101-107. Raz 1986, 102 rightly says that it is a "melodramatic exaggeration" anyway to suppose that every disobedient act endangers the legal order to some significant extent.

[55] Den Hartogh 1998.

[56] In calling the obligation to obey presumptive and defeasible, Finnis 1980, 314-320, does not adequately distinguish between its liability to be overridden and to be defeated. If it may be morally required to deviate from the law in order to secure the very goods the law is supposed to procure, cf. Finnis 1980, 360, 487-489, the obligation to obey turns out to be a selective one after all.

## 5.5. The Possibility of Selective Obligations

On the other side of the fence we find many non-believers misrepresenting the proper force of their arguments as well. They refer to each other as members of the same party.[57] But in *The Morality of Freedom*, Joseph Raz obviously believes that it is at least possible that the "normal justification thesis" sometimes applies to political authority. (According to this thesis authority is legitimate if accepting it makes it more likely for you to comply with the reasons which are valid for you than when you tried to follow these reasons directly). For this is presupposed by his argument that government is sometimes permitted to act in such a way as to restrict the options of autonomous choice it creates for its citizens to morally acceptable ones. Therefore, he should be understood only to deny the general obligation to obey the law.[58]

If the obligation to obey is derived from a more fundamental principle, the fact that something is legally required does not in itself, irrespective of context, create even the presumption that a moral obligation exists. Of course not, I am inclined to say. But this thesis is often confused, by believers and non-believers alike,[59] with the quite different one that the very fact that something is the law never makes a moral difference. (Both propositions can be meant when it is said "that there is no obligation to obey the law just because it is the law", which seems to be the favourite sceptical formulation.)

That these propositions really are equivalent has been argued in an influential paper by M.B.E. Smith.[60] There are two possibilities, he insists. Either the very fact that a valid law is pronounced requiring *x* is enough to make doing *x* obligatory, even if doing it was morally innocent before. In that case, Smith argues, this fact is always relevant, and, what is more, the moral "weight" it bestows on the act of doing *x* is always the same. Or the act of legislation in itself has no moral significance at all. As it

---

[57] Raz 1979, 233; 1984, 139; 1986, 97, aligning himself with Wasserstrom 1963; Smith 1973; Woozley 1979; Simmons 1979; Sartorius 1981; even with Wolff 1970, all refuting "the obligation to obey the law". Green 1988, 231 note 10, cf. Green 1996, 15 note 2, omits Wolff, and adds Feinberg 1995; Simmons 1996c, 34, note 2 adds Lyons 1981, cf. Simmons 1987, 276; Regan 1986, 15, note 1. Cf. also the description of the opposing camp by Honoré 1987 or by Finnis 1984, 116; 1989, 103. Only Smith and Soper mention Brandt 1964, 43-49.

[58] Cf. Raz 1979, 242; Raz 1984b, 142; Raz 1986, 73, 77, 80; and most explicitly Raz 1994, 330-334 Selectivity of obligation is also argued by Wasserstrom 1963; Dworkin 1977, ch. 7 ("Taking Rights Seriously"); Woozley 1979; Feinberg (1979) 1995; Lyons 1981; Lyons 1984, 208-214; Green 1988, ch. 8; Van der Burg 1989; Menlowe 1993; Roberson 1998.

[59] Cf. resp. Finnis 1984, 116; Morris 1998, 217. One explanation is that those authors (cf. also Green 1996) believe that the modern state claims comprehensive or even unlimited authority (see ch. 9.3. at note 20) and then focus on the issue whether or not this claim is valid. Cf. Simmons 1996c.

[60] His argument is endorsed by Raz 1979, 239; Regan 1986, 24; Edmundson 1998. For Edmundson this is a reason to replace the duty to obey the law by a duty not to resist its enforcement. The latter duty supposedly is both general and always of equal weight. I agree that there is no one-to-one relation between the two duties: even if I have no duty to come to a standstill at the crossroads, I may have a duty to resign to my fate if an overzealous policeman halts and fines me. Still, the duty of non-resistance seems to me to depend on the duty to obey: if we do not normally have a duty to obey, the enforcement of alleged duties is nothing but a violation of our liberty which we have every right to resist, albeit not with all means. No-one can have a general right to coerce people to do things which they are morally free not to do. This objection applies to all theorists who believe that state legitimacy can be explained in terms of a justification-right to coerce rather than of a claim-right to being obeyed, e.g. Buchanan 1999, 57, cf. ch. 2, note 11.

is easy to point out cases in which the legal requirement carries only the slightest weight, or not even that, the first alternative is excluded, and only the second remains.

This argument assumes that the obligation to obey the law, if it exists, must be basic. That assumption is unfounded, as the unending quest for the foundations of the obligation shows. It is a famous crux in the divine law theory of ethics to claim that you should comply with someone's instructions, independent of their content, for no further reason at all. But as I argued in section 3, this is both unintelligible and objectionable. (That is the element of truth in the Lockean claim that "man is born free".) However, as soon as you are prepared to look for a further reason, you know that the moral weight of the obligation will be determined by that reason, and hence will probably vary. For example, if the relevant reason is that the authoritative instructions present a focus for the development of mutual expectations, enabling people to avoid a suboptimal outcome in situations of interdependent choice, it follows that the weight of the obligation will depend, among other things, on the importance of the cooperative aim.[61] If no-one's interest, or putative interest, is at stake, or if the relevant interests coincide, no arbitration is needed; and if the interests at stake are slight, the force of the arbitral decision will be slight as well. It is obviously wrong to conclude that in a serious case, the decision has no great force either, or at least cannot derive its force from the fact that it is the arbitral decision in this case. In exactly the same way, the weight of a promissory obligation varies with the risks of reliance. If it is sometimes nil, it does not follow that it is always nil. But if all one wanted to say was that the obligation is conditional and hence selective, it would be rather strange to argue "that there is no obligation to keep one's promises".[62]

Suppose you have a moral reason to spare the feelings of your ageing grandmother, and she would be upset by observing that you disobey the law. Then you might have a non-basic moral reason to obey it, but that is obviously only an accidental fact. I have argued that the obligation to obey the law is a non-basic, and hence a conditional and selective duty. So if the law commands something, does this only accidentally provide a moral reason to do it? This does not follow. One could say that this fact neither universally, nor accidentally, but typically generates an obligation to obey.[63] What does "typically" mean in this context? This is explained by the fact that, to understand the existence of law at all, we have to consider it in the context of the production of a package of alleged public goods, requiring arbitration concerning the composition of the package and the distribution of the benefits and burdens of production. To the extent that the law actually does the job it is supposed to do, it will invoke the principle of fairness and the requirement to accept a fair compromise.[64] But of course, anything

---

[61] Some sceptics argue that, even if authoritative instructions succeed in presenting such a focus, that does not mean that there is a reason to obey the law. I will consider this argument in ch. 6.4.

[62] If no obligation to obey the law exists, not even a selective one, what is our moral position vis-à-vis legal requirements? It is not dramatically different from the position believers think they occupy, as the sceptics allege, cf. in particular Simmons 1979, 29-30, 192-5; 1993, 261-263; criticized by Lessnoff 1986, 89; Senor 1987.

[63] Gans 1992, 76-77.

[64] But note that a considerable part of the law has the function of solving pure coordination problems. To that extent, the law can be functionally described in terms which do not invoke moral principles.

which must essentially be described by its function, can also be used in non-functional ways. We cannot even assume that it will be used in functional ways most of the time.[65]

I have argued that the new sceptical orthodoxy concerning political obligation covers two very distinct positions. The first position only denies that in all cases in which the law prescribes something, we have a moral reason to obey: the principles from which such obligations derive do not always apply. The second position denies that we ever have a moral reason to obey the law because it is the law. There is something odd about this second position which deserves to be mentioned in conclusion. For there is strong evidence that most of the citizens, at least in liberal-democratic states, believe that, normally or even generally, they have an obligation to obey.[66] (Some of them even seem to think that this is the only indisputable duty they have, a legal duty distinguished by that very indisputability from the moral duties all thought to be matters of purely subjective attitudes.) Can they all be wrong?[67]

Well, cannot they? Everyone in the Netherlands believes that it is the rule of the road to keep to the right. Can they all be mistaken?

The sceptical philosophers will reply that this is a preposterous comparison. It does not matter at all whether we all expect each other to keep to the right or all expect each other to keep to the left, as long as we all expect each other to keep to the same side. And given those expectations it is simply stupid not to honour them, only persons in a suicidal mood need a moral duty to prevent them from deviating. On all these scores the alleged obligation to obey the law is something completely different. No one can seriously doubt that it is possible for an evil regime to flourish by the common and willing, but entirely misguided, allegiance of most of its citizens.

On my view the comparison is not so totally mistaken as this reply suggests. The (real) sceptics about political obligation tend to suggest that the reasons for obeying the law can mostly be reclaimed as reasons for doing what the law requires for other reasons than that the law requires them. Such reasons, however, can only be independent ones, for example the fact that some action is good or evil in itself, irrespective of mutual beliefs. But if any political obligations exist, they will, as I have argued, be interdependent ones. Hence the fact that people commonly believe they have such

---

[65] For this reason the thesis that there is not invariably a reason to obey the law does not imply that obedience to the law is always as much in need of justification as disobedience is. If the law does its job tolerably well, this will create a presumption in favour of obedience. Obedience will be the default, cf. ch. 11.9. But though we will tend to require a justification for disobedience and not for obedience, that does not mean that, if required, no further justification for obedience can or need be given, as Murphy 1995 suggests. Murphy is led to this suggestion because he does not distinguish between the first and the second position identified in the next paragraph. However, if there never were any reason to obey the law "as such", surely only a presumption in favour of disobedience could be justified. Note that a presumptive obligation is not identical to a general one: if the presumption is defeated, not even a so-called prima facie obligation is left.

[66] Tyler 1990. Green 1996 argues that the questions used in Tyler's interviews do not discriminate between the belief that one (always) has an obligation to obey the law and the belief that one (mostly) has a reason to comply, for whatever reason. I concede that it is logically possible to agree to a statement like "People should obey the law even if it goes against what they think is right" (82% agreement) without subscribing to the thesis that generally, or even normally, one has a moral reason to obey the law "as such". But it seems to me that you must be a trained, or at least a natural philosopher to be aware of this possibility.

[67] Cf. Hume, *Treatise* III.ii.viii ('Of the source of allegiance'): "...it being certain, that there is a moral obligation to submit to government, because everyone thinks so..."

obligations is unusually significant. Such beliefs have an internal relation to the fact that is the object of the belief: that it is believed is a necessary condition for the belief being true.

It is only a necessary, not a sufficient condition. To this extent the sceptics about political obligation are in the right. The interdependent reasons people may have to honour each other's expectations depend on principles like the principle of fairness or the principle to abide with a fair compromise. And people may believe these principles to apply while actually they do not. But even in that case the existence of the beliefs is a relevant datum. As I will argue, some basic legal principles of fairness and good faith are always relevant to the interpretation of any system of conventions, and in particular of the law. For they express the constraints which are given by the law's claim – even the law's false or insincere claim – to require the obedience of its subjects for moral reasons.

# CHAPTER 6

## LAW AND AUTHORITY

### 6.1. Formal Conventions

If you want to explain the nature of a legal system, it is clearly not enough to characterize it as a system of conventions in the sense explored in the first chapters of this book. It is true that a legal system may, and I think always will,[1] contain many conventions of the type described: patterns of mutual anonymous expectations, largely of an obligatory nature, i.e. appealing to the cooperative dispositions of trustworthiness, fairness, and justice. But these categories are insufficient to understand characteristically legal functions like legislation and adjudication.

To make progress here, we need the concept of a *formal convention*. If you are a participant to a convention as I described it, you have first-order and higher-order knowledge of precisely the things you are expected to do in certain circumstances. Such a convention we may call a substantial one. (We will see later[2] that in order to determine what you should do, it will often be necessary to derive this by a particular type of argument from the explicit content of a given substantial convention. So the knowledge I refer to may be more or less "latent".) If you are a participant to a formal convention, however, your first-order and higher-order knowledge only concerns *the way to identify* the things you are expected to do, the procedure you have to go through in order to discover it. The formal convention only specifies a *source* of substantial practical knowledge, and you need to consult the source (Holy Scripture, the constellation of the planets, the entrails of birds, the result of a judicial duel etc.) to acquire the knowledge.[3]

The most important type of source as a matter of fact, though by no means logically the only possible one, is the intentional communicative act of prescription.[4] If a pattern of mutual expectations exists to do what a certain person, by his words, gestures, or writings, tells you to do, such a convention invests this person with practical *authority* (i.e. authority over your actions). As this is the only type of formal convention existing in modern legal systems, I will permit myself a more restricted use of the

---

[1] Ch. 9.2.

[2] Ch. 11.2.

[3] Therefore the substantial knowledge derivable from a formal convention is also latent knowledge. In due time, however, it may become substantial mutual knowledge; this process is completed when it is no longer necessary for the correct identification of further latent contents to refer to the source. The law enacted by statute may develop into custom, and change in the process. For that reason, the relevance of legislative intention to the interpretation of statute is variable. See ch. 11.5. on the argument from history.

[4] Other sources will usually be conceived of as indirect signs of authoritative, e.g. divine judgments. It is normally difficult to understand how sources that are not created intentionally, can be supposed to give content-independent reasons for action at all. (Unless they do so by providing salience.)

concept of a formal convention: a formal convention bestows practical authority on a natural or artificial person. An artificial person is a group of persons, deciding on the prescription they want to give by following a certain procedure, e.g. voting by majority.

A formal convention, characterized in this way, is not a second-order rule in the Hartian sense but rather an indirect one: it is concerned with actions, not with rules,[5] but it identifies the actions indirectly. However, authority may be exercised in giving general prescriptions, not for a token case, but for a class of cases described in general terms. In that case it is not improper to say that authority creates new rules. The rule, however, is not identical to the prescription; it consists in the pattern of mutual expectations (either manifest or latent) to conform to the prescription.

If you believe that you should do – usually within certain limits – whatever an authority tells you to do, you attribute to the authority's prescription the status of a *content-independent reason*.[6] Content-independence is, of course, also a characteristic of the original Lewis conventions, emerging as they do in games of pure coordination: it does not matter whether we are driving on the left or on the right side of the road, as long as we all do the same. So the convention derives its force, not from what it tells you to do, but from the very fact that it tells you to do it. If people have not yet succeeded in coordinating their actions before, the bare fact that a person tells them to choose one of the equivalent equilibria may give all of them a reason actually to do so, to expect each other to do so, etc., because that particular equilibrium is made salient by the fact. Obviously, this reason is as content-independent as the reason given by a corresponding substantial convention.

Content-independence is characteristic of the reasons to comply with a convention in a Division game as well. Though you may prefer another meeting-point, you strongly want to succeed in meeting the others anyway, and this is (part of) your reason to honour their expectations. When a person's prescription is the actual starting-point of the development of these expectations, your reason to follow the prescription is, again, as content-independent as the reason given by the equivalent substantial convention, though it follows from the nature of the division or bargaining problem that the prescription will be only acceptable within the limits of the negotiation area. So we might expect authority to operate in two types of contexts of interdependent choice: Coordination and Division games. I will refer to both types of authority as coordinating authority. The specific authority operating in the context of a Division game is that of an arbiter.

Formal conventions are functionally equivalent to substantial ones in contexts of interdependent choice in which substantial conventions provide content-independent reasons. This parallellism is absent in other "games" like, for instance, Assurance game

---

[5] Hart 1961, 94.

[6] Hart 1958, 102; 1982, 18, 254. Cf. Lucas 1966, 16; Friedman 1973, 131 (with references to Aquinas and Newman); Anscombe 1981 (1962), 44; Raz 1972, 95; 1986, 35. "Command is, where a man saith, Doe this, or Doe not this, without expecting other reason than the Will of him that sayes it." *Leviathan*, ch. 25, obviously alluding to Terentius' *Sit pro ratione voluntas, Andria* 6, 223. Feldman 1992, 1394, mistakenly describes a content-independent reason as being "a reason for action regardless of the rightness of the action the reason encourages". The authoritative prescription is rather a reason for thinking the action it prescribes to be the right one, irrespective of what it is the prescription prescribes.

or Prisoner's Dilemma. The reason to make a fair contribution to the achievement of the social optimum[7] is not a content-independent one at all. Therefore in these situations practical authority has no role to play: whether it tells you to contribute, or not to contribute, this does not add to your reasons to take either alternative. If government, as is usually assumed, has a specific task to provide public goods, the fulfilment of this task does not require *authority*.[8] However, as we have seen, even in situations with a roughly AG or PD character, the exact specification of the social optimum and of a fair contribution may be the object of bargaining; and to that extent, authority may have a role to play.[9]

If formal and substantial conventions are functionally equivalent, why is there any need of the former?[10] The answer to this question was essentially given by Locke three centuries ago, in his account of the "inconveniences of the state of nature"; with some adaptations, it has been repeated by Hart in *The Concept of Law*, and by many others.[11] Coordination problems can sometimes be solved by a spontaneous process of mutual accommodation (e.g. pedestrians in Bond Street), and very often by communicating one way or the other. Frequently, there are also substantial conventions determining people's choice of action. But quite often it would cost too much time or effort to wait for the outcome of the discussion, whereas sometimes there are no conventions which have unambiguously determined the pattern that must be followed for tuning in to each other's acts, perhaps because the coordination problem confronting us is entirely new. Whether a substantial convention exists at any time when there is a functional need of one, is a contingent fact; there may be none, or there may be a suboptimal convention keeping us "trapped".[12] If we have a formal convention, it is possible for the person invested with the authority intentionally to focus people's expectations over the whole area of his authority (which need not be unlimited), whenever such a focus is needed, or whenever an adaptation of the focus is needed. Even when we could expect a substantial convention to emerge spontaneously in due time, it might take too much time to wait for the completion of this process. This is the legislating use of authority; it provides both a flexibility lacking in the natural development of substantial conventions,[13] and a greater, though still far from maximal, degree of determinacy.

It is not difficult to recognize the authority exercized in legislation as a form of coordinating authority. What about the authority exercized in adjudication? The Lockean explanation of the functional need for the adjudicative exercise of authority is as follows. Occasionally people sincerely believe, or insincerely pretend to believe, to

---

[7] E.g. not to confess, in the original story of the Prisoner's Dilemma.

[8] Cf. ch. 4.8. But the government may have a task of enforcing obligations of fairness.

[9] Ch. 5.1.

[10] As Green 1988, 111ff, asks.

[11] Hart 1961, 89-96, cf. e.g. Finnis 1980, 245: authority settles coordination problems "with greater speed and certainty" than custom.

[12] Cf. ch. 2, note 40.

[13] Although Bloch 1962, ch. 8 calls the customary law of the early Middle Ages one of the most flexible ever known.

follow the existing patterns of expectations, but on some level of their mutual beliefs they fail to converge. In this case, the best way to restore the mutual adjustment of their actions for the future, is a decision about who of them made the mistake in the past. This is also needed if the mistake is a guilty one, deserving punishment or requiring reparation. (When either the mistake is not acknowledged, or no agreement can be reached about compensation.)[14] The identification of the mistake, and the specification of its consequences, can be a matter of endless dispute which is in need of arbitration.

This account assumes that the existing conventions really provide an answer to the question who is right and who is wrong in any of these disputes. Legislating authority says: this will be the law, though it was not until now; adjudicating authority says: this is the law as it stands, you'd better acknowledge it. Legislating authority tells us what we should do in a certain type of case; adjudicating authority what we should have done in a particular case. It seems to follow that, where adjudicating authority is needed, there really is no coordination problem: for each of the disputants, there already are valid reasons determining what he should do, they do not have to be provided. So the question arises whether it really is a form of coordinating authority which is exercised in adjudication.

## 6.2. Epistemic Authority

Authoritative pronouncements can be a reason to believe something (theoretical authority), or to do something (practical authority). Our concern is with practical authority, but in some of its forms it is dependent on theoretical authority. In the relevant type of context, the first I will consider, you have good reasons to have more faith in somebody else's judgment than in your own, for example because you are overtired, emotionally too much involved in a case, or simply because you lack essential information which it would cost too much time and effort to acquire, or which might even be too complex for you to understand at all, whatever the time and effort spent. At the same time there are, in such circumstances, good reasons to presume that someone else is more capable of forming a true insight than you are yourself. That is why you believe that what she says is right, and why you are prepared to act on her advice, without having assessed its soundness, even without having been given an explanation of what exactly underlies it. It is essential in such cases to be sure that you can trust the other person to have the relevant insight which you lack. In this type of context, the reason to act on authority is always derived from a reason to believe that the authority's judgment is true, even if this judgment is not explicitly given. This kind of authority on the strength of expertise, *epistemic authority*, may therefore be a form of both theoretical and practical authority, but the theoretical role is the primary one.[15]

---

[14] Or punishment? In modern legal systems private agreement on the proper measure of punishment does not pre-empt trial.

[15] DeGeorge 1976, 76; Raz 1979, 13-14; Flathman 1980, 16-17; Green 1988, 26-29; Hurd 1991, 1615. The reason supplied by this form of authority depends on other reasons (it is a reason to believe that these other reasons exist), but is nevertheless a content-independent reason: it is a reason to do what the authority tells

An outstanding example of practical epistemic authority is provided by the authority of the medical expert.[16] It is true that nowadays it is generally accepted that a doctor should enlighten her patient on his state of health, and subsequently leave it to him whether he consents to undergo the proposed treatment. This principle is based on the general conviction that a patient is autonomous. But in this context, "autonomy" often cannot mean that the agent decides on his own considered view about the merits of the case. The doctor may provide any amount of information, but its meaning and relevance will typically depend on a background of factual knowledge and unarticulated experience of analogous cases which cannot be fully provided as well. That is why the patient will often, to some extent, have to rely on the epistemic authority of the doctor, not only for adopting correct beliefs, but also for deriving correct decisions from these beliefs. If the final decision is left to the patient, this is only to make sure that the desires and ideals guiding the decision process are his own, and not the doctor's. (The relevant basic value therefore is not autonomy in the sense of self-governance, but rather of authenticity.) But the information given by the doctor can hardly be sufficient to verify the rightness of the decision, given the patient's values and preferences; the patient cannot but trust that the information is not manipulated in such a way that in the end, the doctor's own values and preferences are decisive. (A second opinion may help.)

As this example shows, acknowledgment of authority does not mean that you declare all the premises of your practical deliberation to be irrelevant for your choice of action – including your own desires, needs, ideals or moral principles, or even some of your factual insights. Such an acknowledgment would be unreasonable, indeed it would be the epitome of unreasonableness. What you delegate to someone else may be just a part of the decision process. It is also quite conceivable that you exclude in advance all sorts of possible conclusions. (Exercising your autonomy to that extent.) Submission to authority need not be either blind or total.[17]

In the usual case – medical authority again provides an example – epistemic authority does not concern the essential end of the action, but only the means. In that case it does not command but only advises. Patients are also autonomous in the sense that they are free to brush aside even sound advice; they can only be threatened by natural sanctions. In these cases, epistemic authority only provides "hypothetical imperatives"; it does not impose obligations.

In politics there is a need for expertise as well. Making adequate decisions often requires the digestion of a great deal of complicated information. That is why Robert Paul Wolff's "Proposal for Instant Direct Democracy" – all citizens vote on all political issues through a voting machine attached to their television set – is just a nightmare.[18] The ideal of the autonomy of the citizen, like that of the patient, cannot possibly aim at

---

you to do whatever (perhaps within limits) it is the authority tells you to do. Hurd 1991, 1616, is confused about this.

[16] Even, somewhat inconsistently, recognized by Wolff 1970, 15.

[17] As philosophical anarchists like Wolff 1970 tend to assume. Cf. also the "seamless web" argument of Finnis a.o., discussed in ch. 5.4. Even the acknowledgment of charismatic authority does not require total submission, cf. Raz 1986, 33-34.

[18] Wolff 1970, 34-37.

the elimination of epistemic authority. The justification for democracy does not consist in the substitution of authority by autonomy, but in the pursuit of confining authority to its own grounds and limits, and in the ensurance that authority will be exercised only for the benefit of the citizens. Such an ensurance can never be absolute: as even Locke recognized, the exercise of authority always requires some trust. (That is why the politician who is caught in the act of cheating deserves the severest political punishment.)

Whenever citizens have reason to be trusting to some degree, they have reason to acknowledge the epistemic authority of ministers, civil servants, judges, etc.[19] Usually this only means that they draw on resources of expertise which it would be unwise for a citizen to disregard. This form of authority is of a different kind than the authority claimed by laws, instructions and decrees;[20] it is also different from the authority which can compel obedience, and certainly from the one which is entitled to punish disobedience.

It is not impossible, however, that we really have an obligation to do what epistemic authority tells us to do. This may be the case when we have reason to believe that the authority is in a better position than we are to ascertain the extent of the obligations we already have.[21] It is precisely the task of the authority to "reflect" those pre-existing obligations as faithfully as possible. If we have reason to trust its judgment, this judgment may be morally binding. For example, state officials may forbid you to do something because they believe such action to be harmful to others, and are in a better position to know that it really is. In such cases you may have an obligation to obey.[22] It is fully derived from the obligation not to cause harm. So if you happen to know that the action really is not harmful – taking into account possible effects of your disobedience on the behaviour of less competent third persons – you may have no obligation at all.[23]

---

[19] As shown by an opinion poll from 1977, as many as 42% of Dutch voters at the time held the view that, being a Dutch citizen, one had to accept the decisions of the government because the government knows what is good for the country. (Rosenthal 1981, 125). This shows a surprising amount of confidence; but not necessarily a blind faith (as Rosenthal claims).

[20] Today, anyhow. "Indeed, the elimination of any element of authoritative belief from our present conception of political and legal authority needs to be seen as a historical achievement profoundly tied up with the work of certain modern philosophers..." Friedman 1973, 124. He mentions Hobbes, Spinoza and J.S. Mill, and could have mentioned Locke's classical discussion of the distinction between political and parental authority. Cf. Oakeshott 1975, 149-158 on the "acknowledgment of authority" in "civil association". Arendt 1977 (1958), on the other hand, regards this development as the decline of authority in general.

[21] Accounts of political authority along such lines have been suggested by Bell 1971; Alexander 1990; Hurd, 1991, 1667ff. According to Hurd, for example, the fact that a democratic majority believes that a course of action is morally obligatory is a reason to believe it is. Really? It is hard to believe that elections are generally won on account of the moral superiority of the platform of the winning party.

[22] I did not discuss this form of the obligation to obey the law in chapters 4 or 5, because it is not a distinctive one – you may have a similar obligation to do what your neighbour or your newspaper tells you to do – and because it is rather marginal. Artificial persons like parliaments usually are ill-designed for exercising this form of authority, cf. Waldron 1996b.

[23] Raz 1986, 74, 78. However, in my view such considerations are not extra-legal ones. As I claim in ch. 11.4. at note 34, cf. ch. 7 note 53, the verdict in a case like that of the Huizer vet may be *contra legem*, but it does not involve any strong form of discretion. Cf. also Hayek 1973, ch. 1: within civil society there is always more expertise available than any government can tap, so its epistemic authority can never bind everyone.

The relevant expertise in such cases is not really moral expertise. I certainly do not want to deny the possible existence of authority based on moral expertise: other people may be better placed than you are to identify even your basic duties.[24] However, it is debatable, to say the least, that state officials ever have that kind of moral authority, and even if they had, the obligation to follow their lead would not be an enforceable one as such. That, at least, is an essential part of the political morality of liberal-democratic states. Competent people have the right to decide for themselves, even if they make the wrong decisions. They also have the right to choose their own moral leaders, even if they make the wrong choices. Of course, if you really have the obligations the authority insists that you have, these obligations may be enforceable ones. But that does not make the obligation to obey the authority enforceable.

## 6.3. Coordinating Authority

Even if state enactments are based on expertise, their authority is often not exhausted by its epistemic aspect. The reasons for action such enactments provide are not identical to the reasons provided by the advice of private research organizations or universities, even if the advice is identical in content, and is, perhaps, the actual basis of legislation. The officials exercising legislative authority may have been selected by a criterion of competence; even in that case, however, their decisions do not automatically lose their validity if they turn out to be criticizable on expert grounds. For their authority finally depends on the fact that they *are* selected, for whatever reason. This fact is not only a sign of an underlying personal quality like competence. "The fact that Carl Levin has been elected to the Senate... is not a visible manifestation of the not fully accessible real reason why he... has the authority to make law. It *is* the reason."[25]

Epistemic authority provides independent reasons for belief, and only indirectly for action. Coordinating authority on the other hand provides interdependent reasons, not for believing but for acting. Are these reasons obligatory ones? Not necessarily. Coordinated action often leads to a generally desired result: whoever does not join in, is left behind. Therefore, everybody's own preferences or values provide him with sufficient reason for concordant action. There is no need for either an appeal to moral motives or coercion.[26]

A substantial part of the law has merely a coordinating function: it does not create obligations, but facilities. Good examples are some traffic regulations, all sorts of regulations concerning time (the Gregorian calendar, the seven days' week, summer time, staggering of holidays), nomenclature, weights and measures, coinage, etc. Many other regulations have an important coordinating aspect (although this is not their

---

[24] Anscombe 1962.

[25] I have failed to trace this quotation.

[26] Finnis 1980, ch. 9, sees the law as always creating obligations to obey, even though he only ascribes coordinating authority to it. The reason is that he assumes a fundamental political obligation of every citizen to serve the common good, and it is the fulfilment of this obligation which involves coordination problems. For criticism ch. 5, notes 9, 49; cf. Ullmann-Margalit 1981; Green 1988, ch. 4; Batnitzky 1995.

primary function) as a result of their exact formulation: procedural rules for the conduct of a court case and for constitutional law, technicalities of agreements and wills. Such rules and subrules can have authority without creating obligations. Perhaps they do actually create obligations, but they have authority anyway.

The circumstances under which coordinating authority is valid may, however, undergo subtle changes, and the preferences of the people involved may shift just as subtly. The moment may come that it is no longer your first priority to bring your course of action into line with that of the others, while your previous conduct had been a ground for them to count on you. At that moment, it is a requirement of *reliability* not to let the others down, not to damage their confidence in you. Trapeze artists may, after many years of exemplary cooperation, become gradually disappointed in the division of roles or in each other's fulfilment of these roles. But this is no justification for refusing to stretch out the expected hand at the crucial moment of the salto mortale.

Patterns of interaction in real life do not come with their game-theoretical labels attached. Rarely do we meet a returning problem of pure coordination which we know to be *that*, and only that, precisely and permanently. Road-users may be careless and even suicidal. For this reason, an established pattern of expectations will always be supplemented by an accompanying pattern of expectations distributing the risks of deviating behaviour. Sometimes, people know that they are relying on each other at their own risk. Alternatively, the expectations may assume an obligating character. If these expectations concern focusing on coordinating authority, this authority can therefore create obligations by virtue of the principle of reliability. (Note that even these obligations are not primarily owed to the authority, but to "the others".)

In chapter Five I have argued that legal authority should primarily be seen as a form of arbitration, deciding bargaining problems concerning the execution of our enforceable duties, in particular duties of fairness. The exercise of such coordinating authority creates obligations on account of two principles, working *in tandem*: the principle of fairness, and the principle of accepting a reasonable compromise.

Coordinating authority and the obligation to comply usually go together. Usually – but, I repeat, not necessarily. Formal conventions, like substantial ones, might exist in a society of instrumentally rational non-tuistic utility-maximizers. Hence, the intentional communication of a prescription may create a content-independent reason to obey which is not necessarily a moral reason. It is sometimes held that you cannot properly speak of "authority" (other than epistemic), if you would not allow an obligation to obey it as its correlate.[27] This may be true as a matter of linguistic fact. As I said, it is only to be expected that authority and obligation will go together: authority has a role to play in contexts in which the principles of reliability, fairness and reasonable compromise are relevant as well. This fact may have its linguistic reflection. The point I want to make is that the practical importance of authority is not exhausted by its obligating character: from what is left of authority when its obligatory power is taken away (call it "proto-authority" if you like), you can still derive reasons for action. And it may be true

---

[27] Raz 1986, 27; Soper 1989, 219.

in some pure Coordination games that a person who fails to heed the authority's (or proto-authority's) instructions, is mutually known to do so only at his own peril.

. It is sometimes obligatory to comply with epistemic authority, it is usually obligatory to comply with coordinating authority. But this is not the main difference. In the case of epistemic authority, the obligations as well as the prudential reasons for action should be supposed to exist before its exercise, and to be only reflected by the prism of the authority's superior factual or moral wisdom. Nothing similar can be said of the exercise of authority in contexts of interdependent decision. True, in a Division game the negotiation area may be restricted, not only by the status quo point as it can be reconstructed from the player's options and preferences, but also by pre-existing obligations, and in that case the exercise of coordinating authority should respect those restrictions. (For instance, the bargaining problem should not be solved by forming a coalition to confiscate the property of a weaker party, or forcefully expel him from his land, etc.) It is even true, as we saw, that the bargaining problem may concern the issue of the "distribution" of a pre-existing collective duty. However, these pre-existing duties only demarcate a domain within which it is the aim of coordinating authority to fix a point. It has to respect the duties, but it is not its aim simply to represent them. And unless the person vested with authority also has superior moral insight concerning the nature of these obligations, what she says about them has no particular authority itself; the subjects are left to their own judgment to decide whether the authority remains within the area of her jurisdiction. Within this area, however, what she prescribes gives rise to obligations *that did not exist before*. This will be one of the guiding thoughts of the next chapter.

The discussion so far has deepened the mystery of adjudicating authority. It appears not to be a form of coordinating authority, because it aims at reflecting pre-existing interdependent reasons. But it appears not to be a form of epistemic authority either, because there is an obligation to obey it which is not derived from the pre-existing obligations reflected in its judgment. That is most evident in those cases in which we know this judgment to be wrong. For even in that case, it may be authoritative nevertheless, it need not just vainly pretend to be so; hence, it still has a binding force which mere epistemic authority would lack.

## 6.4. Coordinating Authority and Formal Conventions

For the time being I will leave this problem unsolved, and proceed to clarify some other aspects of practical authority.

Is it possible that coordinating authority is exercised without a pre-existing formal convention?[28] Robert Paul Wolff gives the example of the life-boats of a sinking ship, which must be manned in a very short time.[29] In a situation like this, the mere fact that someone is giving straightforward instructions is a reason for everyone to

---

[28] A similar question can be asked concerning promises, cf. Scanlon 1990.

[29] Wolff 1970, 15-16; cf. the example of the motorist who gets out of her car to direct traffic around the scene of a road accident, Green 1988, 24.

do as they are told. Perhaps the crew members could think of an alternative distribution pattern, at least as efficient as the one that has been pointed out, but the efficiency of potential instructions in itself is no reason for anyone to observe them as long as none of them is salient. And salient is only the instruction which is actually given.

Wolff himself disputes that, in these circumstances, we are dealing with an exercise of authority. He argues that it does not matter who actually gives the instructions, whether it be the captain or just any of the passengers. So there is no particular quality of the person issuing the command which lends authoritative force to his order – rather, it is the very act of commanding which lends it this force. There is nobody who can claim an exclusive right to command.

It is true that epistemic authority can only be based on a supposed antecedent quality (expertise) of the person in charge, but this does not necessarily apply to coordinating authority. A coordination problem arises when all people involved have no ground to choose a particular course of action, unless they can expect others to act accordingly. The difficulty is that everyone has to "wait" until his partners make a decision. As soon as all expect all others to make a certain choice, and know that the others expect the same, and know the others to know, etc., then everyone has a decisive reason to go into action. It does not matter what triggers off the mutual expectations; what counts is only the fact that they are triggered off. It may be either an antecedent quality or a sudden initiative.

Hence, the instructions of the passenger mentioned just now do have authoritative force. They are a reason for the other passengers to stop acting for independent reasons and to comply with the instructions, whatever – within limits – their content. It is not an antecedent authority from which the instructions derive this force; their force *is* their very authority.

So the example really shows how it is possible to have a reason to act on authority without the authority being invested in a person by a pre-existing formal convention.[30] Epistemic authority, of course, provides another example of this state of affairs: in this case, your reason for action is a wholly independent one; it is not necessary that the reason is recognized by other people as well. In the case of coordinating authority, however, our reasons for action are interdependent ones; therefore we either need a salient clue as a basis for building higher-order expectations, or a pre-existing pattern of "substantial" mutual expectations. The second possibility will obviously be more prevalent, in particular if we are dealing with complex schemes of coordination involving many people on many occasions over a long or indefinite period. This explains why *de iure* authority normally requires its general recognition, i.e. *de facto* authority or legitimacy.[31]

---

[30] Winch 1958; Hart 1958; Oakeshott 1975, 149-158; and Flathman 1980 all claim that the concept of authority is essentially rule-dependent. If, as I argued in ch. 2.6., our reasons to converge on a salient equilibrium are already interdependent ones, the claim is true, though not quite in the way they thought. Finnis 1980, ch. 9, argues that coordination can be achieved through either "unanimity" (of judgment) or "authority", 232, 247ff; so he does not recognize that authority (like agreement) *requires* unanimity in order to provide interdependent reasons.

[31] Another example of the "circularity" discussed in Den Hartogh 1998.

In the first section, I explained the emergence of formal conventions by referring to "inconveniences of the state of nature". It could be objected that a rational-choice theory cannot confine itself to such a functionalistic story: even if the exercise of authority has functional advantages, how does it emerge and how is it maintained within a society of rational agents? This problem can now be solved as well. We start from a convention to converge on the salient equilibrium, however the emergence of *that* convention has to be explained.[32] If a person regularly gives directives which solve coordination problems, the very consistency of his success is an obvious form of salience. At some point, people will habitually expect each other to expect each other to comply; salience is no longer needed as a basis for their expectations. And this new pattern of mutual expectations will be self-maintaining in the way described in the first chapter. There is no *distinct* problem about the emergence of formal conventions.

This answer is, of course, highly stylized. Historical variations on the basic theme will be numerous. It is possible, in principle, that people explicitly agree to accept coordinating authority. It is also possible, less theoretically, that the career of authority starts with the exercise of pure coercive power. The subjects find that, if the tyrant gives them orders which solve their coordination problems, they have a reason to obey these orders, even without a sufficient threat of punishment, and the tyrant finds that he is more readily obeyed if he gives orders of that type.[33]

If legislation is a form of the exercise of coordinating authority, it seems that there can be an obligation to obey the laws it provides. It has been objected that this is not strictly true: there may be an obligation to do what formal law tells you to do, but the reason is not that it tells you to do it.[34] So what is the real reason? At this point, the objection can take either of two forms. According to the first form the real reason is that, as a causal result of legislative intervention, other people are now acting in a certain way. In a coordination problem, this is sufficient for me to adjust my action to theirs. This is obviously unsatisfactory, because it treats the decision to comply with instructions of the law as a parametric one.[35] How did the others decide? If there is no relevant difference in our position,[36] there must be a difference in rationality between us. Perhaps we, the rational agents, are in the fortunate position that we can adapt to the irrational worshippers of authority? But then their "irrational" initiative is rationally defensible after all: it anticipated our adaptation. If we are all symmetrically placed, we are only justified in obeying lawgiving authority if a pattern of mutual expectations to obey it already exists. But in that case each of us has the same reason to obey as everyone else.

---

[32] See ch. 2.6.

[33] Cf. Hobbes' analysis of "a commonwealth by acquisition" as basically involving "covenant", Leviathan ch. 20.

[34] Simmons 1979, 194; 1993, 262; Raz 1979, 247-249; Regan 1986, 20; Regan 1989, 1024-1029; Green 1989, 111; Alexander 1990, 7; Roberson 1998, 629.

[35] As Regan 1989, 1026, and Raz 1989, 1188-1189 recognize. Raz calls the person reasoning in this "collectively self-defeating" way a "cognitive free-rider".

[36] It may make some sense to consider citizens to have direct, and tourists to have "adapted" reasons to obey.

The second form of the objection recognizes this, but argues that this reason is not that authority has spoken. Rather, it is the fact that, as a causal result of its intervention, one and only one of the competing equilibria "sticks out". So you have no obligation to obey the law "as such".[37]

This may have some plausibility as an account of the normative effects of instructions given in the absence of formal conventions, as the instructions of the passenger directing people to the life-boats. Even in those cases it is open to doubt. It may be the case that what "sticks out" should in fact be essentially described as "doing what this passenger tells us to do" and only derivatively as "me going to the upper left life-boat". What the passenger does is more than planting a flag at one particular meeting-point and then walking away: it is his actual command we are to consult in decision-making. However that may be, the account certainly misconstrues the production of reasons by existing formal conventions, and it does so in a way I discussed in chapter Two.[38] It assumes that patterns of mutual expectations are built from an independent basis, e.g. salience. But as we saw, if a convention actually exists, there is no independent basis, and salience is irrelevant. If a formal convention exists, people mutually expect each other, know each other to expect etc., to do what the authority tells them to do. So what he tells them to do will become the intentional object of their expectations "as such"; by telling them he does not only cause these expectations to arise.

It is of course true that, even if we have reason to do what formal law commands, the reason is not always that formal law commands it. That is not only the case with avoiding *mala per se*, including the *malum* of making no fair contribution to the cooperative production of public goods,[39] but it may also be the case when formal law corresponds to an established social practice. However, as long as the lawgiving authority is instrumental in establishing the practice, we cannot pass by its commands in our practical reasoning.[40] Moreover, it is not as obvious as it seems at first sight, that no one drives at the right side of the road because the law requires it, for when a government decides that its citizens should start driving at the other side it will probably be obeyed instantly. And in many other cases there is no other custom than the custom to do what the law requires, and even experts in the field may have to consult legal materials in order to find out how their clients are to act. The main point is that we should not consider "it is generally mutually expected" and "it is prescribed by legislative authority" as competing descriptions for our reason for action, for on the one hand what the authority prescribes is only law in virtue of a formal convention, but on the other hand, formal conventions *do* exist, and in those cases we must refer to the authoritative prescription to find out what *is* generally mutually expected.

---

[37] Regan 1989, 1027.

[38] Ch. 2.6.. Cf. also note 26 on Finnis.

[39] But, as we saw in ch. 5.1., the law may be needed for the exact specification of our duty. The same is true for the duty to help people in dire need, and even for the duties not to kill, to rape etc. Boardman 1987, Waldron 1996b, 2200.

[40] As Raz 1994, 336 recognized, cf. Raz 1986, 49-50; Raz 1989, 1189.

Even in cases where only social practice or custom provide us with reasons for action, that does not mean that we have no obligation to "obey" the law. For custom may be part of the law. It may even be the case that we must refer to the actual practice in order to determine the meaning of an "authoritative" statute or judicial ruling.[41]

A person exercises authority over others if her prescription gives them a content-independent reason to act accordingly. Is this sufficient as a characterization? There are phenomena with a similar practical force which cannot be described as authoritative. What makes the difference?[42]

With agreements and promises the difference is clear: these are instructions which the deciding person gives to himself. (You could call this the exercise of authority over yourself.[43]) The same description applies to intentions.[44] As far as conventions are concerned, these are not imposed by any concrete authority at all (but "the authoritative power of the norm" is a very common expression – it indicates that norms, too, are often observed because of their mere existence rather than their content).[45] A threat, on the other hand, does not give you a real content-independent reason; it only gives you a reason to believe that performing a certain action will have unpleasant consequences, and it is this prospect which should compel you to refrain from the action. It follows that a command is not always authoritative: it may derive its weight from an implicit or explicit threat.[46]

It is more difficult to explain why a request is not authoritative.[47] A request usually gives information about the speaker's wishes. How much weight it has, therefore, normally depends on the content of the request. But the fact that a request is made can also be of importance, even if the content is known already. When Prince Maurice of Nassau had his political enemy Oldenbarnevelt, Grand Pensionary of Holland, tried for treason and condemned to death, he was willing to grant him a reprieve, but only on condition that his family would request it. (The family refused to do so.) I should say that even in that situation the weight of the request was not completely independent of the content. This is only the case if the addressee is willing to comply with the request anyway, whatever (within certain limits) it may be: "Ask me and I shall give it to you,

---

[41] See above, note 3.

[42] Cf. Raz 1986, 35-37; on the difference between orders and requests, also Raz 1979, 14-15.

[43] Therefore not surprisingly rejected by the first and most radical philosophical anarchist, William Godwin (*Enquiry*, III iii, "Of Promises").

[44] In my view, the authority one exercizes over oneself in intending is mostly of the epistemic, only rarely of the coordinating type, as it is in promising. See Den Hartogh unpubl.

[45] So Wolff, like Godwin(note 43), should consider promissory obligations and norms to be also in conflict with the principle of autonomy, as Green 1988, 32-34, rightly observes.

[46] Such a command – unlike a warning – can have no epistemic authority either, for it is not based on superior insight.

[47] I must admit that Raz' theory of exclusionary reasons, which I will presently criticize, offers an elegant explanation: someone who makes a request has created a reason and simply asks the addressee to take it on the balance of reasons; he does not ask to disregard other reasons for it.

even if it is half my kingdom." But then I would not hesitate to say that *authority* is conferred on the request.[48]

---

[48] Yet it is a request and not a command because it does not belong to a system of *enforceable* prescriptions.

# CHAPTER 7

## AUTHORITY AND RATIONALITY

### 7.1. Authority and Rationality: Wolff

In the previous chapter I have assumed throughout that it can be rational to adopt and comply with formal conventions. But is this true? Some forms of philosophical anarchism reject the assumption. As we saw, anarchists tend to pursue a negative argumentation strategy, showing the insufficiency of each of the alleged grounds for an obligation to obey the law. But Robert Paul Wolff's essay *In Defense of Anarchism,*[1] published in 1970, is more ambitious. According to Wolff, it is indisputable that no argument whatsoever will ever be satisfying: there are moral grounds which exclude a priori the acknowledgment of political authority.[2] In his view, the fundamental obligation of rational beings to be autonomous underlies these moral grounds. Wolff's reasoning is based on an analysis of the concepts of 'authority' and 'autonomy'.

By 'authority' Wolff means the right to command. By exercising this right, I make a claim on the person to whom my command is directed: I pretend that she has an obligation to obey me. But obedience to a command is not just a matter of doing what you are told. If you obey my command, this means that you do what I tell you, *because I tell you*, without regard to your own opinion about the merits of my command. If you comply with my command simply because you think this is the right way to act, you do not necessarily acknowledge my authority. The command only reminds you of a duty which you ought to fulfil even without being ordered. Acknowledgment of authority, however, always implies a *surrender of judgment.* "Where arguments are used, authority is left in abeyance." "Its hallmark is unquestioning recognition."[3]

To be an autonomous person, on the other hand, means always to act on your own best judgment of the balance of relevant reasons. For Wolff, just like for Kant, the autonomy of man is primarily a fact. Mature and mentally developed people are capable of basing their decisions on practical deliberation, after having listed systematically the available alternatives and having weighed the pros and cons. But moreover, for Wolff – again just like for Kant – autonomy is an obligation, namely the foremost obligation of man, the root as well as the core of all other obligations. It is not incompatible with this

---

[1] The background of Wolff's "philosophical anarchism", which rejects the possibility of legitimate authority in general, is formed by H.D. Thoreau's *Civil Disobedience* (1849) and William Godwin's *Enquiry concerning Political Justice* (1793). Wolff's essay was followed by a flood of critical comments, of which G. Dworkin 1971, Frankfurt 1973 and Pritchard 1973 are the most interesting.

[2] Cf. also Abbott 1976, 74: "The exercise of political authority is simply incompatible with the exercise of conscience."

[3] Hannah Arendt, resp. 1977 (1958), 93; 1969, 45. Cf. Easton 1958, 179 (but cf. comment by Green 1988, 14); Warnock 1971, 65; Friedman 1973, 128-9; Oakeshott 1975, 149, 157 ("authority and obligation do not argue or ask to be approved"); Raz 1979, 24.

obligation to take other people's advice seriously. Complying with the advice without verifying its soundness in advance, however, does conflict with this obligation. The only legitimate function of an advice can be that of a reminder.

Given his assumptions on authority and autonomy, Wolff's argument is easily predictable. Autonomy requires you to consider the pros and cons of a certain decision, and to base your course of action upon this consideration. Authority may allow the first step, but certainly not the second. On the contrary, it requires you to unlink practical deliberation and decision making. If it is our fundamental obligation to be autonomous, there can be no obligation to obey, ergo no authority. Of course, people may *believe* that certain persons or institutions have authority over them, and act according to this belief. But although 'authority' remains an interesting category from a sociological point of view,[4] acknowledgement of authority is always false. 'Legitimate authority' is like the round square: a concept that cannot be exemplified because it contains a contradiction in terms.

As expected, Wolff presents this simple argument several times, either directly or indirectly.[5] Many statements in his argumentation, however, do not fit. His view is obscure or ambiguous on at least three points.

To begin with, the simple argument is that autonomy and legitimate authority are conceptually irreconcilable. In many places in his essay, however, Wolff seems to believe that the invention of a political association which harmonizes both is an unsolved, though not insoluble problem.[6] (Elsewhere[7] he suggests that the creation of legitimate authority by forfeiting one's autonomy – e.g. through a promise to submit – is not unthinkable, though it is morally inadmissible. Such promises are reprehensible, but nonetheless valid. So, in fact, it is only true for an ideal world, and not for the actual world, that citizens can never be obliged to obey.)

Another obscurity is whether, according to Wolff, taking full responsibility for one's actions is an absolute duty which always comes first, or only one of several values to be maximized collectively.[8] When this objective of autonomy comes into conflict with other desiderata, is it allowable to make a compromise so as to achieve an optimum? Or is this completely out of the question?

Finally, the question arises what the obligation of autonomy exactly means: does it demand completely independent deliberation about *every* relevant action we take, or

---

[4] Since Weber, this "empirical" de facto notion of authority is current in sociology. (According to Weber, authority in this sense is a form of power, cf. Wrong 1979). But to be able, *verstehend*, to identify the acknowledgment of the right to command, the sociologist cannot do without a normative, de jure concept of authority either.

[5] "The concept of a de jure legitimate state would appear to be vacuous." Wolff 1970, 19, cf. 18, 71 ("the round square"), also 8, 10, 11; Wolff 1969, 602 ("inherently incoherent"), 607.

[6] Wolff 1970, ch. 2 (unanimous direct democracy as a theoretical solution, esp. 22-23, 26, 27), cf. 72, 78; Wolff 1969, 604.

[7] Wolff 1970, 14, 41-42, 47, 69-72 ("the sin of wilful heteronomy").

[8] Cf. Wolff 1970, 15, 17. According to Graham 1982, Wolff only intends to minimize heteronomy. But Graham, too, believes Wolff's reasoning to be inconsistent; otherwise he would have allowed majority decisions.

is it sufficient to confine ourselves to the *moral* aspects?[9]

These three obscurities are, of course, closely linked: only if autonomy is an absolute duty can it be regarded as conceptually irreconcilable with legitimate authority. But this view of autonomy can only begin to seem defensible when the moral, not the technical part of practical deliberation is concerned.

## 7.2. Authority and Rationality: the General Argument

What is the most plausible argument for philosophical anarchism which can be reconstructed from Wolff's rather incoherent exposition? I think it is the following.

(A) If, after as thorough a deliberation as is necessary, you have made up your mind that, all things considered, you have reason to do *a*, and you have no reason to distrust your judgment, then it would be irrational not to do *a*.

(B) The essential claim of the state – of any state – is to exercise authority over one's actions. (Perhaps even unlimited authority.)[10]

(C) But a person can only be said to exercise such authority if the very fact that she tells you to do something is a decisive reason to do it, irrespective of (at least within limits) what it is she tells you to do.

(D) Suppose the state's claim to be justifiable.

(E) Then it follows from (C) that (at least sometimes) if the state tells you to omit doing *a*, it is rational for you to obey, even if you had decided that on the balance of reasons you have reason to do *a*, and even if you have no reason to mistrust your ability to decide. Authority overrules private judgment.

(F) But this result contradicts our premiss (A). Therefore (D) is false. The essential claim of the state is unjustifiable, for no claim to authority over actions can ever be valid.

This argument differs from Wolff's on two points. In the first place, Wolff makes it immoral, and not just irrational, ever to accept the claims of authority. But even if we accept the Kantian doctrine that we have a duty to be autonomous, it is far from obvious that this duty means what Wolff says it means. (Kant did not think so.) In the second place, as we saw, at least sometimes Wolff seems to believe that we should always try to form our own judgment concerning the balance of reasons that apply to us, and even should act on the outcome of our attempts, irrespective of their success. The argument I proposed, on the other hand, only assumes that *if* we succeed in forming a reliable judgment, it would be irrational not to act on it.

By making the stronger claim Wolff ruined his own case, and made himself an easy prey for his many critics.[11] For it is obvious that the claim is false. Hence the

---

[9] Both these interpretations find support in Wolff 1970, 12-13, compare also 14, 15, 17.

[10] As is suggested by Raz 1975, 149-154; 1979, 115-120; 1986, 76. Raz goes on to argue that at least this pretention is unjustifiable. See my discussion in ch. 9.3.

[11] E.g. Reiman 1972; Bates 1972; Frankfurt 1973; Pritchard 1973; Raz 1990, 12.

ambiguities I pointed out in Wolff's exposition: they derive from a semi-conscious uneasiness about the stronger claim. It is impossible for any person to be an expert on all the relevant aspects of every situation in which she has to make a decision (how to be cured of an illness; how to build a house; how to present a case in court; how to cook lamb). And even if this would be within the reach of any person's abilities, there is no good reason why she should always maximally exert herself.[12]

The irony is that the strong claim is unnecessary. My statement (A) is all that the argument for philosophical anarchism needs. And (A) is not only true, it is a truism.[13]

This does not mean, however, that I am prepared to embrace philosophical anarchism. The argument I presented is certainly invalid. But the mistake is in step (E), not in (A). Authority, as (C) states, gives us content-independent reasons. But it does not follow that it requires any surrender of judgment. That would follow if, in forming one's judgment, one could only take into account *what* has been said by others, and not the fact *that* they say it. Political authority can be legitimate if, properly analysed, it does not require you to refrain from acting on your own assessment of the balance of reasons, but only requests its content-independent reasons to be taken into the balance.

It is true that content-independent reasons have a somewhat unusual position in practical reasoning. It seems natural to say that a person, when trying to decide whether or not to do *a*, does not decide "on the balance of reasons" or "on the merits of the case", as soon as she recognizes the supreme importance of the fact that she has promised to do *a*, or is ordered to do *a*, or advised to do it by a more knowledgeable person. But this way of speaking really amounts to an arbitrary restriction on the notion of the balance of reasons; the essential thing to note is that the content-independent reason can be weighed against the "substantial" merits, and be defeated in the process. That at least is the thesis I will argue for. Let me note straight away that there is nothing in the concept of a 'content-independent reason' that excludes the possibility of taking it into account in the weighing and balancing of reasons.

## 7.3. Exclusionary Reasons

If authority did require a surrender of judgment, it could never be legitimate, for it can never be rational not to act on a reliable judgment of the balance of reasons. This is the kernel of truth in Wolff's case which most of his critics did not see, and which I believe

---

[12] Cf. ch. 6, note 16 on Wolff recognizing the epistemic authority of the medical expert. His predecessor Godwin did clearly recognize the legitimacy of "confidence" in another person's "superiority of intellect or information", Godwin 1976, 240, but not concerning matters of morality, courtesy or political justice, cf. Roberson 1998, 622-624.

[13] Raz 1990, 178-182 sets out to dispel the air of paradox involved in denying (A) by pointing out that, mostly, requirements of rationality have been satisfied if you act in accordance with the reasons applying to you; you need not be guided by them. In Kantian terms, they require "legality", not "morality": conforming, not necessarily complying behaviour. His arguments show, indeed, what is wrong with the Godwin/Wolff view and make room for the indirect pursuit of rationality, discussed in ch.7.5-7.7. But they do not make the denial of (A) any the less paradoxical.

is still worth defending. Although, obviously, the name is not quite appropriate, I will from now on refer to this principle (A) as 'Wolff's principle'.

Though I made rather strong claims for it, I cannot prove that Wolff's principle is true. For present purposes, it will be enough to show that we can fully understand the practical force of legal authority in all its forms, including adjudicative authority, without giving up this principle. Though somewhat more modest, that will be an ambitious aim as well, because the most sophisticated and influential account of the practical force of legal authority presently available, explicitly relies on denying its truth. I refer to the account of Joseph Raz.

The basic concept of his work on practical reason is the notion of an 'exclusionary' reason: a reason not to act on a particular set of (valid) reasons, to exclude a set of (relevant) considerations from being the ground of a decision.[14] Whenever there is such a second-order reason, you should not try intentionally to do what ought to be done on the balance of first-order reasons. The exclusionary reason does not tip the balance, but overrules the result of the weighing process. An authoritative instruction, according to Raz, presents us with such an exclusionary reason. It seems that, if any exclusionary reasons can be valid, both Wolff's argument and my own are refuted. For in that case practical rationality seems to permit a surrender of judgment, any time we meet a valid exclusionary reason. This reason need not be decisive: sometimes just a few first-order reasons are pre-empted, not all of them. Exclusionary reasons "exclude by kind and not by weight"[15]; their scope need not be unlimited, but may occasionally be so.

As Wolff's principle seems to be at stake, it will be worthwhile to consider Raz' views in some detail.[16] It is not my main objective in the following sections, however, to decide whether the concept of 'exclusionary' reason has any instantiations.[17] Rather, my aim will be twofold. It has often been noticed that there are classes of reasons grouped together by Raz as 'exclusionary' which are more remarkable for their

---

[14] Raz 1975, 35-48, 62-65, 159; 1975b, 132; 1979, 16-19; 1986, 42, 59-62 ('pre-emptive reasons'), 1990, 184-185. Raz 1979, 18 defines the further notion of a 'protected reason', i.e. a fact which is a first-order reason to do *a*, and a second-order reason against acting for other reasons. "It enters the tournament field with most of its opponents disqualified from playing," Moore 1989, 851. These concepts have been widely accepted, e.g. by Hart 1982, 254 ('peremptory reasons', i.e. protected ones, but cf. Raz 1986, 39); Finnis 1980, 234; MacCormick 1982, 232; Regan 1987; Green 1988, 37-42; Schauer 1991 (with reservations) ; Shiner 1992; Morris 1998, 206.; Coleman 1998, 269-270.

[15] Raz 1979, 22; cf. 1975, 40.

[16] The conventionalist analysis of obligatory norms, as defended in ch. 1, is also inconsistent with an analysis in terms of exclusionary reasons. This appears particularly clearly from the account of promising both analyses provide, cf. Raz 1972 or Robins 1984 on the one hand, Den Hartogh 1998 on the other.

[17] I leave aside the question whether the idea of weighing reasons can account for the relations between moral and prudential reasons, or between consequentialist and deontological reasons, e.g. reasons of integrity. Kantian moral theories, for instance, prescribe us to act only on first-order reasons which pass a certain test of universalizability. Such a requirement provides us with a second-order reason, because in the complete description of the requirement we must necessarily refer to the first-order reasons. Obviously, it may be the case that such reasons (morally, or rationally, or both) "exclude" acting on some first-order reasons. But they do so by defeating their validity.

differences than for their similarities.[18] What I want to show is that the attempt to provide a unitary account of authority in terms of exclusionary reasons, causes us to misunderstand both epistemic and coordinating authority to some extent, but coordinating authority in particular. The study of the relevant differences is meant to throw some additional light on the nature of legal authority, and in particular should pave the way for solving the mystery of the nature of adjudicating authority. My second aim will be to show that even if some of the reasons provided by authority can understandably be called 'exclusionary', none of them violates Wolff's principle.

This means that, contrary to first appearances, it is not true that the validity of any exclusionary reasons undermines that principle. As we will see, there are at least two different classes of such reasons which Raz groups together, epistemic and coordinating authority providing reasons of each class. The reasons in question belong to the sphere of indirect independent rationality and of direct interdependent (strategic) rationality respectively. Raz is able to group them together because of a certain peculiarity in his concept of 'exclusionary reason'. It is fairly clear what is meant by 'acting on a reason':

(1) The reason is a valid one;
(2) you know, or are tolerably sure, that it is a valid reason;
(3) this more or less confident judgment actually informs or 'guides' your decision.[19]

On the other hand, it is less clear what exactly is meant by 'not acting on a reason'. Obviously:

(1) the reason is a valid one; and
(3) you are *not* guided by any judgment concerning its validity.

But is it also required,

(2) that such a judgment has been made?

It may seem rather strained to say that my shortsightedness is a reason not to act on the reason that the fierce-looking animal in the meadows is only a cow. But it seems that Raz is committed to saying just that; as we will see, some of the examples he employs – those belonging to the sphere of indirect rationality – can only be understood as relevant examples on the assumption that he is.[20] So we can readily distinguish between two categories of "excluded reasons": those which are confidently judged to be valid, and those which are not, or not confidently, judged to be valid. It will be clear that to undermine Wolff's principle (in my amended form), it must be shown that valid reasons

---

[18] See Clarke 1977; Gans 1985; Moore 1989, 854ff; Perry 1989, 927ff; Regan 1989, 1003ff.

[19] "One cannot act for a reason unless one believes in its validity," Raz 1989, 1162. But can one decide not to act for a reason if one does not?

[20] His rejection, Raz 1989, 1156-1157 of the "first sense" of the concept of exclusionary reason identified by Moore 1989, 854-856, might suggest the contrary. But what he finds objectionable in this sense is that Moore interprets some reasons for conforming with Reason indirectly as (first-order) reasons not to engage in deliberation, whereas Raz (as Moore notes) believes that there is often no harm in deliberation, for amusement or exercise, as long as one does not act on it, Raz 1986, 39, cf. 1979, 24. Moore, however, clearly refers to deliberation as a phase in decision making. Cf. note 32 below.

exist which exclude reasons of the first category.[21] What I will deny is that legal, and in particular adjudicating authority provides us with any such case.

## 7.4. Facts, Beliefs, and Reasons

Why does Raz insist on grouping the two categories together? This may be explained by the fact that he rejects, and rightly rejects, a subjective conception of the nature of practical reasons.[22] On his view it is *the fact that* x which gives me a reason to do *a*, not the fact that I believe x to be the case. If there is a cow in the meadow I have no reason to be on the alert, and if I believe it to be a bull, that does not give me a reason to be either. Of course, if I have this mistaken belief, I will also mistakenly believe that I have a reason, and act accordingly. That explains why citations of reasons in explanatory statements may refer to beliefs rather than to facts. But what I mistakenly believe to give me the reason is still an alleged factual state of the world, not my belief itself.

This objective conception seems to run into trouble, however, when belief is less than certain. For then, obviously, this is something which a rational person should take into account. Practical deliberation does not only start from relevant judgments concerning the facts, but also from a *calibration* of those judgments. Otherwise we could hardly make sense of epistemic authority. If I have reason to mistrust my own judgment to a certain extent, then my assessment of the reliability of my judgment (and my assessment of the reliability of my assessment) should be taken into account in the weight I attribute to any purported reason. But then, it seems, what I am weighing in the balance of reasons after all, is my belief about the gender of the bovine animal, for the weight of my reason is determined by the probability I believe my belief to have of being true.

Raz wants to resist this conclusion. Even in calibrating, he suggests, if I understand him rightly, we are still considering only belief-independent facts, including facts about available evidence. "Certain facts are reasons for assigning other facts, which are reasons for action, a greater or lesser weight than they would otherwise merit."[23]

Within the class of such weight-determining factors, however, there is a distinction to be made. Firstly, we have facts like the available evidence, which lead us to attribute some probability to something being the case. It is a moot point in the theory of probability whether or not such probabilities can be analysed in belief-independent terms, but let us assume, for the sake of argument, that this is possible. Secondly, we

---

[21] "The indirect strategy (i.e. achieving conformity with reason, not by attempting to achieve it directly, but by following exclusionary reasons) justifies following rules even in cases in which they require action not justified by the underlying reasons, *even when one knows this to be the case...*", Raz 1990, 197 (my italics). Schauer 1991, 93, complains that Raz "does not address the basic question "Will the rule...provide a reason...even when the justification lying behind the rule is inapplicable?" But at this place he does.

[22] Raz 1975, 16-20; 1978, 3; 1986, 84 ("Reasons precede the will"); cf. Perry 1989, 920-927. Even on the objective account, the existence of a pattern of mutual expectations should be seen as part of the reason, and to that extent it is not belief-independent. See also ch. 1.3.

[23] Raz 1989, 1178, cf. 1163-1164; 1990, 197-198.

have facts like our own lack of expertise, time, composure etc., which determine our ability to form reliable judgments. They may also lead us to rescale the weight of the relevant primary fact to any point between 100 and 0%. But whatever the status of the factors of the first class, those of the second are clearly not belief-independent: they do not depend on an assessment of the data, but on an assessment of our assessment of the data. (As a result, while the factors of the first class have a strictly localized impact on the reasons in the balance of reasons, those of the second class tend to have a general impact.)

It does not follow that we have to retreat from the objective conception of reasons altogether. What we are weighing, when weighing reasons, may still be the relevant facts, given, perhaps, their "objective" probabilities, even though the weight we attribute to these facts is partly a function of the reliability of our judgments. This will of course result in a misrepresentation of the force of those "objective" reasons as they actually apply to us: after all, this animal really *is* either a cow or a bull. We will also know that our weighing operation will inevitably result in such a misrepresentation. It may nevertheless be the best representation available to us.[24]

In this way, we remain committed to the objective conception of practical reasons as firmly as possible, only allowing ourselves to look at these objective reasons from the point of view of the deliberating agent, given his judgmental abilities. Reason requires him to take a reason into account to the extent to which he clearly and distinctly perceives it to be valid; it does not follow that his perception of its validity is the real reason after all.

But neither does it follow that Reason can allow him not to take a reason into account which he perceives to be valid. We may know that our attribution of a weighing factor will, on account of our judgmental abilities, inevitably result in misrepresentation, but it is quite a different thing intentionally to neglect a true representation. Clearly these are two very different moves in deliberation, whether or not they can be given the same description ("complying with an exclusionary reason"). That it can be reasonable to make one of those moves does not prove in any way that it can be reasonable to make the other.

### 7.5. Problems of Calibration

Practical reasoning with an exclusionary force does not just occur in the context of the exercise of authority, according to Raz; he uses the concept in his analysis of decisions, orders, promises, norms ("mandatory rules"), normative powers and obligations as well. What is involved in many of these cases is really the indirect pursuit of rationality.[25]

When Raz first introduced the concept of an exclusionary reason, he used the following example to illustrate it. Ann has been offered the opportunity to make a certain investment, but she has to decide on the offer within a few hours. However, she

---

[24] "Agents do not always deliberate about what to do on the assumption that their reasoning is tracking the objective balance of reasons." Perry 1989, 926.

[25] Gans 1985; Perry 1989; Moore 1989. Cf. note 20 on Raz' criticism of Moore's interpretation.

came home from a day's work being very tired and emotionally upset, so she believes, correctly, that her mental state does not allow her to make a reliable judgment on the pros and cons of the offer. Therefore she decides not to accept it, not because she believes that it is wise to reject it on the merits of the case, but because she is unable to assess the merits.

Why is this is a reason for not accepting rather than for accepting? According to Raz (after all, it is his example), Ann is also too tired or too upset to work out properly how her mental state might taint her judgment; so she cannot correct it for bias either. Instead she appeals to a rule of thumb (*in dubiis abstine*) applying to such situations. This rule, Raz suggests, is a first-order reason for abstention, but her mental state is a second-order reason for refraining to act from any other first-order reason.

Does Ann "surrender her judgment"? The expression is not improper here, but we should be very clear about the sense in which it is not. Ann does not give up her confident assessment of the balance of reasons to the pre-emptive force of a second-order reason; she decides on adequate evidence that she is not in a position to form the confident judgment which a rational person would need as a vindication of her decision. Ann does not deny any valid reasons their due weight in her deliberation, she only decides not to try and assess the validity and weight of those reasons, or decides to disregard any assessment she might inadvertently have made, because she knows such assessments to be defective. So, to be pedantically precise, it is not her "mental state" (being tired, upset etc.) which is the second-order reason for excluding other reasons from consideration, it is her defective perception of those reasons, which she infers from her mental state.[26]

This analysis confirms the conception of calibration I proposed in the previous section: the weight of first-order reasons cannot be determined by reference to belief-independent facts only. For Ann's second-order reason to give no weight to any first-order reason except her rule of thumb, is her assessment of the reliability of her (actual or possible) judgment concerning those reasons.

If we are justified in speaking of a second-order reason at all, it is precisely because it has this "subjective" character.[27] Compare again the two kinds of weighing factors I distinguished in the previous section. If the available evidence compels us to attribute a rather low probability to a certain outcome, that in itself is no reason to neglect this probability in our weighing operations.[28] If we are very uncertain about the reliability of our judgment, it may still be that we should rationally act on it, because we have no alternative way of proceeding. But we must adapt the weight of our reasons to the "subjective" probability of their being valid. (For possibilities which are mutually exclusive and together exhaustive, our rescaling operation will tend to move to 50/50.)

---

[26] Clarke 1977.

[27] I will not pursue the question whether it is possible to account for Ann's reasoning in terms of first-order reasons only. In Den Hartogh 1993 I failed to take into account the considerations of this section: indirect rationality allows us to intentionally neglect the low but not negligible "subjective probabilities" which calibration would lead us to attribute to some reasons.

[28] We may decide to disregard small probabilities in order to save time etc.; that again is a form of indirect rationality.

But suppose we have an alternative way of proceeding which promises better results in terms of conformity to reason.[29] Then we may be allowed to neglect those subjective probabilities altogether.

But if our judgment on the reasons applying to us is sufficiently calibrated, it would be irrational to pursue rationality indirectly. If lack of calibration creates exclusionary reasons, they are no threat to Wolff's principle at all.

## 7.6. Do Plans Provide Exclusionary Reasons?

Similar observations can be made concerning plans and private rules. When a person acts on a long-term strategy, he is said by Raz to give his own resolution exclusionary force.[30] Is this a plausible account? To a large extent it is, but not fully.

Compare two ways of proceeding. In the first case, we form a plan, and then start executing it without bothering to form a complete judgment on the particular merits of any new action at any time later on. This does not of course exclude deliberating on the choice between alternatives within the overall context of the plan. On most occasions the plan cannot be so specific that all particular decisions can be left to the automatic pilot. But it provides some constraints, and these are not to be reconsidered. In the second case we form a complete picture of the balance of reasons before every new action. (In the final analysis, this description is incoherent, for it presupposes that there is just one natural way of breaking a chain of actions into parts. But let that pass.) It is clear that the first way of proceeding can have many advantages. It saves time and energy, and possibly the anxiety of decision. (Modern life may provide us with so many opportunities for enjoyment that "act-hedonism" tends to become counter-productive.) Furthermore, not every time and place is suitable for making up your mind: the heat of battle is surely not. You may have many reasons for distrusting your judgment at times $t2$-$tn$, which did not apply to $t1$, the "cool hour" of planning. Finally, even if your judgment is equally reliable at all times, it may never be completely reliable; in that case you may be well advised to follow a consistent plan, even if it may not be the best possible. Following a second-best strategy may have better results than switching between strategies. In all these cases it is possible that you have good reasons, similar to those of Ann, either not to try and assess the balance of reasons at any later time, or not to rely on any assessment you may (inadvertently) make.

At such later times, we may perhaps be said to have a second-order reason to exclude from consideration any substantial reasons applying to the present time. But the basic reason is not that we have made a plan. Exactly as in Ann's case, it is the fact that our present perception of the balance of substantial reasons is defective, and it is

---

[29] So the availability of this alternative is part of our second-order reason after all.

[30] Raz 1975, 59-60, 65-71. The first attitude to private rules which Raz describes on p. 60 (in every case in which you are not sure whether the rule correctly sums up the relevant reasons, to re-open consideration of the balance of reasons) surely is irrational; it is bound to create more costs (in terms of time, labour, mistakes, instability) than it prevents. Cf. Bratman 1987, ch. 5; Regan 1989, 1010; Elster 1979, 108-109 on "control without rigidity". There is a problem here of identifying, without reconsideration, the right moment for reconsideration.

impossible or inadvisable to try and improve it. This is why we appeal to a consideration which, as we confidently assume, represents or sums up the unknown force of the substantial reasons. It is true that the availability of the new reason is a relevant consideration: if we had not made a plan, we would probably still prefer to act on our assessment of the merits rather than make a random decision. Nevertheless, the new reason is not itself a second-order reason. Rather, its position is analogous to that of the rule of thumb in Ann's case: it takes the empty stage.[31]

This has practical consequences. Suppose that at any time during the execution of your plan, you get a flash of new insight, or are carried along by a process of reflection you are unable to stop in spite of your decision. You become convinced that a particular action provided for in the plan would be clearly suboptimal (either because it is counter-productive to the overall success of the plan, or because the whole plan turns out to be misguided), and you have no reason not to trust your insight. Then it would be irrational not to act "on the balance of reasons" for all that, because you once decided not to do so.[32] Such an attitude to plans is a recipe for disaster.[33]

I conclude that a long-term strategy is not a reason to disregard any reasons known, or reasonably believed to be valid – which would make it a counter-example to Wolff's principle. Nor is it a reason to disregard any reasons insufficiently known to be valid; for the real reason to disregard these is a "subjective" one: the fact that they are insufficiently known.

---

[31] It is not a "protected reason", i.e. a first-order cum exclusionary one, cf. note 14 above. This result can be generalized: no protected reasons exist, purported ones turn out to combine a reason for distrusting one's view of the balance of reasons, and another reason for right action in that condition. Note that Raz did not consider Ann's rule of thumb to be a protected reason! Because it certainly is not what he calls a "maxim which is not a rule", his treatment of the role of rules of thumb in Raz 1975, 37-38 and 59-62 is not fully consistent.

[32] Cf. Clarke 1977. Raz 1989, 1156-1157 discusses an example of a private rule from Raz 1975, 140-141 Jill going on holiday to France each year. He considers three reasons Jill may have: not having to reflect on the relative merits of holiday resorts, avoiding uncertainty as to the future, and the anxiety of having to decide On his view, all those reasons are reasons for adopting the rule, and the rule is the protected reason for going to France. The second and third reason are compatible with calmly considering all relevant competing considerations (hotel prices in Ibiza etc.), cf. note 20 above. But if such calm deliberation leads to the calibrated conclusion that Ibiza is clearly to be preferred on the balance of reasons, it is irrational to stick to the private rule, whatever the reason for adopting it. This is clear for the first reason (which is disrespected by deliberation, not by acting upon its conclusion) and for the second one (which should simply be given its proper weight). The third reason may still have some force, but if it is decisive, one should wonder whether such an attitude towards decision making is not a general obstacle to rationality. The main point is that the private rule is only a first-order reason for going to France, and there should be other reasons, like the first one or, perhaps, the third, for not considering other first-order reasons or not acting on them.

[33] If we find that a strategic decision has been made prematurely, e.g. without full consideration of the available relevant facts, there are some possible reasons to continue acting on it (taking time to reconsider could be disastrous; or we did start to act on it and are in danger of losing our investments), but if none of these reasons applies, the decision will be cancelled automatically, pace Raz 1975, 68. The fact that it had been made has some force only when there is a further reason giving it this (content-independent) force.

## 7.7. Epistemic Authority and the Indirect Pursuit of Rationality

Does acting on epistemic authority imply its recognition as an exclusionary reason? Raz, of course, believes that it does, and the argument for his view is interesting.[34] Suppose we start making up our own mind on the advisability of an action, and arrive at a tentative conclusion, having found reasons pro as well as contra. Unexpectedly, the epistemic authority comes along and tells us what to do. If at this point we did not exclude our original reasons from consideration, we would probably weigh those reasons twice: once as we took them into account ourselves originally, and the second time as reasons taken into consideration by our expert. So we should rather accept the fact that we have entrusted to him the whole business of weighing and balancing those reasons, and withdraw any independent force we had attributed them.

I concede that it is sometimes advisable to completely disregard our own perception of the balance of reasons. But not because otherwise we would commit the mistake of double counting, but simply because, like Ann again, we have good reasons for distrusting our judgment. Even if we know some reason to be valid and relevant, we might be unable to determine its relative weight in relation to other reasons. In the absence of expert advice, perhaps we would have had no alternative but to act on it, but now we have. So, once again, if there is an "exclusionary reason", it is the unreliability of our judgment, not (or not only) the fact of the authority's advice. And accepting it does not bring us up against Wolff's principle.

On the other hand, there are cases where we reasonably take into account expert advice without disregarding our own judgment completely. This shows that scruples about double counting are easily overrated. For instance, I may now decide to refrain from doing *a* because: (1) there is this substantial reason against it, which I had already noted before the expert arrived on the scene, and (2) he advises against it. Perhaps neither reason by itself would have been sufficient to outweigh my substantial reason to do *a*, but together they are.[35] Or suppose I have made my decision on the basis of substantial considerations which I see no reason to doubt, but the expert advises against it, and I know her to be a person of superior knowledge. There is no opportunity for discussion. In that case, I may either consider the expert's judgment a reason to doubt whether I have calibrated my own belief correctly, or I may think my own belief so reliable that I doubt the authority of the expert's judgment on this point. This implies a reduction of either the content-independent force of her advice, or the weight of my substantial consideration, or of both, though to a lesser extent. But at that point I still have to decide to act either on my own view or on that of the authority, and this can only be a matter of weighing. A third example: two authorities of equal reputation give contradictory advice, and so I allow my own judgment, however unreliable, to decide the matter, just as I should have done if no authoritative intervention had taken place. These examples show that what Raz calls a "dependent" reason, i.e. a reason which

---

[34] Raz 1986, 58.

[35] Note the interesting possibility of a *counter*-authority: the fact that someone tells you to do *a* is a content-independent reason *not* to do it.

purports to reflect the balance of reasons, is not necessarily a reason which has to replace or to be substituted for the reasons it reflects, at least not to the full extent.[36]

As a matter of fact, none of these examples necessarily involves any double-counting. Take my first example. If I allow the expert's advice to tip the balance in favour of an alternative I would otherwise have rejected, I may argue that the expert probably had some reasons which escaped my notice, or that he makes a different assessment of the force of some reasons, an assessment probably more reliable than mine. Both these considerations contain a new, additional element, and it is the combination of these new elements which might be said to tip the balance.

Complying with the advice of experts can be a way of overcoming defects of rationality. We do not allow ourselves to be guided by the relevant reasons directly, but by the word of someone else, whom we trust (but cannot verify) to be guided by them. Indeed, the analysis of authority in terms of exclusionary reasons seems to Raz to *follow* from his Normal Justification Thesis: it is rational to defer to authority if and only if we may assume that by doing so we have a better chance of doing what reason *already* requires us to do, than by trying to meet these requirements directly.[37] For if this condition is fulfilled, we should not try to meet the requirements directly.

Accepting epistemic authority certainly should be seen in this perspective; and as I suggested, so should acting on a rule of thumb or a long-term strategy. Content-independent reasons sometimes displace and represent substantial ones, because our perception of those reasons is too dim to be reliable. The theory of exclusionary reasons, however, misrepresents this situation in two ways. In the first place, even when content-independent reasons are taken into account, it is not always the case that the substantial reasons they represent are wholly displaced; occasionally, the two categories of reasons may work in tandem to tip the balance, when none of them on its own could succeed in doing so. In the second place, it is not the existence of the indirect way (the exercise of epistemic authority, the adoption of a long-term strategy) which is our basic reason to leave the direct way, but the fact that, in trying to follow the latter, we are bound or highly likely to be led astray. Hence we may sometimes even decide, on the balance of relevant and valid reasons as we reliably perceive it to be, not even to start forming any conception of the relevant and valid reasons applying to our decision itself. The advice of experts, or our once adopted plan, or the rule of thumb, then supplies us with content-independent first-order reasons for action. And these may still be balanced.[38] For instance, against any other first-order reason we inadvertently come to be aware of.

---

[36] Raz 1986, 41-42, 57-62.

[37] Raz 1986, 53-37; 1989, 1179-1183. Cf. DeGeorge 1985, 36-37: "Legitimate epistemic authority is substitutional in character. Its purpose is to substitute the knowledge of one person for the lack of knowledge of another." Against this, Hurd 1991, 1633, argues that, if one has to decide about any decision whether the Normal Justification Thesis applies, one must consider the balance of reasons for that decision. That argument does not really address the purported exclusionary character of the reasons provided by authority, but their content-independent character. So if valid the argument would, contrary to Hurd's intentions, undermine the possibility of epistemic authority as well. But in that case it is obviously invalid: one may rely on random sample tests or on marks of expertise (diplomas, degrees etc.).

[38] Cf. Flathman 1980, 119; Moore 1989, 872.

So far, I have discussed only "exclusionary reasons" which are forms of the indirect pursuit of rationality. I have assumed that it may be appropriate to describe indirect rationality in such terms, but I have also insisted that it is basically a defective perception of the balance of reasons which provides the "exclusionary reason", not so much the rule of thumb, the plan, or the prescriptions of epistemic authority, even if any such alternative guide to action should be available. It follows that the exclusionary reason can have no force to exclude reasons we know to be valid. So far, therefore, Wolff's principle has not been challenged at all.

## 7. 8. Coordinating Authority and Exclusionary Reasons

It is Raz' aim to provide a unitary account of acting on epistemic and on coordinating authority in terms of exclusionary reasons. So what about coordinating authority, exercised in Coordination and Division games?[39] Its exercise is not a form of the indirect pursuit of rationality, it is therefore very different from the exercise of epistemic authority. If its description in terms of exclusionary reasons has any plausibility, Wolff's principle is really in danger. Happily, it has no plausibility at all.[40] There are three categories of reasons involved in some way or other in coordination problems and their solution by the exercise of authority. None of them has to be "excluded" in the Razian sense.

The reasons which coordinating authorities are supposed to take into account are not "dependent" ones in the same sense as the relevant reasons for epistemic authority. The dependent reasons of an epistemic authority are supposed to represent the full scope of the substantial reasons relevant to the agent's decision, and those substantial reasons are sufficient for determining the answer to the agent's practical problem. (Even if the answer is that it is impossible to make a reasoned choice between several alternative courses of action.) In the case of a coordination problem there are, indeed, a number of considerations which *restrict* the acceptable answers to the practical question – we want to meet, but preferably not on the North Pole – and these considerations should be fully taken into account by the coordinating authority. But they are clearly insufficient to decide the practical problem.

Considerations of this first category are not excluded by the exercise of authority. The agent is not at all barred from being guided by them. On the contrary, they define some of the conditions – in a bargaining problem: the boundaries of the negotiation area – under which he is rationally prepared to heed the decision of the coordinating authority.

---

[39] Coordination is the most important context for the exercise of political authority according to Raz 1975, 64; 1986, 30-31, 49, 56, 75-76; 1989, 1187-1194; 1990, 6-9. Recently, Raz has stressed that he is using 'coordination' in its ordinary, not in its narrow game-theoretical sense, i.e. allowing for other reasons than the maximization of personal utility, and not presupposing perfect mutual knowledge of preferences and alternatives. So do I.

[40] It follows that the appeal to the need for a unitary account fails as an argument for preferring an analysis of indirect rationality in terms of "objective" exclusionary reasons.

The practical problem exists because there are other relevant considerations – we want to meet – which, however, are insufficient to identify the action to be taken. They are, so to speak, reasons in search of an action to be reasons for. The answer to the practical question is underdetermined by reason. Of course, reasons of this second category should also be reflected in the decision of the coordinating authority. But they are not "excluded" by the decision either, for they are and remain the reason to do what the coordinating authority tells one to do. Starting from those reasons, but going beyond them at the same time, the coordinating authority identifies the action which, henceforth, these pre-existing reasons are reasons for.[41] His essential contribution is to create a new relevant fact – a possible focus of mutual expectations – which changes the pre-existing balance of reasons. In a sense, he also creates a new option that is preferable to the existing ones, on the relevant reasons, which the agent still is fully entitled to consider and weigh. Of course, this "new option" identifies an action which the agent was already in a position to perform, but it gets a new description (doing one's part in converging on an equilibrium outcome) which enhances its attractivity.[42]

That the agent is still fully entitled to act on the balance of reasons, is also clear from the fact that the very same "reasons in search of an action to be reasons for" which normally make the new option preferable, may still occasionally dictate a different choice. I will shortly illustrate the point with an example.

There is a third category of reasons involved in coordination problems, besides the reasons for rejecting options as possible solutions and the reasons for identifying other options as such. These are the reasons for choosing an action when coordination fails. In a bargaining game, for example, these may include the reasons for securing the best possible outcome (maximin), or for executing threats used to elicit concessions. Such reasons are, indeed, set aside by the exercise of coordinating authority. That does not turn its judgments into "exclusionary reasons", however.[43] Being excluded simply means here that such reasons either lose their validity – there is no reason to toss a coin if you know where to meet, or to execute a threat if the concession you asked for has been made – or part of their weight. They are "disenfranchised".[44] The exercise of

---

[41] Raz 1986, 30-31, 48-50, 57-60, recognizes that coordinating authority "adds" to the balance of reasons. What he fails to recognize is that the *only* reason which coordinating authority "reflects" (our desire or need to meet each other), is *not* excluded by it at all; the authoritative prescriptions are not "opaque to their background justification", to use the terminology of Schauer 1991. So the "dependence thesis" does not apply, as I argued before in ch. 6.3. The "dependence" and the "normal justification" theses are both modelled on the paradigm of epistemic authority. They imply that a directive can only be authoritatively binding if it is, or is at least presented as, someone's view of how its subjects ought to behave, this view "taking the place" of the subject's own view, cf. Raz 1985, 295, 303. Waldron 1996b, 2195 rightly points out that on that account, the outcome of majoritarian voting cannot be authoritative. In a coordination problem, however, a prescription may have authority, even if it is the result of tossing a coin. Raz 1989, 1192-1194; 1990, 195 suggests that sometimes we had better let authority decide whether a coordination problem exists than judge for ourselves, but this is an exercise of epistemic authority not essentially involved in the exercise of coordinating authority.

[42] It is possible that I did have some other reason to go to meeting-point x rather than y in the absence of authority, so the exercise of authority changes the weight of the reasons to go to x. But not in the way of a second-order reason (Perry 1987, 215, 222-223, cf. Perry 1989, 932; Schauer 1991, 88-93, 116-117), but by simply adding weight.

[43] As Macmahon 1987, 321, suggests.

[44] Moore 1989, 859.

authority has changed the relevant facts: we may now expect to meet each other *at x*. And of course, if the pattern of relevant facts changes the balance of reasons changes as well.

Take the example of a soccer team whose players, before going to play a match, receive special instructions from their coach. Raz believes, as many others do, that a motivated player should consider his personal duty as a ground to disregard all sorts of reasons for making certain manoeuvres which appear to be dictated by the progress of the match. He should be a consequentialist only in the dressing-room, but a deontologist in the field.[45] But let us consider the three categories of reasons just distinguished. (1) There are all kinds of things which the coach cannot forbid or prescribe, because they have nothing to do with the point of his having authority, which is to improve the chance of winning the game, in comparison with noncoordinated or only spontaneously coordinated play. This point is of course fully accepted by Raz: exclusionary reasons may be limited in scope.[46] (2) The players are supposedly interested in winning; that is why each of them, on balance, has a reason to do what the coach tells him to do, in the expectation that the others will do the same. (3) Suppose you had decided about your optimal course of action before the coach gave his instructions; his instructions do not conform to your decision, and you believe your own judgment in the matter to be superior. Nevertheless, you may have a decisive reason to obey him now: you know that the other players will take the instructions of the coach as their cue for forming expectations concerning your behaviour. By stubbornly acting on your superior insight you will fail to coordinate your actions with those of the other players.[47] Following a superior strategy on your own is *not* a way of improving your chance of winning.[48]

You are only required to "surrender" a judgment that, perhaps, *would* have been valid in the hypothetical situation in which no authoritative instructions had been given, or in the equally hypothetical situation in which you had been able to give them yourself. But if you take into account all the facts that are actually relevant, including the existence of a formal convention investing the coach with authority, and the fact that he exercised it by giving instructions, you may have a decisive reason to do what he tells you to do. A reason which is decisive *on the balance of reasons*.[49]

---

[45] This is a quotation, but I cannot trace the source. (My guess is Bernard Williams.)

[46] It is also part of the basis for his argument that there is no *general* obligation to obey the law, cf. ch. 5.5.

[47] The fallacy of Ideal Rule Utilitarianism, e.g. Brandt 1963, cf. Regan 1980, ch. 5.

[48] It could even be the case that, in the absence of any authoritative instructions, we all *would* mutually have known each other to have been able to identify the "best possible instructions", and so would have had reason to follow them; but now must ruefully recognize that we can mutually adjust our actions only by obeying the coach. "These people are trapped," cf. ch. 2.6. at note 40.

[49] This is pointed out by Green 1988, 113-114, 118, but he adheres to the pre-emptive conception of authority and draws the conclusion that no authority can be attributed to the instructions! Similarly MacMahon 1987, 326. Schauer 1991 recognizes at one point (ch. 5) that, if creating predictability is the substantive reason for having a rule, it is possibly rational to decide on the baance of reasons (taking this substantive reason into account) to decide to act on the rule. In that case the rule is neither a rule of thumb nor an entrenched one, so this classification is not exhaustive. In ch. 7 Schauer nevertheless discusses reliance and cooperation as possible reaons for entrenchment.

## 7.9. The Scope of Private Judgment

Does the instruction of the coach, as long as it improves the chance of winning, decisively settle the question of how to play for each player? Should they at least surrender their judgment in that sense? It may in fact be advisable for the players to refrain from speculating at all about the optimal continuation of the match: that will require time and concentration, which might be better invested in their play. But suppose a player suddenly spots a golden chance of scoring; to take this chance, however, he has to make a movement conflicting with his instructions. It may still be wise not to seize the opportunity; perhaps this player has seen such chances before and missed, or has reason to assume that even the slight chance of failure is too risky, because of the resulting damage to his fellow players' confidence in him. What I want to stress is that we are dealing with an ordinary weighing up of relevant reasons; the content-independent reasons provided by the instructions of the coach are only part of them, however weighty.[50] And however explicit the coach may have been in his prohibitions, it will always be a great pity to let a marvellous opportunity to score go by![51]

Could it be objected that, in such a case, we are dealing with a non-excluded reason? No. For how are we to determine which reasons are excluded and which are not?[52] Suppose the coach attempts to provide a complete list of excluded (or of non-excluded) reasons. That would be of no help at all, for in my example I assumed the reason to be explicitly listed as pre-empted, and even so it remained the decisive one in at least some possible cases. Maybe the list is provided, not by the exercise of authority as such, but by the formal convention which vested the coach with authority? It is true that, for any convention, we mutually expect each other to make exceptions (as long as we are rational agents). But we do not expect each other to make them by reference to any "list", or part of the manifest extension of the system of conventions as a whole. For any such list, it is true again that we expect each other to make exceptions. Not by reference to a list, though, but to the shared purpose to win the match. Because we have been assigned duties in order to win, our duty cannot forbid us to do what we know to be conducive to winning.[53]

---

[50] Cf. Gans 1986, 385; Flathman 1980, 110-112.

[51] So there is no reason to stop at a red light on an empty cross-roads, "looking ridiculous to the gods", as Raz 1979, 25 suggests. Raz 1984b, 148-149, argues that, because laws are sometimes roughly drafted in order to be more readily comprehensible or supervisible, a person can sometimes better achieve the aims of the law by disobeying than by obeying it. But this is also an issue which she can only decide "on the merits of the case". I concede that authorities occasionally can be justified in applying sanctions against such justifiable law-breaking. But to decorate a soldier who uses his brains and court-martial him at the same time, as Raz 1975, 43, envisages, seems a rather schizofrenic decision. For court-martialling will only be justified if toleration of the act would undermine discipline etc.; but then decoration would undermine the same effect.

[52] Cf. Gans 1986, 389; Edmundson 1993, 335. See also ch. 9.5.

[53] Cf. the famous decision of the Dutch High Court in the case of the *Huizer Veearts*, NJ 1933, 918, see ch. 11.4. at note 34.

If we see promising as a coordinating device, the same point can be made concerning the duty to keep a promise. If this duty provides an exclusionary reason, how are we to define its scope? If the aim the promisee had in mind in extracting the promise turns out to be better served by not keeping it, we cannot rationally prevent the promisor from taking that fact into account. This is even true when the promise purports, by explicit stipulation, to define its own scope.[54]

The usual objection to this attitude towards promising is that it is counter-productive, and hence self-defeating, because it will not produce sufficient trust to rely on promises. The answer to the objection is, of course, that such results should be taken into account. There is some point at which the decisions of promisors to make exceptions, and of promisees to trust, together produce the best possible results in terms of the shared aims of both. It cannot be excluded a priori that the point is only reached when promisors never make exceptions, but that is a contingent possibility like any other (and a highly improbable one).

Authority is not always a means of overcoming contingent limitations of individual rationality. It is simply impossible to solve a coordination problem by one's own wits; after all, we must bring about a convergence of expectations. If authority helps us to do this, complying with it is itself the "direct way". Coordinating authority is not an antidote against limited rationality; it rather provides a rational way, sometimes an ideally rational way, of coping with the fact that some situations of interdependent decision are underdetermined by Reason. In such cases there is no "optimal action", already identifiable for some person with full knowledge of the relevant considerations, and therefore indirectly accessible to another person with less than full knowledge. It is the exercise of coordinating authority itself which makes the prescribed action the optimal one.

## 7.10. Authority's Halo

Coordinating authority does not forbid to do what is reasonable on the balance of reasons; it changes the balance. This suggests the proper answer to the challenge of philosophical anarchism: an authoritative word does not require you to give up your own judgment about right or wrong, for this very word makes it right to comply with it.[55]

It is revealing that at one point, Wolff himself seems implicitly to recognize this. He raises the question how national defence could be organized in an anarchist society, and replies: on the basis of voluntary participation.[56] There is no need to compel the military to obey the officers because they understand this to be a necessity. The most reliable way to turn a military operation into a disaster is allowing all participants to

---

[54] Raz 1986, 93-94. Cf. note 70.

[55] Cf. Anscombe 1981 (1962), 44. The word of a theoretical authority, of course, does not make the thing true but only plausible.

[56] Wolff 1970, 80.

follow their own judgment. Unity of decision making – in our terminology: the solution of coordination problems – is essential to many collective activities.

This is a remarkable passage. For Wolff's objection to authority was not its incompatibility with freedom, but with autonomy. The problem was not coercion but obedience. After all, Kantian autonomy is asserted at the level of principles, not of preferences.[57] If you fear that your self-legislation is going to be undermined by your inclinations, you have reason to consent in advance that others may compel you to remain autonomous.[58] But even if Wolff rejected not only heteronomy but also coercion, the present passage would be inconsistent. For there may not be coercion in Wolff's anarchist army, but there will be authority.[59] Coordinating authority will be exercised in it, even if its exercise is consented to. But the fact that any soldier in any army has to follow his commander's judgment does not imply that he must surrender his own.

It is true that few commanders are aware of the point. This prompts the objection that my account of coordinating authority is reductionist. The idea of authority has a certain *halo* which my analysis did not capture. And the corresponding notion of obedience has a connotation of bending the knee as well as the head. The exercise of authority may have the effect of solving the problems, but only because people know that they all, independently, recognize its binding force. Everyone sees his relation to the person in authority as a bilateral one of unconditional submission, deference and prostration; everyone is prepared to "surrender his judgment"; and this makes it possible for such persons, if they see fit, to provide clues to the solution of coordination and division problems.

This description may sometimes provide a more accurate picture of people's actual state of mind. Perhaps they often do not understand the interdependence of their choices, and hence of the valid reasons for choosing a certain alternative. But if so, their way of conceiving the binding nature of the state's commands is flawed.[60] To this extent Wolff is right: no state has legitimate authority in that sense. What I claim is that in the context of a coordination problem the instructions of an "authority" can provide a content-independent and interdependent moral or prudential reason to comply with them. No cringing or bowing is required. If that does not cover what people believe "authority" to be, so much the worse for their beliefs.

---

[57] G. Dworkin 1971, 564. Cf. Wolff 1970, 24-25. Autonomy further implies that the agent follows his own judgment as far as he is able to, Wolff 1970, 46. Coercion does not affect this autonomy, as Menzel 1976 believes, any more than a sudden paralysis would. Wolff 1969, 610-611 explicitly acknowledges that coercion towards autonomous individuals can be justified.

[58] Wolff's only objection to Rousseau is that the majority does not automatically know better what I am "really striving for"; apparently, they would be allowed to compel me "to do what I want", if they knew. Wolff 1970, 55-56, cf. 51-52.

[59] In his book Wolff proposes unanimous direct democracy as a theoretical possibility to harmonize autonomy and authority. As is evident from Wolff 1976, 88ff, he allowed himself to be convinced that the proposal failed because, under such a system, anyone who gives his assent to a decision either follows his own judgment – and so does not comply with authority – or follows the community's judgment and is therefore in Wolff's strong sense, heteronomous.

[60] They could also rely on the state as an epistemic authority for identifying coordination problems and guiding them through, as Raz suggests, cf. note 41. That could be a rational response to a defect in rationality.

But should we not say in that case that my account, though perhaps normatively correct, is descriptively false? For what people, rightly or wrongly, believe to be true, *is* true in its social consequences.[61] Here a methodological point should be made. I have argued that the social functioning of authority can be understood without assuming irrationality. I submit that, as a defeasible presumption, such an account is to be preferred, even to what people tell us about the nature of their allegiance. It may be that their report does not do justice to their real underlying reasons. Our ascription of reasons points to an "order which is there",[62] not necessarily to beliefs about this order which are consciously entertained.

It is true, however, that the two accounts do not cover the same range of possible states of affairs. We might find cases of blind and total submission to authority, even against a person's legitimate basic interests, ideals, or moral commitments. In such cases my demythologizing (and perhaps rather Dutch) account of authority can be used to develop a sophisticated form of *Ideologiekritik*. Sophisticated, because I do not claim that all exercise of authority is just so much make-believe, intended to save on the costs of oppression.[63] Such claims always fail to make it intelligible how the make-believe can be successful to begin with. But if we presuppose that the exercise of authority can have a rational force, it becomes understandable how a misrepresentation of the nature of this force can be self-maintaining. To a certain extent the whole complex of social beliefs serves the interests of all, while this particular aspect serves the interests of the people in authority (who might even claim epistemic authority on the nature of authority).[64]

## 7.11. Authority in Adjudication

Consider two parties quarrelling about the question whether the performance of one of them comes up to the terms of the contract they have made. To avoid begging any questions, let us suppose that there exists an answer to this question: one of the parties is right and the other is wrong. They submit the question to the binding decision of an adjudicating authority. This decision differs from the decision of a coordinating authority because there is no problem of underdetermination. Rather, the decision resembles the judgment of an epistemic authority in that it is supposed to be fully determined by the reasons applying to the parties antecedently. Nevertheless, those reasons are fully displaced by the decision. For even if the decision is wrong, *and you know it is wrong*, you are still bound by it if you are one of the parties. As I argued, this has no parallel in the case of epistemic authority. So it seems that in this case at least, the description of the reason as an exclusionary one is fully appropriate, and Wolff's principle is incompatible with its validity.

---

[61] Thomas' axiom, see ch. 1.7. at note 46.

[62] Anscombe 1957, 80. In terms proposed by Pettit 1993 what this rational order explains is the *resilience* of the formal convention.

[63] Cf. Simmons 1979, 195; Green 1990, 263-267.

[64] Cf. Soper 1989, 216 on "double pre-emption".

But consider a slightly different example. Two people playing tennis disagree whether the ball is "in" or "out". The problem is that you cannot say that each of them has a "reason" to go on in a certain way, for they have to agree about the way to go on before starting to do so. You cannot be playing for a match-point if your partner does not think you are. So if these players cannot solve their disagreement, the only alternative for them is quitting the game, which, we suppose, has a lower utility for both players than giving in on the disputed issue. But that is not a reason for either of them to stop believing that it is the other who should give in.

This preference ordering is the characteristic one of a Division game. The difference is that the preferences involved are preferences concerning the results of acknowledging or not acknowledging the facts as they are, and this is a kind of problem one cannot properly describe as underdetermined by Reason.

The solution to a predicament of this kind is to introduce a mixture of coordinating and epistemic authority. On the one hand, the situation is treated as a bargaining game, and the authoritative decision simply identifies the particular equilibrium ("in" or "out") on which the players should henceforth focus their expectations of each other's behaviour. On the other hand, this is not done in an arbitrary way, for instance by throwing a coin: heads is in, tails is out. For the problem could have been solved by reference to the existing pattern of mutual expectations and the actual facts, and to forget this would be unfair to the player who had it right – and perhaps also to the other player, if he was sincerely mistaken. Besides, as a general procedure that would invite strategic behaviour resulting in a quick degeneration of the game. For these reasons, the deciding procedure should be independently informed by the relevant antecedent reasons.

On the other hand, the basic reason for complying with the outcome of the procedure is not that it is so informed; that is the difference with the exercise of epistemic authority. Rather, the players invoke a formal convention for by-passing their disagreement. This is, after all, similar to the case of coordinating authority: a new fact is created which changes the balance of reasons, even if it aims to reproduce the antecedent balance. That the balance is changed is most evident when the umpire makes the wrong decision, for the reason to comply with the wrong decision trumps the antecedent reason to stick to one's correct beliefs. But it can also be shown in a more general way: as in the case of coordinating authority generally, the availability of authoritative decisions creates a *new option*: neither to quit the game or make unilateral concessions, but to precommit oneself to the umpire's decision, in the expectation that the other does so as well. *On balance,* this interdependent choice is obviously better for both players than the two independent options of giving in or quitting the game. Though interdependent, it can be assumed to be accessible because it is symmetrical.[65] The decision to choose it does not require any underlying reasons to be disregarded henceforth. For there are no reasons left to do one's part in converging on the original equilibrium but disenfranchised ones.

---

[65] Which is not a rationally, but a morally relevant consideration, cf. ch. 2.3.-2.4.

Similarly in the case of the contract. The parties disagree about the question what exactly is legitimately expected of each of them. This leads to an impasse. The way out is to create a new option which can become the focus of a new pattern of expectations, without any of the parties, at the time of its creation, already renouncing his claim. They precommit themselves to the result of a procedure which is informed by an independent (and hopefully expert) judgment on the question in dispute; the procedure, however, does not bind as such, but on account of a second convention, a pattern of mutual expectations which was not relevant to the formation of the original expectations.[66] A new equilibrium is identified, but in a way which does not deny that an equilibrium was already identifiable before, and which therefore does not invite disregarding agreements already reached in the hope for better agreements to be reached.

That the balance of reasons is changed is also shown by the fact that altogether new types of reasons become relevant to the decision whether or not to obey the decision. Suppose that the parties to the contract do not expect ever to do business again. So there really is no impasse, only dissatisfaction of one of the parties. The problem which is solved by creating the option of binding adjudication is not really a problem of choice for those parties, but only for society as a whole. It is the "inconvenience of the state of nature" described earlier: insufficient agreement concerning the content of relevant substantial conventions, leading to unending disputes. If the problem is not solved, the result will be that hardly anyone will enter into any contract, because it is still too risky to be the first to perform. So the problem that is solved by the formal convention creating adjudicating authority, is really a problem of defective internalization of the external costs of non-compliance, and the basic reason for complying with the exercise of such authority is fairness.

So adjudicating authority is basically a form of coordinating authority after all: its aim is to provide the *manifest* focus of mutual expectations that was apparently lacking before.[67] But it is a form of coordinating authority which resembles epistemic authority in the scope of its "dependent" reasons. It is a way of reconciling recognition of the force of the original convention with the need to replace it by another, given the failure of the original convention to secure concerted action. The fact that adjudication has this Janus face explains the dual tendency in the history of jurisprudence of overestimating and underestimating its dependence on pre-existing rules.

Adjudicating authority is special in this respect. But that does not mean that it is completely different from legislating authority. Legislating authority says: this will be the law, though it was not until now; adjudicating authority says: this will be the law, because it is the law already.[68] Legislating authority tells us what we should do in a

---

[66] Unless a stage of "juridization" is reached, in which contractual parties only mutually expect that performance to be made which they predict, or even discover, the court will decide to be required.

[67] According to Raz 1980, 215 the point of formal conventions is finality, not certainty or predictability. Properly understood, this does not contradict Raz 1979, 49-52: the function of law is to provide publicly ascertainable standards for the coordination of social life. Hart 1961, 94, suggests that the role of adjudication is to remedy the inefficiency of diffused social pressure, i.e. to solve bargaining problems, not of the parties, but of agents involved in sanctioning or enforcing; but this interprets "finality" in the wrong way.

[68] Does it follow that unregulated disputes (in which the law does not identify who is right before the court does) do not exist? See ch. 12.5.

certain type of case; adjudicating authority what we should have done in a particular case. But because this judgment necessarily determines our expectations in the next case resembling it, adjudicating authority cannot fail to have legislating impact – whatever the official doctrine on the separation of powers.

So, after all, we have found no compelling reason to surrender Wolff's principle. There can be valid reasons to comply with authoritative decisions and orders, but these reasons still have got to win the day in the contest with other reasons.

I recognize that my argument falls short of proving that there are no such things as exclusionary reasons in the full-blown sense – reasons for intentionally disregarding the full weight of first-order considerations that you know to be relevant and valid. If my legitimate sovereign orders me never to take into account the interests of members of a population $P$, or if I promise to do so, then any force the order or the promise might have is obviously the force of a second-order reason. But this is not implied by the fact that an order is given, or a promise made, but only by the fact that *this particular* order is given, or this particular promise made.[69] What, in any case, I take to have shown is that there is no necessary connection between exercising authority and providing exclusionary reasons (in the full-blown sense).

## 7.12. Limited Powers

What about the reasons which should be taken into account in the *exercise* of authority? In certain jurisdictions it may be the case that courts "cannot" declare statutes void for conflicting with the constitution, "cannot" decide not to apply a statute the applicability of which is beyond doubt, "cannot" fail to follow a precedent without pointing to a relevant difference in the case at hand, etc. Some of these "cannots" should not be construed too literally, for if the court exceptionally does what it "cannot" do, its decision will stand. It might seem that these "cannots" should rather be interpreted in terms of exclusionary reasons.

We should remember, however, that coordinating authority is usually created by a formal convention. The formal convention to do whatever $X$ tells you to do, grants $X$ the power to tell you what to do. Given the point of the convention, the power will not be without limits.[70] It is true that if the umpire declares the ball to be out, while it is obvious to all that it is in, his decision stands, but if he makes judgments of that kind

---

[69] Some of the examples Raz offers, cf. Raz 1975, 39; 1979, 17; 1989, 1158-1160; 1990, 190, are misleading in this respect, as Ganss 1986, 392 notes, cf. Edmundson 1993, 332. Whether exclusionary reasons of this secondary class exist is worth discussing. If a promise by its nature only creates a content-independent consideration that may be overridden on the balance of reasons, a promise "never" to consider a certain important range of considerations may be necessarily defective (though not invalid): it may be impossible by any speech-act to make it the case that you will never have any overriding reason not to follow a consideration (perhaps a presently unimaginable one) from that range. A person who leaves a monastic order because he loses his faith may break his vows, but does not act against reason.

[70] See ch. 9.2. And see Schauer 1991, ch. 7, on efficiency and risk aversion as reasons for "entrenching" limitations to decision-making powers. Recognizing this (and only this) form of "entrenchment" is compatible with Wolff's principle, because it is a form of collective rather than individual rationality. The official is not empowered to act on his own better judgment because we do not sufficiently trust his judgment.

ever so often, the convention which grants him the authority will certainly erode.[71] Some "claims to authority" he might make will no longer succeed in creating the concordant expectations; worse, they will not even succeed in making an intelligible claim. If the umpire, or even the highest judge in the land, tells you to sing the Marseillaise, you will probably not even hesitate before disobeying.[72] For someone who is entrusted with the exercise of a certain power, the reasons she can seriously consider are to a large extent determined by that power. Not fully of course, for no power-conferring convention can prevent abuse of power – defined relatively to the power, the reasons for the abuse need not be morally disrespectable. It *is* possible for an authority to consider reasons which are not allowable from the point of view of the formal convention which granted him the authority: independent reasons. Are these not "excluded", if not by his power than by his duty? They are, from the point of view of the *convention* (which, on my view of duty, defines his duty as well as his power), but not therefore from the point of view of *reason*. It need not be unreasonable for an official to weigh independent and interdependent reasons against each other. Though, as I argued, the margins within which it is *possible* for him to do so will not be infinitely wide.

### 7.13. Authority as a Mark of Law

I have suggested that two things are characteristic of legal systems among the larger class of systems of anonymous (and mostly obligatory) conventions: (1) the significant role of formal conventions; (2) the significant role of the exercise of coordinating (and in particular "arbitrating") authority.

　　Although formal conventions may refer to other sources but authoritative decisions, and although authority may be exercised without being identified by a pre-existing formal convention, in reality these descriptions cover the same facts almost without exception.

　　It may be objected that this description does not yet clearly demarcate the area of the law.

　　*First objection.* "Significant" is a very vague term; should one not be more specific? If Hart is right, the basis of a legal system is a coherent system of formal conventions; the remainder consists of the actual prescriptions to be derived from the sources identified by the formal conventions. I intend to comment extensively on this account in the following chapters. But it will be obvious how these comments depend on the discussion in this chapter. The reasons derived from formal conventions do not displace other, content-dependent considerations, they only add to them. In particular, the reasons which restrict and motivate the judgments of coordinating authorities – the reasons of the first two categories distinguished in section 8 – remain relevant, both to deciding what to do and even to understanding what the authoritative prescriptions mean. Of course, I do not deny that with the introduction of authority, a voluntaristic

---

[71] Cf. Hart's scorer's discretion argument, discussed in ch. 10.5.

[72] Pace Raz 1994, 200ff, conditions for the intelligibility of a claim to authority are not independent of the content of the claim.

element enters into the functioning of the system of conventions: what we should do is going to depend to a certain extent on what the person in authority intends us to do. But what he is supposed to intend, in its turn, will depend on the context within which it is rational to recognize his authority: the Coordination or Division game. Therefore, the intentions we can ascribe to him are basically restricted to the range of outcomes which can reasonably be judged to improve on the outcomes of independent rational action (the status quo or state of nature). They are also basically restricted to the prescriptions of actions which may be required from persons characterized by rationality and cooperative dispositions. It follows that a legal system necessarily has to make room – whether this is publicly recognized or not – for fundamental substantial conventions, to be used in supplementing, limiting, and interpreting the prescriptions derived from its formal conventions. For if it systematically fails to do this, rational people cannot be expected to acknowledge its authority.

*Second objection.* There may be systems with adjudicatory, but without legislative authority, or, more speculatively, vice versa. Are all of these "law"? What about decisions made by agencies entrusted with the enforcement of the decisions authoritatively made? On the question whether the existence of legislating, adjudicating and enforcing agencies are essential to legal systems, I have not much to say. On the one hand, we come across systems lacking one or two of those features, which nevertheless look strikingly similar to modern legal systems in a number of other respects. On the other hand, I do not want to deny that the absence of any of these agencies makes a significant difference. So we have significant continuities and significant discontinuities; at which point exactly we should stop talking about "law" seems to me a matter of stipulation.[73]

*Third objection.* Schools, companies, churches, unions and other associations have their formal conventions as well: legislative or adjudicatory agencies, or both. Are these to be considered systems of law? The same point applies, though in this case the relevant continuities are not just logical ones. Not only are such systems of regulations structurally similar to systems of municipal law, they are interwoven with them. For if a system of mutual expectations exists somewhere in social reality, it cannot be fully insulated against other systems. This is even true of the "law" of a criminal organization. (It might be relevant for a judgment of criminal responsibility.)

Even if not all law is state law, it might be asked what makes it distinct from other forms of law. The natural answer is that it also decides on disputes with or between schools, companies, churches and unions: it represents the highest level in a hierarchy of arbitration. As we saw, that is the basic characteristic ("sovereignty") which anarchism is committed to reject.[74] However, the matter is actually far more complicated than this simple formula suggests. On the one hand, the state itself consists of a plurality of agencies, and it may not be possible to identify within this plurality one generally highest level of decision. (Not to mention the increasing importance of levels "higher" than the state.) If we answer that the whole system is structurally ordered, in

---

[73] Essential is "some degree of jural complexity", Golding 1975, ch. 1.
[74] Ch. 5.1.

the sense that for any decision it is decidable which agency has the "final" competence to make it, then it seems that we cannot separate school, company, church and union law from state law at all.[75] Even private persons may have power to make final decisions on some matters, e.g. their religious affiliation or choice of partner.[76]

It may be easier to give an interpretation to the idea that state law has a special place in an ordering if we apply it to another characteristic of the law: that it may authorize enforcement. Of course, non-state agencies may have powers of enforcement as well, but then the individual subject to those powers either has the exit-option to withdraw from their jurisdiction altogether, or has a right of appeal from it to the courts. That state enforcement is special, also appears from the fact that it allows itself to use means – taxation, emprisonment or even the death penalty – which other agencies are strictly forbidden to use.

It is no mystery why these two marks of the law – authority and enforceability – go together. If people disagree about their duties but agree that none of the relevant duties is enforceable, they may either decide to leave the matter unsolved or concur in freely submitting the case to any form of arbitration they may be able to agree upon; however, if at least one of them thinks that he has an enforceable claim, it is clearly unsatisfactory to have only such optional adjudication. If, on the other hand, the enforcing agency is free to disregard judicial decisions, there is no point in making such decisions. For those reasons, it is characteristic for a legal regime that the exercise of the power to enforce without exit or appeal is fully dependent on the decisions of adjudicational authority.[77]

A fully developed legal system will include formal conventions identifying legislating and adjudicating authority and the power to enforce the decisions made by authority. In Hartian terms: rules of change and of adjudication (and enforcement). Is it necessary, in addition to these, to postulate a rule of recognition? There is a problem which has to be addressed: we need some realistic account of the unity of a legal system, to the extent it exists, perhaps we should rather say: of the clustering of (formal and substantial) conventions into one conglomerate. And it does no harm to say that this is a matter of convention. But it would be a mistake to think of this convention as a master-rule from which all other rules derive their binding force. Statutes and court decisions bind in virtue of the rules of change and of adjudication; custom does not bind at all because some other convention identifies it as a proper "source".[78] And we cannot even identify the rule of recognition with the conventions which determine the duties of the court, for the law need not be fully identical to the totality of the norms

---

[75] Even so, this structural ordering may be far from complete, cf. Den Hartogh 1992, 247 with reference to the coexistence of legal regimes in Indonesia in Dutch colonial times. See also Bloch 1962, ch. 8, on early mediaeval Europe. In 19th century Indonesia as in 12th century Italy people had to decide in court for themselves which legal system they wanted to see applied to their case.

[76] It will be objected that this is not a supreme power, because it only exists as long as it is recognized by the state. I discuss this objection in ch. 9.3.

[77] These powers are indivisible, Hobbes, *Leviathan* ch. 18. Even in this case, though, Morris 1998, 219-221, may be right when he argues that all state powers have some room for manoeuvre vis-à-vis each other, whatever their constitutional hierarchy.

[78] Ch. 9.2.

which the courts are duty-bound to take into account.[79] Hence, though I accept that it is a matter of convention whether a norm belongs to the law, I do not subscribe to the Hartian doctrine of the rule of recognition as it is usually understood.[80]

---

[79] Ch. 10.4.

[80] As a result the thesis to be developed in the next chapters that legal argument cannot exclude all moral considerations, is not threatened by the argument that the resulting legal norms can make no practical difference beyond the difference made by the rule of recognition giving legal status to such considerations, Shapiro 1998, discussed by Coleman 1998.

# CHAPTER 8

## MORAL ARGUMENT AND CONVENTION

### 8.1. Hart's Block-ups

One of the perennial questions of legal philosophy is whether it is possibly or even necessarily true that the existence and content of at least some legal obligations can only be established by an appeal to moral argument. When Hart in *The Concept of Law* argued that law is a system of social rules, and that the essential characteristic of a rule is that the people following it believe they have non-coercive reasons for doing so, he seemed to open the door to a positive answer to this question.[1] For it seemed plausible to assume, firstly, that at least some of those non-coercive reasons could only be moral ones, and, secondly, that the existence and content of a rule cannot always be established without consideration of the reasons people have for following it. Indeed, that is precisely what I intend to argue in this chapter.

Hart, however, did not want to endorse these assumptions, and in developing his theory he made sure to build in a number of block-ups to stop the movement from moral argument to identifiable law. In this and the next chapter I will consider these block-ups, as they have been presented by Hart and in some cases elaborated and supplemented by others, notably by Joseph Raz. And I will argue that they all fail.[2]

Some of the block-ups do not depend on the special characteristics of systems of legal rules, they apply to all social rules as such. I will consider the following theses.

(a)  The non-coercive reasons to comply with the rule do not necessarily include moral ones.

(b)  Even if social rules depend on the belief that there is moral reason to comply with them, such beliefs only constitute a positive social morality. From the point of view of "critical morality" these beliefs may be considered false, and even morally pernicious. And critical morality is what moral argument is about.

Other block-ups refer to the nature of law as a system of formal conventions.

(c)  The authority established by formal conventions presents content-independent and, Hart believes, pre-emptive reasons, but moral argument requires us to weigh reasons on their substantial merits. The whole point of having formal conventions is to bypass the coordination problems which inevitably arise from the controversial nature of moral argument.

---

[1] The argument also rules out a view of the law as a self-contained system of hypothetical prescriptions which we can fully develop before asking which reasons people have to comply with it. Such views are criticized by Raz 1979, 10; Lyons 1985, 325, 339-342; Detmold 1984, 22-30.

[2] A similar argumentation strategy is followed by Postema 1987c; by Goldsworthy 1990 and to some extent by Shiner 1992.

(d)   Even if it is true that an appeal to values and principles is common in legal reasoning, the relevant values and principles can either be derived from formal conventions, or they must be considered as extra-legal materials which judges are free (or perhaps even duty-bound) to appeal to when the law is silent.

(e)   Even if the law – and perhaps all law – claims or pretends to generate moral obligations, the pretension may be insincere and/or the claim false. The external observer is not committed to accept either the claim or the pretension.[3]

I will consider the first two theses in this chapter, and the others in chapters Nine and Ten. In this chapter we stay in the "protolegal" world of substantial conventions, making the transition to the legal world of formal conventions only in the next.

"Legal positivism" will be a convenient label for conceptions of law which deny the relevance of moral argument for deciding questions of legal validity.[4] If moral argument is not relevant, what is? All legal argument starts with relevant "social facts": statutes passed by competent legislators, precedent rulings given by competent judges, custom. In most cases, these facts obtain in virtue of what I have called formal conventions, determining "competence". Some of these facts may obtain in virtue of substantial conventions, existing among either legal subjects or judges. The positive claim of positivism is that this is all there is to identifying valid law: the appeal to conventional facts. It will be clear that I have no objections against the positive thesis. But I will argue that, perhaps surprisingly, it does not entail the negative thesis, but rather its denial.[5] The establishment of some "social facts", in particular facts which obtain in virtue of the existence of conventions, requires moral argument. (If it is objected that this stretches our usual conception of "social fact", I agree.) Whether the resulting position should be called "positivism", because of its acceptance of the positive thesis, or "antipositivism", because of its denial of the negative one, is not in itself a very fruitful issue to discuss. But as we need labels, and as the position I criticize usually goes by the name of "positivism", it seems natural to call my own position "antipositivism".[6] This is not to deny, of course, that valid law may be highly deficient from a moral point of view (who would deny that?), and that this may be one possible reason why it fails to create the obligations it claims to create. My point is that, even so, the fact that it makes the

---

[3] As another block-up one might consider Hart's thesis that the belief that there are non-coercive reasons to comply with the law only needs to be shared by the officials of the legal system, not by the law-subjects generally. What he means is that the basic rules of the system may only be "accepted" by an oppressive élite, whether or not the élite consists of the officials of the system as identified by its rules. On this thesis cf. ch. 3.5. and ch. 10.5. at note 51. Though Waldron 1999 recognizes that it is "misleading to say that a system of law exists among the coercers, their troops, *and* those who feel nothing but the sharp end of their bayonets" (176), he nevertheless (and inconsistently) endorses Hart's thesis.

[4] The term "positivism" often is attached to doctrines denying other connections between law and morality, in particular: that the very fact that something is a valid law creates an obligation, perhaps only a prima facie one, to obey it; or that anything which is utterly without moral merit cannot be a valid law. I share both denials, cf. ch. 5.4. Some natural law theories, e.g. Finnis 1980 are positivistic in my sense of the word, and so is Kant's legal philosophy.

[5] Paulson 1992, 320, argues that the inseparability of law and morality cannot be asserted consistently in combination with the reduction of law to social facts.

[6] "Antipositivism is the ultimate sophisticated positivism", Shiner 1992, 99.

claim makes moral argument relevant to interpreting the "obligations" it purports to create.

The history of legal positivism since 1961 can be largely read as the story of a strategic retreat: one by one the lines of defence have been surrendered. Hart himself came to accept that the appeal to values and principles can be an intrinsic part of legal reasoning, without the values and principles deriving their legal status directly or indirectly from formal conventions other than the rule of recognition. He still insisted, though, that this need not to be the case.[7] Raz never made that particular concession, but he accepted that judges as judges may be duty-bound to appeal to values and principles. But what they are duty-bound to do should be called changing the law, not applying it.[8] He also accepted that the reasons people think they have for complying with legal rules necessarily include moral ones, a point Hart was never prepared to concede.[9]

It is doubtful whether the remaining positions, in particular the one combining all concessions, differ in any interesting way from the antipositivist position I defend, though formally they are still forms of positivism. That does not mean, however, that the topic of the relevance of moral argument has lost its intrinsic interest, but only that the cluster of positions which can be taken on the issue with some initial plausibility, should not be arranged along a single dimension.

It is my contention in these three chapters that the conventionalist theory developed so far provides a clear and independently plausible answer to the question. This result will bolster the reasons for subscribing both to the theory and to the answer it provides.

## 8.2. The Internal Point of View

Hart's account of a rule has been discussed in chapter One. It can be summarized as follows. A social rule exists in a group if, and only if
(1)   the behaviour of the members of that group shows a certain regularity $R$;
(2)   the members are able to identify deviations from $R$;
(3)   they tend to take a critical attitude towards such deviations;
(4)   expressions of this critical attitude tend to be followed by self-correction (or by justification, excuse and so on), hence by a return to $R$-behaviour;
(5)   the deviation is considered to be a reason for criticism and self-criticism; $R$-behaviour is considered to be justified.
All these elements are present in the conventionalist conception of a social rule as a transparent pattern of mutual expectations. However, one necessary element is added: the

---

[7] Following Hart I will call this position "soft positivism"; it has also been called "inclusive positivism" (Waluchow) and "incorporationism" (Coleman). Adherents include: Soper 1977; 1984; Lyons 1977; 1982; Mackie 1977b; Ten 1979; Coleman 1982; 1989; 1998; Brink 1985; Hart 1994, 247, 250-254; cf. 1961, 199; Waluchow 1994; Kramer 1999.

[8] See ch. 10.3.

[9] First in Raz 1979, ch. 2 and 12; cf. Raz 1984c, 130; and for his earlier views Raz 1975, 147-148; 1979, 155; 1980, 235. See already Beehler 1978; MacCormick 1978, 64, 139-140. For Hart's refusal to accept the point see Hart 1982, 264-268; Hart 1994, 243, 257.

interdependent character of the relevant reasons. For suppose that each of the members of the group believes that each has reason to conform to $R$, whether or not the others have. In that case these persons would not be following a social rule. People are only doing so if they are intent on coordinating their actions in order to avoid a suboptimal outcome. If there is no cooperation, there is no social rule.[10]

The difference between a rule and a mere regularity of behaviour lies in the attitude of the people concerned. You can only be said to be following a social rule, Hart claims, if you take what he calls "the internal point of view". A minimum description of this point of view would be that it is the perspective taken by a person who considers what reasons she has for choosing one out of several alternative courses of action, and in so doing takes account of the existence of the rule. On this minimum description it would be possible, for a free-rider, a conscientious objector, or others, to decide "from the internal point of view" not to follow the rule. Contrary to Hart's intentions, I see no reason to go beyond the minimum description.[11] Note, however, that a person who decides to comply with the rule (i.e. to do what the rule happens to require) because of a sanction attached to it, is not taking the internal point of view. For what matters to him is not that the action conforms to the rule, but only that it avoids the sanction. He need not even know that the behaviour which is sanctioned is also required by a social rule.

If law is a system of social rules, then what kinds of reasons do people who take the internal point of view towards these rules, believe they have for conforming to them? Hart always resisted the view that moral reasons are necessarily included. In his view the supporting reasons may be of many kinds: "fear, inertia, admiration of tradition, long-sighted calculation of selfish interests as well as recognition of moral obligation",[12] and it is not even necessary for people to attribute any particular reason to each other. We can only be sure that they cannot be exclusively motivated by the fear of punishment. It will turn out that the defensibility of this position is crucial to the success of Hart's whole enterprise of finding a middleway between traditional natural law and traditional positivism: a type of positivism which recognizes the "normative" (non-coercive) power of the law.

Of the possible reasons Hart suggests, unreflecting routine will not do because it is not a reason at all: it will produce only Austinian habits, not Hartian rules. Rules require a "critical reflective attitude". However, the routine may simply be the result of the internalization of the relevant reasons: we do not normally consciously decide to drive on the right side of the road. Such a second nature is compatible with a critical reflective attitude, precisely because it remains dependent on the relevant reasons still being in force. What we need to explain is, in the last analysis, not the actual compliance with the rule, but the resilience of such compliance. The fear of punishment is a reason, but not, as

---

[10] See ch. 1.2.

[11] Of course, the rule can exist only if sufficient people decide to comply with it. Because Hart introduces the concept of the internal point of view in order to explain the nature of social rules, it is understandable that he concentrates on those people.

[12] Hart 1958, 93, cf. ch. 1.2, note 13. Cf. Hart 1961, 111-112, 198 , 226; 1982, 158, 256-257, 265; 1994, 256-257. Cf. Raz 1975, 148; 1979, 155; 1980, 235; Green 1996a, 1694-1697; Waldron 1999, 176.

we saw, a reason accessible from the "internal point of view".[13] Like habit, it belongs to the world of Austinian legal theory which Hart superseded. Of the other possible reasons Hart mentions, we should at least require that they are not independent ones. Conformism satisfies this requirement, but it is by its very nature a parasitic reason: if everybody only wants to go where the others go, it will not be decided where to go. And even to the people actually moved by it, it is hardly a reason which they will acknowledge, either to themselves or to others, to be a good reason.[14] If these reasons are all insufficient, and moral motives not necessary, only long-calculated prudence remains to carry the burden.[15]

Is it up to the task? In chapter One, we have seen that this depends on the nature of the interaction pattern in which systems of mutual expectation subsist. In games of pure coordination – if any exist – people do indeed simply maximize their own utility by conforming to the pattern. In Assurance and Division games and iterated 2-person Prisoner's Dilemma games such prudential motives are also relevant, but if there is less than perfect mutual knowledge of the relevant utilities and/or a more than token discounting of the future, patterns of mutual expectations exclusively relying on such motives may still be relatively unstable. Therefore, I argued, participants to such conventions actually tend to rely on cooperative dispositions for justifying their expectations. And in still other forms of strategic interaction, e.g. one-shot and $n$-person PD games, conventions simply require such cooperative virtues for their existence. For agents who are only interested in maximizing their personal utility would have dominant reasons not to follow such conventions at all. As it is obvious that the law covers cases of all types, and in particular the $n$-person game of producing public goods, moral reasons for complying with its rules turn out to be indispensable.[16]

The conclusion that we need moral motives can be strengthened by observing that if it is necessary that some people have them, it is also necessary that most people have them. For the sense of moral obligation is characterized by reciprocity: people will not consider themselves to have an obligation of fairness to do what they are expected to do, if they believe that most of the others do so routinely, from conformism, from fear or for purely self-interested reasons. Conversely, if your own reason for compliance is one of these, you can hardly hold other people to have a duty.

## 8.3. Moral and Legal Obligation

---

[13] Hart 1961, 88, contrasting, as Bayles 1992, 57 observes, with some of the passages referred to in the preceding note.

[14] Holton 1998, 604.

[15] Social psychologists report that citizens of liberal democratic states tend to believe to have moral reasons to obey the law, cf. ch. 5, note 66.

[16] As we have seen, ch. 4.6., note 64, Hart 1955 suggested founding political obligation on a principle of fairness (mutuality of restrictions in the context of a cooperative enterprise). Significantly, this perspective is totally absent from Hart 1961, cf. Hardin 1985, 414-416.

That people should believe that they have moral reasons for compliance, is a conclusion Hart cannot consistently refuse to draw. At least two of his well-known doctrines require it.

The first of these is his conception of obligation. In his view, some social rules are rules of obligation, other rules are not.[17] And surely he is right in this, even if we disregard for the moment the status of power-conferring rules. Conventions arising in games of pure coordination ("Lewis conventions") will not be obligatory rules, for people expect each other to heed the convention for prudential reasons, and this is quite sufficient for the convention to be maintained. If, exceptionally, your preferences change in such a way that there is no longer any allurement in the original "meeting-point", it stops being a meeting-point, and so you have no reason to go there anymore.

(It may be the case, however, that you still have a moral reason of solidarity to go there, because of the harm that failure to turn up will cause to the other party. A pattern of expectations built on this motive would be obligatory indeed.)

It is clear that at least some legal norms are obligatory. How is it possible for Hart to maintain that even these norms, or the formal conventions determining their validity, do not require for their "existence" the belief that moral reasons exist for complying with them? The answer is that Hart believes "obligation" to be a generic concept, of which moral obligation is one species, legal obligation another.[18]

How do obligatory rules differ from Lewis conventions? Hart suggests three characteristics: deviations from the rule must standardly meet with serious criticism and pressure for restored conformity; the rule must be considered to protect the existence of the group or some highly prized feature of its life; and people may be required to sacrifice their personal interests in order to conform to it.[19] The problem with this account is that he does not explain how these characteristics are linked.[20]

The first characteristic might give the impression that Hart wants to interpret obligatory rules as rules made effective by coercion.[21] But this cannot be his real intention.[22] We should remember that he is talking about social rules; rules require "taking the internal point of view", and for Hart this excludes fear of sanctions as the dominant motive. It should not be the case that the expectation of unpleasant consequences in itself gives people reason to conform; rather, the reasons to conform are at the same time reasons to "punish" failure to conform.

If this is the correct interpretation, then the second characteristic rather than the first appears to be the more fundamental one. Interpreting obligatory rules as patterns of mutual expectations now points the way to the relation between the three characteristics. A cooperative enterprise is undertaken, mutual expectations govern the distribution of

---

[17] This is his view since Hart 1961. According to Hart 1958 all valid legal rules establish obligations.

[18] Hart 1982, 146-147. But see note 24 below. According to Hart 1958, the concepts of duty and obligation are "really at home" in the legal world, and exported from there to the spheres of positive and critical morality.

[19] Hart 1961, 84-85.

[20] Beehler 1978, 1986.

[21] Lucas 1977, 97, and other authors discussed by Bayles 1992, 52.

[22] Hart 1961, 175, 82, 88, cf. note 13 above.

costs and benefits within it. Important social values are at stake, and the problem of suboptimality to be addressed is not just a problem of pure coordination. It follows – the third characteristic – that it may not always be in everyone's best interest (as defined by the preferences constituting the problem) to conform to the expectations. It also follows that one necessary condition for it being reasonable to appeal to anyone's motives of trustfulness and fairness is the assurance that the others will take their share as well; nobody is going to have a free ride on the readiness of his fellows to contribute. This is the main reason for adding the threat of sanctions: it is not meant to supply the principal motive for conformity, but only the assurance that people will not take advantage of each other's conformity.

At this point we are handicapped by a well-known crux in the interpretation of *The Concept of Law*, caused by the fact that Hart does not discuss legal obligation in relation to these three characteristics, while it is clear that it does not fully satisfy them all. As he explicitly observes, not all legal obligations protect "important" social goods.[23] And even if it is reasonable to suppose that in the case of legal obligation social pressure should be replaced by legal sanctions, it is only generally, and not universally, true that sanctions are attached to legal obligations.[24] However this may be, it seems incontestable that his third characteristic applies: obligatory ("duty-imposing") rules are supposed to apply to people irrespective of the fact whether following them maximizes their personal utility or not. Indeed, it is obvious that it often does not. Once we exclude the fear of sanctions, what other than *moral* reasons can these people possibly have, or think they have, for complying with those rules, if they take the internal point of view? A mere Lewis convention could have no binding force in any intelligible sense.[25]

The law can only create obligations, and hence only claim or pretend to create them, by appealing to the principles we found relevant in chapters Four and Five: the principles of fidelity, fairness, and being prepared to accept a reasonable compromise, or some similar principle of cooperative virtue. If it eschewed such appeals, the claim to create any "legal obligation" would not be intelligible at all. The view that the law has a binding force sui generis is too mysterious to be accepted.[26] So we should conclude that there is only one kind of obligation, moral obligation, and legal obligation is the form of moral obligation created (sometimes) by the existence of the law.[27]

---

[23] Hart 1961, 170.

[24] Cf. Hart 1961, 212. Because of these observations some authors, e.g. Shiner 1992, believe that Hart did not intend his general account of obligation to cover legal obligation. But then his ten page presentation of this general account, far from being a "necessary preliminary to understanding it in its legal form" (Hart 1961, 83) is entirely unmotivated, Hill 1970, 60. On this problem of interpretation, cf. also Siegler 1967, 342; Hoffmaster 1977, 1312-1314; Hacker 1977, 4; Duff 1980, 66; Beehler 1986, 6; Bayles 1992, 43-53.

[25] Cf. Green 1996a, 1697.

[26] Ch. 5.3. Cf. Den Hartogh forthcoming, § 9, commenting on Ian Brownlie.

[27] Raz 1981, 455. Cf. Den Hartogh forthcoming, §9.

## 8.4. The Minimum Content of Natural Law

The second famous Hartian thesis which actually requires recognizing the essential role of moral reasons, is the doctrine of the minimum content of natural law. As this minimum content consists of duty-imposing rules, my discussion of the doctrine will also illustrate and confirm the argument of the previous section.

The "highly prized feature of social life" in this case is the survival of the members of the group. Under the 'circumstances of justice' (human vulnerability, approximate equality of natural ability, limited resources, limited altruism) this is threatened by the escalation of conflict, by the possibility of a surprise attack, by the unreliability of information, by the insecurity of investment. Therefore it is to be expected that obligatory rules will develop, protecting life, truth, property and contract.[28] Without them society could barely exist; therefore such rules will be found as the hard core in every system of social rules, whether "morality" or "law".

Why exactly is it to be expected that such rules exist? I do not believe that Hart is arguing on functionalist lines here, claiming that the existence of social phenomena can be explained by showing that they are indispensable for the continued existence of society or important features of it.[29] We should expect his argument to be reproducible "from the internal point of view", and this is confirmed when he sums it up in the formula: "what reason demands is voluntary cooperation in a coercive system". The role of coercion in this system is the complementary one I described: if the majority of the citizens follow the rules voluntarily, it is possible to bring the rest into line by the threat of sanctions, thereby assuring the voluntary cooperators that they will not be exploited. It is a remedy against the instability in the pattern of expectations caused by limited rationality and will power.[30] But why should reason demand voluntary conformity to the rules in the first place? Hart seems to argue that it is in everybody's interest that (almost) all should be prepared to accept some restrictions. But, as the PD shows, it does not follow from this that everybody should be personally prepared to accept the restrictions. It could be argued that we also need sanctions to cover that possibility. "Voluntary cooperation in a coercive system" would then mean: you should be prepared to contribute to the production of the punishment necessary to motivate anybody to accept the restrictions. But, as we have seen, this only shifts the problem to a higher level: everybody may have reason to desire that (almost) all should contribute, but this does not necessarily imply that everybody has reason to do so himself.[31]

It would require an extended excursion into state of nature theory to identify the games people play in the state of nature.[32] It is often assumed straight away that they are playing PD games all the time, but this is far too simple. People in the state of nature

---

[28] An obvious omission are rules concerning sexual conduct and child-raising, cf. MacCormick 1981, 98.

[29] Though his concentration on the value of survival to some extent suggests it. Such an account would be a specimen of the group-selection theory which is generally held to be largely discredited within evolutionary biology. (But see Sober and Wilson 1998.)

[30] Cf. ch. 3.5.

[31] Ch. 3.2.

[32] Hampton 1986, ch. 6; Den Hartogh unpubl. ©.

have a number of different decisions to make, and we cannot assume that they can all be described by one matrix. For example, given the availability of any natural resource not yet appropriated, they must decide to attempt taking possession or to abstain from any such attempt. Depending on their actual preference orderings, this choice may confront them with any of several possible games, including the so-called Chicken game. Alternatively they may decide to share the value of the resource, but that confronts them with a Division game. Another decision they have to make is whether or not to use any opportunity for reducing the natural power of a competitor. The relevant choice ("first strike" or "lie low") may again take the form of several games, including Assurance game and PD, especially when the resulting *overall* distribution of competitive power is taken into account, and not just the possible gains and losses in relation to this particular opponent. So the state of nature would confront people with a cluster of suboptimality problems, not only Assurance games, as Hart suggests,[33] but also PD and Division games. It should also be stressed, as Hobbes, Hume and Hart all do, that we should not assume "purely rational players", but players of limited rationality, inclined to short-sightedness, in particular to excessively discounting the future.[34] This means that even in Assurance and Division games, in which people have self-interested reason not to deviate from the rules, this may not be sufficient to stabilise them. For all these reasons, even the minimum content of natural law presupposes that people are susceptible to appeals to trustworthiness and fairness. This part of the rules at least will consist of rules of obligation, and this means that Hart's third characteristic will be present: conformity to the rules will frequently require some self-renunciation. So, even in order for the law to have the "minimum content" Hart claims it necessarily has, it has to draw on the resource of cooperative virtue.

The doctrine of the minimum content is significant for another reason. To introduce this, let me bluntly ask the following question: did Hart not, in positing a minimal natural law, accept a necessary connection between law and morality? The short answer is that he did. The rules protecting life, truth, property and contract are as necessarily a part of "morality" as of any system of law. To that extent, the content of law and morality must overlap. It is sometimes said that this is just a contingent fact, not a conceptual necessity.[35] But such a distinction would completely trivialize Hart's argument. For his aim is not to sum up logical possibilities and then decide to which of them the label of "law" must be affixed. That would be a matter of description of conventional use, or of stipulation to be determined by the pragmatic needs of theory construction. The aim is rather to find elements of social reality that form a structural whole, that go together because there is a "deep" explanation for their connectedness. Conceptual analysis, Hart says, is interested in words in order to enhance the understanding of things, and the analysis of law is in this sense a matter of "descriptive (or rather theoretical) sociology".[36] Therefore, when Hart asserts that the universal

---

[33] Cf. MacCormick 1992, 185: the more people have moral reasons to accept the rules, the more others have prudential reasons.

[34] Hampton 1986, ch. 3; Ainslie 1992.

[35] Soeteman 1986, 40; Duff 1980, 67.

[36] Hart 1961, Preface; on "natural necessity" p. 195, cf. 188.

presence of certain types of rules is a matter of natural necessity – think them away and there is no recognizable human interaction left –, he is making a statement on the most fundamental level of "conceptual analysis". It is only on the basis of "contingent facts" about human nature and the world that such things as a system of social rules or a system of law develop; it is for this reason that an understanding of those contingent facts presents us with the essential aspects of the concepts of 'social rule' and of 'law'.

Hart would not deny having pointed out a necessary connection of sorts, he would only stress that it does not amount to much. It does not exclude the possibility of legal systems that are morally criticizable to the highest degree. For it is not "necessary" that everyone who is subject to the rules gets any protection from them, it is not necessary that the rules regulating the use of force, property, or voluntary obligation are decent ones,[37] nor is any necessary content to the rules specified beyond the minimum. Everything that really matters is variable.

For the moment, I do not want to dispute these points. Even so, the doctrine of minimal moral law is arguably far more significant than Hart allows. One of the basic divisions in legal theory, related to but distinct from the division along the positivist/non-positivist line, and possibly more important, is that between instrumentalist and what I will call teleological accounts. In both views, law offers a means which can be intentionally used for achieving social aims. But in the instrumentalist view, its essential characteristics only relate to the nature of the means: it is a special technique, which can be used for any conceivable social aim whatsoever. In the teleological view, by contrast, law is primarily characterized by the aims for which it can be used, and its specific instrumental nature, which is not denied, can be fully explained in terms of its function.[38] The most prominent form of instrumentalism – I am inclined to call it "vulgar instrumentalism" – defines the technique of the law as the intentional changing of the pay-offs attached to alternative options of choice.[39] In Hart's more sophisticated view, it consists in the intentional creation of reasons that can be recognized as such from the internal point of view.[40] What the doctrine of minimal natural law shows is that this conception of legal instrumentality cannot fail to import some constraints on the possible aims of the law, and hence to introduce some "teleology". Why cannot a legal system exist which does not contain the minimum content? Reply: because there is no more fundamental interest than the interest in survival. But why cannot a legal system fail to address that fundamental interest? Reply: because in that case it would not provide a reason – it could not even intelligibly claim to provide a reason – for "voluntary cooperation in a coercive system".

The law cannot fail to provide protection of life, property and contract, because if it did, the people whose basic interests would be left unprotected could not possibly be expected to believe that they had obligations of fairness or fidelity to comply with its

---

[37] Cf. Raz 1975, 169.

[38] Teleological accounts are not restricted to forms of natural law theory, e.g. Finnis 1980 (the function of the law is to coordinate action for the common good); Moore 1985. Less substantial descriptions of the aims of the law are given by Raz 1979, 169-176, cf. 1986, 47-53.

[39] Cf. ch. 3.5.

[40] Hart 1994, 249; Green 1996a, 1711: law is a modal kind, not a functional kind.

provisions. But if this argument is allowed, it cannot consistently be ruled out that there may be other constraints on the possible aims of the law.[41] True, even if some things are basic goods for human beings universally, it clearly does not follow that every legal system will be in the business of providing them, and certainly not of providing them to all its subjects. There is no guarantee that all such basic goods will be recognized as such.[42] I do not even claim that any interesting list can be made of goods which really are universally recognized, or of which every human society recognizes at least a substantial number.[43] But the least we can say is that the aims of the law should be such as to make it understandable that people conceive of them as "goods", or at least as plausible components of an indivisible package of goods, to be chosen by bona fide arbitration.

### 8.5. "Accepting" the Rule

So far, I have described the internal point of view towards a social rule in terms of the possible reasons people might have for complying with it. Hart usually prefers to characterize it by saying that it is the point of view taken by people who "accept" the rule, and this indeed is a common description.[44] I have objected that one might also take the internal point of view towards the rule and reject it, but this seems a minor quibble. Let us say that the internal point of view is taken by people who either accept or reject the rule, the external point of view on the other hand by persons who – at least for the purposes of the enterprise in which they are presently involved, e.g. building a legal theory – do neither.

I believe that this way of putting it is seriously misleading, because it usually betrays a mistaken conception of the role of "acceptance" in moral reasoning, and in practical reasoning generally. As this mistaken conception informs the next objection against the relevance of moral argument for identifying the requirements of social rules, we will have to deal with it.

The mistake is brought to light in MacCormick's analysis of what it means to take the internal point of view.[45] MacCormick identifies a cognitive and a volitional element. The cognitive element consists in knowing that the members of a certain community display a certain regularity in behaviour, take a critical view of deviations from it, etc. The volitional element consists in accepting this pattern of behaviour as a guide to one's own actions. The cognitive element is shared between the internal and the ("moderately")

---

[41] As Finnis 1987, 63, notes, Hart 1967 proposes as the final point of the law not mere survival, but "enabling men to live and organize their lives for the more efficient pursuit of their aims".

[42] This is the basic deficiency of the kind of natural law theory expounded in Finnis 1980. Cf. Duff 1980, 81-87; Shiner 1992, ix.

[43] Nussbaum 1992, cf. Scanlon 1993.

[44] Hart 1961, 87; 1982, 154; 1994, 242, 255; Raz 1975, 126; 1979, 154; MacCormick 1978, 63-64, 139-140, 288.

[45] MacCormick 1978, 288-292; 1981, 33-34. Cf. Gibbard 1990 for a similar analysis, and my criticism in Den Hartogh 1999a.

external point of view, the volitional element is distinctive of the internal one. This means that the rule is relevant to one's practical deliberation only because one endorses it.

This analysis still does not take into account the interdependence of reasons. It can only be a fully adequate description of being guided by a private rule; hence in so far as it describes a "community", the community consists of people who concur in being guided by the same private rule. The mistake of the analysis is its *monadological* character.

Suppose you are a tourist coming to a country in which people are used to driving on the lefthand side of the road. Then you have a reason to do so as well. It is not necessary for you to make any decision to "accept" the rule; indeed it makes little sense to say that you have decided to conform to the rule because you accept it. The relevant pattern of expectations exists as a matter of social fact; given your preference orderings (or your value beliefs), you cannot consistently deny this fact to give you a reason to do what you are expected to do. There is a "volitional element" involved, but it is only an ordering of preferences over possible outcomes, not an attitude towards the rule.

The situation is more complex when it comes to moral reasons to comply with a duty-imposing rule. As I have argued, such reasons do not result from patterns of expectations and "antecedent" preference-orderings only; it is also necessary that *cooperative dispositions* are widespread within the relevant population. Such dispositions have an internal reference to the existence of conventions: being trustworthy, for example, means being prepared to honour legitimate expectations, and being fair means being prepared to renounce exploiting them. From the fact that such dispositions are required for the maintenance of the corresponding conventions, however, one cannot conclude that the existence of the conventions is only practically relevant for people "accepting" them. For, on the one hand, one cannot decide to be trustworthy or fair with reference to one particular convention only. If you have those general dispositions, the question whether you have reason to follow a particular rule in a particular case is a decidable one. The dispositions do not allow you to pick and choose the rules of your liking. On the other hand, even if such dispositions must be widespread for the convention to exist, that does not mean that the convention only "applies" to the individuals who have them.[46] Even if you lack the disposition you will be expected to act as the convention requires, and people will know that you know they are expected to do the same. Whatever your volitional state, you belong to the people who do the expecting and who know themselves to be the object of it. And this fact cannot fail to be relevant to your deliberations, whether eventually you decide to comply or not. It is not on account of your attitude or decision that it becomes relevant. For example, it cannot be the case that you are only properly held liable for harm caused by your negligence if you are prepared to "accept" the relevant principles of liability.[47]

To the extent that a volitional element – the existence of cooperative dispositions – is necessary, it is presupposed in the cognitive element: the convention could not exist without it. But if the cognitive element is given, no further volitional element is needed for you to take the internal point of view.

---

[46] Cf. ch. 2.9.

[47] Cf. my criticism of the consent theory of political obligation, ch. 4.2.

I have conceded – indeed, I want to stress – that for any person of cooperative virtue the question whether a particular convention generates reasons for conforming action in a particular case, may be open to debate. Perhaps the cooperative enterprise sustained by the pattern of mutual expectations does not appear to be aimed at any "good" or package of goods at all, but is destructive of social capital. Or the distribution of the benefits and burdens is such that you cannot be said to have a requirement of fairness to contribute. If your answer to these debatable questions leads you to conclude that you have reasons to conform, then you may be said, innocently, to "accept the rule". But this acceptance is only a practical belief, possibly incorrect, about the relevant reasons for your decision; it does not create any new reasons.[48] You do not decide to let the reasons count, you only recognize their weight. So the debate cannot be settled by each of the participants making his own "decision of principle". You cannot opt out of being the proper object of other people's expectations by making any such discretionary choice. Therefore, if you say that you follow the rule because you accept it, this cannot be the final explanation; it makes sense but it is hardly informative. You will be asked why you accept the rule, and your answer will explain why you follow the rule directly, without any reference to your acceptance.

Throughout *The Concept of Law,* Hart strove to avoid making any commitments to meta-ethical views. However, it is clear that the notion of "acceptance" has its source in a non-cognitivist view, and discrediting the notion implies discrediting that view.[49] Non-cognitivism may perhaps more appropriately be called speaker-relativism. It is the doctrine that anyone making a normative statement refers in the end to standards which take their relevance from the fact that she, autonomously, has "chosen" them, has "committed" herself to them, or has a "pro-attitude" towards them. As an analysis of the general notion of "having a reason", this is quite implausible. A has a reason to do x, if doing x is the one and only way to realize his standing projects or to satisfy his needs; I cannot but assent that he has this reason when I learn the facts of the case; it does not matter in the least what standards I adhere to personally.[50] For the notion of "following a social rule", speaker-relativism is an even more implausible doctrine, as it makes every reason necessarily an independent one. It suggests the monadological picture of a number of people each of whom, independently of the others, decides for personal reasons to take one particular private rule as a guide to his actions and his judgments. When these people come together, they will as a matter of fact display a regularity in their behaviour and judgment, but the convergence will be accidental; they are not following a social rule. This will even be the case when their decisions to "accept" the rule are causally related to each other. The picture is monadological because each person can only take an external

---

[48] In Den Hartogh unpubl. (b) I argue that intention normally only has epistemic authority.

[49] Cf. Hart 1961, 188; 1963, closing pages; 1982, 159; 1994, 254. Interestingly, Hart's early criticism of the excessively "protestant" character of the meta-ethics of his time, Hart 1958, 100, seems to address its speaker-relativism.

[50] Den Hartogh 1980. This is consistent with the amended Humean view of reasons I considered in ch. 1.3. (facts only constitute reasons for an agent against the background of her actual desires) because that is a form of agent-, not of speaker-relativism.

point of view towards the reasons that move the others. Of course I can endorse your reasons, but that is strictly irrelevant to your reasoning.

I conclude that people taking the internal point of view may eventually come to think that they have reason to accept or reject the rule, but it is not by their acceptance or rejection that they actually *take* the point of view. The internal point of view towards a convention is taken by a person who is a participant to the convention in the sense described (expecting others to act in a certain way and being expected by them to act in the same way), and who now tries to figure out what she should do on a particular occasion to which the convention is relevant.

The external point of view towards a rule, on the other hand, is occupied by a person who either is not a participant to the convention at all, or who is presently not involved in practical reasoning but in describing or explaining the practical reasoning of the participants. The external and the internal points of view are both purely cognitive. Does it follow that the external point of view fully reproduces the cognitive judgments made from the internal one? Not quite.

To articulate the difference, let us first add a further refinement to our description of the internal point of view, once more deviating from Hart in doing so. To the distinction between points of view, Hart wants to correlate a distinction between types of statement. In *The Concept of Law* he simply defined the internal statement as a statement made by someone who takes the internal point of view towards a rule, i.e. accepts it as providing guidance to his actions. Such a statement would be: "I ($X$) have now (at time $t$-1) a reason to do $x$, because there exists a transparent pattern of mutual expectations requiring it." But this same statement: "$X$ has at $t$-1...etc." can be made by myself at another time, or by anyone else at any time, without changing its truth value. In both cases, as Hart recognized in later work, a normative judgment is made applying the rule.[51] Hence, even in the second case, the statement is not just the external statement of an observer reporting possibly false beliefs. However, the distinction between the cases is not that between a "committed" and a "detached" use of the rule, as he went on to say. For I may be wholeheartedly "committed" to the rule, but nevertheless apply it in a judgment which has no practical consequences whatsoever, simply because the conditions are not satisfied under which it would have such consequences. I am not, at that particular moment, involved in a process of deliberation, to which the pattern of mutual expectations is relevant. But I am involved in practical reasoning (and not in description or explanation). My conclusions may be true, and I may even be prepared to commit myself to act in conformity with them as soon as they become relevant. But at this time they are not. The main difference between a judge and a writer on Roman Law lies in the fact that the statements of the latter have no legal consequences. But the reason is not that he has not accepted the rules of the system, or accepted them only "hypothetically". The reason is that he has no normative authority, and therefore is not in a position to deliberate on an authoritative pronouncement. (He may have epistemic authority, however, and this shows that drawing conclusions from practical reasoning is a

---

51 Hart 1982, 153-155, following Raz 1975, 171-177; 1979, 153-157; 1980, 234-238; cf. Finnis 1980, 234-236; MacCormick 1981, 38-40.

cognitive enterprise anyway, whether or not at the present time it is also a pertinent contribution to deliberation.)

So we should redescribe the internal point of view as regards a system of conventions in the following way. It is taken by anyone who tries to figure out what *any participant to the convention* should do on any possible occasion to which the convention is relevant.

Still, the notion of "detached" engament in practical reasoning seems to make sense. Suppose you are a Dutch legal scholar discussing a case of French law. You may recognize that it is debatable whether e.g. the clear wording of a statute really creates reasons to act accordingly, and you may be inclined to give a negative answer to the question. Nevertheless, you may know that the French legal community, wedded to a legalistic attitude as it is, will answer the question in the affirmative, and you may go on taking their view as a premiss of your reasoning. As a matter of fact, you need not have any view on the matter at all, you may simply suspend belief. Still, you are involved in practical reasoning, not in description or explanation, but now you are really reasoning in a "detached" way. Note, however, that what you fail to be committed to is a matter of belief, not of attitude!

Obviously, the option of detached reasoning is also open to participants to a convention. The conclusion of such an argument is not: you are legitimately expected to do *x*, nor: you will actually be expected to do *x*, whether legitimately or not, but: if you are legitimately expected to do *x*, you are also legitimately expected to do *y*. But then, of course, such an argument may also be reproduced from an external point of view, in reporting, explaining or predicting behaviour. The observer may know people to take a certain position, rightly or wrongly, and be able to predict that they will also take a second position, simply because it follows from the first. What distinguishes his point of view from the internal one, is that he is not committed to the truth of any of the beliefs he reports. But, again, that is a difference in belief, not in attitude.

So even if it is the same body of beliefs to which internal and external statements refer, they do so in different ways. The typical form of the internal reasoning is: given those beliefs, it follows that *x*. The typical form of the external statement is: given the truth of those beliefs, we may predict people to believe *x* as well.

Usually these statements will be closely related. For given the fact that people have a certain belief *x*, the prediction that they will have another belief *y* is usually explained to everyone's satisfaction by pointing out that *y* follows from *x*. If it does not, we need far more extensive explanations. It follows that, if certain forms of argument are necessary to see the connection between *x* and *y*, the external observer must be competent in that form of argument in order to make the corresponding predictions. And the points that compel her to suspend belief are precisely the points at which she owes us additional explanations.

To summarize, we have a series of different positions. The first position is that of an agent involved in deliberation and considering what is required by a system of conventions relevant to his decision. The second position is taken by anyone who is not trying to reach a decision to be executed presently, but only for a past or a possible case. The third position is taken by a person who, involved in similar considerations, suspends his rational acceptance of some of his premises or intermediate conclusions. The fourth position is that of a person who is involved in describing or explaining the beliefs and actions of the participants of the system of conventions. The second, the third and even the fourth position must to a large extent "mirror" the first one. The first and second position are characterized by zero tolerance for known and identifiable error: whoever reasons, reasons *sub specie veri*. On the third and fourth position some identifiable errors can be allowed, but only against a background of true belief, shared with the first and second position.[52]

## 8.6. Positive and Critical Morality

I have argued that, in protolegal systems of duty-imposing social rules, people taking the internal point of view will by and large consider themselves to have moral reasons for complying with the rules.[53] They will only do so if they believe that such compliance contributes on the whole to the realization of some worthwhile end or package of ends, and if minimum conditions for the appeal to the cooperative virtues of trustworthiness and fairness are satisfied. When it is not immediately obvious what the rules require, they will try to identify the required action by extrapolating from clear cases. In doing so their reasoning will be constrained both by their understanding of the value of the cooperative enterprise as a whole, and of the principles of fidelity and fairness which are supposed to sustain it. Hence moral argument is relevant to the identification of the relevant requirements.

Hart would make the following final objection against this line of argument: what it shows, at best, is the relevance of considerations of positive or social morality, not of critical or enlightened morality.[54] "Positive morality" is something to be studied by social science; normatively it has to be judged by the standards of critical morality, and

---

[52] Hart 1961 almost always deliberately takes the external point of view. He does not say: people have reason... etc., but only: they think they have reason..., cf. e.g. p. 54-56. But on p. 82 for once he says that deviations from the rules *are a reason or justification* for hostile reactions. This is significant, for he has argued before that the statement *'X* has an obligation" is not a psychological one, translatable in terms of *X*'s beliefs and motives; presumably it rather suggests correct or justifiable beliefs. But then we cannot leave out the notion of correctness from the external point of view altogether. "Universal mistake is unthinkable... because... massive error erodes the background of true belief against which alone failure can be construed." Davidson 1980, 221, cf. 290. Cf. ch. 10.5.

[53] Holton 1998, 611 ff., suggests that this is compatible with denying the relevance of moral argument to questions of legal obligation, because it does not follow that legal obligation statements are identical in meaning to moral obligation statements, they may only pragmatically imply them. But on the one hand, this is implausible because, if legal obligation statements do not themselves assert anything about rule-following which is relevant to practical reasoning or critical reflection, it is hard to understand what they could mean at all. On the other hand, even if it is true, it is enough to establish the relevance of moral argument, for in interpreting what people say we assume them to be committed to the pragmatical implications of their assertions as much as to their meaning.

[54] The terms "positive" and "critical" morality are introduced in Hart 1963, 20. The term "positive" morality is taken from Austin, cf. Hart 1961, 252, note on p. 165. Hart 1961 speaks of the "conventional" or "accepted" morality of a social group (165, 188, 196) or "social" morality (167). "Enlightened" morality is social morality in so far as it survives moral criticism in terms of rationality and universality, cf. 176-179; MacCormick 1981, 47-50; Coleman 1989; Bayles 1992, 108-110.

this is the real object of moral philosophy. It may be true that people tend to situate the moral reasons they believe they have for following social rules or declining to follow them within the context of their moral beliefs as a whole, but that does not show that moral argument in the proper sense is relevant for their decision. Hart would also maintain that this is true irrespective of one's meta-ethical conception of "moral argument in the proper sense". It is true for someone who, like Hart, adheres to a speaker-relativist conception, for in that case no one is committed to accept the validity of "considerations of positive morality", unless he has the appropriate pro-attitude or has made the appropriate decision of principle. But it is also true for a moral realist who holds that moral beliefs are true or false and that their truth and falsity is *independent* of any human beliefs or conventions.

In my reconstruction of the argument I have deliberately used the concept "considerations of positive morality" in an ambiguous way. It may either mean considerations that express, or considerations that refer to, existing moral beliefs.

If the first interpretation is correct, the argument cuts no ice at all. It is certainly true that people using moral argument to identify what is required of them by social conventions may make mistakes, either in the premises or in the conclusions of their reasoning. It is also true that it is possible either to reproduce their reasoning in a detached way or to report it from an external point of view, without being committed to the truth of either the premises or the conclusions. But for persons taking the internal point of view, no such distinction can be relevant: the moral argument they are involved in is moral in the sense of critical morality. For what they attempt to do is derive true conclusions from true premises, whatever their personal conception of "truth" in these matters, if they have any. (Even the attenuated sense accessible to speaker-relativism might do, but for reasons to be discussed shortly.)

The fact that scientists make mistakes does not justify us in distinguishing "positive" and "critical" science, and claiming that canons of critical science are not relevant to positive science.

On the second interpretation, the moral argument that people taking the internal point of view are involved in belongs to the sphere of "positive morality", because it refers to the beliefs of other people within the relevant community.[55] And on this supposition critical morality does not.[56] The reason is that it claims the right to judge those existing beliefs from the point of view of a true – or on a speaker-relativist interpretation a "true", meaning an authentic – morality. However, this conception of the relation between positive and critical morality must be rejected for two reasons.

Firstly, if critical morality is to be used as a criterion to test the validity or worth of social or "positive" morality, then it must provide us with *better* standards of cooperation. But then it cannot be independent of the beliefs of others. For the standards of such an independent morality will be worthless as rules of cooperation, whatever their content; precisely because they have no social existence, and therefore do not provide a shared

---

[55] Cf. Raz 1975, 170: the normativity of law is belief-dependent, not validity-dependent.

[56] According to Hart 1958, 82 the obligations of critical morality do not derive from rules, cf. Hart 1961, 165, 178. (What about the obligation to keep a promise?) This is overlooked by Lyons 1984, 52-53. Hart 1994, 256-257 seems to deny that even social morality is conventional.

orientation to a group. They are unable to create interdependent reasons.[57] You may enter the football game with the best conception of a winning strategy, but if it is only your conception, it will be disastrous to act on it.[58]

Secondly, though, every positive social morality contains within itself the criteria to criticize it.[59] For the pattern of "manifest" mutual expectations is, for a person taking the internal point of view, not an ultimate datum. What matters is in how far it provides relevant reasons for action, even for people who have the required cooperative dispositions. There are several reasons why it may not do so. It may depend on false beliefs about matters of fact. Or it may regulate a cooperative enterprise oriented towards a goal that has no real value whatsoever (or no value anymore, owing to changed circumstances or changed preferences).[60] Or it may appeal to moral motives of fairness, trustfulness or willingness to accept a reasonable compromise, under conditions which do not justify making such an appeal. This may be the case because the distribution of the costs and benefits of the enterprise is very unfair; or because some people have independent reasons for supplying the total value of the enterprise, regardless of the contribution of others; or simply because it is common knowledge that almost nobody will in fact make the required contribution. Such conditions of legitimate expectations are themselves a matter of shared understanding on some deeper levels; they belong to the common structure of all stable and pervasive patterns as such.

It is therefore possible to criticize positive morality on the grounds of false beliefs, values, or principles. These criticisms do not immediately produce an alternative positive morality, though they may suggest one. They may give reason either to go on contributing whilst trying to convince others of the necessity of a change, or to stop doing so in order to stimulate the necessary change.[61] You may have a critical moral belief which, for the time being, nobody shares. Even then, you will claim that everybody else *should* share your belief, not because it is true or because you have universally prescribed it, but because you believe this to be implied by the beliefs you actually do share. (Vegetarianism is a case in point.) Critical morality is a reconstruction of positive morality from its *raison d'être*, not a shift to an entirely different topic.

It may not just be needed for criticism, but also to identify your duty in concrete cases. A social rule arises only in contexts in which people are regularly confronted with

---

[57] That positive and critical morality cannot be unrelated is also shown by the well-known work of Lawrence Kohlberg on the development of moral reasoning. The transition from thinking in terms of social rules to thinking in terms of values and principles occurs between the second and third level (fourth and fifth stage). Because Kohlberg thinks of those values and principles as the product of autonomy, he is unable to explain the transition in terms of his own explanatory framework of differentiation and integration. If we interpret the values and principles as the underlying values and principles *of* the heteronomous system of social rules, it is easy to see how their recognition enables us to solve problems which are unsolvable on the level of the rules themselves. Den Hartogh 1996, 63-65.

[58] See ch. 7.8. and note 47 on Ideal Rule-Utilitarianism.

[59] "The seeds of criticism lie in the morality itself," Strawson (1961), 1974, 40. Hart 1961, 178, seems to agree with this view, cf. MacCormick, 1981, 50. That might explain his criticism of "excessive Protestantism", cf. note 49.

[60] I do not deny that social rules may be dysfunctional, cf. ch. 2.10. But I claim that to acknowledge a moral reason to comply with them entails a belief that complying contributes to the realization of some value.

[61] Cf. Hooker 1994.

a pattern of causal ties and preferences posing the same problem of suboptimality. But of course the pattern will almost never be quite the same. If it is just a little different, it may not be immediately clear what exactly is to be expected from everybody involved. The participants will then try to discover this, and to this end they will look at the whole system of mutual expectations as embodying some values and principles. But in this case, it is even more obvious that those values and principles cannot derive their relevance to "critical" argument from being either true or self-legislated. For if that is all we can claim for them, we cannot expect other people to rely on the outcome of our reasoning, and hence adhering to this outcome could certainly not be a requirement of either fidelity or fairness. Nor could "critical" considerations of fairness and trustworthiness justify us in deviating from manifest expectations. When we take values and principles into account, the aim is still to identify *interdependent* moral reasons, reasons that can sustain coordinated action for the good.[62] This means that our arguments should aim at convincing not just ourselves but our fellows. Critical moral argument is justificatory argument addressed to a forum. The forum is constituted by the participants to the patterns of mutual expectations shared within a community. In that sense, critical moral argument is an exercise of public reason.

Such arguments have a dual character. On the one hand, they aim at discovering the truth: what really belongs to the *implicit extension* of the pattern of mutual expectations, taken as a whole. As such they are constrained by canons of truth-finding argumentation. On the other hand, they create new expectations by making explicit what was only implicit before. They will thereby cumulatively change the terms for later discussions. This is the way in which a positive morality generally develops.[63] In this sense it is true that morality is not changed deliberately,[64] though it may be the case that over a certain period, some people voluntarily enter into explicit agreements which then cumulatively produce a change in mutual expectations, even between people who were not themselves party to any of those agreements. (Sexual morality provides examples.)

Social morality may have some universal aspects, a "minimum content of natural law". Its non-universal aspects, however, are not arbitrary. If we think of social rules as the outcome of rational choices in a certain type of situation, the historical development must be conceived as a collective learning process, in which people adjust their terms of cooperation to changing circumstances, changing distributions of power, changing beliefs and changing values. Whether a society is primarily organized so as to realize some

---

[62] In spite of his appeal to Hobbes, Kramer 1999 fails to appreciate this point, accepting instead Dworkin's view that moral consensus is a matter of convergent rather than of interdependent beliefs. Law, on the other hand, cannot exist in his view unless it is largely settled – otherwise it cannot have a coordinating function; hence we can expect it to be independent of such contingent convergences. Because of this separation of domains, Kramer's defence of soft positivism fails. For to the (predictably rather marginal) extent that any rule of recognition can acknowledge moral criteria of legal validity, it is no longer a matter of convention, but only of convergent convictions.

[63] Kramer 1999 is entirely right in criticizing Dworkin's view that conventionalism has to insist on "a crisp distinction... between arguments about and arguments within the rules", Dworkin 1986, 137, preventing it to recognize the possibility of change as a result of self-reflective argumentation.

[64] Hart 1961, 171 ff. This immunity to deliberate change characterizes morality only on the basic level; adaptation to local circumstances and conventional specifications may be left to authority, agreement or mutual adjustments, MacCormick 1981, 51-52.

substantial idea of the common good, or so as to provide the conditions for the private pursuit of individual ideals, may well depend on historical factors such as the size of its population, its class structure, the diversity of its economic activities and exchanges with the outside world, or the development of a plurality of religious and political views. (Of course a tradition may for a long time resist any change, even to the point of "imprisoning" its participants in a pattern of suboptimalizing choices.)

The concepts of "positive" and "critical morality" are necessarily connected with each other, like "belief" and "knowledge". So we should certainly not conceive of "positive" and "critical" morality as two independent systems. Rather, they are two dimensions within social morality itself. Social rules may have one or both of two properties: they may be recognized generally, accepted, effective, or they may be justified within the system as a whole. "Rules" that are justified but not recognized, are for the time being only ideal entities.

This conception is not meta-ethically neutral. It is clearly incompatible with speaker-relativism. If I am asked why I condemn the contribution expected from a certain person as an unfair burden, I cannot simply answer: because it violates a principle of fairness I personally subscribe to. As pointed out before, the answer is inappropriate for two reasons. In the first place, why should my subscribing to a principle be relevant to justifying the choice this person (living perhaps 2000 years ago) has to make? But, in the second place, if we all follow self-chosen principles in this way, we will not succeed in mutually adjusting our actions, or succeed only by coincidence.

It is more difficult to decide whether the conception of public reason is compatible with moral realism. At first sight, a realist need not deny that the existence of a pattern of mutual expectations makes a moral difference. His position is: there is one right way to respond to such expectations, and that this is the right way is independent of any further human beliefs. In the end, however, this is open to the same objection we made to speaker-relativism. For the expectations other people have of our behaviour can only be justified by the response they anticipate from us. Our disposition to respond in certain ways is internal to the expectations. The fact that our response is right or wrong in the realist sense is irrelevant to the justification of these expectations. Justification should be transparent.

The realist might reply to this objection by claiming that moral truth in the realist sense actually *is* accessible to all. (Or at least to some people, competent to exercise moral authority over the others.) This is the classical natural law conception.[65] It is not plausible, given the actual extent of moral disagreement. If we do not allow any

---

[65] As revived in the school of Germain Grisez, see e.g. Grisez, Boyle and Finnis 1987.

separation between moral truth in the realist sense, and public accessibility, the appeal to one of them can only be a form of lip service.[66]

[66] Cf. note 42. The realist claim tempts its adherents to violate important postulates of rational discussion, in particular the postulate not to assume bad faith in one's opponent. For instance: natural law opponents of the legalization of euthanasia routinely assume that proponents want to get rid of unwanted human life. Apparently they cannot believe that these proponents *really* think that human life is not always a good to the person living it.

# CHAPTER 9

## MORAL ARGUMENT AND LAW: REFUTING THE POSITIVIST ARGUMENT

### 9.1. From the Protolegal to the Legal World

In chapter One, I argued that the reasons for following conventions, as recognized from their internal point of view by participants to a system of conventions, necessarily include moral ones. This is true for legal as well as protolegal systems. For if no appeal to moral reasons can be made, then in many cases e.g. of the one-shot or $n$-person PD type, no other reasons are available; only reasons for *deviating* from the conventions. The fact that an appeal to moral reasons is indispensable, however, creates constraints on the possible content of the conventions. Identifying those constraints will often be relevant for determining what is required by a convention, in particular in an unfamiliar case. Hence the identification of conventional obligations, including legal ones, calls for moral argument.

Positivism resists this conclusion, even when it concedes the premiss: the indispensability of moral reasons. Positivists typically argue that, even if the argument succeeds for protolegal systems – systems in which no differentiation between law and conventional morality has taken place – it fails for legal systems. Law has special characteristics which exclude, or at least possibly exclude (if we follow soft positivism), the relevance of moral argument for the determination of its content.

In chapter Six I discussed Hart's Lockean description of the transition from the protolegal to the legal world. Three deficiencies of the protolegal system, three "inconveniences of the state of nature", are remedied by the transition: lack of coherence, lack of flexibility, and the instability created by conflicts about the proper interpretation of the conventions and the rules of enforcement. The remedy consists in introducing, by means of formal conventions, different forms of authority. Perhaps the most salient moment in this process of transition concerns the nature and scope of adjudicative authority. As soon as it is possible for people to put their conflicts before an arbiter who is identified according to a procedure, and not simply called in because they trust his wisdom, and as soon as they are bound, not merely advised, by his decisions, the decisive step into the legal world has been taken.

It is clear that the entrance into the legal world has substantial advantages. But Hart does not describe it as an unambiguous form of progress.[1] In discussing the second deficiency of the protolegal system – the impossibility of changing the rules

---

[1] Green 1996a, 1698-1699; Waldron 1999. This is also true of Locke, cf. Den Hartogh 1990a.2. Hart's description is often interpreted as a hypothetical contract theory: identifying the elements that would be lacking in a protolegal world and hence justify us to stay in the legal world. However, as Hart does not claim that the transition from the protolegal to the legal world is on the whole beneficial and hence justified, I prefer to read his description, again like that of Locke, as a kind of speculative history, open to empirical corroboration, see e.g. Bloch 1962, ch. 6.

deliberately if circumstances require this – he remarks that the lack of a moral legislator is generally a good thing. Cooperation according to moral rules is oriented towards very fundamental values, and it is rather fortunate that this orientation cannot be abolished by decree. The deficiency only concerns the specification of these values in terms of the concrete conditions of cooperation, which are partly conventional in nature. It is desirable to be able to adjust these to changing circumstances, without having to wait for the incremental effect of imperceptible adjustments of interpretation. But we pay a price for introducing flexibility by enlarging the scope of legislative, executive and adjudicative authority. For we lose the guarantee that the newly created authorities will respect the fundamental values which were unchangeable in the protolegal world.[2]

The same point can be made about the other deficiencies: legislative authority will be able to avoid the indeterminateness and incoherence of the protolegal system, at least to a certain extent, but there is no guarantee that the clear and coherent prescriptions it provides will satisfy ideal or even minimal moral requirements. And if legal subjects disagree about the proper interpretation of the law on moral grounds, the controversy will be settled by the decision of the court, but again, it may be settled in ways which are morally criticizable to the highest degree.

From these considerations we can reconstruct a series of interlocking arguments against the necessary, or even possible, relevance of moral argument for establishing the existence and content of legal norms.[3] We start with an argument from function. If it is the main function of legal authority to provide clear and determinate prescriptions and to short-cut endless controversy concerning their interpretation, then its pronouncements should be taken as they come, and not be subjected again to interpretation and amendment appealing to the very sources of indeterminateness and controversy, in particular moral considerations.[4] We should exchange substantial conventions for formal ones. Here the argument from function connects with arguments from the nature of authority. For formal conventions establish authority, and authority is able to fulfil the required function in virtue of its defining characteristics. Firstly, the reasons authority provides for complying with its norms are content-independent ones, they do not require the substantial, especially moral considerations which give rise to indeterminateness and controversy. Secondly, those reasons are exclusionary ones. This means that on the one hand they aim at making people act on the reasons which apply to them, including moral reasons (as we will assume on the basis of the argument of the

---

[2] Hart 1961, 197-198.

[3] Elements of this reconstructed argument are to be found in Raz 1975, 169-170; 1979, ch. 3: 1989, 1190-1191; 1994, ch. 9 (1985); Dworkin 1986, ch. 4 (criticizing "soft conventionalism", 124ff); Finnis 1980, 245ff., and already in Hobbes and Kant, cf. for Kant Waldron 1996a. Discussion: Waluchow 1994, 117-141, 182-190 (cf. Himma 1999); Postema 1996.

[4] Dworkin 1977, ch. 3 insists that the controversial nature of much legal argument as such is incompatible with a conventionalist understanding of the criteria of legal validity. Against this, Coleman 1982, 156 has objected that a consensus about the criteria of validity (formal conventions, in particular the rule of recognition) does not exclude dissensus about the content of requirements of valid law. The objection is cogent, even though, as Coleman 1998 recognizes, too much dissensus about the content of a rule would render the claim of applying the "same" rule unintelligible. That does not help Dworkin, for there are limits to the amount of dissensus he can allow himself, cf. note 39.

preceding chapter). But they do so by giving people reasons not to consider those moral reasons directly themselves, but to follow instead the content-independent norms prescribed by authority.

The appeal to content-independence, or the formal character of legal validity, is the most basic of these arguments. It is required to complete the argument from function, by presenting an alternative to the deficiencies of substantial conventions, and it is presupposed by the appeal to the pre-emptive force of authority. Exclusionary reasons are necessarily content-independent, but not vice versa. The appeal to content-independence by itself, however, is not conclusive. Law must have room for formal conventions that identify ways of generating alleged content-independent reasons by authoritative pronouncements. But this leaves it undecided whether there is more to law – possibly more (soft positivism), or even necessarily more. The argument from function aims at excluding this "more", by showing it to be incompatible with a basic functional requirement. The appeal to the exclusionary character of the reasons provided by authority also has this more ambitious aim, for it intends to show that the appeal to substantial reasons, in particular moral ones, is "pre-empted" by authority. But even then some argument from function, either the one presented or any other, seems to be required, for it needs to be explained why we cannot be trusted to follow the relevant moral reasons directly, without taking the detour of submitting to authority. I do not believe any successful functional explanations of this kind have been provided.[5] However, in considering the argument from the pre-emptive character of the reasons provided by legislative authority (section 5), I will assume that some such explanation exists.

The preceding chapter has shown that people have moral reasons to obey the law, if they have reasons to obey it at all. The arguments under consideration suggest that the relevant moral reasons are reasons to do whatever it is authority tells you to do, and in order to identify what it is authority tells you to do, no moral argument is needed or allowed.

## 9.2. The Role of Custom[6]

Even in the most thoroughly formalized legal systems, the systems of civil law, substantial conventions still exist. Legal development in modern municipal systems involves an ongoing process of the replacement of custom by legislation and jurisprudence, resulting in a seemingly very marginal role for custom, but the process is never fully complete. Positivists do not deny that some law is customary law; they usually list custom, rather misleadingly, as one of the "sources" of law.[7]

---

[5] Cf. ch. 7.

[6] This section heavily relies on Scholten (1931) 1974, 97-124; cf. also Fuller 1981.

[7] If law derives from a source, it should be possible to identify the brute fact of the operation of the source (the pattern of the chicken's entrails, the pronouncements of authority) and the institutional fact of its legal consequences separately. But if you have identified the custom (a regularity in behaviour plus the *opinio iuris*), you have ipso facto identified a legal norm.

The role of custom is not really as marginal as it seems. This optical illusion is created by the fact that legislatures are apt to codify customary rules, and judges habitually follow them. Murder and rape are not crimes because the Penal Code says they are, rather the Penal Code says so because they are. Codification and jurisprudence only settle disputed questions, e.g. whether physician-assisted suicide counts as murder, whether rape is possible within matrimony, etc.[8] By its recognition the legislative has not made new law, but only deferred to the binding power of the old one. The legislature does not invent marriage and wills either, but only specifies the details of these institutions: the procedures to be followed, and the exact legal consequences of following them. It makes provisions in the margin, but leaves the existing core intact.

In this way many legal norms derive their binding force from both custom and legislation, or from both custom and jurisprudence. Their validity is overdetermined. That does not mean, however, that custom really is redundant. (Why not say legislation is, except in so far as it settles marginal disputes?) For the extent to which the norm succeeds in guiding the behaviour of citizens (and not only the behaviour of their representatives in the courtroom) often depends on the fact that the norm is already firmly entrenched as a substantial convention.

That custom precedes statute is therefore not only a historical statement. Public legislation does not create the power of "private legislation", but only specifies the conditions of its enforceability.[9] Modern municipal systems of law recognize the freedom of individuals to choose their own arrangements, they do not even always stipulate formal requirements. So one clearly cannot say that it is not the contract which binds the parties, but only the statutory rule stipulating the legal consequences of a legal fact.[10] The law consists of the mutual expectations that the parties to the contract are justified to entertain; these expectations are evoked by their free acts; they may sometimes change when conditions change in unforeseen ways.[11] In case of a conflict the judge has to ascertain what the parties could reasonably expect of each other, given the actual "clues" for reaching a shared understanding that can be found in the terms of the contract and the developing context of their interaction. And this part of his activity is already to find the law, not to find the facts to which the real law must then be applied. Agreements between states have binding force, but it has not been given them by any higher authority.

Again, property is not created by statute, for then statute would have to provide an exhaustive list of the rights of enjoyment and the powers of disposal of the proprietor. If it attempted to do that, property would disappear in the process. In reality, laws only specify restrictions on those rights and powers; what is left is the unspecified

---

[8] Boardman 1987; Waldron 1996b, cf. ch. 6, note 39

[9] "Alle wettiglijk gemaakte overeenkomsten strekken degeen die dezelve hebben aangegaan tot wet." Art 1374 lid 1 BW. (All legally made agreements have the force of a law to the agreeing parties.)

[10] Cf. note 30.

[11] "De gebondenheid aan dat woord ligt in de verhouding zelf precies evenzeer opgesloten als de gebondenheid aan het bevel dat van het gezag in de gemeenschap uitgaat, in het bestaan der rechtsgemeenschap." Scholten 1974, 19. (The binding force of the statement is implied in the relation between the parties in the same way as the binding force of the authoritative command is implied in the existence of the legal community.)

area of the original "moral" right. And you cannot say: what the law does not forbid, it permits, for the right of property is not a liberty only; it has the obligations of others as its correlate.[12]

The informal ordering of society may compel recognition, even if this is explicitly forbidden by statute. In Dutch civil law between 1838 and 1956 the institution of a foundation ("stichting") was not recognized by statute, and the courts were prohibited by statute to consider as a source of law what was customarily done and considered proper.[13] But the High Court – then in its formalist heyday – had to declare nevertheless that the continuity of the legal order was of such prevalent importance that custom in this case had to be considered valid law.[14]

Professional duties (e.g. the right of a journalist to refuse to identify his source) and other social duties may overrule legal requirements, and the courts have to recognize this ("necessity"). It is their duty to do so, and it is not only their duty because it has been their practice all along: they may fulfil their duty by *starting* the practice.[15]

Because formal law supervenes on a system of mutual expectations that is of constitutive significance for social interaction, it is as impossible to rule out the force of custom generally by an act of legislation, as it is impossible to rule out the force of precedent. Expectations will simply go on converging on the customary. It follows that what is called the plain meaning of a statute is not simply the context-independent meaning which someone who has learned to master the language is able to extract from its wordings, it depends on the existing legal context in which the statute is meant to interfere, and this importantly includes informal patterns of mutual understanding already existing within the society.

For that reason the hidden power of custom makes itself felt in adjudication as well, for instance when out of two possible interpretations of the wordings of a statute, or two constructions of the ratio of a precedent, that one is chosen which best fits in with existing practices in social interaction.[16] Sometimes this criterion is relevant for establishing the intention of the lawgiver, on the assumption that, as he shares the relevant interpretative context, he knows how his words will be taken. But such adjustments often go beyond legislative intention as well, in particular when the interpretative context changes. By such processes a legal norm, as laid down in a statutory provision, may change its meaning over time almost beyond recognition. Indeed, it should be acknowledged that the binding force of many "old laws", whether or not the impact of the norm has changed in the way described, can no longer be derived from the authority of the lawgiver (who may have functioned in a constitutional order that does not satisfy minimum requirements of legitimacy according to present standards), but only from the fact that it is embodied in existing practices.[17] Its force is

---

[12] Scholten 1974, 14-16.

[13] Art. 3, Wet A.B. (1829). Art. 5 adds that statute can only be repealed by statute, not by custom.

[14] Scholten, 1974, 92, 113.

[15] On the role of custom in international law, cf. Den Hartogh 1998a.2; Den Hartogh forthcoming, § 9.

[16] Even the plain meaning of a statute can be set aside by appeal to "the requirements of social intercourse", cf. *Maring/Assuradeuren*, discussed in ch. 11.11.

[17] Raz 1996a, 277-279; 1996b, 357-358.

the force of custom. Even Kelsen was compelled to recognize the power of custom (*desuetudo*) to undermine the validity of a legal norm over time; he called this rather impure phenomenon ("ein Sollen durch ein Sein zerstört") "juristisch ein Mysterium".[18]

So custom is really far more important than it might seem at first. Norms created by legislative authority must be broadly congruent with and integrated into the existing practices of a society, and will be interpreted on the assumption that they are.[19] Now custom, as a remnant of the protolegal world, is covered by my arguments in the previous chapter, but not by the argument from the function and the nature of authority developed in section 1. A customary rule must be applied and interpreted by reference to values and principles. If we find ourselves in a situation in which, by strict application of the customary rule, we should do *x*, but doing *x* is counter-productive, or it is highly unfair to require it in this particular situation, then we will not expect people to expect us to do it. And hence we cannot say that doing it is required by custom, precisely because such moral argument is relevant to the identification of its requirements.

By a law passed on December 3, 1964 the Netherlands claimed legal powers over an artificial island that had been built outside the Dutch territorial waters specifically to facilitate forms of commercial broadcasting at that time forbidden in the Netherlands. The island was sealed up. For this action no justification could be found in international treaties or explicit customary rules of international law, except "the custom that lacunas in international law are filled by the interested party in accordance with principles of reasonableness". Calling this a custom may suggest that its validity is content-independent, but it clearly is not. The only reason why the reasonable action does not conflict with existing legitimate expectations is that it *is* reasonable.


### 9.3. An Unlimited Claim to Authority?

Positivists could with relative equanimity accept the argument that their appeal to the function and nature of authority in law does not cover customary law. They would insist that in municipal law, custom is really nothing but a marginal phenomenon, a remnant from the protolegal world. To the extent that legislation does indeed tend to reproduce custom, that is a contingent fact explained by legislative prudence. In the end it is only from legislative authority that such laws derive their legal validity. Even the validity of pure customary law, moreover, depends on its being tolerated by the lawgiver. Older positivists used to hold that customary rules fully derive their validity from being silently adopted by the sovereign. But even if the silence of the law is not a sufficient condition of the validity of custom, it clearly seems a necessary one. For the lawgiver is empowered to decree that a custom will no longer be valid. And this power is

---

[18] Kelsen 1911, 344.

[19] Postema 1994, 374. "If a law is to work it must not go too much against the grain of the forces of spontaneous order," Sugden 1986, 5, cf. ch. 1, note 53. Thiss is confirmed by the almost total unenforceability of some laws, e.g. those regulating the use of drugs.

unlimited, it does not only apply to morally unsuspect cases. The lawgiver is not restricted by the moral constraints that would be relevant for the application and interpretation of the customary rules themselves.

True, it may be the case that the "normal" lawgiver, say the government and a simple majority in parliament, is bound to some moral norms, for example because they are incorporated into a written constitution. But, as Joseph Raz remarks, the same constitution usually provides a procedure for changing the constitution.[20] This procedure, one could say in traditional language, identifies the real sovereign. (For example: the government and two successive parliaments, the second decision being taken by both houses in united session by a majority of two out of three.)[21] The highest lawgiving authority has power to remove any value or principle whatsoever from the constitution, even human rights or the principle of equality.

It could be objected that a constitution may also explicitly provide that some articles it contains cannot be changed.[22] But in that case the argument could be completed according to the pattern set by Hobbes and Austin: such self-binding is necessarily futile, for if an authority has power to create such limitations, it has power to repeal them as well, whether or not this is recognized in the constitution. For the constitution derives its normative force only from being enacted by this very same authority. The only way in which limitations could be made effectively, is by having them made by an even higher authority, but then of course the higher authority itself is not restricted by them.

Even if this final argument is not accepted,[23] one may still hold that authority can only be limited by authority. That is the basic claim to be considered. It presents the appeal to the nature of authority in its strongest form: the claim of the law to provide content-independent and pre-emptive reasons does not recognize any antecedent limitations of its scope. Then it follows sure enough that, in as far as legal subjects and officials wish to stay within the framework of the law, they cannot appeal to moral arguments, except when this appeal is explicitly required or silently permitted by the lawgiver. So we need to study the argument carefully.

Obviously, one other difference between Hobbes and Raz remains: both agree about the unlimited character of the claims of the law, but while Hobbes believes that these claims are necessarily true, Raz holds that they are necessarily false.[24] This should create some suspicion: if the claim is necessarily false, what reason can the bearers of the mask of "the law" have for making it – even making it, allegedly, always and everywhere? It cannot be implied in any claim to undominated authority as such, for even supreme authority need not be comprehensive authority. Medical doctors may

---

[20] Raz 1986, 76-77; cf. Raz 1975, 150-152; 1979, 116-119, 30-31 (law's claim to authority is comprehensive and supreme); Green 1988, 82-83 (distinguishing the claim to supreme and unlimited authority); Morris 1998, ch. 7. For Hart's discussion of legal limitations on legislative power, see Hart 1961, 64-76. For a more extended discussion of the claims of the state, see Den Hartogh forthcoming.

[21] Dutch Constitution, Art. 137.

[22] Bundesgrundgesetz.

[23] Cf. Hart 1961, 145-146.

[24] For evaluations of Hobbes' argument see Hampton 1986, ch. 4; Den Hartogh unpubl. (c).

claim "supreme" authority on questions of medical diagnosis and treatment, but not therefore on questions of Thai cooking as well. What is so special about legal authority that it is compelled to make false claims?

A contrary view would be the following. Just as I argued that codified law in many cases should be seen as a recognition of the continuing force of existing substantial conventions – statute does not create the conventional facilities of contract or marriage –, the constitutional lawgiver should be seen as recognizing the antecedent force of basic moral constraints on the exercise of lawgiving powers. It is not because of the authority of the state that we should recognize human rights and equality before the law, rather it is a condition of the authority of the state (at least in certain societies) that it recognizes them.

On this view, the state need not formally be precluded from withdrawing recognition; indeed, there may be a recognized procedure for doing so. But that does not show that the recognition itself is nothing but an exercise of authority. Consider the following analogy to Raz' argument. Every speaker necessarily has to claim to be omniscient. For suppose that, at the present moment, he confesses to have no knowledge at all of a factual domain $x$. As soon as he changes his mind and proceeds to make pronouncements about $x$, it will be inconsistent for him to admit that he is in no position to do so. So the "limits" he recognizes on his competence, are only limits as long as he recognizes them, hence really no limits at all.

What is wrong with this argument? If I change my mind and make some statement about $x$, I will necessarily claim that I have the competence to make that judgment with the amount of assurance I happen to display. But of course it is quite compatible with this that I now believe, and believe truly, that I have no such competence at all. In the same way, when a legislative body now recognizes that it is outside its powers to declare $x$ to be a valid rule, from the moment it changes its mind and declares $x$ to be valid, it will have to claim that it has authority to do so, but it does not follow that at this moment it is mistaken. Nor does it follow that there are no limits to its authority otherwise than those it temporarily imposes upon itself.

Is it possible to decide between these competing views? I think it is.[25] Suppose we hold on to the formal mode of reasoning, asserting that authority is necessarily unlimited because any limits it authoritatively states, it may authoritatively repeal. It then follows that the highest lawgiver can also legitimately decide to change the procedure for identifying the highest lawgiver, as it is described in the constitution. But this saddles us with a Münchhausen paradox: the lawgiver derives his authority from the "rule of change" as Hart would call it, but the rule derives its validity from the authority of the lawgiver.[26]

The way out of this paradox is by recalling that the rule of change (or perhaps an even more fundamental "rule of recognition" from which the rule of change derives its validity) is itself a customary rule, a "formal convention". This of course is the Hartian

---

[25] Another way to decide the issue is to attend to the limitations of sovereignty recognized (increasingly) in international law. States are not granted the power to massacre or expel parts of their own population, whether or not they signed any international treaties to that effect. See Den Hartogh forthcoming.

[26] Van den Bergh 1975.

view. Custom does not derive its force from authority, because authority in the end derives its force from custom. This was stated in a famous passage in the *Digesta*: "For, as the laws have binding force for no other reason than being accepted by the *iudicium* of the people, it is right that whatever the people judges to be good without any written form whatsoever, will be binding to all. For it does not matter whether the people declares its will explicitly or by actual behaviour."[27]

To the extent that the constitution is seen as consisting of formally valid rules, the relevant legislative authority cannot be created by the constitution, but only be recognized by it. The same can be said of the binding force of jurisprudence. In Dutch law, for instance, the principle of *stare decisis* has never been explicitly recognized by statute. There even exists a statutory provision, dating from 1829 and never repealed, which explicitly forbids any form of judicial legislation.[28] In former times it therefore used to be legal doctrine that even Supreme Court decisions had no binding force: it was not the decision which had authority, but only the motivation. (In other words: it had only epistemic authority.) But of course it has always been the practice of the courts to follow Supreme Court decisions, as well as significant trends in lower jurisprudence. This practice was accompanied by an *opinio iuris*, and hence a form of customary law.

If legislative authority itself is not created but only recognized by the constitution, the same may be true about the limits of authority. But then it does not matter that formally valid rules do not, or perhaps even cannot, preclude the repeal of this recognition. That does not mean that moral constraints on the exercise of authority are only in force as long as they are recognized by authority. For they derive their force not from authority, but directly from the conventions that establish authority.

If the constitution provides for a way of changing the constitution, that should not be seen as giving a blank cheque to the "sovereign", but rather as enabling the legislative to reflect developments in basic mutual understandings of political morality concerning the limits of the law. That is the point of flexibility. The existence of a recognized procedure for changing even the most basic constitutional provisions may not be a sign of arrogance but rather of modesty: the constitutional lawgiver recognizes his own fallibility.

Indeed this is arguably the case. At this point, the argument first developed for substantial conventions in protolegal systems, and later applied to customary rules in mature legal systems, becomes relevant again. Conventions may provide content-independent reasons, for instance when they are used to settle bargaining problems in Division games. However, these reasons are only content-independent within certain limits, defined by the values at stake in the cooperative enterprise and by the conditions triggering the appeal to principles of fairness and fidelity in the distribution of its benefits and burdens. If that is true for substantial conventions, it is true for formal conventions as well, as they have exactly the same role, e.g. solving bargaining problems by arbitration.

---

[27] Dig I.3. (Julianus).
[28] Art. 12, Wet A.B.

This has in effect been recognized by Hart in his doctrine of the minimum content of natural law. If the authority of law is unlimited, it is not inevitable for the law to reproduce social morality at any point.[29] But if it cannot fail to do so at this point – the social requirements for individual survival – without losing any semblance of authority, why at this point only?

If reasonableness and fairness set limits to the interpretation and application of customary rules, they set limits to the interpretation and application of legal norms as well, not because this is authoritatively prescribed, but because the recognition of authority is itself a matter of customary rules (formal conventions). The article in the new Dutch civil code, providing that contractual provisions are only binding if compatible with requirements of reasonableness and fairness, is therefore strictly redundant.[30] It may show a kind of legislative arrogation, in as far as it suggests that these constraints on the binding power of contract would not be in place if the code did not authorize them.[31] It is the same arrogation we came across in that old law stating that custom has no validity unless it is explicitly recognized by statute. Such declarations are ipso facto futile: it is begging the question to take the question of the priority between statute and custom to be decidable by statute. Ironically, the law excluding statute from being repealed by custom, has itself de facto been repealed by custom.

Principles have legal validity because their validity is a presupposition of the moral force of conventions, including formal conventions. Hence, if the validity of principles is overdetermined by custom and statute, it is statute which is redundant, not custom. This is also shown by the following argument. When a principle is relevant to a range of cases, it is rarely of equal relevance to all: the "weight" of the principle may be different from case to case. Pornography as well as criticism of the present government may be protected by freedom of speech, but the protection is more easily overruled by countervailing considerations in the one case than in the other. If, however, principles derived their validity from the authority of statute, this could not happen, because their validity would be content-independent.

## 9.4. The Costs of Legality

We are now in a position to see why Hart was mistaken in his description of the dangers involved in the transition into the legal world.[32] In his view, the gains in determinateness, flexibility and finality obtained by the introduction of formal conventions have their price: the potential abuse of norm-creating powers. This view rests on the presupposition that authority, once introduced, cannot be restricted. But if the substantial conventions of the protolegal world require a background of shared

---

[29] Cf. ch. 8.4.

[30] Art. 6.2 BW. Cf. Art. 6.1: natural and contractual obligations can only be derived from statute.

[31] Cf. the discussion between Schoordijk and Abas, reported in ch. 11.10.

[32] Endorsed by Green 1996a, 1700-1702; Waldron 1999. Of course the transition may involve the acquisition by state officials of powers (in the non-normative sense) which may be abused by coercion.

moral understandings for their application and interpretation, there is no reason why a similar or even the same background would not be required for the formal conventions of the legal world as well

Hart may have been misled to some extent by the functionalist language of his account. (Although, even if you want to explain the process of juridification by referring to the need for removing deficiencies, it seems the explanation only succeeds if the process results in some net improvement.) The point can hardly be missed if you describe the transition into the legal world in intentional terms, i.e. from the internal point of view of the participants to the relevant conventions.[33] This can be shown by an explicit Althusian or Lockean thought-experiment. Imagine the members of the protolegal society coming together to discuss what should be done to remedy the inconveniences of the state of nature. It is clear why they would agree to accept the introduction of legislative, adjudicating and enforcing agencies. It is equally clear that they would never agree to entrust those agencies with an unlimited authority. "This is to think that men are so foolish that they take care to avoid what mischiefs may be done them by polecats of foxes, but are content, nay think it safety, to be devoured by lions."[34] So the parties will frame the relevant formal conventions in such a way that not only powers are conferred, but also disabilities. In particular they will make sure that authority will be restricted by the very moral constraints on the application and interpretation of norms that are already in place. For the reason why moral values are "immune from deliberate change" retains its full validity when the step into the legal world is made. In the Althusius/Locke tradition the point would be expressed by saying that the political community reserves the sovereignty for itself, and only delegates legislative and adjudicative powers to state institutions and officials. These powers are a "trust", given on conditions. The conditions are derived from the aims of the political community: the protection and promotion of security, justice and prosperity. The content of these conditions are partly given as a "minimum content of natural law", but they have to be specified over and over again in a historical learning process.[35] If the authorities act beyond their powers in clear, drastic and systematic ways, and if it is not possible to find redress within the law or by "civil disobedience", the same "rules of change" legitimize violent means of overthrowing them.

What such thought-experiments really aim to bring out are the conditions for the possible appeal to cooperative dispositions. If legislative or judicial pronouncements would redirect the cooperative enterprise towards goals that are generally considered socially disastrous, or if they order people to contribute on terms which do not activate a principle of fairness, of loyalty, or of reasonable compromise, voluntary participation can no longer be mutually expected.

Rules conferring authority are themselves patterns of mutual expectations arising in circumstances requiring cooperation for the avoidance of suboptimal results. It is inescapable that they appeal to moral motives of trustfulness, fairness, and

---

[33] Openshaw 1986, 149.

[34] Locke, *Two Treatises*, II.7.93, quoted before in chapter 3.3, at note 13.

[35] Den Hartogh 1990a, 207-210.

reasonableness; hence they are limited to conditions under which such an appeal makes sense. Otherwise they can have no stability at all. And it does not matter whether or not these disabilities are explicitly stated. The constitution does not create them, but only recognizes (and specifies) them.[36] Constitutional law on the whole is strongly overdetermined in the way codified customary law is, as indicated above. But again, that does not mean that custom is redundant. On the contrary: legislation cannot override custom on these points, because they belong to the conditions for recognizing its authority. The same is true for values and principles structuring specific legal domains. Whether or not they are recognized by the lawgiver, explicitly or even implicitly, is not relevant to their legal status.

In a similar way we can also explain, and thereby confirm, the ongoing significance of substantial conventions that I argued for in section 2.[37] When Hart realized that a Kelsenian pure theory of law, fully isolated against social reality, could not be had, he made the minimum adjustment necessary, relating pure law to social reality by means of the pineal gland of the rule of recognition. But this is a self-defeating policy; the rule of recognition, after all, is only one convention among others, often relevant to the same areas of mutually adjusted behaviour. Such conventions cannot fail to determine each other's scope and interpretation. If we realize that a particular action is expected from us on account of one convention, the fact that it is forbidden by another is necessarily relevant to our decisions. That is true for conventions arising in games of pure coordination: if two equally prominent Lewis conventions send us into opposite directions, we clearly have a higher-order coordination problem. But it is even more obviously true for obligatory conventions constituting fair terms of cooperation among cooperatively disposed persons. Norms deriving their force from formal conventions must be broadly congruent with and integrated into the existing pattern of substantial conventions if they are to have any authority, for otherwise it could not be a matter of fairness to comply with them. Because such norms at least claim actually to have authority, the total framework of the existing substantial conventions also provides a context that cannot fail to be relevant to their interpretation.

Basically, what matters is not conformity with the intention of a legislative authority, but mutual adjustment of actions on fair terms. If the focus of mutual adjustment provided by the exercise of legislative authority systematically deviates from legislative intention, as it tends to do in the case of "old laws", then legislative authority has nevertheless done its job.[38]

---

[36] Cf. Hart 1961, 67-72 on constitutional disabilities created by the rule of recognition itself; cf. 145-150. These passages confirm Hart's claim, Hart 1994, 247, 250, that his theory has always been a form of soft positivism. (This is disputed by Green 1996a, 1705-1707.) Cf. MacCormick in MacCormick 1986, ch. 6.

[37] Cf. Fuller's argument for this thesis as reconstructed by Postema 1994.

[38] See ch. 11.5. on the argument from history.

## 9.5. The Scope of Exclusion

In the first section I formulated a composite argument against the relevance of moral argument for the identification of valid law, appealing to both the function and the nature of legal authority. I have so far argued that the moral constraints on the application and interpretation of substantial conventions are equally relevant to the application and interpretation of formal ones. This takes account of that part of the original argument which referred to the content-independent character of legal validity. Not only formal conventions create content-independent reasons, some substantial conventions do so as well, for example those which "solve" Coordination and Division games. But these reasons are only content-independent within limits, and the limits are relevant in applying the conventions to new cases.

It could be objected that, as long as such "substantial" considerations are allowed, the system will fail to generate the clear and determinate guides to behaviour that are required for an improvement upon the protolegal system. This objection, however, overrates the controversiality of moral considerations as such. In moral discussion we tend to focus on points of disagreement, and this may blind us to the extent to which there is agreement. A public morality, providing a platform of moral argument capable of attracting wide and transparent recognition, will perhaps fall short of ideal morality, precisely because it does not press controversial points; but that does not automatically take away its binding force, though it may do so in extreme cases.[39] If the controversial character of moral considerations as such would lead us to exclude them from consideration altogether, we would succumb to the danger Hart discerned in the formality of law, and we might end up "being devoured by lions". We expect this danger to be *commonly* recognized, and precisely this fact shows the existence of shared moral views.[40] This is not simply a factual observation; as I argued in the preceding chapter, we should conceive of morality, or at least of the morality of rights and duties, as essentially providing interdependent reasons.

One strand in the argument from the formal nature of authority is still to be discussed. I refer to the claim that it is part of the nature of authority to provide exclusionary or pre-emptive reasons. This claim does not deny that, in any case in which an authoritative prescription is made, there may be relevant moral considerations for and perhaps against the prescribed action. But the point is that, whenever we really have reason to obey the prescription, we should not aim to act on those relevant considerations directly, but rather trust the authority to have taken them into account. Legislative authority should acknowledge moral constraints, but it does not follow that in interpreting its pronouncements or in deciding on their force, legal subjects or judges

---

[39] Postema 1995b; cf. Postema 1987a, criticizing Dworkin's "Protestant" view of the judicial responsibility to reconstruct the political morality embodied in the law. Dworkin recognizes that, to function properly, law requires a substantial amount of consensus, but he argues that this consensus can be a confluence of independent moral convictions, an "overlapping consensus", to use Rawls' term. "Nothing *need* be settled as a matter of convention in order for a legal system not only to exist but to flourish," Dworkin 1986, 133.

[40] Waluchow 1994, 122-123, 185. Raz does not deny the point, see Raz 1980, 215-216; 1994, 215; cf. Green 1996a, 1708.

should refer to those very moral constraints by appealing to legal values and principles, for that would be to deny the exclusionary force of legislation.

Of course, this argument must be supplemented by explaining when and why it is rational to submit to authority in this way. I argued in chapter Seven that the proponents of this conception of authority have failed in their explanations on this point, in particular when they appeal to the coordinating or arbitrating function of the exercise of authority. These functions only require that the reasons provided by authority are (within limits) content-independent, not that they are pre-emptive.[41]

Even so, I have explicitly allowed for the possibility that exclusionary reasons have a role to play in role moralities.[42] In "trusting" or "delegating" specific tasks to professionals, we usually must allow them some space for making their own judgments as to the optimal way of fulfilling the task. However, we may have reason to restrict this space by disabling them to appeal to certain considerations that we believe can be better represented in the decision-making process in other ways. As I argued, it would be irrational in our private deliberations to exclude a consideration that we confidently believe to be valid and relevant; but it is not irrational to exclude certain considerations from someone's professional deliberations, even though the professional might confidently believe them to be valid and relevant. We might know, for instance, that his confidence is often mistaken.[43]

This type of argument may also apply to the exercise of authority by legal officials. Exercising authority may be subject to exclusionary considerations, even if it is not on account of the very fact that authority is exercised. In liberal states, religious truth is never an argument in a court of law. On the other hand, it need not be. So we cannot decide in an a priori way whether moral considerations in general, or only moral considerations of a particular kind, are "excluded" in the exercise of adjudicating authority. We must look and see.

Let us first note that moral considerations may be "excluded", not because of the validity of any exclusionary reason, but because they simply are not relevant to the task at hand. Judges are supposed to decide whether in a particular case the existing pattern of mutual expectations justified the plaintiff to expect the defendant to do what she actually expected him to do. The private moral conviction that judges might have with respect to the pattern as a whole or aspects of it is irrelevant. They cannot appeal to principles and values they personally subscribe to, and not even to "true" principles and values: the relevant critical morality is a public one.[44]

---

[41] This is also true for the role of legislative authority in settling matters of moral controversy. It does not "replace" any reasons we had before, because if we disagree, we do not have the option of cooperating on our terms.

[42] Ch. 7.12.

[43] In recent political philosophy two ways of dealing with moral controversy ("the fact of pluralism") may be distinguished: the method of avoidance (Rawls), i.e. excluding the controversial issues from being considerations for political authorities, and the method of compromise, cf. Den Hartogh 2000a. Interestingly, Raz is one of the foremost critics of the former method! Raz 1986, ch. 6; 1994, ch. 3. His preferred solution combines compromise on the level of legislative decision with avoidance on the level of legal subjects.

[44] Ch. 10.2.

The basic question, therefore, is whether the public morality that is expressed in legislation and consists of the underlying values and principles of the law, is always directly relevant to the practical deliberation of judges, or whether such considerations may be "excluded" because they are supposed to have been adequately considered by the legislature.

Whatever the claims of the law, positivists enjoin us to be critical about them. The very fact that a legislative or judicial authority has made a pronouncement applying to us, does not automatically mean that we have any moral reason to obey. That is not only true for "authorities" of dubious legitimacy. If the lawgiver, on the whole, exercises his authority in a morally acceptable way, Raz believes that citizens have an option to take up a general attitude of respect for the law, but they may also prefer to follow a more selective policy. If they take the first option, they will have a general obligation to obey laws "as such", i.e. simply because they are valid laws. But even then this general rule is not unlimited, for there are things we should never do, whether or not the law commands us to do them. Law's claim to unlimited authority can never be accepted.

I take it that for officials of the legal system, and in particular for judges, taking up this general attitude of respect is not optional. But even for them it remains true that occasionally they may decide not to apply the law, to deviate from what the lawmaker, given the natural meaning of the wording of his laws, obviously intended them to decide. Positivists agree that it is at least permissible for them occasionally to make such a decision, and Raz, for one, accepts that they may even be duty-bound to do so.[45] This description clearly conforms to the actual practice of the courts in legal systems of the liberal-democratic type. Two other possible descriptions are thereby ruled out. In the first place, we could imagine a legal system in which the courts mutually expect each other to accept the law's (supposed) claim to unlimited authority. This requires a moral justification of unlimited authority. Such justifications are not unheard of. We will shortly come across a descendant of the original Hobbesian argument which claims a lexical priority for the value of peace, and suggests that any deviation from the commands of the sovereign returns one to a state of nature and hence of war with every other citizen who might oppose the deviation. A second possible argument is the radical democratic one which claims a similar priority for the value of submission to the general will. In both cases the common belief of the legal community might be that legislative authority covers all cases which may possibly come up for adjudication, but it need not be. It may also be commonly assumed that the law in the books has lacunas, to be filled by judicial lawmaking. In that case the authority of the lawgiver has some limits, but the limits are determined by the plain meaning of statute. To put the point in Hartian terms, it is only when we arrive at the boundary between the "core of certainty" and the "penumbra of doubt" that the judicial duty to make law begins. But the positivist view of the actual practice of the courts in modern legal systems rejects that picture as well, and rightly so. For it is clear that in those systems, judges often deviate

---

[45] The relevant duties being the duties of his role, recognized by a publicly available role morality, see ch. 10.2.

from the natural meaning of statute if the latter would render a very unreasonable or very unjust result.[46]

On the other hand, it is also obvious that judges do not simply proclaim the result which is the most reasonable and just one, leaving the wording of statute to function only as a tiebreaker. How are they supposed to decide on the priority of formal or substantial considerations? On the exclusionary reason account the answer is that this is determined by the *scope* of the exclusionary reason. For such reasons do exclude other reasons from being weighed in the balance of reasons, but not necessarily all other reasons. That is why it may be legitimate for a judge to decide that it would be too unreasonable or too unjust to decide in accordance with the clear meaning of statute.

The idea that the exclusionary reasons provided by authority have a limited scope, is fully compatible with positivism. It is not even a form of soft positivism. The positivist will say that it is only in determining what the presumed exclusionary reasons require within their proper scope, that we are involved in identifying the law as it is. If we go beyond that scope, we are no longer stating the law but changing it. For such considerations it is even futile to claim the status of "law", for that does not make any difference to their relevance for practical reasoning.

But how are we to establish the scope of such reasons?[47] One might suggest that it must be determined by the lawmaking authority itself.[48] Such scope-limitations, however, would only be apparent. For the sovereign's authority, on this view, is only limited by self-imposed boundaries, which it is at liberty to remove. If scope-limitations derive their validity from authoritative decisions, this validity is still content-independent. So, if the legislature makes explicit room for an appeal to either values or principles, by instructing the courts to respect boundaries of "good faith", "equity" or "due care", the courts in complying will still not give any weight to moral considerations as such. Their procedure can be compared, as Joseph Raz suggests, to the courts following an authoritative instruction to decide a case in accordance with foreign law.[49] In doing so they do not recognize the authority of the foreign law itself.

As a matter of fact, judges will make judgments in terms of good faith, due care and equity anyhow, whether or not their practice is covered by sufficiently elastic provisions of statute.[50] And hence, as I argued, we should not conceive of any such provisions as *setting* limits at all, but only as recognizing them.

---

[46] Hart 1961, 119. See ch. 11.3. at note 25.

[47] Cf. ch. 7.8. at note 53 on following the instructions of a soccer coach.

[48] This is presupposed by Stokes' claim that formalism is the only theory of judicial responsibility compatible with positivism, Stokes 1994.

[49] Raz 1979, 46, 62.

[50] Three famous Dutch High Court decisions illustrate the point. *Lindenbaum-Cohen*, NJ 1919, 161 (the Dutch equivalent to *Donoghue/Stevenson*): liability for harm may result from lack of "the due care appropriate in social intercourse", even if there is no relevant statutory prescription. The first clear deviation from the volitional theory of contract, introduced by the appeal to *bona fides* in *Eelman-Hin* 1960, 230: you can be held to more, or less, than you have explicitly committed yourself to. And finally *Quint-Te Poel*, NJ 1959, 548, allowing considerations of equity to stand, even if they do not derive from statute but only "fit into the system of the law".

If real limitations to the scope of authority cannot be derived from authority, they can only be a matter of right reason. Courts do not have to believe that the legislature would have authority whatever it decided, but only that the limits it actually tends to set itself, are really adequate for the protection of its authority. Hence even when the scope of authority is identified by the lawgiving authority itself and the courts do not question its identification, the courts do not simply accept the authority of the legislature in this matter. Any suggestions made by the legislature must be checked by the courts, otherwise they run the risk that their own claims to adjudicative authority are unjustified.[51] In the end, the scope of the exclusionary reasons provided by lawgiving authority to the courts has to be identified by the courts themselves without reference to authority. The same can be said about the exclusionary reasons provided by the *ratio decidendi* of an authoritative precedent, for in considering the precedent the court must always decide whether or not to "distinguish" the present case.

But this is actually inconsistent with claiming that those reasons are exclusionary ones. If a subject to an authority is to determine the "scope" of an exclusionary reason by reference to the extent to which following it would violate some substantial value (like reasonableness or fairness), then what he really does is draw up a balance of reasons, weighing the reasons for complying with authority against other reasons. If the limits to the pre-emption of reasons are to be determined by weighing, no pre-emption takes place.[52] The point to keep in mind is this: the very fact that a law has been made may have a content-independent weight of its own, because it provides a focus for mutually adjusted behaviour. That is why even an adverse judgment from the point of view of the relevant values and principles does not immediately outbalance its weight. The choice may be between a suboptimal form of adjustment and no adjustment at all. The judge is trying to establish what the parties had reason to expect of each other. Usually, it is only when an explicit statute is very unreasonable or very unjust, "manifestly absurd or morally repugnant",[53] that the parties may be justified in mutually expecting each other to deviate from it. But the very fact that such strong and comparative language is used, shows that making this decision is a matter of weight, and not of scope.[54]

Content-independent reasons provided by the exercise of legal authority are weighed with and against moral considerations. Moreover, as chapter Eleven will amply show, both types of consideration are inextricably interwoven. This interdependence is overlooked when it is claimed that courts normally judge on formalist grounds and only change over to moral considerations on arriving at the boundaries of the reason-giving force of authority.

---

[51] Of course the courts may as a matter of fact close their eyes to illegimate scope-claims of the legislature and accept it's authority blindly Is not that fact sufficient to prove the positivist's case? See ch. 10.2.

[52] Ch. 7.9. Cf. Postema's criticism of Schauer in Postema 1991b.

[53] *Becke vs Smith* 1836, quoted by Waluchow 1994, 35 note.

[54] It might seem that this objection can be accommodated by Perry's conception of second-order reasons as not excluding first-order ones, but only changing their weight, Perry 1987; 1989. But see my criticism in ch. 7, note 42. As weight is a relative notion when it comes to balancing, adding new first-order reasons changes the weight of others. That is no reason to consider the added reason a second-order one.

# CHAPTER 10

## MORAL ARGUMENT AND LAW: FURTHER CONSIDERATIONS

### 10.1. The Internal Reconstruction Thesis

What the law is in a particular case, how it allocates rights and duties, should not be decided just by looking at the conventional meaning of the instructions of a lawgiver; we must consider the law as a whole, taking it as a realization of a range of shared values and principles. We cannot know what it is the law requires, unless we interpret it against this background.[1] Suppose we want to decide whether it is permissible to extend the scope of a norm by analogical reasoning, or whether this is not allowed (as the *argumentum a contrario* alleges), or whether its scope should even be restricted by "refinement" – in all those cases we must consider the *ratio legis*.

We need this reference to a background of values and principles not only when it is unclear whether the meaning of a term used in a law or judicial decision requires its application to the case at hand. As I suggested in the previous chapter, Hart's "avocado" model is misleading from the start: if you have isolated the "core of certainty" from the "penumbra of doubt" for all the terms of a legal provision, you may still find that occasions arise in which what may reasonably be expected conflicts with its "core" meaning.[2] Whether the provision applies, given the facts of the case, obviously does not depend exclusively on the terms used in it; it may also depend, for instance, on its purpose. The law must always be interpreted as providing the terms of a cooperative enterprise; if by attending to the ordinary meaning of an authoritative document we get results which are plainly counter-productive, it cannot be the correct determination of the law.[3] (And sometimes not even the correct interpretation of the document.)

The thesis that the correct determination of the law requires attention to values and principles is not in itself inconsistent with positivism. A reception of Dworkin's criticisms of Hart has been defended (even by Hart himself) in which we start, as we

---

[1] This conception is now mostly associated with Dworkin 1986; however, it is already to be found in Scholten (1931) 1974 and the work of his predecessor Gény and his contemporaries Cardozo and Heller. On Heller cf. Dyzenhaus 1996. See also Postema 1995b; 1996; 1997.

[2] According to Hart the penumbra is desirable, because unforeseeable circumstances may arise in which we have reasons to make a different decision than a formalistic interpretation would allow. But why should this not happen within the core? Waluchow 1994, 253. Cf. ch. 11 at note 25.

[3] MacCormick 1978, ch. 6. Some Dutch examples: *Water- en Melkarrest* NJ 1916, 681 (no punishment without *mens rea*), *Opticiensarrest* NJ 1923, 1329 (extension of the concept of 'necessity' or 'force majeure' to include conflict of duties), *Van Oppen/Ontvanger der Successierechten* NJ 1926, 723 (*Fraus legis* decision: a legal provision is applicable if the sole aim of an action has been to avoid the legal consequences the provision aimed to create), *Grensoverschrijdende garage*, NJ 1971, 89 (abuse of property right if another's loss strongly outweighs the owner's advantage). Most clearly *contra legem*: *Huizer veearts*, NJ 1933, 918, cf. ch. 7, note 53, ch. 11 at note 34.

used to, with the rule of recognition and the sources of valid requirements it identifies: legislative enactment, administrative promulgation, custom, precedent and so on. Perhaps we will find some values and principles already explicitly recognized by these sources.[4] Subsequently we ask ourselves: if we interpret all this material as the realization of a coherent system based on fundamental values and principles, then which values and principles could be adduced? We find the constitutional foundations of law by means of an internal reconstruction.[5] What the law requires in any given case, will be that decision which provides maximal coherence with the total body of legal standards found in this way.

Does not this account concede the relevance of moral argument for identifying legal obligation? In a way it does. But it does not recognize the relevance of moral argument as such, but only, on Raz' foreign law model, as in an odd way "required" by legal norms.

But why should we recognize this requirement? Why should we interpret the explicit provisions of the law as the terms of a cooperative enterprise contributing to the realization of some worthwhile goals, and involving an appeal to principles of good faith, equity and reasonableness, if there really *is* no such enterprise going on, and if such appeals have no motivational impact whatsoever, or only accidentally so?[6] Why bother to construct principles which have no pedigree of their own, unless they have their own "gravity"?[7] Suppose that it is possible to organize a body of law in terms of a set of principles which would not be recognized as right and relevant by either the legislature, the courts or the legal subjects, would it make any sense to take these principles into account? On the other hand, if there is such a collective enterprise, and if it relies on the moral motives disposing people to cooperate on fair terms, then we will not necessarily always have to go through the motions of "finding" our values and principles by way of the internal reconstruction of the legal system. We may sometimes as well derive them from social morality directly, or find them by *its* internal reconstruction, i.e. by arguments of critical morality. And even if we elicit them by internal reconstruction, this is not an exercise in the construction of a possible world, but a way of discovering the real one.[8]

---

[4] That may not be decisive. "De vrouw is aan haar man gehoorzaamheid verschuldigd, zegt art. 161 B.W. Dit wil een rechtsbeginsel beduiden; het is doode letter." Scholten 1974, 65-66. (A wife owes her husband obedience; this claims to be a legal principle, but it is a dead letter.)

[5] Sartorius 1966, 183-190; 1971 ("recursively characterized"); MacCormick 1978, ch. 7, e.g. 155, 166, ch. 9, 226-246, cf. 106; MacCormick 1986, ch. 7; Soeteman 1986, 160ff; Brink 1985, 371-373 ("quasi-justification"). Cf. *Quint-Te Poel*, quoted ch. 9, note 49. If the test of institutional fit leaves us with alternative sets of values and principles, we could then apply the test of moral fit as a tiebreaker. (This is Dworkin's original stance, Dworkin 1977, ch. 4.) The internal reconstruction thesis is not a form of soft positivism, because the validity of legal principles is not derived from the rule of recognition directly, but indirectly, by way of legal norms.

[6] Cf. the similar question I asked about the revealed preference conception of utility, ch. 1.3.

[7] Shiner 1992, 194-199; cf. already Scholten 1935, 269-270. MacCormick 1978 says on the one hand that the "underpinning reasons" for the recognition of the rule of recognition refer us to "some conscious commitment to underlying political values" (140), on the other that the appeal to principles is a postulated requirement of coherence in the law (152).

[8] That is why legal dogmatics should avoid fictions, cf. Scholten 1974.13.

I am not denying the importance of the test of "institutional fit"; far from it. If law is a specification of a publicly accepted morality, there may often be no surer way to identify the fundamental tenets of this morality than by trying to rationalize the actual requirements of the law in terms of underlying goals and principles. But if we have captured the sense and point of the whole system in this way, we have unearthed the actual foundations of the law, and not just found a peculiar way of making the system coherent. Internal reconstruction has only a heuristic value.

Why should we even want to make the system coherent? It is often said that the function of principles is to rationalize the norms of a legal system within a systematic framework. But this is putting things upside down. Surely the norms themselves, conceived as ideal normative entities in Popper's third world (or as the commands of a sovereign), do not require being rationalized or systematized. Rather, the principles and values require to be specified authoritatively for particular types of circumstance. Principles and values do not get their legal importance because they provide us with a way to organize law; rather, we want to organize law around them because law can only claim to provide authoritative norms by being alive to our sense of fairness.[9] Principles belong to the *skeleton* of the law; authority only provides the flesh.

We must refer to values and principles in order to determine the implicit extension of conventions, both substantial and formal ones. That is the reason why they are relevant for the interpretation of the norms which derive their validity from formal conventions as well. The alternative would be to consider them as part of the implicit extension of the norms themselves. I have argued that this is implausible: if we take the rules as ideal normative entities only, there is no reason to suppose that they have any implicit extension. If we know that doing $x$ is required by a valid norm, and doing $x$ implies doing $y$, we cannot conclude that doing $y$ is required by a valid norm. It depends on what it means for a valid norm to exist. If valid norms are expressions of a sovereign power, the conclusion is not warranted, for the power may not know that doing $x$ implies doing $y$. If valid norms are patterns of mutual expectations, the conclusion is not warranted either, for belief is equally subject to referential opacity as volition is. That is one reason why a pure theory of law is impossible: if we have not determined its ontology, we have not determined its logic either. Therefore, if a principle is part of the best internal reconstruction of the law, it is not on that account necessarily part of the law.[10]

It may seem that this argument undermines my own account as well. As soon as we use values and principles in an inferential argument, the referential opacity of mutual expectations will not allow us to interpret our conclusions as part of the law. From the fact that $x$ (the rule) is part of the pattern of expectations, that $y$ (the value) is so as well, and that $x$ and $y$ together entail $z$, it does not follow that $z$ is also part of this pattern. The answer to this objection is that it does not always follow, but it sometimes does: to a certain extent people are able to mirror each other's practical arguments from

---

[9] Cf. ch. 12.4. on the ideal of coherence.

[10] Raz 1994, 212-213; Scholten 1974, 45-46, referring to Jhering's famous criticism of Karl Bergbohm's "Begriffsjurizprudenz": from a command one cannot conclude that the commanding authority also "wills" its implicit extension.

given clues.[11] Sometimes we can be assured that (almost) everyone involved will follow the same inferential path, be assured that the others will follow it, etc. This is especially the case with formal conventions: for the procedures they specify for norms to acquire validity may include forms of inference as well.[12]

So each convention has what I will call a *latent extension*, which includes all the applications to possible cases that can be reached by *interdependent reasoning*. Indeed, every legal norm created by authority could be said to belong to the latent extension of a formal convention, at any rate at the beginning of its existence. (It may develop into a substantial convention.) For it has to be arrived at from the formal convention (do what *X* tells you to do) by inference (*X* tells you to do *x*, therefore do *x*). However, because the core meaning of such a legal norm is already fully at our disposal, I will take it to be part of the manifest extension of the convention. Finding the latent extension requires actual reasoning.

Legal argument has the double aspect we found in critical moral argument: it makes latent extensions manifest, and thereby enlarges the actual range of the mutual expectations which are fully at our disposal. In the propositional sphere the aim of the activity is to discover the truth; in the sphere of social interaction it is to create new manifest expectations (at least within the community of legal experts in a certain area of law).

This view of the nature of legal argument, to be developed more extensively in the next chapter, has some important consequences. First it illuminates the role of doctrine. Doctrinal theory is related to law as critical morality to positive morality: in fact, it is an extension of the same normative activity.[13] For this reason, doctrine is as much a necessary "source" of law as custom and precedent: as soon as it exists, it cannot fail to shape the convergence of expectations. The law is found and made at the same time.[14]

The same is true about judicial argument in hard cases. A hard case is a case in which the correct decision is not fully at our disposal as part of the manifest extension of the relevant conventions. But it may be part of the latent extension, and hence be discoverable by interdependent reasoning.[15] In that case the judge does not have the strong discretion positivists usually think he has. He is duty-bound to decide the case in a certain way, because that is antecedently the right way to decide it.

This account is even meant to cover those epoch-making judicial decisions that break through legal norms which are held to "exist", but have come to be widely

---

[11] This also explains why seemingly aesthetic requirements (simplicity, naturalness) are relevant to the assessment of a legal (esp. "constructive") argument, Scholten 1974.13.

[12] A system of formal conventions may recognize a metaconvention providing that everything which is logically implied by valid rules is a valid rule, cf. ch. 11.2. at note 16.

[13] Though it may be "detached" to a certain extent, cf. ch. 8.5.

[14] Scholten 1974 considers the "systematic" or constructive method to be a matter of coherence only, resulting in universal propositions which have merely "internal validity"; but analogical reasoning in his view aims at finding principles with "external validity", "tendenzen, welke ons zedelijk oordeel aan het recht stelt" (84, "tendencies which our moral judgment imposes on law").

[15] On possibly remaining indeterminacies see ch. 12.5.

perceived as "traps".[16] From their internal point of view – to borrow the form of argument Hart himself uses against Austin's adoption theory – the judges deciding such a seminal case do not intend to create a right, but to finally recognize it. They understand that following the well-trodden path would be "manifestly absurd or morally repugnant" to such an extent that it can no longer be expected.

## 10.2. The Objection from Wicked Legal Systems

A pure system of substantial conventions (custom), as well as a mixed system of formal and substantial conventions, and even, if it exists, a pure system of formal conventions, should all be conceived in the same way: as systems of mutual expectations, enabling participants to contribute to the achievement of aims they believe to be worthwhile, by appealing to each other's cooperative dispositions. This requires that the interpretation, both of the substantial conventions and of norms validated by formal ones, and in particular their non-routine applications to relatively unfamiliar cases, should be informed by the relevant values of the cooperative enterprise and the relevant principles of cooperative virtue. Hence the indispensability of moral argument.

A standard objection to views of this kind is to point to the existence of wicked legal systems, e.g. German law during the reign of the Nazi's, the law of Eastern-European states under communism, Argentinian or Chilean law under military dictatorship, or South-African law during the Apartheid regime. How are we to understand the relevant values of those cooperative enterprises: the supremacy of the Aryan race, the dictatorship of the proletariat, the protection of existing property relations? Is the argument in those terms really to be considered an exercise in "critical morality"? Positivism prefers to distinguish between the law as it is – norms produced by legislative authority, valid (or "valid") irrespective of their content – and the law as it should be, informed by the values and principles of a really enlightened morality, whether or not it still has any public standing in this particular society. This leaves good-willing judges in those systems with a clear and sober view of their options: to exercise their discretion in filling the gaps left by legislative authority in the most humane way they can get away with, to sabotage evil law by intentional misinterpretation, or to retire from office.[17]

As a rule, the appeal to wicked systems is made in a rather casual way. But the case of South African law under Apartheid has been extensively studied by David

---

[16] On conventions as "traps" see ch. 2.6. at note 40. Dutch examples of such trail-blazing decisions include those mentioned in ch. 9, note 49, and ch. 10, note 3. Cf. the Dutch judicial legislation on euthanasia and assisted suicide, described in Griffiths 1998. In NJ 74, 68 the High Court signalizes to the lawgiver that a person who in good faith uses a legal instrument in a formally defective way (or too late) should not be duped by his oversight; in NJ 76, 502, the Court itself decides in this way. Lord Atkin in *Donoghue vs. Stevenson*: "I do not think so ill of our jurisprudence as to suppose that its principles are so remote from the ordinary needs of civilized society... to deny a legal remedy where there is so obviously a social wrong," Similarly Scholten 1974, 122 on *Lindenbaum/Cohen*: the law might not have been changed, if the defendant's action had not been so obviously wrong.

[17] Hart 1982 150-153; Raz 1994, 208.

Dyzenhaus.[18] From the moment the Nationalist Party acquired power in the elections of 1948, South African courts were confronted with cases in which people designated in the offical racial classification as Blacks and Coloureds contested statutory and (mostly) executive measures aiming at segregation or at "national security", i.e. the silencing of protest and opposition. The courts responded in two fundamentally different ways. The first group of judges considered the common law tradition of South African law to be the basic framework for interpreting all law, including the new Apartheid legislation. Constitutive for this framework are individual human rights, protecting liberty, especially against the executive, and establishing equality. Now it was obvious that the new legislation continuously created "fundamental inroads" on these principles. Common law judges would uphold the legality of executive measures if they were *expressis verbis* allowed by the new legislation, but they would refuse to extend violation of common law principles in any way, arguing that the Legislature could only be held to intend such violations if it did so explicitly. In other words, they started from the presumption that the Legislature intended to be faithful to the common law tradition,[19] and in their interpretation of statute "screened out" all less than decisive pointers to the contrary. For instance, even if it had been explicitly decided that public amenities (like a post office) may be segregated into white and black compartments, it did not follow in the view of the common law judge that it could be part of legislative intention to allow substantial inequality in the quality of service, for example by reserving all first-class railway coaches for whites.[20]

The other group of judges had a different view of judicial responsibility. Some of them also expressed their uneasiness at what they recognized to be violations of the common law principles. In their view, however, the task of the court consisted only in applying the law as the Lawgiver really intended it to be applied. For that reason, they would extensively consider evidence of legislative intention not contained in the wording of statute (the 'historical design" test)[21] and be prepared to set aside the common law as the relevant interpretative framework if sufficient indirect indications existed that the Legislature intended it to be set aside. Such "counterpointers" included stipulations that could hardly have had any point when the principles were fully in force, and the extension by analogous argument of the explicit intention of a law to a disputed matter not formally covered by that law. Dyzenhaus calls this the "plain fact approach".

During the period of Nationalist ascendancy, the room for manoeuvre of common law judges steadily decreased. Extensive legislation was introduced to give

---

[18] Dyzenhaus 1991.

[19] That way of constructing the relevance of common law principles should clearly be considered a legal fiction or "pious fraud"; it formally accepts the idea that valid law is what the political authorities intend it to be.

[20] *R. vs. Abdurahman* 1950, Dyzenhaus 1991 63ff. The government reacted in a characteristic way by making a law explicitly allowing substantially inequal treatment.

[21] In a pioneering decision of this approach, in 1911, Chief Justice De Villiers interpreted legislative intention against the background of the "positive morality" of white superiority, noting that "we may not from a philosophical or humanitarian point of view be able to approve this prevalent sentiment..." Dyzenhaus 1991, 56.

limitless discretionary powers to the executive, powers to be exercised on purely subjective criteria of reasonableness. ("A member of a Force may, without warrant of arrest, arrest... any person whose detention is, in the opinion of such member, necessary for the maintenance of public order or the safety of the public or that person himself...") Furthermore, there was a series of judicial decisions, motivated by the plain fact view, that willingly acceded to the executive any power it claimed to have. By 1970, the Appellate Division had made it crystal clear that judges should be alert to the legislative intention that security officers are not required to observe any common law principles of reasonableness, fairness and equality in using their powers, and by 1986 it had in all but form abdicated from controlling power in any way. But even then some remarkable common law decisions were still made. For example, when statute allowed the detention without warrant of arrest to be extended beyond fourteen days by a simple written notice of the Minister of the Interior, a common law judge required a fair hearing of the prisoner before the notice was given, and when the government responded to his decision by making a law explicitly denying this requirement, the judge concluded that fair hearing then should take place afterwards. For it can only be assumed to be the intention of the legislative to set aside the *audi et alteram partem* principle to the extent that it does so explicitly. Then at last the tide started to turn in 1988.

What lessons can be learned from this case study of law in wicked systems? For the defenders of the indispensability of moral argument, it shows a way of dealing with the standard objection. If coercive systems try to avail themselves of the benefits of the semblance of legality, they provide the courts with an opportunity to counteract their oppressive policies, if only on a small scale. Not only in the ways positivism envisaged, by exercising discretion and perhaps by sabotage, but by using the moral resources of the law itself. For by the very use of the legal form such regimes connect themselves to a legal tradition that, as such, embodies moral values and principles opposed to their aims. Of course, it depends on the courts to what extent these resources are actually used.[22]

Dyzenhaus believes that he can turn the tables on positivism by associating their view with the plain fact approach. But what is really revealing in the history he relates is rather that Hartian positivism has not been represented at all by any group of judges.[23] Of course not, one could say: if any judge had actually taken the stance positivism enjoins her to take, she would hardly have done so openly. But that is precisely the point. The conventional understanding of the judicial office, to which the judge cannot fail to be publicly committed, cannot allow judges to fill the gaps of the law by appeal to their private moral views.[24]

---

[22] Cf. Cover 1975 arguing that the American legal tradition had the interpretative resources that could and should have enabled judges not to deliver fugitive slaves to their masters.

[23] Cf. Dyzenhaus 1994, 81 about the "esoteric" character of legal theory as conceived by positivism.

[24] I do not deny that a judge in a wicked system may sometimes have a moral duty secretly to obstruct the law from taking its course, but that is not a duty of his role. Even in such systems, their judicial role "typically" (in the sense explained in ch. 5.5., i.e. as a default-rule) provide judges with moral reasons to comply with the requirements of their role, at least as long as they are justified not to resign, or even excused

Courts make two claims. In the first place, they claim to identify the reasons for action which the parties antecedently had, and which derive from substantial and formal conventions, in particular from the exercise of legislative authority. In the second place, they claim to make this identification authoritatively; they take the stance that their decisions are worthy of obedience as such, even if they, occasionally and unintentionally, fail to make good on their first claim. It follows that judges must be partners to a convention of adjudication,[25] such that they can hold (or, in the parasitical case, can at least seriously pretend to hold)[26] that their appeal to legislative authority results in authoritative decisions. But in that case both the moral reasons for obedience and the essential conditions for having such moral reasons (if these are recognized) should, in the shared view of the judges themselves, be capable of being publicly ascertained.[27]

This is obviously true of the common law judges: they did not appeal to their own moral views or to moral truth, but to the basic values and principles of the common law. But it is also true of the plain fact judges. For even their practice of absolute deference to legislative authority presupposes a moral understanding of the judicial role. Dyzenhaus makes a convincing case for identifying this political morality as a quasi-Hobbesian one: the lexical priority of the value of *Rechtssicherheit* to all considerations of justice. This position is often considered to be a form of positivism; indeed it is the position Gustav Radbruch had in mind when he denounced positivism for paving the way for the German courts' slavish submission to the Nazi's.[28] But on Hart's understanding, it is not a form of positivism at all, because it establishes a necessary relation between law and morality: all law, as such, has overriding moral significance. It is rather a weird kind of "natural law" theory.[29]

---

from not resigning. Raz accepts that the duty of judges to obey the law tends to be more extensive than the duty of legal subjects, cf. Feldman 1992, 1412-1417 with references.

[25] A "complex, but normally concordant, practice of the courts, officials, and private persons identifying the law by reference to certain criteria", Hart 1961, 107.

[26] As private individuals they may only be interested in furthering their career, avoiding conflicts with the executive etc. Such reasons are irrelevant to the conventional understanding of the duties of their station.

[27] Raz recognizes that courts, to be courts, must profess to a moral understanding of the judicial role, Raz 1975, 139, 171; 1979, 113; 1994, 207. But he does not understand this morality as a matter of "public reason".

[28] Radbruch 1946. It has been shown that his accusation is historically inaccurate, Müller 1987; Rüthers 1989; Rottleuthner 1983; Ott & Buob 1993. "Positivism" was associated with the deference to democratic decisions that was part of the political morality of the Weimar republic. The German judiciary was quite happy to decide in accordance with the "values and principles" of the Nazi regime – often, but not necessarily, on the instruction of party bosses. Hence it was often not even necessary for the regime to change the law to make it more concordant with its wishes. This shows that a form of jurisprudence that allows the appeal to values and principles can be as disastrously wrong in its execution as any plain fact approach, to the extent of completely undermining any claim to respect and obedience. It is not an implication of conventionalist antipositivism to deny this possibility, as it is of Dworkin's views. Note that the German judges did not bother to make any moral appeal to their victims, but were content to simply treat them as enemies of the people.

[29] Cf. Finnis' formalist natural law theory, resting on his view of the law as a seamless web, cf. § 5, note 49. But Finnis requires a minimal level of performance of the law in its coordinative function for the common good. Cf. Raz 1975, 165-170 on the compatibility of positivism and natural law: a theory may identify law by non-moral features but argue that these features are such as to ensure it some moral value. This is a rather common understanding of positivism outside the English-speaking world (and the source of the basic misunderstandings between Hart and Radbruch).

On neither of these views is there any room for the appeal to moral standards in the exercise of strong discretionary powers of decision. That is not accidental: there can be no such room on any understanding of the judicial office. The point can be made by using the Lockean thought-experiment again. Imagine the topic of the role of judges coming up in the general meeting in which the transition into the legal world is discussed. Suppose one of those present proposes that, as a matter of public responsibility, they will only be bound to source-based norms, on the understanding that gaps left by insufficient determinacy of, or conflict between these norms will be filled by judges appealing to considerations they deem to be relevant, including moral ones. This proposal will be clearly unacceptable. If the participants to the meeting agree that moral considerations should be relevant, they will insist on taking into account only considerations they can share, and therefore on making them *publicly* relevant.

The proposal of the positivist suffers from three shortcomings. The first one is a common place by now: the proposal does not respect the fact that the judicial role is essentially concerned with the past. If they exercise discretion, how can they be in the business of identifying pre-existing reasons for action, content-independent or not? The problem is not only that the parties are supposed to have had those reasons at the time of action, it is that such reasons can only derive from patterns of mutual expectations already in place at that time.[30]

Suppose that a positivistic judge in giving his verdict says to the parties $A$ and $B$ what he believes to be true: "In your case there is no legal fact of the matter, the relevant considerations either underdetermining it, or being in unresolvable conflict with each other. Morally, however, it is preferable that $A$ wins. So I decide he wins." It is not, as Hart and Raz suggest, a matter of psychology that judges commonly refrain from saying such things; rather it would, in any jurisdiction, undermine their authority. The parties could only feel offended and/or baffled, the winner $A$ as well as the loser $B$. For even $A$ thought he deserved to win because he had a legitimate expectation concerning $B$'s behaviour, which $B$'s actual actions did not honour. That is what their dispute was all about. So if neither of them was right on the issue in dispute, how can the judge be empowered to make any decision at all? Why should his private judgment that the world would morally be a better place if $A$ wins, be relevant? Why should even the fact that this private judgment happened to be true, be relevant?

It could be objected that it is impossible for the judicial role to be fully backwards-looking, because legal norms can never achieve the degree of determinateness this requires. Here we come upon the second defect of the positivist proposal: it underestimates the resources of a system of conventions to identify its latent extension, in particular by reference to its underlying values and principles. (Formalists, of course, cannot use this plea in their defence.)

The third defect of the proposal is its monadic conception of "critical" morality. It sees judicial responsibility from two unrelated points of view: the conventional point

---

[30] Even if a judge is instructed to put himself in the place of a wise legislator in cases in which he seemingly runs out of legal considerations – as he is by the code of the Schweizerische Landesgericht – he does not necessarily exercise discretion by following the instruction, for it may still be supposed to be publicly ascertainable what he will decide.

of view and the point of view of morality. It is possibly (soft positivism) or universally true that the rule of recognition only identifies social facts as generating judicial duties. If that is the case, then whenever a judge finds that what he is expected to decide is morally wrong or dubious, it is not a matter of mutual expectations if he attaches any consequences to the fact, but only a matter of his individual conscience. Legal duty is public, a matter of interdependent reasons, moral duty is private, a matter of independent reasons.[31] However, this is shown to be wrong by the very fact that even a formalist understanding of the judicial duty itself, which excludes the relevance of moral argument, has to justify itself on the public forum by arguments of political morality.

So there is no possible "internal point of view" that judges can take and from which moral considerations are seen as relevant, but not legally, i.e. conventionally relevant; from which such considerations are only seen as relevant because of the extensive leeway judges have to follow their own moral convictions. When Hart says that, for a decent regime following a dictatorship, it is a moral quandary whether to punish oppressive actions of the former regime by retroactive legislation, or to let such actions go unpunished, that is obviously a statement of *public* morality.[32] Judges have only two options: to believe that they must apply content-independently valid norms in accordance with the plain meaning of authoritative texts and the intention of its authors, even if this leads to absurd or repugnant results, or to believe that they must prevent such results by reference to values and principles which can be assumed to be publicly recognized or recognizable, and hence to be taken into account by legal subjects as well. In both cases they must appeal to a public morality in order to justify their conception of the duties of their station, and in both cases this public morality will fail to give them strong discretionary powers of decision.

I have argued in the preceding sections that the first option is not really available either. This invites the objection, however, that even if this conception of judicial responsibility is mistaken, it may be the conventional understanding that judges actually hold, as the plain fact judges did. In that case my argument would only warrant a soft-positivistic conclusion. Before dealing with this objection (in sections 4 and 5), I must consider one last way in which positivism might try to deny even the possible relevance of moral argument to questions of legal validity.

## 10.3. Two Kinds of Duties?

One particular argument for denying the possible relevance of moral argument to establishing legal validity ("hard positivism") starts with conceding most of the points I have made. It is a fact that, at least in some jurisdictions but perhaps even in all, courts engage in moral argument in order to arrive at their decisions. It is not only a fact, it is

---

[31] Cf. Ch. 8.6.

[32] Hart 1961, 204ff; Hart (1953) 1983, 72-78.

part of their duties *ex officio*. But whenever the courts fulfil this particular duty, they are no longer in the business of applying the law, but rather of making it.

How are we to make this distinction? We did consider the argument that whenever moral reasoning is required, the result is too controversial to be predictable, and we concluded that this argument overestimates the controversiality of moral judgment as such. In response, the positivist could claim that questions of reasonableness and fairness may be fully decidable, but even so, they must be decided before the answer can be law. Therefore the law is changed, even if the judge is duty-bound to change it, and even if she is duty-bound to change it in this particular and predictable way. (After all, legislatures may be duty-bound in similar ways, e.g. in criminalizing *mala per se*.) If an appeal is made to the authority of the legislature, there *is* law, which only has to be reproduced by adjudication. The courts are involved in interpretation. But as soon as moral argument is required, the courts are no longer involved in interpreting or reproducing pre-existing law, they are making new law, to be reproduced by later decisions.[33]

At this point we may start wondering whether the remaining distance between positivism, even so-called "hard" positivism, and antipositivism is still worth caring about. Both positions agree that judges qua judges are duty-bound to ascertain the plain meaning of statute on the one hand and to make judgments of reasonableness and equity on the other, and to take both types of judgment into account in arriving at their final judgment. How important is it whether what the judge is duty-bound to do, is called applying the law or changing it (with retro-active force!), in particular when the outcome of the activity is predictable and hence can be relied upon?[34]

Nevertheless, for what it is worth, I believe that positivism has to surrender even this last ditch. Let us focus on a judge who is not considering statute but custom. Strictly speaking she is not involved in the business of interpretation, for a convention has no "meaning", it does not refer to anything outside itself. On the other hand, the movement of thought involved in establishing the "latent extension" of a convention – whether and how it applies to a case with relevant properties not met before – is so similar to interpretation, that it can hardly be inappropriate to use the term.[35] If you ask people who know the custom what it involves, they may all give you the same text which needs only to be enacted to become statute. Establishing what, if anything, this custom requires in an unfamiliar case, cannot be a very different intellectual activity from establishing what the corresponding statute requires.

In any case, it is clearly a matter of reproducing something which has an independent existence. And that is no less true when the judge considers that a certain prima facie plausible application of a convention produces absurd or unfair results. For

---

[33] This is how I understand Raz' present position: Raz 1996a; Raz 1996b. Cf. Raz 1979, 182.

[34] For Raz it is important because it follows from his "dependence"-conception of authority: weighing moral reasons belongs to the deliberative stage of reasoning in which an authoritative judgment is made, in the executive stage of reasoning these reasons are displaced by the dependent reasons given by authority. This distinction of stages is introduced in Raz 1980, 213-216. Cf. Morris 1996, 827.

[35] That is why Michael Walzer's description of moral argument as interpretative (of a social practice) is not as improper as Raz 1991 suggests, at least not for some forms of moral argument.

he still claims that the parties to the convention could and should have drawn the same conclusion, he is still "mirroring" their reasoning in the way each of them is supposed to "mirror" the reasoning of the other.[36] The absurdity of a possible conclusion is simply a clue for identifying the proper result, in the same way as the salience of a particular property or the temporal closeness of a precedent is.[37] In the case of a substantial convention, therefore, the appeal to values and principles is relevant for establishing what the convention requires, and the convention is not thereby "changed", except in the way in which the meaning of a text can also be said to "change" in the history of its interpretation.

As we have seen, old laws have a tendency to develop into substantial conventions.[38] Interpreting the meaning of the law in such cases does not involve attending to the natural meaning of its words, but to the mutual expectations of the partners to the convention. If this requires the appeal to values and principles, it follows that this appeal is directly relevant to "interpreting the meaning of the law". However, the main point is that the meaning of the law is not what we are basically interested in at all, we are interested in establishing what is required by convention.

So why should this be suddenly different in the case of a recent statute? It is true that here the appeal to values and principles may happen to instruct us to deviate from the meaning of the statute. Interpreting the meaning of statute is no longer identical to establishing the law. But that does not alter the fact that there is a pre-existing reality that is reproduced by establishing the law, the same conventional reality as in the case of custom and of old laws. Why should the requirement that "applying the law" should be a form of *reproduction* now address itself to a different object?

Applying the law means establishing what is implied by the pattern of mutual expectations that governed the interaction of the parties. This may require to consider statute, but that is only one clue among others. If legal subjects know that the courts will be duty-bound to deviate from statute in their case, they may have no reason to comply with statute at all. But how can what they have no reason to do, and no reason to expect each other to do, nevertheless *be* the law?

I said that in the case of a recent statute, the appeal to values and principles may happen to instruct us to deviate from its meaning. This may happen to be so, but it need not. Suppose that a statute can be read in two different ways, but gives reasonable and fair results on one of those readings only. This is not just a reason to prefer that particular interpretation, but on many occasions we should also say that only this interpretation gives the plain or natural meaning of the statute. Common understandings of the relevant values and principles of the law belong to the necessary context of interpreting its wording. The lawgiver is a participant in the same community of understanding, and so must be supposed to have anticipated the relevant standards to be taken into account in the interpretation of his text.

---

[36] See ch. 11.1.-2. on " vicarious reasoning".

[37] This is more obviously the case for common law reasoning: you can only decide whether or not to distinguish by moral argument, Goldsworthy 1990, 466ff.

[38] As Raz agrees, cf. ch. 9, note 17.

It follows that it is impossible to separate legal reasoning neatly into two groups – considerations relevant for establishing the law, and considerations relevant for changing it – and to relegate moral arguments exclusively to the second group. At first sight this may seem a plausible move for cases where the appeal to the plain meaning of an authoritative text, and the appeal to reasonableness and fairness, give different results. But there are also cases – and they are not sharply differentiated from the first type of case – where the appeal to reasonableness and fairness is relevant for interpreting the plain meaning of a text, or (in the case of an old law) the meaning it has acquired as an expression of an existing convention. This shows that the plausibility of this neat view is superficial: it takes the appearance of the law, which is authority, for its reality, which is convention.

## 10.4. The Law and Judicial Duty

As I suggested at the end of section 2, it might seem that my arguments in this chapter do not refute soft positivism, but rather tend to confirm it. After all, it can hardly be denied that it is possible for a plain fact or "seamless web" jurisdiction to exist.[39]

In section 5 of the previous chapter I argued that considerations of reasonableness and equity are not "excluded" by the exercise of legislative authority. All I showed, however, was that they are not necessarily excluded, because they are not excluded in the legal systems of liberal democratic states. It does not follow that there could not be legal systems in which they are excluded. After all, I have conceded that, even if the existence of exclusionary reasons is not implied by the recognition of authority, it is quite possible for the power-conferring rules instituting judicial offices to contain exclusionary clauses. Would not it be possible for such clauses to exclude all moral considerations? Maybe Hart had a point after all when he stressed the danger that juridification could lose sight of its inherent moral limitations. All that is necessary to actualize the danger is the perhaps not quite accidental meeting of real coercive power with a formalist legal theory. Why should it be impossible for a legal system to embody formalism to any, even the fullest extent?

In this section and the next one I will develop two arguments aiming to refute this objection. Both take their starting point in an argument by a self-styled (soft) positivist, Waluchow and Hart respectively.

The first argument addresses a question I have considered before. Law is a subset of all the numerous conventions that exist in a human society. How is the subset to be identified? The indisputable fact that legislative and adjudicative authority are so important in law has led legal theorists to suggest that it is the role of these authorities, and in particular the role of adjudicative authority, which separates legal norms from others. This thesis has been proposed in different forms, which I will discuss in the order of the stringency of the proposed relation.

---

[39] "Pineal gland" formalism, however, cannot be instantiated, as I argued in ch.10.2.

In the strongest form of the thesis, the *differentia specifica* of a legal norm is that it is directly addressed to adjudicative authorities. According to Kelsen, for instance, legal norms command the courts to apply sanctions (in his wide sense of "sanction" which includes all legal remedies). A somewhat weaker form of the thesis says that legal norms are the norms the courts are duty-bound to recognize as such. According to Dworkin, for instance, legal norms specify the rights and corresponding duties which can be claimed in court and which judges are obliged to grant. This is a weaker form than the first thesis because it does not deny that it is primarily the conduct of citizens which the legal norm seeks to guide.[40] The weakest form of the thesis only says that legal norms are the norms the courts should take into account in reaching their decisions, whether or not they are duty-bound finally to "apply" the norm, or perhaps rather to change it. In this form the thesis is accepted by Raz.[41]

The stronger forms of the thesis, as proposed by Kelsen and in particular by Dworkin, have been subjected to thorough criticism by Waluchow.[42] He points to the fact that in some jurisdictions, the Hohfeldian powers of lower and higher courts may differ, and that as a result they are instructed to treat the same case in different ways. He gives an example from a common law jurisdiction where the lower courts are duty-bound to follow the *ratio decidendi* of a precedent if the case at hand is not reasonably distinguishable, even when the judges consider this outcome manifestly absurd or morally repugnant. They may, though, sometimes explicitly express their wish that a higher court on appeal will use its power to give a more acceptable ruling.

Even the highest courts may suffer from similar incapacities. In many European states, including the Netherlands, not even the Supreme Court is allowed to assess the compatibility of a formal law with the national constitution.[43] In a famous case, the Dutch High Court had to give a judgment on the question whether a law aimed at implementing a significant reduction of students' allowances should be upheld, even if this law had been given retroactive force.[44] The Court found that by reference to the constitution, the law was thoroughly objectionable, but that it could nevertheless not be annulled.[45] (Interestingly, the reason given was that annulment would violate a basic

---

[40] In his discussion of Dworkin's view, Waluchow 1994, 46ff, does not recognize this difference between Kelsen and Dworkin. It is true that Dworkin occasionally says that the moral rights belonging to the law are rights to win the law suit, Dworkin 1977, 89, or rights to a decision, Dworkin 1986, 152, but this cannot be their full description, for in that case the decision by itself would vouchsafe those rights, irrespective of its execution. But it is clear that for Dworkin the relevant rights are rights to the goods that the decision should make available. This certainly makes it incoherent for him, as Waluchow points out, to index the rights according to the court which decides your case, cf. Dworkin 1986, 452-453 note 1. That would be possible if you have rights to decisions, but not if you have rights to goods. For this reason, Hart's criticism of Kelsen (the primary aim of the law is to guide people's conduct, not judges') does not apply to Dworkin.

[41] Raz 1975, 139; 1979, 113; 1996b.

[42] Waluchow 1994, 46-58.

[43] On Dworkin's view this would mean that citizens of such states do not have constitutional rights against the legislative. It should be noted that Dutch courts have the power to annul statutes if they are incompatible with regulations of international treaties, and the power to stipulate that strict application of a statutory norm should be omitted if this would conflict with so-called general principles of decent administration.

[44] *Harmonisatiewet-arrest.* HR 14/4/1989, NJ 1989, 469.

[45] The minister of education took the hint and redrafted the law.

principle of the politico-legal system, the subordination of the courts to the legislative powers of the crown and parliament. The court should rather, by reference to the very same constitution, have stated that it simply lacked the Hohfeldian power to annul.)

So when the law is said to be identifiable in terms of what a legal authority is instructed to pronounce, Waluchow wants to know which authority we have to look at. The lower court, which is bound by precedent, or the higher one, which is free to disregard it? The supreme court, which cannot assess the constitutionality of a formal law, or parliament, which has the constitutional duty to make this assessment?

Waluchow rightly concludes that we cannot read off the law from the duties of legal authorities, we should rather distinguish between the grounds of the law and its "institutional force", i.e. what legal authorities are to make of it. When a judge or a jury in a criminal case has to establish the facts of the matter, they are not allowed to consider all possibly relevant considerations on their merits, but they are subject to all kinds of restrictions as to what they are permitted to allow as proof or as evidence. In view of this it would be very strange for someone, even if he subscribed to some odd constructivist conception of truth, to suggest that the factual truth is what the judge or the jury is duty-bound to regard as the truth. There may of course be very good reasons for these restrictions: they must be seen as forms of indirect rationality, allowing courts to approximate the truth as much as possible, given the inherent limitations of human judgment. They are designed to eliminate well-known sources of mistake, such as bias. But what is true about fact-finding, is true about law-finding as well: courts are subject to a number of restrictions in their reasoning, restrictions which are motivated by the aim of approximating legal truth indirectly.[46] Courts are not fully allowed to balance relevant legal considerations on their merits either, they are bound to indirect adjudicative justice. That it is impossible to identify the law with the outcome of any of their prescribed proceedings, is shown by Waluchow's argument: the outcome may be different for different authorities.

The odd thing is that he does not quite seem to realize the force of this conclusion himself. In his exemplary case, he believes that in the end it is the lower court which is duty-bound to state the law – it is fixed by the precedent case -, while the higher court has the freedom to change the law in the interests of rationality and justice. But how does he know this? The difference between the two courts is that the lower court is duty-bound to give preference to a consideration concerning a source of law – the authoritative decision in a precedent case -, while the higher court must consider "content-dependent" reasons of rationality and justice as well. Both types of consideration have a clearly recognized standing within the legal community; there is no systematic difference in the self-understanding of a judge appealing to either: he will always believe that he is attempting to discover what the law is. It is simply positivist prejudice to consider the former set of considerations as relevant to "stating the law", and the second to "changing it".[47] Moreover, if this distinction could be made so

---

[46] Cf. ch. 7.12.: in role moralities, considerations of indirect rationality may be developed into exclusionary reasons.

[47] It also seems to contradict Waluchow's "inclusive" (soft) positivism, which accepts that appeal to content-dependent considerations, in particular considerations of basic political morality identifiable by reference to a

confidently, the force of Waluchow's example or even of his argument would be undermined. For then it would be possible to say about the jurisdiction Waluchow refers to, that in this system the law can be identified by what the courts are duty-bound to say it is, even when some of the courts, the higher ones, have been given the power to change it.[48]

That would, of course, considerably weaken and perhaps destroy Waluchow's case against Dworkin. For if Waluchow is to be allowed his positivist prejudice, Dworkin is to be allowed his antipositivist one; and so Dworkin can make the analogous move, claiming that it is rather the duties of the higher court from which we can read off what the law really "is". Then Waluchow is reduced to arguing why it is more implausible to pick the higher court than the lower one. Indeed, that is what he tries to do, but not very successfully. If we take our clue from the lower court, he says, then the court that "changes" the law at least does so for the better; while if we prefer the higher court, the lower court is condemned not only to violate the law, but to violate it for the worse. That will hardly be a consolation, either for the party against whom the lower court is duty-bound to make the manifestly absurd and morally repugnant decision, or for the party who loses his legally valid case before the higher court.[49] It is law as it is, not as it may be altered, which is supposed to guide citizens' behaviour, so on this construction they are to follow an occasionally absurd and repugnant guide, fully aware that the court of highest appeal will not countenance their compliance. In this way we are in danger of losing the basic thrust of the original argument, which is to show that we do not have a choice to begin with: courts do not simply aim at establishing the law, they do so in artificially filtered ways, and therefore we cannot find in their briefs the criteria we are after for the identification of legal considerations as such. It is clear that in Waluchow's example it is precisely the lower court which is strongly restricted by such filters. So to present his argument in its strongest form, we should say that no court which is bound systematically to disregard manifest absurdity and moral repugnance in favour of clear precedents, as this lower court is, can ever be fully trusted as a guide to legal truth, even if it never makes mistakes, or precisely if it never makes mistakes.

We should not try to determine in any general way which of the courts "state", and which of them "changes" the law. The decisions of both count as authoritative judgments about legal truth, even if only one of them (at most) can be fully correct. If we could decide this question in a general way, there would be no need for the filters to begin with.

---

system's rule of recognition, may be required for determining the validity or content of a purported legal norm. Cf. his argument, Waluchow 1994, 161, that a decision of that kind determines the legal status of the actions which gave rise to litigation, hence *before* the law has been "changed".

[48] For this reason, Waluchow's own version of the third thesis (law is what the courts are duty-bound to apply or to change) is also incompatible with the distinction between the grounds of the law and its institutional force, at least as long as the courts are supposed to apply or to change the law *knowingly*.

[49] Cf. Postema 1996, 100: judicial role morality cannot allow a citizen to know her behaviour to be consistent with pre-existing law, and yet to lose her case because, all things considered, it is morally preferable that her opponent in litigation wins.

Waluchow's distinction between the grounds of the law and its institutional force is essential to the conventionalist view. For on that view, the law is to be identified with a set of legitimate expectations which the members of a community, or the inhabitants of a territory (including the officials) have or may have of each other's behaviour. These expectations form nested sets, and the inner sets of the series are only available to groups of experts, groups of decreasing sizes. But the most basic pattern of mutual expectations necessarily involves the legal subjects. This basic pattern concerns the recognition of legal authority – a recognition perhaps combined with only the vaguest notion about the way it is distributed – and of its fundamental limits.

It is the task of adjudicative authorities to find out what these expectations are. They are instructed to do so in certain ways, perhaps using certain filters. That is why we cannot say that what they are duty-bound to establish as the law, really *is* the law. It is at best the best possible approximation of it.

In their pronouncements they will sometimes ascribe to their legal conclusions more determinacy than they really deserve to have. For instance, both clear precedents and considerations of equity are legally relevant considerations, and it may not be determinable in a particular case which of the two should be given precedence, even if one court or the other is instructed to give precedence to only one of the two sets. On the whole, the scope of indeterminacy in the law may be larger than judicial officials are allowed to recognize.[50]

We can now see that even the weakest of the three proposed theses concerning the relation between the law and the duties of judicial authorities cannot be accepted without reservation. According to this thesis, the law consists of those conventions and conventionally validated norms which the courts are duty-bound to take into account. However, a lower court may be prevented by its brief from establishing the legal truth, e.g. because it is instructed to follow a clear precedent, while at the same time appeal to a higher court is ruled out for some reason or other. In the form I gave it, on the other hand, the thesis is too weak, because courts may find occasion to take the existence of non-legal conventions, e.g. linguistic ones, into account, if not to "enforce" them.

I suggest that only the following fourth form of the thesis is true. Legal conventions are those conventions about which the members of a community, or some relevant subset of them, interdependently have reason to expect that they *should* be enforceable by adjudicative authority. This belongs to the *opinio iuris* that is a condition for the existence of the convention. For each convention, it is mutually known whether it is in this sense a legal one or not, and if it is, it is the task of constitutional law to design the judicial office in such a way as to make it enforceable. But this is a task that can only be executed imperfectly.[51]

It follows that, even if the courts consider themselves to have certain systematic disabilities in considering a range of moral considerations, we should not conclude that these considerations are really irrelevant for settling a question of legal validity. Public

---

[50] I will argue in ch. 12.6. that the wish to avoid having to recognize real indeterminacy where it exists, is not a good reason for installing filters. But I do not deny that it may be the actual reason why they are installed.

[51] See ch. 7.13.

discussion within the legal community or in the society at large may establish the discrepancy (and proceed to discussing the appropriateness of the disabilities.)

Of course, the two sides of this discrepancy cannot be isolated against each other. If the legal system of a society is dominated by a strongly formalist ideology, this very fact will influence both the mutual expectations legal subjects will develop, in particular vis-à-vis the officials, and the forms of their actual social interaction. On the other hand, the fact that those expectations necessarily rely on a shared interpretation of this interaction as a cooperative enterprise for some good, will continue to exert its influence on legal interpretation, if only in the fictional form of attributing intentions to the legislative that it does not have. If the discrepancy grows too large, it will threaten to undermine the legitimacy of the legal system. For that reason the ascendancy of an uncompromising formalist ideology tends to be rather short-lived.[52]

If this ideology takes the stronger form of recognizing a lawgiver's unlimited claim to authority, it will suffer from other pathologies as well. As the example of the South-African plain facts judges suggest, a legal system of the quasi-Hobbesian type will tend to withhold the protection of basic rights from its subjects or from certain classes of its subjects. It will then confront these subjects as a system of pure coercion, "a gunman writ large".[53] From their internal point of view they have no reason at all to take it into consideration. It cannot sincerely claim to have authority over them, because it cannot sincerely claim to give them, as Raz would say, "dependent reasons" for obedience. Of course, a purely coercive system can attempt to achieve any additional credibility it can get by making a *hollow* claim to legal authority, and I will not insist that it is linguistically improper to call such a system a system of law. Such linguistic decisions do not serve any substantial point. But, at least as regards some of its subjects, it lacks an essential attribute of law. Therefore, as a system of law it is highly defective and, as I argued before,[54] for any functional entity $x$ there comes an indeterminate point at which a defective $x$ is no longer an $x$.

## 10.5. Scorer's Discretion

This point can be reinforced by another argument. The classical objection against arguments like the one I made in the last section is the following: it is rather futile to say that the courts may get it wrong. For when all is said and done, it is the judgment of the courts that counts; this is the judgment that will be enforced, not the possibly more "correct" judgment of the learned legal author. Judicial judgments have a finality all other legal statements lack. That is what we need them for.

---

[52] In the Netherlands this was the dominant ideology between 1848 and 1880, Kop 1982.

[53] Cf. ch. 8, note 5.

[54] Ch. 3.5. That no great theoretical weight should be given to borderline cases is a view generally shared by Hart 1961, e.g. 79, 208, cf. Finnis 1980, 14; 1987, 62, 68; Shiner 1992, 132. In requiring only the officials of the system to participate in accepting the rule of recognition, Hart deviates from this "central case technique" (Lacey 1986, 225).

So if it is possible for judicial authority to deviate from existing patterns of mutual expectations to the extent of leaving all moral considerations out of account in determining legal validity, it is only a pityful gesture to insist that to that extent it is likely to be mistaken. What you mean is only that law *should* be under the control of values and principles. But it is just wishful thinking to claim that it always *is*.

The answer to this objection can be found in a very elegant argument Hart himself made in discussing the "realist" thesis that law is what the judge says it is.[55] Suppose a competitive game is played, in which the players themselves collaborate in keeping their own scores. At a certain moment they feel the need to enlist the services of an arbiter. This will enable them to concentrate their energy on the game, and prevent unpleasant discussions. From now on the position in the match will be what the arbiter says it is; his decisions will count even if they are mistaken. The realist concludes from this fact that it will no longer make any sense to say that he is "mistaken": no consequences follow from the fact. This is incorrect, Hart says: it is and remains the job of the arbiter to apply the rules of the game. If he stops trying seriously to do so, if his mistakes cease to be incidental and become systematic, if his decisions have only a random relation to the rules of the game, and if the players nevertheless continue (perhaps under compulsion) to accept his decisions, then the game has changed. For a game is defined by its rules; and the new game has just one scoring rule: "the score is what the scorer says it is". It has become the game of "scorer's discretion".

Hence, the introduction of an arbiter does not remove the relevance of the players' judgment. Their position, as Lucas stressed, is even stronger than Hart recognizes: if they continue to keep the score for themselves, they are not just, as Hart says, doing the same thing as the arbiter, only without "legal force". Their results are the criterion for deciding whether the arbiter *is* really arbitrating, or rather changing the game to that of scorer's discretion.[56]

In the same way, the pronouncements of legal authority remain dependent on the shared moral understandings of a society. The legislative and adjucative officials of the system are supposed to regulate the cooperative activities of the citizens for their common good, to uphold the rules that counted before, to change them only for good reasons, and to give detailed specifications of them only when necessary. The citizens had their moral reasons for being prepared to make their contribution, and these reasons should be respected by authoritative decisions.[57] But these are not only normative statements, to be used to assess the quality of the officials' work. They are also criterial statements, to be used to assess its nature. (Of course, in the criterial statements only minimal levels of performance are to be specified, not ideal ones.) Officials may supplement the existing pattern of mutual expectations, correct its details, adapt it to changing circumstances, even try (gradually) to bring it into closer harmony with its underlying values and principles, but they cannot change it substantially, or replace its foundations. If they cease "doing the same thing", if they require obedience merely on

---

[55] Hart 1961, 138ff.

[56] Lucas 1977, 94.

[57] Cf. Raz' dependence thesis, Raz 1986, 42-53.

account of the formal-procedural validity of their requirements, they "change the game", that is to say they try to control the behaviour of the others from a position of superiority exogenous to the game.[58] And, indeed, if they no longer attempt to create obligations, if they no longer appeal to moral motives, it does not matter any more whether their requirements are flawless in the formal-procedural sense either.[59] Formal authority is only relevant against the background of mutual expectations that its results will be accepted. An appeal to authority that is really just meant to camouflage the exercise of compelling power, will therefore always be attended with an attempt to uphold moral appearances. And even this will to some extent constrain the possible constructions of the content of the commands.

## 10.6. The Positivism of Wit

It has often been suggested that the whole debate between positivism and antipositivism, as exemplified perhaps most clearly by the discussion between Hart and Dworkin, rests on a misunderstanding. Antipositivists describe the law from the point of view of the committed participant, in particular the judge, positivists on the contrary describe it from the external point of view of the neutral observer, say the legal anthropologist or the judge outside working hours. If seen that way, the descriptions are fully compatible.[60] For instance, it may be true, as I insisted, that courts do not claim to "exercise discretion", but that does not prove, as I also conceded, that in every new case the law is fully determinate. For at a distance we can see that the law changes over time by judicial decisions, and presumably not just by judicial mistakes. Similarly, moral *argument* may be necessarily relevant to the participant, but the observer is only interested in moral *belief*.

I am not denying that those different points of view exist, and that the legal world looks a bit different from either perspective, or from the "detached" internal point of view. But the comparison between this last point of view and the external one is revealing. In detached reasoning we may either state that some particular premiss of the argument is false, or stay uncommitted on the point. But we can hardly make similar claims concerning all premisses of the argument and concerning the logical relations between the steps of the argument as well. At some point detached reasoning ceases to be reasoning. My contention is that a similar relation exists between the internal and the external point of view. A detailed description from the external point of view will contain the same elements and the same relations which are used in full-blown normative argument.

---

[58] As I described this position in ch. 3.3. Of course legal authority may also in good faith act in such a way as to forfeit its claim to authority, e.g. by pursuing politics which are actually destructive of nature or mankind.

[59] That is the kernel of truth in Fuller's famous thesis of the "inner morality of law".

[60] Finnis 1980, 21; 1987, 357, 367; Hart 1994, 240-244; Schauer 1994 (claiming that Fuller's views makes some sense if taken to describe the lawyers' internal point of view). Cf. Postema 1987c, 84-85 on participant and observer theories; Waluchow 1994, 19-30.

In a postscript to a Dutch collection on contemporary legal theory, the editors P.B. Cliteur en M.A. Loth support the proposal to reconcile positivism and antipositivism by assigning each to a point of view.[61] To illustrate their point, they adapt an analogy used by the leading antipositivists Fuller and Dworkin.[62] Suppose you want to retell an anecdote you recently heard. What you actually do will be informed by two elements: firstly, your recollection of the original story (the dimension of fit), secondly your idea of what is funny about it (the dimension of justification). In many a detail you will, intentionally or unintentionally, deviate from the original story, guided by your conception of its point. So you will not make any distinction between the anecdote as it "is" and as it "ought to be". Every new attempt to retell the story tries to be an optimal realization of the humoristic values it embodies. In the same way every application of the law to a new case necessarily attempts to be an optimal realization of the values and principles embodied in the law.

Cliteur and Loth believe that the analogy supports their view. You should distinguish, they argue, between different tasks a person can try to fulfil, say as possible assignments given to you in a theatre school course:
(a)    retell the story in the funniest possible way;
(b)    reproduce the story as you heard it, as exactly as possible.
In executing the second task you must distinguish between the authentic and the optimal form of the story. Only by doing this will you be able to explicitly identify possible improvements on the authentic version. It is true that in executing the first task you cannot make this distinction between the story as it is and as it should be, but the reason is, as Cliteur and Loth put it, that you are instructed to *tell* the story, not that you are instructed to tell the *story*. The distinction can be made if you are instructed to analyse the tale, i.e. from the external point of view. Humorist values ("natural laughter") are only relevant to the practice of *making* jokes.[63]

The two tasks are clearly distinct, but there is no reason to surrender the second one to positivism. For a serious attempt to execute the second task must also be guided by a "conception of the point of the story". You cannot do a good job by simply parroting. In reproducing a funny story, many elements matter: words, pace, rhythm, intonation, mimicry; and you can only approach the original model if you know how each of these elements contributed or failed to contribute to the realization of its aims, hence if you treat them as an embodiment of humorist values. The same is true for the audience which has to evaluate the success of your attempts. For you cannot fail to deviate in many unintentional ways from the original models; how are they supposed to decide how important each of these deviations is for the faithfulness of your reproduction? They can only do so by establishing whether the imitation succeeds, or fails, in being funny in the manner in which the original version succeeded, or failed. You can only understand the production of a series of sounds as "telling a joke", or even as "spoiling a good joke", if you have an idea of what is supposed to be funny. If there

---

[61] Cliteur & Loth 1992, 253.

[62] Fuller 1940, 8; cf. Dworkin 1986, 17 (on interpreting a poem).

[63] Waluchow 1994, 26, makes a similar point against Dworkin: the thing that we aim at making the best of its kind in observer theory is the theory, not its object.

is no agreement in sense of humor, it is impossible not only to retell an anecdote well, but also to reproduce it exactly.

The use Cliteur and Loth make of Fuller's analogy emphasizes the point of the "scorer's discretion" argument, showing it to be relevant to the external observer. It often happens, of course, that people tell jokes without really trying to do it well. Similarly, you can participate in all kinds of communicative practices without aspiring to optimal performance, halfheartedly, only to keep up appearances, or even in parasitic ways, aiming at goals that are incompatible with the normal outcomes of the activity. (Parodying someone who tells his jokes very badly can be very funny.)

You can play a game of chess with your son with the intention to let him win. Even in that case the normal goal of winning will inform your moves to a certain extent, for otherwise you are not playing chess at all.[64] In making such distinctions, the underlying values of the practice are a necessary point of reference.

---

[64] Cf. Raz 1975, 119.

# CHAPTER 11

# A CONVENTIONALIST THEORY OF LEGAL ARGUMENT

## 11.1. Interdependent and Vicarious Reasoning

Linguistic communication depends on Lewis conventions. It does not matter whether you call those well-known objects with roots, branches and leaves "trees" or "arbres" or "bomen". There is no problem as long as by using one of these words, or any other, you intend to refer to trees, are taken to intend to refer to them, correctly believe that you are taken to intend to refer to them, are supposed to believe correctly etc. You succeed in referring because there is a self-reinforcing pattern of mutual beliefs concerning the intentional use of the word.[1] In any particular conversation we need mutual beliefs about reference and a lot of other things: the illocutionary force of our utterances, the facts we do not state but presuppose, our mental models of the domain of discussion.[2]

How exactly does a hearer succeed in reconstructing the speaker's intentions? He relies on two types of reasoning: from above and from below. When he comes across a sentence containing the word "trees", he takes the speaker to refer to trees because he derives this intention from the standing pattern of mutual beliefs. ("He intends to refer to trees. Why do I think so? Because I assume that he knows that I will take him to refer to trees.")[3] But sometimes this reasoning from above leads to an unacceptable conclusion: the sentence containing "trees" makes no sense at all if we ascribe to the speaker the intention to refer to trees. The sentence starts to make sense, however, if we take the speaker to intend to refer to other things which are somewhat similar to trees, for example to the pictorial representation of games in extended form. In such a case the similarity is a *clue* to our understanding. It "indicates to us" that the speaker intends to refer to the similar things. And he, of course, perceives this indicating force as well; indeed, he intentionally makes use of it. He reflects our way of thinking, even anticipates it. We, from our side, are able to reflect his reflection; therefore, our clue not only indicates to us that the speaker intends to refer to game trees, but also that he knows that we will take him to intend to refer to game trees, knows that we believe that he knows, etc. The pattern of mutual beliefs is built up from below, starting from the

---

[1] Lewis 1975.

[2] For example, if we say that $A$ is to the right of $B$, and $B$ to the right of $C$, can $A$ be to the left of $C$? It depends on whether, in our common description scheme, the points are arrayed on a straight line or on a circle; Garrod & Anderson 1987, 197.

[3] Lewis 1969, 52-57 takes the relevant reasoning to be a reasoning from below: the fact that speakers using the word "trees" regularly intend to refer to trees, is a reason for assuming that this speaker does; others can see that this reason applies; they will assume I can see it applies, etc. In ch. 2.6. I have argued that no such independent foundation needs to exist.

clue.[4] Higher-order beliefs are derived from lower-order ones by a mirroring process.[5] But in this process we presuppose the standing pattern of mutual beliefs concerning the normal use of "trees". So we have two processes of adjustment: first the reasoning from above by which we derive the lower-order belief that the speaker intends to refer to trees from the standing higher-order belief that people using the word "trees" generally do so. Having realized that *this* speaker does not, we use the similarity between trees and game trees, and the perception that a reference to game trees makes sense in the context, to ascribe to him a new intention, and, reasoning from below, go on constructing new higher-order levels of belief.

These local adaptations are very common. The use of indexical terms, for instance, requires them. In communication people often must *do* something in order to establish mutual intelligibility. Occasionally they may start out by explicitly negotiating a common conception of their domain of discussion. But most of the time they will attempt to minimize collaborative effort[6] and therefore to solve their problems in a more implicit way. The listener, for instance, tries to reconstruct the speaker's description scheme, and then uses this reconstruction as the basis of his own utterance. At this point, any discrepancy between the assumptions made will usually become apparent.[7] But as long as you can make sense of the other's utterance on the basis of your own scheme, you presume that his scheme is identical to yours. In this way a conversation often takes the form of a process of trial and error, resembling the mutual adjustments of people walking in opposite directions on Bond Street.

The common characteristic of both types of reasoning, top-down and bottom-up, is that we always proceed *interdependently*, that is: conscious of the fact that no step is valid unless our partner or partners can be expected to expect us to make it. Such interdependent reasoning can be found in all kinds of contexts. In a Dutch television program people were asked to guess the popularity rankings of quizz masters, pop artists etc. within the population at large. Present economic theory is unable to explain the yo-yo movements of the stock market, because (on the short term at least) they cannot be related in any clear and consistent way to external factors (the success of firms, government policies, etc.). The reason might be that stockbrokers do not look at such external factors independently, but only with an eye to the anticipated responses of their colleagues, all of whom are thinking in the same way. The smallest signal of a general trend in these responses may therefore start an autonomous spiral of enlargement.

Suppose you are present at a conversation in which some misunderstanding arises concerning the "local" meaning of one of the expressions used. You happen to record the conversation and, playing the tape at home, you find a plausible explanation for the misunderstanding. And you might conclude that A was after all *justified* in

---

[4] Even this form of reasoning "from below" relies on further patterns of mutual belief, e.g. on common notions of salience, cf. ch. 2.6.

[5] But since we always rely on transparent patterns of mutual belief, we are never "windowless monads", as Lewis 1969, 32 suggests, cf. ch 1.6. at note 43.

[6] Clark & Wilkes-Gibbs 1986.

[7] Garrod & Anderson 1987, 207-212.

expecting *B* to understand his point: the available clues would normally have been sufficient. Thus comparing the actual course of the reasoning pattern of *A* and *B* to your *vicarious reasoning,* you may be able to distribute the responsibility for the failures of interdependent reasoning over its participants.


## 11.2. Interdependent Reasoning in Customary Law

Let us now look at a simple legal or rather protolegal system: customary rules or "substantial conventions" requiring people to act in certain ways or to omit certain actions, and giving them the elementary powers of promising and transferring property. There is no authoritative way of settling controversies about the application of the rules, let alone a centralized´way of executing such decisions. (People may defer to the judgment of certain persons because of their superior wisdom. But that, as we saw, is not adjudication.) Grievances are discussed in village and clan councils; when a settlement is achieved, this restores the harmonious social relations between the parties. If a compromise is beyond reach, war follows, ending with the killing or expulsion of the losing party. The danger of this alternative outcome will probably be the main incentive for accepting the compromise.[8]

Let me remind you that when I call this a system of conventions, I am using the word in its extended sense.[9] It does not matter whether you say "tree" or "arbre", as long as you are understood. But it *does* matter whether the prohibition to kill people extends to new-born children, adulterers, or foreigners. (It matters at least to them.) Linguistic communication is a pure Coordination game: for example, every possible combination of sounds, not extending a certain length and a certain measure of pronunciability, is a more or less equivalent equilibrium for people who want to refer and to understand references. But social interaction regulated by law obviously consists of games of other types besides pure Coordination games: Assurance games, PD games, Bargaining games etc. I have adopted the convention of calling the rules that arise in these patterns of interaction, and that enable people to avoid suboptimal outcomes, conventions as well, because they have the same structure as conventions governing pure coordination problems: they are patterns of mutual expectations of different orders concerning individual decisions. Lewis conventions are stable to a certain extent, because people whose only relevant desire is to meet each other have a decisive reason to conform to them. At the other end of the spectrum we find *n*-person PD-games; to explain the stability of the conventions emerging in such games, we have to suppose that to a certain extent, people respond to the existence of such patterns in a morally constrained way: they do not want to betray, or to exploit, the expectations of the others. So patterns of mutual expectations are built on the mutual ascription of either rationality and nothing else, or of cooperative virtues of reliability and fairness as well. In the latter case the rules are obligating ones.

---

[8] Cf. Ottley & Zorn 1983 on the traditional Melanesian law system of Papua New Guinea. The authors deplore the transition from a reconciling to an adversarial conception of doing justice.

[9] Ch. 1.7.

In the protolegal world, even in small communities, the relevant expectations will also be *anonymous*: they do not depend on acquaintance with individual characteristics, but only on the ascription of rationality and minimal cooperative virtue to the average qualified member of the community as such (and at least some fear of punishment to the remaining members).[10]

In this world we will find the two processes of replication that I identified in linguistic communication. Sometimes people find themselves in a situation in which it is unambiguously clear that the rule applies. Then they will know what they may expect each other to expect, and hence what to do. Perhaps they even use exactly the same words in articulating the rule. But often problems will arise concerning its applicability. The situation does not quite meet the criteria, or, though it does meet them, it has additional features which may also be relevant. Or the application of the rule leads to collision with other conventions, either generally recognized within the society as a whole, as (some) norms of justice are, or constitutive of some particular social group. In such cases the standing pattern of expectations only serves as a starting point, rendering a *default expectation* which may be overridden by interdependent reasoning "from below", starting from any salient clue that might be given. Perhaps in going through this procedure people will regain their confidence. But they may also have to conclude that the relevant clues they can assemble provide insufficient ground to ascribe to each other any particular higher-order expectation.

Cannot we solve these problems by simply discussing them? No principle of minimizing collaborative effort stands in the way this time. And indeed, it would be easy to achieve mutual understanding if we had only problems of pure coordination on our hands. But in mixed motive games, the problem is to identify a particular distribution of the benefits and burdens of cooperation. If we know that the expectations of all of us explicitly converge on one and the same distribution, we all have a reason to conform to them: otherwise we risk incurring cumulative negotiation costs. But when our specific expectations diverge, it is not only the elimination of vagueness and ambiguity that interests us. Each of us is also the partisan of a particular interpretation. Therefore it is not enough for me to reveal my reasoning to you to obtain your agreement, I must also *justify* it. What does it mean to "justify" my reasoning? Here we come upon a central thesis of conventionalism, or of my brand of conventionalism anyway: I justify my reasoning by showing to you that you, as a rational (and virtuous) participant to the standing pattern of expectations, *should* have found the same path on your own, given the available clues for local adjustment. Therefore I was right in expecting you to find it. For example, I point out to you why the similarities between two cases are more prominent than the dissimilarities, or vice versa.

Every time interdependent reasoning has failed to achieve mutual understanding, the question arises: which party (if any) is justified in expecting the other to mirror his reasoning; and which party (if any) is mistaken? This question is answered by vicarious

---

[10] Ch. 2.9.

reasoning. This reconstruction of the proper path of interdependent reasoning does not aim to reproduce actual mental states of mutual belief, but only potential ones.[11]

When a judge in a case of contract law is filling in the gaps where the parties in their original declarations have been silent or ambiguous, he is commonly understood to do a job of vicarious reasoning: his interpretation of the implied terms should "mimic the market"; he should bind the parties to the provisions reasonable parties would have made, had they cared to do so.[12] I want to claim that every form of legal reasoning is of the same kind: it attempts to determine the locus of legitimate mutual expectations.

This analysis also *explains*, independently of a general contextualist theory of justification derived from either Wittgenstein or Gadamer (or both), why it is an appropriate criterion of the soundness of legal argument that it should be capable of defence "before an ideal audience". The suspicion of circularity this criterion naturally evokes (is not the ideal audience the audience that allows itself to be convinced by good arguments?) is dissolved by the explanation: the relevant standard of correctness of the reasoning is its capacity of being replicated. Replicated, I mean, by people of normal rationality and at least minimal cooperative virtue who have the available information at their disposal.

In recent legal philosophy it has been quite a popular undertaking to develop this criterion of justification into a list of canons of argumentation and interpretative principles, specifying a sense of the propriety of arguments widely spread within (at least) the real community of legal experts.[13] These canons and principles are to be tested against our intuitions about concrete cases, in a process analogous to the specification of linguistic rules. But if we only intend to apply the rules in order to test their validity, is it not perfectly pointless to try and specify them? It is not, for the canons and principles help us to extrapolate from the actual achievement of mutual understanding in a series of concrete cases, to its vicarious achievement in a contested case. Once this is done, they cannot fail to provide a focus as well to the development of interdependent reasoning in the future. (Similarly, books of grammar simply cannot fail to exercise some minimal prescriptive force, even if they explicitly deny any intention to do so.)

By vicarious reasoning I may point out to you that some premises we both accept (i.e. know each other to accept etc.) logically imply the conclusion I defend. That will normally be decisive. But will it always be? Could you not occasionally reply that I should not really expect people of normal rationality to follow such convoluted chains

---

[11] Sperber & Wilson 1986, 42-43, show that such reasoning is often sufficient to achieve definite reference as well: I know that you do not know which trees I am talking about, but also that you have sufficient material to work it out on your own, if you wish.

[12] "If the parties to a contract have used in it an expression which is liable to be misunderstood, and if they turn out to interpret this expression differently, the answer to the question whether a valid contract has been made, depends on what they have both declared, and what they have inferred from each other's declarations and actions, *in accordance with the meaning which they could reasonably attribute to these declarations and actions.*" If it is the case that "the meaning one party has given to the expression would lead to a result which does not square with what the parties intended to achieve by the contract", this fact is especially significant. HR in *Bunde/Erckens*, NJ 1977, 241, my translation and italics.

[13] Cf. Bell 1986. Principal authors: Aarnio, Alexy, Peczenik.

of deductive argument and especially to follow them interdependently, i.e. confident that the others will follow them as well? It seems that in interdependent reasoning, even conclusiveness may not be enough.

But it is a rather hazardous enterprise to determine to what extent people of normal rationality can be expected to identify logical relations. If this is required, the area of undecidability will become pretty large. Suppose we all acted on the presumption that people are able to determine whatever may be logically[14] implied by the manifest content of their mutual expectations and statements of public fact; then we would predictably make a number of mistakes, but we would nevertheless on balance succeed in meeting each other more often. Such a metaconvention would provide one analogy in the sphere of interdependent reasoning to the indirect rationality of acting on a plan.[15] This metaconvention can actually be found to be operative in the legal world;[16] it partially explains how a form of interdependent reasoning can get so technical.

There is a useful function for legal dogmatics here: by doing its vicarious reasoning publicly, it contributes to the prevention of mistakes. Suppose a legal expert proves an unexpected conclusion to be logically implied by indisputable premises; then by the very act of making this reasoning explicit, the intensional opacity of mutual belief is overcome. To this extent legal dogmatics has a self-fulfilling power.[17] (Perhaps fortunately, this does not go very far, because lawyers tend to disagree at least as much as other human beings.)[18]

A further point aptly illustrated by the analogy with linguistic competence is the fragility of mutual belief. To arrive at correct conclusions by vicarious reasoning is quite an achievement. It requires that the persons mirroring each other's reasoning are very similar to each other, by nature and certainly by education: otherwise they could have no confidence in their own ordering of the importance of similarities and dissimilarities being mirrored by the others. But even then, most communicative performances beyond the very simple ones – for example, trying to get across the point of this paper – can only be expected to succeed to a limited extent, far more limited than we usually care to admit. Similarly, ambiguity and confusion are endemic in the application of any system of customary rules: they belong to the main "inconveniences of the state of nature".

---

[14] I will argue that the relevant logic is not really a deductive, but rather a non-monotonic logic.

[15] The game in which it emerges can be interpreted as an Assurance game.

[16] This metaconvention has its cost: a person may fail to win his case, even if he could not really be expected to be able to identify his obligation (or to hire an expert to identify it).

[17] Ch. 10.1. at note 14.

[18] "In legal philosophy the critical question is not whether a theory is true, because in law, theory does not just attempt to mirror reality; rather, the law also structures reality to follow theory. In this sense, law becomes what we believe it to be." Coval & Smith 1982, 480.

## 11.3. Forms of Interdepent Reasoning in Legal Argument: Textual Meaning and Authoritative Intention

Lacunas in decidability were one reason (adaptability to changing circumstances was the other) for making the transition into the legal world.[19] Enters *authority*. Its exercise in legislation and adjudication does not depend on superior knowledge and competence, highly desirable though these qualities may be; it is itself a matter of convention (in the extended sense). People mutually expect each other to take notice of the laws in the statute book and the decisions of the courts, whatever (at least within certain limits!) their content. Conventions of this type I have called formal conventions.

To what extent will formal conventions succeed in eliminating undecidability? I will consider that question in the next chapter.

In the legal world, the real community of interdependent expectations, and the "ideal audience" of vicarious reasoning, to a large extent only consist of legal experts, or even of experts in some particular area of the law. The relevant "systems of mutual expectations" are capable of guiding the actions of citizens (individuals *and* corporations) only indirectly, by the mediation of the experts. (The primary agents only expect each other to abide by legal advice, whatever it is.) But this can never be true about the law as a whole: other parts will continue to try and guide the behaviour of ordinary private citizens directly, and in those cases the relevant community of mutual expectations continues to be the "civil society" of those citizens. Suppose we found a legal system within which the judiciary systematically ignored the attitudes and expectations of the law-subjects, in particular their attitudes and expectations regarding the acts of the judiciary. Such a system would not succeed in its primary aim: the guidance of the behaviour of its subjects.[20]

Even when the legal community is the final forum, it should be interpreted as representing civil society. The ideal legal audience is the community of citizens, miraculously equipped with the relevant legal knowledge.[21] The power of legal experts is held *on trust* (in the Lockean sense). Law is never the business of lawyers alone.

Suppose that we have a system of conventions with the salient features I have described in this book. Can we predict what *forms* of interdependent reasoning will be used to determine at any time what the system requires?

Let me start by recalling those salient features.

(a)   A system of conventions, i.e. transparent patterns of mutual expectations of higher and lower orders, governing a significant part of the interactions of a group of people.

(b)   A mutually known commitment to the avoidance of certain specific suboptimal outcomes as the mutually recognized point of the system.

(c)   Mutually ascribed cooperative dispositions.

---

[19] See ch. 6.1., ch. 9.1.

[20] Postema 1982, 190-191.

[21] Bell 1986, 55.

(d)   The existence of one or more formal conventions: the mutual recognition of the authority to specify what the system requires. (Legislative and adjudicating authority.)

So here I am, wondering what to do. Obviously, I should first look whether any relevant provision has been made by the legislative authority. These provisions are communicated, and henceforward available (in the collective memory of the elders, inscribed in stone tables etc.) in language. So the first type of argument I might profitably use will be this.

(1) The argument from the meaning of the legislative statement (LS).

This requires linguistic competence: knowledge of the possible "lexical" meanings of the words used, of syntax etc. If a word has more than one possible lexical meaning, I have to eliminate the meanings that result in absurdity. Occasionally, perhaps, the LS with the meaning I consider will be absurd "in all possible worlds", a mere senseless concatenation of words. No propositional content can be established. But most of the time the sentence in the interpretation I consider will make "abstract" sense, but will nevertheless be absurd: the propositional content cannot be interpreted as referring to any possible state of affairs in the actual social world. Hence, to establish the relevant meaning of the LS I should also be able to muster general knowledge about the actual social context within which the language of the LS is used. At this stage, however, only general knowledge is relevant. If I want to ascertain that the provision at least prima facie applies to my actual condition, I must of course know the relevant features of this condition as well. But at this stage, this knowledge will not be relevant to identify the meaning of the provision. The argument from meaning is to this extent *relatively context-independent.*

Some judicial authorities have sometimes pretended that this first argument is the only one they need – in France to a large extent they still do.[22] But this cannot be true. The first reason, by now almost universally acknowledged by word, and universally by deed, is that it may be impossible to determine in a straightforward way whether and how to apply a LS in a concrete context. Even with the absurd meanings eliminated, more than one possible meaning of a word may remain (ambiguity). Or we do not know whether a given aspect of the case falls within or without the boundaries of a concept (vagueness). In these cases the other types of argument have a supplementary function. *However, if these arguments are available, they may also be in conflict with the argument from meaning,* and so they may have a countervailing function as well. (Of course they may also have a supportive or reinforcing function.)[23] This possibility could only be excluded if we had any reason to attribute to the argument from meaning absolute (lexical) priority. As we shall see, we have no such reason. And so the appeal

---

[22] Troper, Grzegorczyk & Gardies 1991, ch. 6. The father of the Code Civile, Portalis, did not share this legism.

[23] Cf. the appeal to the principle of indemnity by the defendant in *Maring Assuradeuren,* discussed in ch. 11.11.

to the other arguments should not be considered only in the perspective of the solution of "hard cases". The appeal sometimes *makes* hard cases.[24]

It has been rightly observed[25] that to some extent Hart allows for such countervailing considerations in his well-known discussion of the "core of certainty" and the "penumbra of doubt".[26] When he introduces this distinction, he seems to be making an observation about linguistic meaning: we reach the penumbra when we are uncertain whether a certain term applies or not. But he goes on to comment that we have reason to be pleased with the existence of the penumbra: it gives the judge some room for manoeuvre when the formalistic application of existing rules would have unfortunate results. Of course, such results may follow as well from the application of the rules in question to cases where they undoubtedly apply, if we just consult the meaning of the rules. So Hart's discussion seems to recognize a second conception of "the penumbra of doubt" besides the linguistic one: we reach it when the literal application of the rule gives us inappropriate results.[27]

This distinction between a supplementary and a countervailing appeal to purpose, principles, precedent etc., seems to me to be far more important than the usual distinction *praeter/contra legem*. It turns out that there is a very large grey zone between these concepts, which leaves hardly any room for indisputable instances of *contra legem* decisions. Most of the time countervailing considerations can be accommodated by activities of "interpretation", for instance by extending or restricting the normal extension of a term.

In the argument from meaning, the "text" of the LS is considered as if it had been written on a paper found in a bottle on the shore. Actually it is the text of an authoritative enactment. An enactment is an intentional communicative act (a "speech act"). So when we ascribe a meaning to the text, we at the same time attribute an intention to the legislative authority (LA). If we treated it simply as a "proposition", we would in effect deny the legislator's authority. It follows that we should admit another type of argument as well.

(2) The argument from subjective legislative intention.

This may take two forms. Sometimes we have at our disposal additional material besides the LS (and other texts of the same status), material that throws light on the LA's intention.[28] But even if this is not the case, it is possible to reach another layer of meaning of the LS, if we interpret it, as we should, as communicating the LA's intention. To do so, we must make certain presuppositions about the LA as an agent, for instance that he is rational, i.e. that the LS is enacted as a means to some intelligible end.[29] By accepting this presumption we do not exchange the actual subjective

---

[24] See ch. 12.5.

[25] In an excellent paper by Atria 1999; cf. Bayles 1992, 85-90.

[26] Hart (1958) 1983, 63-64; cf. 1961, 121-132 on the open texture of law.

[27] See ch. 12.5. for a similar observation on MacCormick's claim that legal reasoning often has a deductive form.

[28] In Sweden and Finland the use of travaux préparatoires to establish legislative intention is common, in the UK it is explicitly forbidden. Summers 1991, 470.

[29] Cf. *Maring/Assuradeuren*.ch. 11.11. below.

legislative intention for a hypothetical one.[30] For this presupposition is needed for the understanding of any intentional act whatsoever.[31] Reading the text as an expression of intention also warrants supplementing or countervailing the argument from normal meaning by appealing to the (normal or local) meaning the same expressions have at other places in the same text.

### 11.4. Forms of Interdependent Reasoning: Values and Principles

So far, we have only taken into consideration the fourth feature of the system of conventions mentioned above. If we take the other ones into account, it turns out that they generate other types of consideration, to be used either in a supplementary or in a countervailing way. To begin with:

(3) The argument from substantive values.

I agree with Fuller that a legal system, unlike social morality, is strictly a system of mutual expectations, not of mutual evaluations.[32] The law does not give marks. Of course, the armoury of normative concepts within the law is not restricted to "obligation", the law knows powers, disabilities, immunities etc., but these are all to be defined in binary terms, mostly with either obligation or permission as the basic concept. That does not mean that values are irrelevant to legal argument, however, for it will often be the case that a norm, or rather a system of norms, can only be understood by reference to its point.

We mutually know that the system is meant to avoid some specific suboptimal outcomes in situations of interdependent choice. So if one of the possible meanings of the LS, or intentions of the LA, is such that complying with the LS in this interpretation would itself clearly lead to one such suboptimal outcome, that is a relevant argument against ascribing that meaning or that intention. Again, this does not lead us from the actual intention into the realm of fiction: for it is mutually known that the LA is in the business of promoting the common good, so it is reasonable to accept a presumption against ascribing to him a contrary intention.[33]

---

[30] As suggested by Troper c.s. 1991, 181.

[31] Davidson 1980, quoted ch. 8, note 32. It is often alleged that no actual legislative intention can exist, because the legislative in modern systems is a composite body of persons, each of whom may have had different things in mind. The answer is that even in face-to-face communication we do not read people's minds, but construct their intention from their actions, given the context, and given some presuppositions concerning their rationality and possible aims. It is inconsistent to ascribe authority to a legislative act, and at the same time to deny that it expresses an intention to prescribe, permit etc. This collective intention may differ from any of the individual intentions constituting it.

[32] Fuller 1964.

[33] Cf. the 'Mischief Rule' from Heydon's Case (1584), quoted by Bankowski & MacCormick 1991, 367: "And it was resolved by them that ... the office of all the judges is always to make such construction (sc. of a statute) as shall suppress the mischief, and advance the remedy ... according to the true intent of the makers of the Act, *pro bono publico*." "For though a wrong Sentence given by authority of the Soveraign, if he know and allow it, in such Lawes as are mutable, be a constitution of a new Law, in cases, in which every little circumstance is the same, yet in Lawes immutable, such as are the Lawes of Nature, they are no Lawes to the same, or other Judges, in the like cases for ever after. Princes succeed one another; and one Judge passeth,

The argument can also be used in a countervailing way. For instance, suppose the LS states that it is forbidden to bring sick cattle into contact with healthy cattle. At the very start of an epidemic, a veterinary surgeon starts to do precisely the opposite.[34] It is clear that he does what the LS forbids and what the LA intended to forbid: no possible interpretation of the meaning of the LS, and hence no possible interpretation of the intended force of its communication, could accommodate his actions. But he argues that the newest epidemiological view is that, contrary to received opinion, his action tends to halt the spread of the epidemic by giving the healthy animals the opportunity to develop antibodies. We assume that the LA intended to stop, not to promote, the spread of epidemics; therefore we conclude that, if the surgeon is right about the facts, he acted with the LA's blessing, even if it was contrary to what the LA actually intended to communicate at the time the regulation was introduced. In this way, the second and third argument can be used in combination to defeat the first.

The second feature of the system that generates additional types of argument is the role of cooperative dispositions. The members of the group must suppose each other to be generally trustworthy, fair, prepared to compromise, and perhaps also to execute retribution; if not, their mutual expectations cannot be sustained, at least not in some important types of situations of interdependent choice. They therefore cannot expect each other to comply with an LS which a just, fair and trustworthy person would not willingly comply with. So we get:

(4) The argument from principles.

I conceive of legal principles as the norms that necessarily belong to any system capable of enlisting the willing support of cooperatively disposed persons. The foregoing chapters contain, one might say, a "transcendental" argument for the necessity of recognizing at least some legal principles as relevant legal materials. No legal system could fail to contain these materials, given its nature as a pattern of mutual anonymous expectations that can only be self-maintaining if supported by cooperative dispositions.

Of course, the principles will have to be specified to some extent in order to be useful, and the specifications will differ between legal systems, and even between different areas of the same system. Such different specifications may be due to divergences, and even defects, of reflective understanding of the nature of the system. Nevertheless, these differences can be seen as variations on basic common themes. The Rule of Law, to take the most fundamental example, in requiring acts which are either

another cometh, nay, Heaven and Earth shall passe; but not one title of the Law of Nature shall passe; for it is the Eternall Law of God." Hobbes, *Leviathan*, ch. 26. Perhaps the clearest statement of his antipositivist view. Cf. also. the practice of the common law judges under Apartheid described in ch. 10.2. In a decision of March 3, 1998 the Dutch High Court argued that a recent change of law involved a radical departure of existing provisions of the penal law without any indication being available that the legislature no longer subscribed to these provisions or to their rationale. The Court concluded that the actual wording of the new provision "by mistake" omits a narrowing clause.

[34] *Huizer veearts*, NJ 1933, 918, cf. ch. 7, note 53; ch. 10, note 3. *Cessante ratione legis cessat lex ipsa.* For another example, cf. Alexy & Dreier 1991, 79: the German Civil Code prohibits an authorized agent to make a legal transaction with himself in the name of the principal. The Federal Court of Justice in Civil Cases decided (1972) that the wording of the regulation exceeded the actual purpose of protection, and therefore allowed the act when it could be to the advantage of the represented person and to him only.

forbidden, permitted or mandatory, to fall under known general descriptions, simply sums up the whole point of having a system of conventions. For only acts that can be identified before the doing, can be said to be "expected". Most principles can be interpreted as those limiting norms of the legal system, or of certain areas of law, which represent the outer boundaries of the possible appeal to cooperative dispositions. For example, people mutually know each other to be retributive, and hence will mutually expect to be punished for crimes. But they will not expect to be "punished" for what they did unintentionally (and non-negligently): such "punishment" would not be a proper expression of the disposition of retributiveness (and therefore really no punishment at all). Hence the *mens rea* principle. In many areas of the law we find principles that can be seen as specifications of the principle of fairness. And *bona fides* is not only basic to contract law.[35]

I do not want to claim that everything presently called a legal principle can be accounted for in this way. A principle is often considered to be a basic norm -*any* basic norm – that is specified by, or incorporated into, a relatively large body of other norms. This use of the concept is responsible for very heterogeneous collections of things called "principles". How many specifying or incorporating norms are needed to call the norm thus specified or incorporated a principle? And what do we mean by "basic" – can a principle be shown to be a specification of an even more basic norm, and remain a principle? It seems preferable not to say that such "principles" form a distinct group of norms, but only to speak about *relations* between norms, relations of specification or incorporation that may be used to arrange norms into "trees".

A purely logical way of distinguishing between principles and "rules" has been proposed by Dworkin.[36] In his view, rules are binary standards but principles are not. If two principles conflict, they could therefore both be satisfied to a certain extent: principles tolerate compromising or trading. Rules, by contrast, are intolerant: they are either satisfied or not satisfied.

There is indeed a logical distinction here, but the relevant terms to be used are values and norms respectively. It may be true that some so-called legal principles are better thought of as representing the aims of the collective enterprise that is regulated by the law, and therefore as exhibiting the characteristic maximizing structure of values rather than the binary character of norms.[37] (E.g. individual freedom, the satisfaction of individual need, collective welfare etc.) But if that is so, then in the interest of clarity we should call these "principles" values.

Earlier, I agreed with Fuller that values do not belong to the law in the way principles do: legal provisions do not have a maximizing structure. It may seem easy to point to counter-examples to this thesis. Indeed, some legal discussions seem to concern the question whether a legal standard should be seen as a strict norm or as a value. For

---

[35] For example, it is now a basic principle of Dutch fiscal law, explicitly recognized for the first time by HR 1979, 533, that if the actions of fiscal authorities give you the reasonable conviction that some explicit tax law will, to your advantage, not be strictly applied to you, your trust is protected, cf. Happé 1996, 86 and passim.

[36] Dworkin 1977, 26-28. And more or less endorsed by Alexy 1985, 75ff: principles are norms commanding that something be realized to the highest degree possible.

[37] Cf. ch. 1.2.

instance, in the Netherlands (and presumably elsewhere), there is a discussion about the interpretation of constitutional positive rights (to housing, employment, health care etc.), a discussion regarding the scope of the corresponding governmental obligations: is the government bound to guarantee each individual person the unhindered access to these goods, or is it held only to make a reasonable effort, compatible with its other aims and obligations? In the second interpretation, the legal standard seems to posit not a norm but only a value. However, while "effort" is a term with a maximizing structure, "reasonable" is a binary term: it points to a mark on the continuous scale of effort, just as the standard for passing an examination points to a mark on the scale of student performance. Because the scales are continuous, the identification of the mark is necessarily arbitrary to a certain extent; and a term like "reasonable" is also, obviously, pretty vague. But if the relevant application of the standard yields a legal judgment, it is either the judgment that the government has met its obligation or that it has failed to do so. So even this legal standard is a binary one, and hence a norm.

Dworkin's own favourite example of a principle – "No one should profit from his own wrongs" – is clearly a binary standard. If Elmer had been given his inheritance, he would have profited from his wrongs, and that's the end of it. It would have been a form of satire to say that in that case the principle had been satisfied to a certain extent, for the extent would have been nil. Now it is true that a court could recognize the principle as a principle of law, and yet, for some reason or another, consistently allow Elmer his inheritance. But this is just to say that the relevant norm here is stated incompletely by the formulation of the principle. A more complete formulation would also have stated under what conditions a person should be allowed to profit from his own wrong. Again, it is true that we cannot expect these conditions to be exhaustively stated in advance by any formulation of the norm at any time. But as we will see presently, the same can be said about (almost?) any formulation of any norm: we can never exhaustively identify the possible circumstances in which countervailing considerations appear to be relevant. The meaning of a norm formulation is never perfectly manifest.

When talking about a "strict" or "intolerant" norm, we seem to have in mind the French ideal: we interpret the authoritative formulation of the norm in its relatively context-independent meaning, we find the conditions specified in the formulation satisfied, hence we necessarily know the legal position. Someone reminds us that this "necessarily" is wrong, that there is (almost?) no norm formulation which we cannot imagine to be ever defeated by countervailing legal considerations. We answer: all right, then we will take the completed norm, including the possible countervailing considerations, even if this is only an "ideal type" or "regulative idea"; this completed norm will be "strict" or "intolerant". That is a logical point about norms. What is stressed in this way is nothing but the binary nature of the norm: making an exception to a binary standard is different from trading away one value for another. I agree, but then there is no reason why we should not classify principles as "strict norms".

I conclude that principles cannot be identified by any logical features. We are able, to a certain extent, to identify them in an intuitive way. My suggestion is that the great majority of norms so identified can be seen as representing the force of cooperative dispositions as necessary presuppositions of a system of obligatory conventions. It is this fact that explains why principles have a particular "aura".

Principles can obviously be used in a supplementary as well as in a countervailing role.[38] They are also used in the reconstruction of subjective legislative intention: we presume the LA to intend to remain within the limits prescribed by them.


## 11.5. Custom

So far I have argued as if the only conventions relevant to legal argumentation were formal ones. But this is not true, and hence we have:

(5) The argument from substantial conventions.

This argument is available in two forms. The most obvious form is the appeal to an "unwritten" custom.[39] Such an appeal will be relatively rare in modern legal systems, because the force of custom there is represented (and specified) by authoritative statements, either in the form of codification or in the form of judicial pronouncements. As we saw before, that state of affairs may create the illusion that the force of custom is exchanged for, rather than incorporated into, the force of legislative authority. In many cases, however, the authoritative statements did not change anything – and if they had attempted to change much, they would not have succeeded. Hence it is wrong to say that these ongoing patterns of expectations have legal standing because they are "adopted" by the legislator. It is the other way around: legislation has legal standing because it is "adopted" by practice.[40]

That this is the true state of affairs appears in the other, more frequently used form of the argument from substantial conventions, which we might call the argument from history.[41] When a legislative statement has been enacted recently, we must interpret it as an expression of legislative intention; otherwise, as I argued, we would not take seriously the legislator's authority. But if the LS really has a role in social conduct, it will begin to function as a substantial convention. In the first place, most of the time people will simply know what to expect from each other without having to take recourse to evidence concerning the LA's intentions. But as circumstances change, there will also occur that slow incremental process of adaptation of the content of their expectations that is characteristic for all conventions. After, say, a decade or two, the pattern of expectations will have changed significantly. At that point the real, complete meaning of the text of the LS (if it is still in force) will not be the meaning as addressed by the argument from meaning: namely, what the words would standardly be taken to

---

[38] A famous case, usually considered to be *contra legem*, is the Soraya decision, discussed by Alexy & Dreier 1991, 80, in which the Federal Constitutional Court awarded compensation for non-material damage, though the relevant statute explicitly restricted this to cases statutorily identified – which did not include completely fictive interviews. Cf. also the Dame Lamotte case, discussed by Troper c.s. 1991, 182.

[39] Cf. *Maring/Assuradeuren*, ch. 11.11. below. Even in France the decision in the case Abbé Olivier (1909) limited the statutory powers of local mayors to issue police regulations on the matter of religious funerals, and did so with reference to local traditions.,Troper c.s. 1991, 189.

[40] Ch. 9.2.-3.

[41] Summers 1991, 469.

mean by a competent speaker, disregarding his legal knowledge. It certainly would no longer have the meaning as addressed by the argument from subjective legislative intention: no one could really believe that the convention as it has now developed was intended to come into force by a legislator from the beginning of the nineteenth century. The meaning of the text is determined by the way it is used, i.e. by a substantial convention. There is no need at all to conjure up the image of a hypothetical (or even ideal) present-time legislator and the "intentions" he could have had in enacting the LS. That is only a way of hiding the real force of substantial conventions behind a façade of legislative authority, a move which betrays its idleness by the wholly fictional nature of its suppositions.


## 11.6. Analogy and Precedent

Some other types of argument follow from the nature of interdependent reasoning as a search for "clues". The first is:

   (6) The argument from analogy.

   When there is an important similarity between a case covered by a clear rule, and the case under consideration which is not, then the solution will be suggested by the similarity. This is just a way of applying the principle of salience.

   In some cases, analogous reasoning will also be required if, using a presumption of rationality, we try to discover the subjective intention of the legislating authority, when this is too inadequately expressed to be identified by the argument from normal meaning. For instance, if the buyer has been explicitly awarded a right to compensation when the seller malevolently conceals a defect of the good, we may assume the legislator to intend to award a similar right when the seller malevolently pretends to a non-existent quality.[42] But not every use of the argument from analogy can be plausibly constructed in this way. (The clear rule from which we take the analogy may itself be a substantial convention!)

   From its very nature, the argument from analogy can only have a supplementary character. If the first five arguments have supplied us with a satisfactory solution, we have no reason to look around for analogies.

   The applicability of the argument from analogy results from the fact that one way for an equilibrium outcome to acquire salience is by being prescribed by legislative authority. Obviously the same is true about adjudicating authority. Hence the principle of salience also yields:

   (7) The argument from precedent.[43]

   When there is an important similarity between a case which has already been decided, and the present one, the similarity will again suggest a decision.

   If the argument from precedent is allowed, this necessarily invests judicial decisions with a certain amount of legislative authority. Given the nature of

---

[42] A German decision of 1907, discussed by Alexy & Dreier 1991, 79.

[43] On Lewis' account, precedent has an essential role in the development of conventions anyway. But cf. ch. 2.6.

interdependent reasoning, this consequence is unavoidable. Even if the appeal to precedent is *expressis verbis* forbidden by an LS, in the name of legislative supremacy, precedent will nevertheless irrepressibly exert its focusing power.[44]

The official doctrine in civilian law systems tens to be that earlier decision only has authority if it is legally correct on its merits.[45] But this would mean that it has no content-independent force, hence no authority at all, but at most only a heuristic value. Which is to deny the obvious facts of judicial practice even in such systems. Earlier generations understood the authority of precedent to be epistemic: the totality of past decisions was supposed to represent "the accumulated wisdom of the ages".[46] But in the practice of the courts precedent turns out to have a content-independent force which cannot be seen as merely declaratory of an antecedent truth of the matter. What is still lacking is a generally accepted explanation of this force. It is often pointed out that the constraining power of precedent contributes to the uniformity of legal decisions within a jurisdiction, but this explanation only succeeds in displacing the mystery, because it leaves it unexplained why uniformity is desirable if it is not the uniform prevalence of the truth. This is often explained in its turn by the value of equal treatment, but this explanation is unsatisfactory for similar reasons. If you treated A in a certain way, that is no reason to treat B who is similarly situated in the same way, if your treatment of A was an improper one to begin with.[47] The basic explanation is that in a context in which people try to mutually adjust their actions, and conflicts about the proper forms of adjustment are decided by authoritative adjudication, such decisions cannot fail to shape the formation of mutual expectations for the future.

As I said, in some legal systems this is denied, however vainly. In other systems the lawmaking power of judicial authorities is not only recognized, but also regulated. In such systems the argument from precedent may be used in a countervailing way; otherwise it will only be used in a supplementary way.[48]

---

[44] Cf. ch. 9.3. at note 28. In German legal theory it had been assumed for a long time (e.g. by Esser and Larenz) that the force of precedent was exhausted by the quality of its reasons. But recently the focusing power of judge-made law has been recognized to some extent: according to Kriele 1976, 243 ff, it establishes a presumption of the reasonableness of a particular decision in a certain type of case. See Alexy and Dreier 1991, 44. Such focusing power is also inevitably exerted by legal doctrine, whether "the argument from the *communis opinio doctorum*" is legally allowed or not, see ch. 11.2. above at note 17. The force of precedent, therefore, does not wholly depend on the fact that the preceding decision was made by a recognized authority. Some focusing force is exerted, and hence some authority exercised, by any decision competently made.

[45] See the chapters in MacCormick & Summers 1996 on Germany, France and Italy, and comments by Bankowski c.s., 484, and Marshall, 508.

[46] Blackstone, quoted by Postema 1991b, 1165. This was also the view of Carl von Savigny and his historical school, cf. Bankowski c.s. 1996. 483.

[47] Postema 1991b. In this paper Postema implicitly rejects the conventionalist theory of precedent, asserted (and attributed to Hume) by Postema 1987b. Postema now argues that reliance on a decision, like equal treatment, is only warranted if the decision is independently justified. This argument overlooks the specific nature of coordinating authority. Postema's new account points to the value of a community being true to its own identity. This seems too grandiose an explanation to cover the routinely constraining force of many humdrum judicial decisions in which the community's identity is hardly at stake.

[48] Glossing the results of MacCormick & Summers 1996, this seems, by and large, to be the remaining difference between the common law and the civil law countries.

Looking back again at these seven types of argument, we find that (2), the argument from subjective intention, has a special status: it is often made implicitly when other arguments are made explicitly. As I indicated, this is especially true for the arguments (3) and (4), from substantive values and from principles.[49] For these arguments may be made in the form of applying presumptions concerning the lawgiving agent: that he aims at the common good, accepts the limiting force of the principles, and as a rational agent does not normally issue inconsistent prescriptions. So the argument from subjective intention is "transcategorical".[50]

Exactly the same point can be made concerning the argument from substantial conventions.[51] A statute may over time come to be interpreted in accordance with an evolving understanding of its purpose or of the principles embedded in it. An argument appealing to this new understanding will not establish the intention of the legislator, but it *will* establish an actually existing pattern of mutual expectations.

About these seven types of argument, I claimed that their use can be predicted for any system of conventions answering my description of its salient features. And lo and behold, they turn out to be actually used in all (modern) legal systems, and can even be said to be the most prominent types of argument used in those systems. Some years ago an impressive comparative study has been made of the actual arguments used by courts in the interpretation of statutes. (The study concentrated on judges, not because their form of reasoning is different from legal reasoning by other persons, but because they have a duty or make it their practice to explain what they are doing, and therefore tend to do it more self-consciously.) This study resulted in a list very closely resembling the one I developed in this chapter.[52] I take this to be a corroboration of the conventionalist account. Conventionalism can go beyond the mere enumeration of forms of legal argumentation, and provide an explanation of their use.

Canons of acceptable argumentation and interpretative principles are sometimes seen as articulating a common feeling of propriety developing within the community of legal experts. But this is not a *basic* social datum, a "form of life".[53] What is to be considered proper depends on the nature of the legal enterprise.

---

[49] And of (5), the argument from analogy, and (8), the argument from inconsistency, cf. ch. 12.3.

[50] MacCormick & Summers 1991, 522. But I do not accept that all the other arguments may be involved: (1) establishes a meaning independently of speaker's characteristics, and (6) and (7) do not establish a meaning of the LS at all.

[51] Which is therefore also "transcategorical". An example is given by the appeal to custom in *Maring/Assuradeuren*, ch. 11.11. below.

[52] MacCormick & Summers 1991, cf. the summary by MacCormick & Summers, 512-515, and cf. Summers, 464-465. Their "argument from substantive reasons" can be distributed over my third and fourth arguments. The forms of reasoning covered by their "contextual harmonization" and "logical-conceptual" argument are mostly covered by my arguments from inconsistency (ch. 12.3.), and from subjective intention. Their classification seems to be inspired by a disputable ideal of coherence, see ch. 12.3.

[53] Cf. Aarnio 1986, 213-229.

## 11.7. The Role of Rules in Practical Reasoning: Deductivism and Act-deontology

It has long been, and still is, highly controversial to what extent "rules" are essential to practical reasoning, whether prudential, moral or legal.[54] The reason is, it seems to me, that arguing from rules is usually constructed on a deductivist model. One starts by identifying the relevant rules with the relatively (or completely) context-independent meaning of rule formulations, for example statutory law. It can then be shown that the deductivist model fails on two counts. In the first place – to summarize my argument so far – the reconstruction of any "argument from above" on a deductive model must start by claiming that the rules it wishes to introduce as its major premises are the *only* true and relevant premises. But we have no warrant for this claim. Perhaps Dworkin overstated a valid point by saying that we "never run out of valid arguments"; the valid point would be that it is often possible and even probable that other persuasive and relevant arguments *might be* discovered. And yet that does not mean that we must suspend our judgment. Part of the explanation for this puzzling state of affairs is that in interdependent reasoning it does matter whether a convincing argument really *is* advanced. If it is, the parties will be justified in expecting each other to take it into account; if it is not, then even if one party is aware of the argument, he may sometimes be justified in neglecting it, because he cannot possibly expect the other to replicate his reasoning.

In the second place, the deductivist model only describes the phase of "reasoning from above"; but by trying to apply "the rules" to a concrete case, one may fail to achieve a determinate result, and it may then be necessary to appeal to "arguments from below" or local adaptation arguments. Deductivists will incorporate this phase into their model by adding the "rules" found in this way to their list of major premises. For example, the *ratio decidendi* of a precedent, which shows the precedent to be relevant to the present case, may be formulated as a rule covering a class of cases containing both the precedent and the present case. But this fails to account for what it is really the decisive step in the whole process: the mutual recognition of a salient clue.

Deductivist theories tend to make a sharp distinction between heuristic and justificatory arguments. If these theories fail in the ways described, it follows that this distinction is not all that sharp. It is true that not every way in which an idea urges itself on me is relevant for the purpose of justification. I have to ask whether I may expect the idea similarly to urge itself on others. But if so, that fact *is* relevant for the purpose of justification, and deductivism cannot account for this.

When I say that legal argument is not deductive in form, I mean that it never is. Some authors argue that there are many run-of-the-mill cases of legal reasoning that provide counter-examples. It is true that we can often reconstruct a justificatory text by listing some premises, and showing that the conclusion drawn actually follows.[55] But this reconstruction fails to bring out the real justificatory force of the argument. To bring out that force, we would have to add a ceteris paribus proviso to every

---

[54] From the extensive literature in applied ethics I mention Jonsen & Toulmin 1988; Winkler 1993 and (in defence) Beauchamp 1996. See Den Hartogh 1999a.

[55] Alexy 1989b, 121, calls this the "internal justification" of a legal proposition.

prescriptive premise, and a separate premise to every justificatory step, stating that things really *are* equal.[56] But these premises are purely ornamental, we simply assume them to be true until the opposite is shown to be the case.

If deductivist theories fail, what follows about the role of rules? The most radical alternative is to deny that rules have any role to play at all. So how does practical reasoning proceed? One might suggest that in each individual case it is simply, contingently, true that an act is obligatory, permitted etc. The provisional nature of rules is then explained by their inductive character: so far we have found that conditions so and so have such and such normative consequences.

The basic deficiency of this kind of theory – particularism or *act-deontology*[57] – is that it is unable to account for interdependent reasons. I will argue for this point by starting from another problem: act-deontology seems at first sight unable to recognize the *supervenient* nature of normative properties. It seems to assume that the relation between "killing the innocent" and "wrong" is similar to the relation between "car" and "yellow". Supervenience needs to be explained in different ways for different properties exhibiting it. But at least sometimes, when people have interdependent reasons, it must be explained by reference to the fact that the non-normative properties of an act cause them to develop converging expectations about the doing or omitting of it.

That does not mean automatically that any rule is involved. One might suggest that all practical reasoning is reasoning-from-below, that it starts from a salient clue which "indicates to us" that we should do or omit something. Precedent has been claimed to be such a salient clue, by Lewis and others. In this way act-deontology could account for supervenience: it stands for the relation of "indicating-to-us". It is easy to integrate the inductive conception of rules into this view of practical reasoning, for a regular pattern of behaviour is simply one clue among others.[58]

I have argued, however, that it is typical for a convention that the reasons it provides for complying cannot be derived from any independent basis. What any fact indicates to us (plural!), is already a matter of common belief. That is true of salience in the relevant sense as well. And only in such cases are we really dealing with interdependent reasons. If there is an independent basis, the equilibrium solution to our practical problem is individually accessible.[59]

It is therefore false that all practical reasoning is reasoning-from-below. Substantial conventions do exist, as well as formal conventions identifying legislating authorities. But such conventions consist in patterns of mutual *general* expectations to act in certain ways. For example, it is in the nature of legislation that it makes

---

[56] Cf. ch. 12.5. at note 25.

[57] Frankena 1963, 21-23. A forceful statement of particularism is Dancy 1993.

[58] To be more precise, on this view one person has an independent reason to choose the salient option, the others have independent reasons to adjust to his choice. Or perhaps the first person has no reason, but only a natural inclination to go for salience. I believe that reasons of the second, and, if they exist, of the first type, in the end also resist a particularist analysis: we have reasons in this *type of* case to adjust to this *type of* choice.

[59] Ch. 2.6.

regulations for classes of cases described in general terms.[60] The radical view of practical reasoning which denies that rules have any role to play, can only get off the ground by also denying the practical significance of all such authoritative pronouncements. That is a *reductio ad absurdum,* if anything is.

## 11.8. What Does It Mean to Know a Rule?

In the previous section I have argued only that some legal arguments involve an appeal to rules. As a matter of fact, I hold the stronger thesis that all arguments aimed at establishing a legal position (and not just matters of relevant non-legal fact) do so. That is also true for seemingly "bottom-up" arguments, for example the argument from precedent and from analogy. They do not start from any "independent basis" either. Considering these cases, however, will also show us a kernel of truth in act-deontology, and will thereby explain to some extent why people feel attracted to that kind of position.

It has often been observed that an appeal to precedent is not that much different from an appeal to a rule. For by appealing to precedent, we judge that the present case is similar in a relevant respect to the precedent, and by this judgment we "project" a rule for all cases similar in that respect. Courts may even be obligated in their justificatory statements to spell out that rule: the *ratio decidendi.*

In the argument from analogy the reference to a rule is even more obvious, but also slightly disturbing. In using this argument we judge that a certain case is similar in a relevant respect, not to a certain case, but to a certain class of cases identified by a rule, though the authoritative formulation of the rule does not specify the relevant respect, at least not if interpreted in terms of its relatively context-independent meaning. This is a reason either to reformulate the rule, or to reinterpret the meaning of its formulation. In this case it is possible to appeal to the normal meanings of words in order to distinguish between the "direct" and the "analogical" application of the rule.

Looking back at the case of precedent we find a similar distinction to apply. For even if a *ratio decidendi* has been authoritatively articulated, the compelling force of a precedent is not exhausted by any such formula. It is always possible that in the next case, we must decide that the precedent is relevant, though its relevance cannot be derived from the relatively context-independent meaning of the statement of the *ratio decidendi.* Then we have to adjust the statement, or our interpretation of its meaning.[61] So it seems that the rule is established by the mutual recognition of the precedent, and derives its force from that, not vice versa.

Let us now return for a moment to the protolegal world of customary rules. No formal conventions have started to develop as yet. In this world it will be difficult to

---

[60] Opponents of the rule model in applied ethics often recognize the fact, and then identify the rule model with "juridical" reasoning about ethical issues. This shows that they have a false deductivist conception of legal argument.

[61] This observation does not show that no rule is involved, for something quite similar will presently be said about the extension of a rule.

distinguish between direct and analogical applications of the rule. For the extension of the rule is not to be determined by reference to any formula, but only by reference to standard cases. It is possible that a new case arises, very different in some respects from the standard cases, but nevertheless immediately and mutually recognized to be sufficiently similar in the relevant respects to be treated alike. Here we obviously exercise the same capacity that is used in the mutual recognition of precedents.

If people in this society now try to formulate the existing rule, and agree about the appropriateness of some formulation, this will inevitably have some influence on the subsequent channelling of their expectations concerning such "new" cases, but in the main the meaning of their formulation will be determined by their responses to such cases, and not the other way around. It is only because of this pre-existing agreement in responses (in form of life), that such general formulas succeed in acquiring a more or less definite meaning, and this in turn is a precondition of the possibility of authoritative legislation.

In this way we can explain something about the role of rule formulas in interdependent practical reasoning by reference to the role of precedent and analogy. People are able to a certain extent to discover the relevant similarities of a new case to either the precedent case, or to paradigm cases of the application of the formula, and to do so interdependently. The difference is only that in the case of a "rule" there is a series of precedent cases which *have* already been mutually and explicitly recognized as such.[62]

How do we teach a person to follow a norm? There seem to be two possibilities: we can either communicate a statement of the norm in general terms, which we may expect a competent speaker of the language to understand, or we can present this person with a series of relevant cases, pointing out the required behaviour in each.[63] How do we know that our pupil has understood the lesson? This is clear in the second case: he has understood it if he is able without further guidance to recognize a further relevant case, and to identify the required behaviour in it. But this is also the correct answer in the first case; if our pupil only knows the formula we have taught him, and is (mysteriously) able to explain its meaning by giving adequate reformulations, without knowing what to do in a concrete case, we would consider our lessons to have been in vain. This means that even to really know the meaning of the statement of the norm, one must be able to continue the series. On the other hand, in using the second method our aim has not been to teach our pupil something about the "particular cases" we present, but rather to be able to *extrapolate* from these to an indefinite number of new cases. But if we are using statements in general terms as a vehicle, our aim is exactly the same, for to understand the meaning of such statements also involves being able to refer to paradigmatic cases, and to extrapolate from these to new ones.[64] Cognitive psychology

---

[62] The cases need not actually have happened, and in the limiting case their number may be restricted to one.

[63] Hart 1961, 121ff.

[64] This leaves us with Kripke's famous problem, to explain how a rule can fix its own future application; for an exhaustive discussion see Stein 1997. But, as Kripke 1982 recognizes, any thorough scepticism concerning the very possibility of rule-following (expressed in general terms!) would be obviously absurd. Hence Kripke's problem has an answer, even if we do not yet know it.

tells us that our mastery of general concepts is like this; my suggestion is that our appeal to general considerations in practical judgment is not at all different.

Note, however, that talk of "particular" cases should not necessarily be taken literally; abbreviated sketches of such cases, which themselves really stand for classes of cases, may be sufficient. The point is just that a grasp of the general always consists in the ability to extrapolate or project from some of its instantiations to others. That is not, as has often been suggested in the claims for the superiority of casuistry over principlism in applied ethics, a form of knowledge alternative to knowing a rule. It *is* knowing a rule.

We have now found the kernel of truth in particularism. Pointing to particular cases (or to descriptions of relatively concrete classes of cases) has more than a heuristic value only: it fixes the meaning of general (or higher-level) considerations, and as such it has an indispensable informational value. Even if in any specific case this value is dispensable, that is only because the relevant consideration is part of a network of belief which is fixed in this way at innumerable places. On the other hand, cases are only relevant as models or paradigms of rules. The appeal to precedent is therefore perfectly understandable.

## 11.9. The Defeasible Character of Legal Reasoning

I have argued that deductivism misrepresents legal argument, but that legal argument nevertheless invariably exists in the appeal to general considerations. Clearly this calls for explanation.

The problem about particularism was that in each case in which an action is obligatory or permitted, we can point to some properties of the action or its context that combine to make it obligatory or permitted, and this must be explained by appeal to a valid norm in virtue of which these properties make the action obligatory or permitted. But the problem about deductivism was that it turned out to be generally true about all general statements of the rule that they clearly cover some possible particular case without dictating the proper legal result in it. How is it possible to combine these two insights? If two new situations have the same properties as one precedent or paradigm case, picked out as relevant by an explicit rule or *ratio decidendi*, how is it possible that the action which was obligatory in the old case, is also obligatory in one of the new cases but not in the other?

---

Here is one answer. How do we know that 'plus' means addition, and not: addition until time $t$, and always summing to 5 after $t$? Kripke himself suggests that this is a matter of the convergence of blind inclinations of the people making up a linguistic community. But that does not explain why a person who says 68+57=5 is mistaken, rather than only deviant. However, people are not only blindly inclined to act in certain ways, they also expect each other to be so inclined, and adjust their own actions to their expectations. If I get only fl. 5 instead of the fl. 125 which I expect, I will be angry. Normative language expresses mutually adjusted reactions to successes and failures in coordination.

How is it possible for our reactions to be so adjusted? Take two computing machines, one with the function 'plus' = addition, the other with the time-index at $t$. The second clearly is dysfunctional for purposes of coordination, as the millennium-bug reminded us. So there may be a functional (evolutionary) explanation for "the convergence of blind inclinations".

Consider the following. If some action is right for being *A*, and another action wrong in spite of (or even for) being *A*, this must be explained by pointing to some other property that the second action has, which is lacking in the first (or vice versa); therefore the original norm identifying *A* as a right-making characteristic has to be qualified. As the particularist will be quick to point out, this is not the end of the matter: for similar reasons, the qualification must itself be qualified, etcetera ad infinitum. But that does not preclude that, each time a qualification is added, it covers *a class of* possible cases. So any statement of a general consideration has a clause for exceptions or default assumptions built into it: "when *C* you should do *A*, except when also *C-a...n*'. Some of these exceptions can, with some thought, be stated in advance by anyone with sufficient moral competence and experience, but this rider is nevertheless always an open one: we can never be certain that no unthought-of type of situation will be exemplified in fact or in fiction, forcing us to recognize it as a new condition for making an exception.

So exception clauses have exception clauses built into them as well, and all these clauses have the same open-ended character. By means of these exception clauses, all principles are related to each other in a network of belief, some relations being established, and others remaining to be discovered at any time. That is why supervenience works in a *holistic* way, as particularists rightly observe.[65] If we are only looking at some of the properties of the action etc., we can never conclude that it has a certain moral property as well. We must inspect the other properties, and any one of these may be relevant to the final judgment. To establish any moral judgment conclusively, we would have to go through the whole chain of exception clauses to exception clauses (without making mistakes in reasoning). We could never do that exhaustively.

Why not? It seems to me that the limitations of our understanding are only part of the explanation. The other part is that any system of conventions is to some extent "invented" by the community of the agents supporting it as they go along.[66] In any new situation we may be sufficiently constrained by the relevant considerations to be warranted in believing that our conclusion is a discovery and not an invention. But nevertheless, when this conclusion is added to the relevant considerations for the next problem, we start a cumulative process of constructive thinking that inevitably results in the network of moral beliefs being revised, and this not only by our mistakes.

It follows that the conclusions we actually reach are always provisional, open to challenge. But it also follows that the considerations we appeal to in justification are always general. It makes sense to refer to other cases, and to explain their relevance in terms of a *ratio decidendi*, which is one chain of a norm with exceptions, exceptions to exceptions etc., cut short at some point, and for that reason open to further challenge. It is also never true that all the actual properties of a token context are relevant to determining its normative character, nor that any subset of them is sufficient to (logically) identify the situation uniquely. If the situation requires a certain judgment on

---

[65] Platts 1979, ch. 10; Dancy 1993.

[66] Cf. Beauchamp 1996, 90-91.

account of a certain constellation of its properties, we can always imagine the same constellation requiring the same judgment in other cases. Most of the time we are actually acquainted with such cases, and sometimes routinely.

The idea of open-ended chains of exception clauses to exception clauses may seem very discouraging. In going through this process, how can our rational confidence in any conclusion ever *grow*? And this seems to be a minimal requirement, even if we are accustomed to the idea that it will seldom grow to something resembling certainty. We may suspect that a ceteris paribus clause to a rule will undermine its claim to being a rule at all: things are never equal, but we cannot decide whether the dissimilarities are relevant by reference to the rule. So how do we decide whether we are within the domain of the "rule" or of its exceptions, otherwise than by looking at the particular case?

To give our generalist account some initial plausibility, we must introduce something like a "ripples-in-the-pond postulate". The postulate says that in going through the chain, our chances of meeting any unforeseen exception will normally be reduced, and be reduced substantially. If we are to be able to apply the whole network of relevant considerations with any degree of confidence, the complexity of its relations to the world must be finite, so that our grasp of the network as a whole, though necessarily incomplete, is sufficiently firm to enable us, by and large, to tackle this complexity. This constraint on holism explains why it is not wholly absurd to say, with W.D. Ross, that the validity of a principle, notwithstanding its defeasibility, implies a "tendency" to fix the moral property of cases to which it applies.[67]

This postulate, however, is only a superficial answer to our worries about default rules. The main point can be introduced by noting a characteristic aspect of the language used in normative reasoning. Statements of general considerations appealed to in justification will show their character as default assumptions by taking the form "normally if $c$, then $p$". And the conclusion they allow us to draw will therefore be of the form "presumably $p$". The applicability of these concepts presupposes a certain distribution of the *burden of proof*: we will only be fully satisfied by a denial of $p$ if some relevant defeating consideration is adduced.

Let me illustrate the point by a simple example from moral reasoning. Suppose you have been told that a person did something morally wrong; you ask what made his action wrong, and the answer is that he lied (intentionally led another person to believe a falsehood). The answer, if a bit short, is satisfactory. Now suppose you have been told that another person did something morally laudable; you again ask what about his action made it so, and the answer is once more that he lied. To be intelligible at all, this requires elucidation. Default rules reflect this asymmetry in their ordering of the relevant features.

---

[67] Van Willigenburg 1999, 51-52 objects that in appealing to a moral consideration ("that would be lying"), we do not claim that there is a certain probability of, say, 80%, that the property referred to will actually determine rightness or wrongness, cf. Dancy 1993, 99-100. We certainly do not, because in such statements we (provisionally) claim to be at the end of the chain.

If you hold that, normally, human beings are one-legged, you will not only have many exceptions to explain, but, more fundamentally, it will be very hard to explain them.[68]

This means that, though it is true that the moral character of an action or a person (or a society) results from the relevant properties of the action, the person or the society as a whole, it is also true that this moral shape can be analysed, or broken down. Each relevant feature makes a difference, but the difference must be explained against the background of other features. If the background is kept constant, the significance of the feature will be the same. If we have been informed that the action has the property *A*, we conclude that it is right (say, courageous), if we now learn that it is also *B*, we consider it wrong (say, foolhardy). With every new property the moral meaning, and even what Dancy calls the 'polarity' of the old ones may change, but it does so in a universally valid way. At every particular point we may stop this process, and then we know the moral truth for all cases in which it is proper to stop at this point. The moral "shape" of a case is built up step by step from the differences each of its salient features *generally* makes at its own particular point in the building process. There may be several routes to the same final holistic conclusion, each taking a different starting point, e.g. in the properties invoking one of two conflicting principles. But not every possible ordering of the relevant properties is equally acceptable.[69]

Default-generalism, as we might call it, is a modest doctrine: it only asserts that moral shapes are analysable in this way. It accepts the holistic idea that a salient feature does not make the same difference everywhere. But it does not accept that if a feature makes the same difference here and elsewhere, this is entirely accidental.[70]


## 11.10. Do Principles Have Derogatory Force?

In this chapter I have identified seven types of argument that, given my conventionalist account of the nature of law, should be expected to occur in legal reasoning, and do in fact occur. Is it possible to flesh out the description of default-generalism given in the previous section, by giving a general account of the place of these types of argument in an "ordering of defeat"?

If a question of law has to be decided, then in modern systems there will usually be at least one authoritative statement, licensed by an existing formal convention, which is directly applicable. In interpreting the authoritative statement we proceed as we do with any communicative act: we first establish (top-down) its relatively context-independent meaning. But sometimes reasons can be given why this is not satisfactory, and then we have to look around (bottom-up) for other clues available for interdependent reasoning. And even when we have made sure what the relevant

---

[68] Veltman 1989, 215. Cf. ch. 5.5. on the obligation to obey the law as a default.

[69] This fact may partly explain Dworkin's mistake about the logical character of principles, a mistake I discussed in ch. 11.4. above. Because principles belong to the first level of this ordering, they are most obviously open to an indefinite number of exceptions.

[70] On the logic of defeasible reasoning (non-monotonic logic), see Veltman 1996; Hage 1997; Prakken 1997.

authority intended to prescribe, that does not always settle the question of what the law is; for substantial conventions, values and principles have an independent supplementing or countervailing force of their own.

So we can, disregarding the argument from custom, subdivide the process of reasoning into two stages, and the first of these into two substages. The whole process aims at settling the question of what the law is. At the first stage we try to identify the communicative intentions of the relevant authorities. At the first substage we do this by using the argument from normal meaning. This has therefore a special status: it usually establishes the first default interpretation, and thereby determines the burden of proof.[71] At the second substage we make the necessary local adaptations. The result is an answer to our central question, but again only a defeasible one. Arguments may be adduced for going beyond the intentions of the relevant authorities.

The argument from substantive values and the argument from principles can be used either at the second stage or at the second substage. For at the second substage we presume that the relevant authorities had the substantive values and principles in mind. (Therefore the argument from subjective intention was said to be "transcategorical".) But this presumption notwithstanding, it may turn out to be beyond reasonable doubt (given the evidence of the *travaux préparatoires*, for example) that the authority intended to give a ruling which conflicted with the values or contradicted the principles. It is obvious, for example, that the Dutch lawgiver in the Penal Code of 1881 intended to include euthanasia under his description of the criminal offence of homicide. So when a Dutch court for the first time declared that, under certain conditions of careful action, euthanasia could be justifiable, it clearly could not appeal to legislative intention.[72] I do not suggest that it is always clear whether one should appeal to the presumption or declare it defeated; it may not make any difference for the conclusion anyway. Take the law on the public violation of modesty: did the legislature intend to forbid what he supposed to *be* offensive, timelessly, or what will be mutually deemed to be offensive (and therefore be offensive) at any particular future time of application? The discussion about the exact range of the proper appeal to legislative intention is therefore doomed to be endless. However, as with any fuzzy border, there are clear cases at either side of it.

This distinction between stages and substages can be used to settle a recent dispute in Dutch legal theory concerning the relation between the interpretation of statutes and the principle of *bona fides* ("good faith" in the old, "reasonableness and fairness" in the new civil code).[73] Art. 6.2 NBW (the new Dutch civil code) stipulates explicitly that a legal rule governing the relation of creditor and debtor is inapplicable if

---

[71] Cf. Bankowski & MacCormick 1991, 366 on "the argument from undisplaced obvious meaning": no sufficient reason obtains for displacing the presumption in its favour. The only exception is a case in which no authoritative legislative statement is relevant, but only a substantial convention.

[72] Perhaps to the intentions of an ideal legislator? Cf. MacCormick & Summers 1991, 522. But he is only characterized as ideal because he adheres to the relevant values and principles. The expression misleadingly suggests that even at the second stage, we are acting under the aegis of legislative authority.

[73] Abas 1989; Schoordijk 1985; cf. Hesselink, Oosting & Du Perron 1990. Schoordijk's position can be found in many of his works, canonically in Schoordijk 1972.

it is unacceptable on criteria of reasonableness and fairness. Art. 6.258 applies this principle to the binding force of contracts when new circumstances arise:
"The judge is empowered, on request of one of the parties to a contract, either to change its legal consequences, or to dissolve it wholly or partially, when circumstances arise unprovided for in the contract and of such a nature that the other party cannot reasonably and fairly expect unrevised application of its provisions."

According to Abas this is an unfortunate article. For cases may arise that cannot be said to be "unprovided for"[74], in which it would nevertheless be unreasonable to expect complete fulfilment of the requirements. For instance, a firm $Y$ undertakes to supply crude oil to $Z$ for a period of fifteen years at a certain price, which may be adjusted once in six months to market prices, but with a maximum of 45%. Then suddenly the market price of oil goes up by 700%. Does the maximum apply?

Schoordijk objects that this argument shows an inadequate conception of legal argument. The words used in contracts and laws are always in need of interpretation, and in interpreting them we should presuppose that they are made by reasonable and fair persons. (This is sometimes called "normative interpretation".) In this case we should suppose that the stipulations concerning price adjustment do not cover increases in the order of 700%. So the new situation was *not* provided for.

Abas, on the other hand, is happy with Art. 6.2, while Schoordijk is not. According to Abas we always start by identifying the literal meaning of the provisions of the rule. In some cases, however (not only when unforeseeable circumstances arise, but also in cases of necessity, error, etc.), the rule does not suffice to determine the legal position. In those cases the principle of *bona fides* must be used, either to fill the gaps left by the rule, or even to deviate from the clear outcome of the application of the rule, in order to arrive at an acceptable result. This "derogatory force" of the principle seems to be recognized by the article.

Schoordijk, on his part, does not want to accept any derogatory force. (Although, as we shall see, he rather inconsistently accepts a supplementing force.) Words never have a *sens clair*, they always require normative interpretation. We should read the law through the glasses of bona fides. The courts will never find themselves in a position in which they have to set aside any valid rule, for they will always be able to interpret the rule in such a way as to avoid unacceptable results.

I will argue that *both* authors misdescribe the situation to some extent. Words, even vague words, *do* have a *sens clair*; otherwise Schoordijk could not communicate to us his "normative interpretation". Knowledge of the meaning of words, of the ways words can be combined to form sentences (syntax), *and* of the fairly permanent background conditions that give the rule its point, are sufficient to determine the normal meaning of the text of either a statute or a contract. This establishes a default interpretation of the intentions of the lawgiver, or the contracting parties. But this interpretation may be either supplemented or corrected when we recognize that local variations in context bring into play the principles of reasonableness and fairness; by

---

[74] The actual Dutch word is ambiguous, it can also be interpreted as "unforeseen"; Abas' interpretation derives from the history of the introduction of the article.

taking these into account, we fill in the gaps left by going through the first substage – we may even deviate from its outcome.

Schoordijk's mistake is not to recognize this two-step sequence. He seems to think that we cannot identify any clear meaning of the text of a contract without interpreting it straight away in terms of *bona fides*. However, we *do* in fact note that the maximum provided for in the contract would result in no more than a 45% rise, and we do judge this outcome to be unfair; we do not go straight to any "fair" outcome without even noting the problem.

Abas' mistake, on the other hand, is to believe that by taking this first step we arrive at "*the* meaning of the provisions of the contract" (or of the statute), whereas the second step brings us to the actual legal consequences, by the "derogating" force of the principle of fairness. So he does not distinguish between the second substage and the second stage. Making a contract or a statute, however, does not just consist in uttering a formula or writing a text, it is an intentional speech act which aims at a change of the normative situation, and – unless it "misfires" -succeeds in doing so (even if the actual change may not necessarily fit the intended one!). Understanding this speech act means understanding the intention of the speaker. So the contract or the statute has no "meaning" that can be distinguished from its intended legal consequences. We can isolate sentences used in a document from the actual context in which the text of the document should be applied, and ascertain their "normal meaning". But if we want to identify their *present* meaning we must take into account the actual context.[75] The meaning of the contract or statute consists in the legitimate expectations it creates; identifying the normal meaning of the words does not result in discovering those legitimate expectations per se, but only in a default expectation that must be corrected in order to arrive at the right result.

Schoordijk's mistake is to suggest that the *formulas* used in the authoritative acts of contracting or legislating do not have any clear meaning outside the framework of "normative interpretation'. They have. Abas' mistake is to believe that this clear meaning of the formulas determines the *legal* force of the legislative acts, which then has to be overruled by an appeal to other standards. But we should rather appeal to these standards in determining the force of those acts in the present circumstances. For the acts aim at changing the 'normative situation", an aim that only makes sense against a normative background already structured by those standards. I accept the idea of "normative interpretation", but it applies to speech acts, not to words and sentences.

Having seen that the stipulations for price adjustment do not cover the actual case, how should we proceed in determining the legal position? Van Dunné proposes to extend the theory of "normative interpretation" in the following way.[76] The judge should simply apply the principles of reasonableness and fairness, and the results he arrives at are then to be considered to be the real meaning of the contract. Schoordijk, on the other hand, believes we have found a lacuna in the meaning of the contract: it did not succeed in determining the legal position, and the judge must fill the lacuna by his

---

[75] Cf. MacCormick & Bankowski in 1989, 42-43.

[76] Van Dunné 1985.

application of the principles of reasonableness and fairness. The principles have no derogating force, but they do have a supplementing force. This strikes me as an inconsistent position, as I said before: Schoordijk now only brings the principles into play when the meaning of the contract has already been established, and that seems to be a complete surrender to Abas' position. Schoordijk is forced to do this because he recognizes, quite rightly, that the proper result cannot be derived from the words used in the contract. (However, that it would be improper to insist on the maximum of 45% cannot be derived from these words either. So if this criterion is sufficient to recognize a supplementing force, it should also lead to the recognition of a derogatory force.) Again it is not the formula used, but the act of contracting that should be the object of the normative interpretation. As long as the application of relevant principles gives a determinate result, which can be arrived at by vicarious reasoning, it ipso facto fixes the meaning of the contract: the parties could, and should, have arrived at the same conclusion.

To this extent Van Dunné is right. However, it is perfectly possible that such a conclusion cannot be reached at all. The evidence might show that the lawgiver or the parties really intended the unreasonable or unfair result. It may still be possible to determine the legal position by appealing to the principle of reasonableness and fairness. But then the legal position can no longer be said to be the meaning of the statute or the contract. People may create unintended results by their intentional acts. So Van Dunné makes the same mistake as Abas: he does not distinguish between the second substage and the second stage. Though he assimilates the stage to the substage, while Abas did the reverse.

This sequential order also illuminates the notion of "gaps" or "lacunas" in the law. Do we fill the gaps by interpretation or do we find them? The puzzle is solved by realizing that gaps may remain at the end of each stage or substage; sometimes, but not always, those gaps can be filled by proceeding to the next stage (if there is one). On the other hand, gaps can also be *created* by countervailing considerations at a later stage.

Did I not play into the hands of the positivists by separating between the stages in the way I did? The appeal to authority is made at the first substage. Following Joseph Raz[77] (and Abas), could we not say that this substage establishes what the law *is*, while the other substages establish what the courts, using their discretion in non-arbitrary ways and thereby possibly changing the law (as they ought to), decide the legal consequences to be? There are two reasons why this move cannot succeed. The first reason is that the first substage is incomplete without the second: we cannot fully establish the prescriptions of legislative and judicial authorities unless we interpret their pronouncements against the background of relevant substantive values and principles. The second reason is that, even if at the end of the second substage we have established the content of the relevant authoritative prescriptions, we have not established their *authority*. The whole of the present chapter confirms the thesis of chapter Seven that we should not interpet this authority as providing exclusionary reasons. For it is always possible that at the second stage we meet countervaling considerations that need to be

---

[77] See ch. 10.3.

balanced against the reasons provided by authority. Such considerations refuse to be excluded.[78]

## 11.11. A Case Study[79]

When Maring's old farmhouse burnt down, he turned out to be very well insured indeed. Just a few months before, he had made a substantial addition to the insured sum, as a result of which the total sum amply sufficed to cover the expenses of rebuilding. The insurance company, however, refused to pay more than the price the building would have made in sale.

The court (*Rechtbank*) concluded from the amount of the insured sum that the parties to the agreement intended the insurance to cover rebuilding costs. (A run-of-the-mill case of vicarious reasoning, using the argument from subjective intention, in this case the intention of the contracting parties as "private legislators".) The question whether such an agreement can be legal was answered affirmatively with a reference to art. 29 of the Lease Act, which places a duty on a lessor to rebuild after fire, provided only that it had been open to him to take insurance against rebuilding prices. The court of appeal (*Gerechtshof*) confirmed the decision. It consulted experts who reported that it had become the general custom of the trade to insure against rebuilding prices. In times past, greater stability of prices had made it possible for private persons to make reservations for write-down, but this method nowadays was generally considered unsatisfactory.

The insurance company was not convinced. And, indeed, it seemed to have an unusually strong case. For the Sale of Goods Act (1838), art. 289, forbids insurance to cover more than the market value of the object, explicitly bound to a maximum of 3/4 of the expenses of rebuilding. And this was not an arbitrary provision, but, according to the company, a rule motivated by a general principle of indemnity underlying other articles of the Act as well: insurance should cancel the adverse effects of a calamity, but the insured person should not be able to *improve* his net position as a result of its occurrence. This whole defence had been treated by the court of appeal in a rather cavalier way.

The High Court (*Hoge Raad*) accepted the relevance of the principle of indemnity, but considered the practice of insuring against rebuilding prices not to be incompatible with it. For it is a requirement of the continuity of the conduct of business that a firm can rebuild the accommodation in which its activities take place. Therefore, the harmful consequences of the fire can only be taken away by rebuilding. This is a clear example of the argument from substantive values.

The High Court did not deny either that article 289 applied to the case. So it accepted the argument from normal meaning, but went on to defeat it. For it considered that the restrictions thereby placed on the practice of insurance against fire had proved

---

[78] Cf. Atria 1999, 566-576. And cf. ch. 9.5.

[79] *Maring/Assuradeuren*, HR 3/3/72, NJ 1972, 339.

not to be in accordance with the needs of social conduct, and were therefore properly disregarded by custom. This custom, furthermore, had received the blessing of the legislator, as shown by art. 29 of the Lease Law. In this way the combined efforts of practice and legislation had caused art. 289 to lose its legal force.

So the High Court, spurning the prevarications of the court of appeal, clearly recognized the inconsistency between the Sale of Goods Act and the Lease Act. From a purely logical point of view this was not inevitable: it would have been possible to conclude from art. 289 that the condition stipulated by the Lease Act could never be fulfilled. That would have meant, however, to declare art. 29 of the Lease Law unapplicable and therefore pointless. If the article had to be given a meaning, it could only be taken to imply a recognition of the new custom of trade. Here we find the argument from subjective intention again, based on the presumption that the legislative authority has some intelligible aim.

The main interest of the decision, however, is its use of the argument from substantial conventions to justify a decision usually supposed to be *contra legem*. The court recognizes that the custom of trade is not an arbitrary convention, but a way of meeting a clear social need. In circumstances differing from those of 1838, the risk of fire could only be made controllable by having the option of insuring against rebuilding prices. Insurance companies had fully cooperated in the development of the new pattern of mutual expectations; never before had they appealed to the diverging legal prescription. (The reluctance of the insurance company in Maring's case was exceptional, due perhaps to the obvious convenience of the occurrence of the fire.) But when conventions develop which enable participants in social conduct to avoid suboptimal outcomes without any harm to third parties, it cannot be the task of legal institutions to frustrate their cooperation. The decision of the High Court recognizes this basic fact of "legal immunology".

# CHAPTER 12

## COHERENCE AND DECIDABILITY

### 12.1. Inconsistency in Systems of Mutual Belief

Let me start again in our protolegal world of customary rules. Suppose we come upon an inconsistency in our system of rules: you are required to do $p$ under conditions $a$, and to omit doing $p$ under conditions $b$, but conditions $a$ and $b$ obtain at the same time. It is a contingent inconsistency: it does not arise from the requirements alone, but from the requirements in combination with a true description of the actual state of affairs. It may be possible in this situation to find a clue for postulating the priority of one of the requirements (i.e.: for believing that you may *reasonably* expect the others to agree with your assessment of priority); for instance, that everybody can see that following the one rule is in line with the point of having those rules, and following the other is not. But perhaps we do not find a clue. The result is the same as when our choice is *underdetermined* by the rules: we have no ground to expect each other to form any specific expectations.

Hence it appears that, properly speaking, in our protolegal system *there is no such thing as inconsistency at all.* For it cannot be the case that people mutually expect each other to do and to omit $p$ at the same time. What at first sight seemed to be an inconsistency, turns out to be a form of undecidability. In reasoning "from above" we come to inconsistent results; but this does not end the matter. However, when we try to go on by reasoning "from below", we find no clues, or, alternatively, we find equally prominent clues pointing in different directions. The outcome is a gap in our pattern of mutual expectations, a failure of coordination. It could be described as a case of ambiguity by overdetermination.

When we take a closer look, even this ambiguity may seem to vanish. If we are not justified in expecting a person either to do or to omit $p$, surely it follows that he is free to make his own choice? But then the normative position is unambiguously defined. The burden of proof always rests on the person who claims a (positive or negative) obligation to exist; there is always a presumption of freedom. Given the framework of a conventionalist theory of obligation, this is not so much a substantial moral truth as a logical implication of the framework.[1]

But rules for the distribution of the burden of proof, even unambiguous ones, do not completely rule out ambiguity. A presumption of freedom is just one consideration, it may be evenly balanced by reasons for attributing obligation. For instance, if wages are taxed, do the contributions that employers make to pension programs count as

---

[1] Similarly, there is a "natural" (salient) distribution of the burden of proof for the application of other types of legal rules: those establishing the existence of legal entities, legitimizing inferences to be drawn from evidence, assigning powers and liabilities etc. Cf. Hart 1955 (retracted Hart 1983, 17).

wages? The consideration that no taxation can be legitimate without proper title hardly decides the matter. We have to inquire into the reasons for choosing wages as a basis for taxation.

Undecidability cannot be completely avoided by the adoption of canons of proof. But is it true that all forms of prima facie inconsistency within patterns of expectation resolve into undecidability? There seems to be a cogent argument to the contrary. Suppose that, given the standing pattern of mutual expectations and the data available to me, I have good reason to believe that either you do believe that you ought to do $p$, or at least that you should believe this. It might be the case that, given the same pattern of expectations and the data available to you, at the same time you have good reason to believe that either I believe you ought to omit doing $p$, or at least that I should believe this.

Would this be possible, even if we both have access to the same data? At first sight it seems that it might. Similarly, it seems reasonable to believe that two literary critics may have sufficiently good reason to defend contradictory interpretations of a poem, even if none of them appeals to data not available to the other one.[2] But I think this intuitive affirmation leads us quickly into paradox. It seems that the assertion that both critics have sufficiently good reason (an assertion made on the basis of the same data as theirs) cannot but pretend to be *itself* the superior judgment on the merits of the case.[3]

Leaving this case aside for the moment, it seems safe to affirm that it is at least possible for two persons plausibly to ascribe to each other information which the other party does not in fact have, and therefore to assume mutual knowledge which does not exist. Attempts at interdependent reasoning, therefore, even if they meet all standards of reasonableness and successfully identify a clue to start from, may still result in inconsistent conclusions. Does a certain contract bind when circumstances have changed in unforeseeable ways? The parties may have diverging views of the matter, each believing, *on good grounds*, that they may expect the other to concur. (I do not say: on equally good grounds, for I wish to leave open the possibility that the force of valid and opposing reasons is sometimes incommensurable.)

But does this add up to an inconsistency in our pattern of mutual beliefs? It does not. One party is justified in believing one thing, the other in believing the opposite. There is no inconsistency in affirming both. From this double affirmation it follows, however, that they could not be expected to succeed in mirroring each other's reasoning: if they failed to converge, they did so blamelessly. And therefore, in reasoning vicariously, we can only conclude that on the level of *mutual* beliefs the question was undecidable.

I conclude that a conventionalist theory should deny the possibility of inconsistencies in the law. Things look differently from other philosophical perspectives. If you assume that law is the expression of the will of a powerful person, then inconsistency is certainly possible. It is to be expected that this person sometimes

---

[2] Cf. John Wisdom's story of the garden, Wisdom 1964, 154-155.

[3] Cf. ch. 12.6. below.

wants you to do *p* under conditions *a* and to omit doing *p* under conditions *b*, without realizing that you may be in conditions *a* and *b* at the same time. It is even more to be expected if law is the expression of the aggregated will of several persons; for social choice theory has shown that under many circumstances, no aggregation process can exclude the possibility of inconsistency.

We cannot therefore discuss the notion of legal consistency within a *reine Rechtslehre*; we only start talking about law when we have given (or presuppose) our interpretation of the kind of reality we take law to be (our "model" or description scheme). You cannot speak about logical relations between legal statements in Popper's third world, without taking a position on the question of the nature of law as a phenomenon in the second world. Suppose we find, in two sources of law of equal status (for example two statutes, published in the *Staatsblad* on the same date), two norms containing logically contradictory requirements. What is the legal position of the citizen to whom both norms apply? On some theories, he is always at fault, whatever he does, because the "commands" are equally valid, and apply to him. On other theories, he must search for a priority rule beyond the formal status of the norms, and it is certain that there is one only waiting to be discovered. On a conventionalist theory, such a priority rule *might* exist, but it is also possible that it does not. Sometimes the conclusion is warranted that our citizen has no legal obligation either way and is left to his own discretion. But we cannot a priori exclude the possibility that no final decision about his legal status can be made at all; the attempt to create mutual expectations may have failed, leaving only confusion.

## 12.2. Formal Conventions and Ambiguity

Lacunas in decidability were one reason for making the transition into the legal world. Is it really possible to overcome the inconveniences of the state of nature by the introduction of formal conventions? What we see is rather a process resembling the evolutionary race between predator and prey: the increase in complexity of social relations invites a corresponding expansion in the exercise of legislative and judicial powers, which in its turn is one causal factor in the increase of social complexity. The labyrinth grows with the length of Ariadne's thread. A similar development occurs *within* the legal system: the desire to eliminate ambiguity by underdetermination, produces ambiguity by overdetermination. I would venture to suggest that beyond a certain point, especially when legal regulation in any field proliferates beyond the encompassing power of the mind of any single individual, the net result of both processes might be an increase in ambiguity. (If we start from the lack of identifiability and flexibility as the main deficiencies of the prelegal world, it is rather paradoxical to observe that legislating authorities increasingly, by the use of vague terms, rely on informal conventions to provide either identifiability or flexibility or both.) As the whole point of legislation is the focusing of expectations, this would mean that legislating activity is becoming increasingly counterproductive. In any case, the time that the idea of law as a seamless web could even begin to be believable is long gone.

Ambiguity is not necessarily an unmitigated evil for everyone. (Even outside the legal profession, which of course relates to ambiguity as the medical profession relates to illness.) For instance, it may create room for manoeuvre for individuals to change their status (e.g. in the order of succession to a chiefdom) through litigation.[4]

It is one of the great illusions of rationalism (personified in Jeremy Bentham) to believe that by making the law subject to intentional production, we can overcome the limitations of our capacity to achieve mutual belief. We have made some progress indeed; legislation and adjudication are stronger means of focusing expectations than the opinions of wise men, which may diverge. These means permit local victories on ambiguity, but never a final one. The problem is not only that legislating authorities cannot possibly foresee in what ways the rules they produce might become relevant. The problem is also that law is never created from scratch; "new" laws only fill in, or marginally change, the details of existing conventions. If these constraints are neglected by legislators who wish to use the law as an instrument of social change, we will sooner or later enter the domain of legal pathology. (Laws that nobody expects anyone to comply with, that were proclaimed in order to guide behaviour but are only used for the allocation of liability, that have no more than symbolic value, that are only introduced to build an image of vigour or to satisfy electoral appetite, etc.)

Authority is only one source of conventions, its products have to fit into the whole body of mutual expectations. Statutes and verdicts can only guide the reasoning from above, but never the reasoning from below. It is therefore beyond the power of authority to determine people's obligations exactly the way it wants. Its exercise is subject to certain laws of legal *immunology*.[5] Legal principles in particular exercise powerful immunological functions.

## 12.3. An Argument from Inconsistency

In chapter Eleven, seven types of argument were listed that seem to me distinctive of reasoning within a system of formal conventions. It is widely assumed that there is a further important and distinct type of legal argument, called "the argument from coherence".[6] Let us see whether this is true.

What do we mean by coherence? The least one could say is that there should be no inconsistencies between allegedly valid legal statements. Now suppose that we find an apparent inconsistency (usually it will be a contingent one) on the level of our first type of argument, i.e. the appeal to the normal relatively context-independent meaning of the words of statutes of judicial decisions. I will here disregard the principle that you

---

[4] As is common practice with the Tswana, as described by Comaroff and Roberts 1981: for example, through the settlement of disputes the status of a woman may be redefined from wife to concubine. (Cf. the practice of medieval European monarchs.)

[5] Cf. ch. 1, note 52. These limitations on the exercise of authority are often concealed by adoption theories: whenever authority is forced to recognize existing law, it is assumed to make it into proper law by its very act of recognition, cf. ch. 9.2.;

[6] MacCormick & Summers 1991 consider 9 out of 11 of the types of legal argument they identify to be "systemic" arguments, aiming at coherence.

can derive any statement you like from a contradiction, a principle that may not be valid within the sphere of interdependent reasoning. Even so, there are at least some possible cases in which we would not be able to decide between conflicting prescriptions. Suppose we come upon one such case. Then we will have reason to act on the following maxim: if a suggested interpretation of the meaning of a concept leads to an inconsistency with an apparently valid legal proposition, the inconsistency should be removed, either by rejecting the interpretation under consideration, or by re-interpreting the meaning of the conflicting proposition.

This is a second example of a metaconvention. Its function is the same as that of the first example we came across, the metaconvention to consider as valid law anything that can be validly derived from valid law.[7] Both metaconventions decrease the area of undecidability. This particular one establishes within the system of conventions an immunological reaction to inconsistencies: it tries to drive them out.

But if we are to comply with this maxim, we cannot normally remain on the purely propositional level, we should appeal to arguments of at least one of the other types.[8] If we have used these arguments, and found a solution that can be supposed to be mutually replicable, the inconsistency is removed. If no solution can be found we must conclude, as I argued in section 1, that there is an undecided question of law. So in this case there is no distinct argument from inconsistency that by itself leads to any identifiable conclusion.

Suppose, however, that in a relatively context-independent interpretation we do not find an apparent inconsistency, but rather an ambiguity: e.g. a term which, with equal plausibility, can be given one of two possible meanings. And suppose that, if we attributed one of those meanings, an apparent inconsistency would arise. That indeed is a reason to prefer the other meaning. (Not necessarily a decisive reason, we also have the option of removing the apparent inconsistency by drawing on the other types of argument; we could also appeal to them to decide which option to prefer.) So we find a special type of argument after all:

(1a) The argument from inconsistency.[9]

It is a bit different from the other types, because it does not follow from the nature of the system but rather from the maxim of avoiding inconsistencies, a maxim that should be seen as a metaconvention. It is one of the usual means of "local adaptation" in every system of conventions, including every system of linguistic communication; it should therefore not be seen as a distinct type of argument on a par with the other seven types, but rather as one of the concrete forms our type (1), the argument from meaning, may take.

---

[7] Ch. 11.2. at note 17.

[8] Because the inconsistency leads to undecidability, and the use of the other type of argument fills this gap, I would consider this to be a supplementary rather than a countervailing use, though technically the argument will conflict with at least one valid legal statement in its "normal" interpretation.

[9] Perhaps there is an argument from undecidability comparable to the argument from inconsistency: if one interpretation of a term leaves a larger area of undecidability than another, this is a reason to prefer the second one. A maximum of decidability seems to be part of the ideal of coherence.

Even if the argument from normal meaning has a clear conclusion, arguments of the other types may still, as I suggested, generate countervailing considerations. Sometimes this will again generate an apparent inconsistency; we may then once more appeal to our metaconvention, and try to find a replicable interpretation of the apparently conflicting legal propositions which reconciles them. In this case there is no distinct argument from inconsistency to appeal to. Such an argument can only be of any help if the countervailing considerations generate an indeterminacy of meaning, and one of the possible interpretations would lead to an apparent inconsistency. (Even then, as I said, the argument will not be automatically decisive.)

To participate in a discussion about the consistency of the law is a rather confusing experience most of the time. Someone claims that a particular legal system, for instance the Dutch one, is full of inconsistencies. Someone else asks him to give an example. The first person proceeds to do so, and the second one, predictably, denies that it is an inconsistency: a certain concept should be interpreted differently, a latent proviso added and so on and so forth. The parties suppose they have an argument, but they have not. The first one is thinking within the framework of a restricted repertoire of appropriate arguments, probably consisting of arguments from normal meaning only, or perhaps also consisting of arguments attempting to reconstruct the subjective intentions of the legislative authority (LA). Within this framework, he may be quite right. Even if we adopt a principle of interpretative charity, as we should, we may sometimes be pretty sure that an explanatory statement of an LA or a justificatory one by a court contains an inconsistency.[10] With any luck we may even find a court identifying an apparent inconsistency in the relevant legal materials, and not finding a way to remove it.[11] The second person then appeals to the maxim of dealing with apparent inconsistencies and concludes, also impeccably, that the final word has not been spoken (though the sentence may have been entered!), and that we should enlarge the domain of acceptable arguments in order to find a solution.

But when all legal argument has been exhausted, there are no inconsistencies left, only gaps. That is not an unduly optimistic assessment of the quality of legislating performance, it follows from the nature of the system.

## 12.4. The Ideal of Coherence as an Argument

If a system does not contain inconsistencies, this does not mean that it is maximally coherent. Coherence is a rather elusive concept, but let us suppose it means something like maximum mutual support of relevant considerations. Do we have room for any other appeal to coherence as a distinctive form of argument?

---

[10] One example is provided by the Dutch judicial decisions on euthanasia. Here a justificatory ground ("necessity") that can only be appealed to in conditions which the legislation could not foresee, is used to proclaim a new legislation. See Den Hartogh 1995.

[11] Brouwer 1991 discusses an interesting example: a traffic law (1974) making the owner of a vehicle responsible for violations of the law committed by the driver, a provision in obvious conflict with basic principles of criminal justice.

It is true that coherentist considerations often figure in our use of the other types of argument. For instance, by presuming the LA to be rational, we suppose him to pursue his aims not only in a consistent but also in a coherent way (until the opposite conclusion turns out to be inescapable). And in arguing for the relevance of a certain legal principle, in particular for some specification of it, it is important to show that the principle enables us to "make sense of" a whole domain of the law, or at least of a good deal of legal material – authoritative pronouncements, custom – within the domain. But even in this case, we do not recognize the principle on the ground that by doing so, we improve the coherence of the domain. Rather, we use the coherentist argument to show that this is a principle we had implicitly recognize all along, that it belongs to the latent extension of our conventions.[12]

It is even more obvious that the acceptance of valid arguments often contributes to the mutual support of relevant considerations. The appeal to precedent is a clear example, in particular if the *ratio decidendi* is spelled out. The appeal to analogy might also be adduced, if we were to accept analogy between considerations as a form of mutual support. But again, we appeal to these "sources of law" because they are relevant, not because in doing so we maximize mutual support. For we also take them into account as countervailing considerations, i.e. when they are a source of conflict between relevant considerations, rather than of mutual support. When, as a result of this, the law becomes unsettled, that is no reason at all to disregard that particular argument.

But if we have exhausted these arguments, I cannot see any room left for an independent appeal to coherence. If any of our types of argument, on its own or in combination, gives us an unambiguous answer to our legal problem, we are satisfied. Whether any of those considerations is relevant, is decided on its merits and on the question whether a reasonable person can be expected to replicate it. Accepting the conclusion, or any of the arguments, may result in a greater or lesser degree of mutal support for the totality of the considerations explicitly recognized to be relevant to any case; but this circumstance can hardly be a countervailing consideration. It would be rather paradoxical to use it that way. But if an argument cannot be used in a countervailing way, it cannot be used in a supplementing way either; it simply lacks the necessary independent weight.

And anyway, it is hard to see how mutual support of considerations can be established independently of the relations fixed by our other considerations. Suppose, for example, that a statute is very old, and pretty inefficient but not totally so; a significant part of the community complies with it, but another significant part deviates from it. How do we decide whether enforcing it would make the law as a whole more coherent, rather than the opposite, if not by using the arguments from history and from value?

What should we wish to make more coherent: the manifest extension of our system of conventions as a whole, or the full extension, including the latent part? I cannot see much independent attraction in the ideal of coherence if it is restricted to the manifest extension. It will always be the case that if a proposed legal judgment creates

---

[12] See ch. 10.1.

some incoherence, one of our seven arguments can be advanced against it: it will disregard a valid statute or precedent, deviate from custom etc. So the ideal can only have an independent status if it applies to the latent extension as well. But in that case it presupposes a foreknowledge of contingencies such as we can never achieve. This does not just mean that we fail to realize the ideal, it means that the ideal is misguided. For the system should be able to guide our decisions, given the actual state of our knowledge. Hence a short chain of justification, perhaps ending at a simple but clear precedent that has no visible further justification, may be more helpful than a long chain, the cogency of which depends on factual information we do not possess.

I conclude that there is no "argument from coherence" on a par with the other seven types of argument. Once we have used all other valid and relevant arguments, there is no argument from coherence left.

## 12.5. Principles, Coherence, and Decidability

The transition from the protolegal to the legal world was made in order to increase our powers to decide what it is we mutually expect from each other. I argued in section 2 that the quest for decidability is never ending; we will always meet new and unexpected gaps. But, surely, that is only true if we restrict our attention to authoritative enactments and the intentions behind them? If it is accepted that we can enter the second stage, that we can supplement the gaps left by authoritative intention by using the arguments from substantive values, from principles, from substantial conventions, from analogy and from inconsistency, then perhaps these new instruments will enable us to find the Holy Grail of final decidability. In principle at least, for people are of course fallible. But if we maintain that in each dispute there will always be at most one disputant in the right, perhaps we cannot be refuted.

A seemingly hard case can sometimes be solved – and solved easily – by an appeal to value or principle. But it is equally possible that a hard case is *created* by taking policy or principle into account. We have learnt to look at these dimensions of the legal system as resources for the reduction of indeterminacy of meaning,[13] but that is not their *raison d'être* at all. They are relevant as interpretative clues because of the kind of reality law is; whether their net effect is the reduction or the creation of decidability cannot be decided a priori.[14]

The same point can even be made about the pursuit of legal coherence. I have interpreted this ideal as the attempt to maximize the number of *justificanda* and to minimize the number of *justificantia*, and I have testified to some scepticism about it.

---

[13] E.g. MacCormick 1978, 152-153: the relevance of the appeal to principles follows from the requirement of coherence; Van Hoof 1987. Cf. ch. 10.1. Dworkin 1977, ch. 2 ("The Model of Rules I") argued from the binding character of principles as legal standards to the denial of strong discretion. But if principles *can* dictate a result, it does not follow that they always do, Raz (1972) 1984d, 74-76, 82.

[14] Brouwer 1990, 28-29; Wiarda, 1988, 111. Llewellyn 1950, referred to in Sunstein 1990, 809, boasted that in any specific case, for every interpretative principle proposed, he could find a principle of equal weight pointing in the opposite direction. Nieuwenhuis 1979, 4, suggests that principles create system, precisely by pointing in opposite directions ("a system of checks and balances").

My argument was that under human conditions, this enterprise does not necessarily reduce undecidability;[15] it may create it as well. So we should not decide to treat the law as a unified system *in order to* reduce indeterminacy. To a certain extent we cannot help taking a holistic attitude towards the law, because similarities and dissimilarities force themselves upon our attention as relevant clues. But a form of incoherence may create no problems at all,[16] because the relevant patterns of mutual expectations have become compartmentalized, applying to conditions which are isolated against each other, either in reality or in people's minds. We should remember here that the primary application of legal norms is made outside the courts, by individuals, organizations and even state agencies hardly interested in the law as a unified system. By explicitly forging a link, for example by trying to judge such conflicting patterns of mutual expectations against a single set of principles, a court might well succeed in *making* them relevant to each other's domains, and tap a new source of indeterminacy precisely by doing so.

The best-known argument against (identifiable) undecidability is, of course, Dworkin's.[17] He conjures up the image of an ideal judge, Hercules, who would be able to identify all valid and relevant arguments. Whenever it seems to us, mortals, that the weights in the balance are equally poised, all we have to do is realize that we did not come up to Herculean standards, and then we will concede that we did not really run out of relevant considerations to tip the balance.

Why do we ever run out of considerations that would restore it? Perhaps Hercules would find the countervailing arguments we overlooked. It is hard to decide what an ideal judge could do. That is the paradox of Dworkin's argument: he suggests that we cannot decide that a question is undecidable, because we lack the relevant powers to make that decision. How then can we decide that a question is decidable? Whence the asymmetry? Dworkin appeals to the practice of the legal community and its self-understanding. Courts have a legal duty to decide every issue brought before them, *and* to justify their decisions, and judges appear to comply with both duties without showing any awareness that they may be incompatible. Dworkin seems to believe that this places the burden of proof on the person who thinks they are, and he then argues that we can never be sure that we have run out of arguments.

This would perhaps be convincing if, as Dworkin also suggests, it would be necessary from the insider's point of view to believe that the right answer is there, only to be discovered by finding the right argument. This belief would then be a kind of "regulative idea" necessarily informing the court's exertions. But I fail to see why this should be so. If he did not act on this regulative idea, Dworkin says, a judge would come into the position in which she must say to the parties: it is not the case that one of

---

[15] This is taken for granted in most discussions of the role of coherence in adjudication, e.g. MacCormick 1978, ch. 7; Dworkin 1986, ch. 7; MacCormick & Summers 1991, 535: the ideal of coherence follows from the Rule of Law.

[16] This is even true of inconsistencies, if we disregard the metaconvention discussed in ch. 11.2.

[17] Dworkin 1977, chs. 2-4; 1978; 1984; 1986 ch. 5; 1991.

you is right and the other wrong, but nevertheless I am deciding in favour of $A$.[18] But this is only true if she thinks that a decision *has* to be made.

Moreover, it seems to me that Dworkin does not offer any consolation to the parties at all. Why is it reassuring, from a moral point of view, to know that there *is* a right answer, if ordinary human powers are insufficient to identify it? Justice seems to require that the parties themselves, or at least their lawyers, can determine the rights and wrongs of the case.[19] It is not the existence of the right answer but its identifiability that matters.

But in a conventionalist perspective it is impossible to distinguish existence and identifiability at all. Whatever a Hercules can do is irrelevant to deciding any question of law, for the question *is* what a person of ordinary capacities may expect the others to expect him to do. We cannot solve an indeterminacy of meaning by appealing to an ideal interpreter, if we have no reason to assume the speaker and the hearer to be ideal interpreters. Dworkin's fundamental mistake is not to recognize the vicarious nature of legal argument.[20] The really great lawyer is the person about whose conclusions the others always say: that is an insight I should and could have achieved myself.

Nevertheless, Dworkin's position has a kernel of truth. It is also wrong to identify *Rechtssicherheit* with compliance to the letter of statute or judicial decision, and then to assume a permanent conflict between considerations of legal certainty and of justice. If law is a system of conventions, then every consideration needed to identify a justified mutual belief is ipso facto a consideration of legal certainty. If it is necessary to extend or to narrow down the meaning of the terms of a legal provision, or even to pronounce it *contra legem* in order to avoid absurd or patently unjust results, this is not a sacrifice of legal certainty. What you may legitimately expect is never automatically identical with "the law in the books". For "books" are only used in an attempt to focus expectations, but the attempt may fail.

When an explicit legal norm or a traditional legal principle (e.g.: *caveat emptor*) comes into conflict with the requirements of trade and social conduct, or with changed views of social morality, undecidability cannot be avoided by a legalistic attitude. Even if the judiciary publicly disclaims legislative powers, and time and again reconfirms its traditional interpretation of the ruling norm, the mutual expectations of the citizens concerning each other's behaviour, and even concerning the decisions of the next judge, will fail to fall into line. Hence the law cannot be treated as settled, whatever the courts say. It is the mistaken loyalty to the letter which *creates* uncertainty in these cases, and it is the seemingly "free" decision that ends it, by "pushing out" an interpretation that has become a *Fremdkörper* within the system of conventions as a whole. When the decision in the case *Zutphense Juffrouw* confirmed the narrow legalistic interpretation of "tort" – nothing but breaches of explicit statutory regulations counted as such –, this only led people to wait for the next occasion to change it: which turned out to be the

---

[18] Dworkin 1977, 84.

[19] As Dworkin 1977, 86, partially concedes; cf. 162: "It is unfair for officials to act except on the basis of a general public theory that will constrain them to consistency, provide a public standard for testing or debating or predicting what they do..."

[20] Cf. Postema 1987a.

"epochal" *Lindenbaum/Cohen* case (the Dutch equivalent of *Donoghue/Stevenson*). [21] Since that time, actions not in accordance with the due care that is judged becoming in social conduct, constitute actionable private wrongs as well. If even on that occasion the traditional interpretation had been followed, the period of legal uncertainty would simply have been prolonged.[22]

Suppose we have a seemingly easy case: a consumer is harmed, the producer cannot be proved to have omitted exercising reasonable care, the supplier delivered goods that were clearly not of marketable quality.[23] Statute assigns strict civil liability to the supplier. No relevant customs or precedents can be appealed to for making an exception. So the supplier has to pay up, even if no one could possibly expect her to check thoroughly all the goods she sells. As a result she might face bankruptcy. As Lewis J. conceded, this is a harsh judgment on a perfectly innocent person; and if it is, the case is certainly not an easy one. The problem is not, as legal positivists allege,[24] whether or not the judge is (morally) justified not to act on unambiguously clear legal requirements. When the law allocates burdens that are unfair under any conception of fairness, the relevant requirement as such cannot be unambiguously clear. This conclusion does not follow from a "free" conception of the law, which gives the judge the discretion to follow his own moral judgment, disregarding considerations of legal certainty. It follows from a correct understanding of the idea of legal certainty itself.

It is the same legalistic fallacy in reverse to believe that every time the "law in the books" uses vague terms (*Generalklausel*), all judicial decisions appealing to those laws are "autonomous" ones, exercises of judicial discretion.[25] A reference to what counts as seemly in social conduct can, on occasion, be quite determinate (as it was in *Lindenbaum/Cohen*; afterwards a similar case would not have been a hard case at all).[26] Vague terms require the judge to exercise vicarious reasoning, but such reasoning can have a uniquely predictable outcome. The mistake is to believe that only legislation and

---

[21] Resp. H.R. 10/6/1910, W. 9038; H.R. 31/1/1919, NJ 1919, 161. "I do not think so ill of our jurisprudence as to suppose that its principles are so remote from the ordinary needs of civilized society and the ordinary claims it makes upon its members, as to deny a legal remedy where there is so obviously a social wrong." Lord Atkin's speech, quoted by MacCormick 1978, 109.

[22] Another classic example is the "complete bar rule", in force in England and the USA since *Butterfield vs Forrester* 1809: if you have been negligent to even the smallest degree, you have no remedy against another person's total negligence. This "harshest doctrine known to the common law" was tested time and again, until one state court after the other repealed it. An analogous situation at the present time: Dutch employers have the legal right to delegate, to whomever they please, their authority to assign tasks to employees. But employees who expect their employers to consult them, strongly resent their omitting to do so, often to the extent of again bringing the case to court, despite unambiguous past rulings. They will surely continue to do so until a legal remedy is provided.

[23] *Daniels vs. White* (1938), 4 All E.R. 258, presented by MacCormick 1978, ch. 2, as a paradigm case proving that sometimes it can be shown conclusively, by means of a purely deductive argument, that a given decision is legally justified. It is rather a paradigm case of a defeasible argument! For a similar comment Atria 1999, 558.

[24] Lyons 1985.

[25] E.g. Wiarda 1988, 28.

[26] "Sometimes extremely general terms give rise to largely uncontested meanings, as in the Scottish and English occupier's statutory duty to take 'reasonable care' for persons on the premises occupied..." Bankowski & MacCormick 1991, 360.

precedent create the fixed points in law. Vague terms have their own "core of certainty", which they owe to informal patterns of mutual belief existing in society.

## 12.6. Compromising Decisions

By conceding and even stressing the existence of indeterminacies of meaning, resulting from either underdetermination or overdetermination, as an unescapable fact of life, I do not want to embrace the positivist conception of strong judicial discretion. It is a remarkable fact that these two positions – "always a right answer" and "strong judicial discretion" – are almost always taken to exhaust the possibilities. But if there is no satisfactory way of filling a gap, why should the judge not recognize this?

It is true that reasonable conventions for distributing the burden of proof will often save him from this predicament. If the evidence is not sufficient to hold a person guilty, she ought to be held not guilty; if there is no sufficient reason to believe the house was sold, it is not sold. But there is a relevant difference between these two judgments: the first concerns a fact of nature, the second a fact of law. Either Jones killed Smith or he did not; *tertium non datur*. But legal facts are belief-dependent, and beliefs have all the troubling aspects of intensionality. There might be sufficient reason for *A* to believe that the house was sold, and for *B* to believe that it was not sold, even if both recognized that in order to draw this conclusion they had to mirror each other's reasoning.[27] In that case it is not true that either the house was sold, or it was not sold. So why should the judge say it is?[28]

It seems to be one of the fixed points of legal conviction (in modern Western legal communities)[29] that judges should "make up their minds", either on sufficient or on insufficient legal grounds.[30] Of course, judges have a whole arsenal of legal means to narrow the gap between the decision that *A* is right, and the "mediating" recognition that neither *A* nor *B* has any better right than the other. Let me mention a few. The contract is not binding, but *A* has obligations to *B*, because he excited "precontractual

---

[27] Cf. in particular contracts made under a misunderstanding that cannot be blamed on either of the parties. *Locus classicus*: the *Peerless* case (1864; 2 H & C, 906, cf. Nieuwenhuis 1979, 86): a parcel of cotton was sold "to arrive ex Peerless from Bombay", but it turned out that at about the same time two ships named Peerless sailed from Bombay. It is usually concluded that in such cases no contract has been made. But this verdict will sometimes mean a disproportional loss to one of the parties who had equally good reasons for his interpretation as the other (e.g. *Bunde/Erckens*, NJ 1977, 241, cf. ch. 11, note 12). This unjust result might then itself tempt the judge to conclude that a contract *has* been made.

[28] "De regter die weigert recht te spreken, onder voorwendsel (*sic*) van het stilzwijgen, de duisterheid of de onvolledigheid der wet, kan uit hoofde van *regtsweigering* vervolgd worden." (The judge who refuses to decide, pretending that the law is silent, obscure or incomplete, can be prosecuted for *deni de justice*.) *Wet Algemeene Bepalingen* (1829), art. 13, taken from de Code Civil. This is not the only obsolete article in this law.

[29] Solomon's famous decision, while not itself a compromising one, clearly presupposes a legal context in which it is normal practice to allocate equal parts of a good to claimants presenting an equally good case for being entitled to the whole.

[30] Scholten, 1974, 133-134; cf. comment Leyten 1989: "Each of the opposing positions rests on equally good reasons, I have no means of deciding who is right; so I solve the problem by arbitrarily deciding in favour of one of you." Compromising verdicts have already been defended by Meijers 1916.

expectations"; it was binding, but $B$ is not assigned full (or even any) compensation.[31] The good has been stolen from $A$, and bought in good faith by $B$: $A$ is the owner, but he owes $B$ the purchase price. The good has been borrowed from $A$, and bought in good faith by $B$: $B$ is the owner, and the intermediary (if he is not insolvent) owes compensation to $A$. We always recognize jurisprudential illusions by the subtle ways judges find of circumventing them. Such manoeuvres make it possible to continue to uphold the *tertium non datur* doctrine. But why is it so important to do so, even when this amounts to denying the facts? Of course the judge has to make a ruling for the future. (And, to forestall another objection, by making a ruling she will also create a precedent preventing the same problem of undecidability to rise again.) But why should she not recognize that it existed so far, if it really did?[32]

The recognition of existing undecidable issues does not detract from the value of *Rechtssicherheit*; on the contrary, it would contribute to it. It is obvious that strong discretion is in conflict with this value, but the same is true about any "right answer" that cannot be arrived at by interdependent reasoning.

At one point in his convoluted discussions of the issue of discretion, Dworkin objects that this position is not really an alternative to the right answer thesis, but rather a variant of it.[33] It may be the case, indeed, that there is no pre-existing right of either party to win the case, but rather a tie in the contest between their claims. In that case *this* is the right answer.

I accept the objection. But Dworkin, in the end, does not. For he goes on to suggest that in a complex legal system with very diverse types of relevant considerations, we never *have* to conclude that there is a "tie". Again I agree: the notion of a "tie" suggests a neat picture of balancing with commensurable weights, which does no justice to the variety of types of legal argument. But in my view the fact of incommensurability does not undermine, but rather reinforces, the thesis that sometimes the right answer is that we have no decisive grounds to decide one way or the other, and therefore should proceed to make an equal division of the contested good or right.[34]

Dworkin, however, draws the opposite conclusion. He argues as follows. Either the litigant, or the defendant, has the antecedent right to win, or none of them has.[35] *Quartum non datur*. In an advanced system, "thick with constitutional rules and

---

[31] Cf. Atiyah 1981, 6, 140.

[32] Part of the explanation is perhaps that lawsuits in our culture have an *agonistic* character: they are a ritualized way of fighting, following the tradition of medieval legal combat. (Cf. Jhering 1874, 16). And so we would be disappointed if no winner was identified. In other legal systems (cf. note 5 above) the value of reconciliation is given a central place; a "winner takes all" attitude is strongly disapproved of as harmful to social cohesion. A prayer of the Anafo (Togo): "God give us a man with a needle to fasten the relation, and guard us against the man with the knife who wants to cut it," Van Rouveroy van Nieuwaall 1981, 305. Contrast Jhering: "Der Kampf um's Recht ist eine Pflicht des Berechtigten gegen sich selbst," irrespective of the costs involved: Michael Kohlhaas is a "Märtyrer seines Rechtsgefühls", ibid. 63. Cf. the difference between the Lozi and the Tswana as discussed by Comaroff and Roberts 1981.

[33] Dworkin 1977, 70; 1978, 285.

[34] Mackie 1984, 165; Peczenik 1989, 191.

[35] In which case the judge would be permitted, he says, to award the palm to either of the parties. So strong is the hold of the principle that the judge should "make up his mind"!

practices, and dense with precedents and statutes, the antecedent probability of a tie is very much lower; indeed it might well be so low as to justify a further ground rule of the enterprise which instructs judges to eliminate ties from the range of answers they might give."[36] It is true that if the force of the claims of the parties sometimes cannot be "weighed" in any straightforward sense, the probability of a tie is lower. But so is the probability of one party having the stronger claim! Incommensurability of claims really *is* a "fourth" possibility.

The argument is not only a non sequitur, it amounts to a surrender of the position Dworkin set out to defend.[37] Suppose a tie exists; Dworkin does not rule out the possibility, only the possibility of being very sure about it. In that case the rule that forbids recognizing the tie, *creates* room for strong discretion. For it requires to decide in favour of one of the parties, even if he really has no better claim than the other. So Dworkin is forced to recognize that it *is* possible for a judge to exercise strong discretion; his new thesis is just that he should *act on the assumption* that he does not. For if he acts on this counterfactual assumption, his chances of "hitting" at the right answer improve.[38] The right answer thesis is no longer a thesis about legal truth, but about the right way to counteract the consequences of judicial fallibility.

That this is not the original thesis should be clear. For the original objections to strong discretion equally apply to the new thesis. Suppose a judge, after due consideration, tentatively but rightly believes that a tie exists, but because of the new "ground rule of the enterprise" decides in favour of one of the parties. By doing so he "makes new law and applies it retroactively in the case before him". And Hercules, at least, would know he did.

I conclude that we cannot be sure a priori that legal reasoning will allow us to identify the stronger case. The facts suggesting incommensurability of relevant considerations give us reason to believe that this is not just a logical possibility, but a very real one indeed. Therefore the right answer thesis can only be saved by recognizing this possibility: the right answer may be that there is no right answer.

---

[36] Dworkin 1978, 286-287; the argument can be found already in Sartorius 1971, 158-159 (and many other places, see references in Hoffmaster 1982, 45, note 39). I agree, of course, that such a convention or metaconvention exists in many legal systems, but I contest that it is a reasonable one.

[37] Cf. Hoffmaster 1982, 48-52.

[38] Cf. ch. 7.5.-6. on the indirect pursuit of rationality; ch. 10.4. on judicial incapacities.

# REFERENCES

Aulis Aarnio. *The Rational as Reasonable: A Treatise on Legal Justification.* Dordrecht: Reidel 1986.

Pieter Abas. *Rebus Sic Stantibus: Een Onderzoek naar de Toepassing van de Clausule Rebus sic Stantibus in de Rechtspraak van Enige Europese Landen.* Deventer: Kluwer 1989.

Philip Abbott. *The Shotgun behind the Door. Liberalism and the Problem of Political Obligation.* Athens: Univ. of Georgia Press 1976.

George Ainslie. *Picoeconomics.* Cambridge: Cambridge Univ. Press 1992.

Larry Alexander."Law and Exclusionary Reasons". *Philosophical Topics* 18 (1990): 5.

Robert Alexy. *Theorie der Grundrechte.* Baden-Baden: Nomos Verlagsgesellschaft 1985.

Robert Alexy. "On Necessary Relations between Law and Morality". *Ratio Juris* 2 (1989a): 167-183.

Robert Alexy. *A Theory of Legal Argumentation: The Theory of Rational Discourse as Theory of Legal Justification.* Oxford: Clarendon 1989b. (First German ed. 1976)

Robert Alexy & Ralf Dreier. "Statutory Interpretation in the Federal Republic of Germany". In: MacCormick & Summers eds. 1991, 73-121.

Robert Alexy & Ralf Dreier. "Precedent in the Federal Republic of Germany". In: MacCormick & Summers eds. 1996, 17-63.

Judith Andre. "Blocked Exchanges: A Taxonomy". *Ethics* 103 (1992): 29-47.

G.E.M. Anscombe. *Intention.* Oxford: Blackwell 1957.

G.E.M. Anscombe. "Brute Facts". *Analysis* 18 (1957b): 69. Repr. in: Anscombe 1981, 22-25.

G.E.M. Anscombe. "Authority in Morals". (1962) In: Anscombe 1981, 43-50. Also repr. in Flathman 1973, 157-163.

G.E.M. Anscombe. "On the Source of the Authority of the State". (1978) In: Anscombe 1981, 130-155.

G.E.M. Anscombe. *Ethics, Religion and Politics: Collected Philosophical Papers, Vol. III.* Oxford: Blackwell 1981.

Hannah Arendt. *On Violence.* New York: Harcourt etc. 1969.

Hannah Arendt. "What is Authority?" (1958): in: Hannah Arendt. *Between Past and Future.* Harmondsworth: Penguin Books 1977.

Richard J. Arneson. "The Principle of Fairness and Free-Rider Problems". *Ethics* 92 (1982): 616-633.

P.S. Atiyah. *Promises, Morals. and Law.* Oxford: Oxford Univ. Press 1981.

Fernando Atria. "Legal Reasoning and Legal Theory Revisited". *Law and Philosophy* 18 (1999): 537-577.

Robert Aumann. "Correlated Equilibrium as an Expression of Bayesian Rationality". *Econometrica* 1 (1987): 1-18.

Robert Axelrod. "An Evolutionary Approach to Norms". *American Political Science Review* 80 (1986): 1093-1111.

Michael Bacharach. "A Theory of Rational Decision in Games". *Erkenntnis* 27 (1989): 17-35.

Annette C. Baier. "Trust and Antitrust". *Ethics* 96 (1986): 231-260. Repr. in: *Moral Prejudices: Essays in Ethics.* Cambridge Mass.: Harvard Univ. Press 1994, 95-129.

Annette C. Baier. *The Commons of the Mind.* Chicago/la Salle: Open Court 1996.

Douglas G. Baird, Robert H. Gertner, Randal C. Picker. *Game Theory and the Law*. Cambridge Mass.: Harvard Univ. Press 1994.

Judith Baker. "Trust and Rationality". *Pacific Philosophical Quarterly* 68 (1987): 1.

Zenon Bankowski & D. Neil MacCormick. "Statutory Interpretation in the United Kingdom". In: MacCormick & Summers eds. 1991, 359-405.

Zenon Bankowki, D. Neil MacCormick & Alfonzo Ruiz Miguel. "Rationales for Precedent". In: MacCormick & Summers eds. 1996, 481-501.

Stanley Bates. "Authority and Autonomy". *Journal of Philosophy* 69 (1972): 175-176.

Leora Batnitzky. "A Seamless Web? John Finnis and Joseph Raz on Practical Reason and the Obligation to Obey". *Oxford Journal of Legal Studies* 15 (1995): 153-175.

Michael D. Bayles. *Hart's Legal Philosophy: An Examination.* Dordrecht: Kluwer 1992.

T.L. Beauchamp. "The Role of Principles in Practical Ethics" In: L.W. Sumner & Joseph Boyle eds. *Philosophical Perspectives on Bioethics*. Toronto: Univ. of Toronto Press 1996, 79-95.

Lawrence C. Becker. *Reciprocity* . London: Routledge & Kegan Paul 1986.

Rodger Beehler. "The Concept of Law and the Obligation to Obey". *American Journal of Jurisprudence* 23 (1978): 120-142.

Rodger Beehler. "Societies, Populations and Law". *University of Toronto Law Journal* 36 (1986): 1-18.

Nora K. Bell. "Nozick and the Principle of Fairness". *Social Theory and Practice* 5 (1978): 65-73.

John Bell. "The Acceptability of Legal Arguments". In: Neil MacCormick & Peter Birks eds. *The Legal Mind*. Oxford: Oxford Univ. Press 1986, 45-66.

Avner Ben-Ner & Louis Putterman eds. *Econmics, Values, and Organization.* Cambridge: Cambridge Univ. Press 1998.

Jonathan Bennett. *Rationality: An Essay towards an Analysis*. London: Routledge & Kegan Paul 1964.

Harry Beran.*The Consent Theory of Political Obligation.* London: Croom Helm 1987.

Cristina Bicchieri. *Rationality and Coordination*. Cambridge: Cambridge Univ. Press 1993.

Ken Binmore. *Game Theory and the Social Contract, Vol. I: Playing Fair*. Cambridge Mass: MIT Press 1994.

Brian Bix ed. *Analyzing Law: New Essays in Legal Theory*. Oxford, Clarendon 1998.

Marc Bloch. *Feudal Society*. London: Routledge 1962. (First ed.: *La Société Féodale*. Paris: Michel, 1939-1940, 2 volumes.)

William S. Boardman. "Coordination and the Moral Obligation to Obey the Law". *Ethics* 97 (1987): 546-557.

Richard B. Brandt. "Toward a Credible Form of Utilitarianism". In: Hector-Neri Castañeda & George Nakhnikian eds. *Morality and the Language of Conduct*. Detroit 1963, 107-143.

Richard B. Brandt. "Utility and the Obligation to Obey the Law". In: Hook ed. 1964, 43-49.

Michael Bratman. *Intentions, Plans, and Practical Reason*. Cambridge Mass.: Harvard Univ. Press 1987.

David Braybrooke. "The Insoluble Problem of the Social Contract". *Dialogue* 15 (1976): 3-37.

David O. Brink. "Legal Positivism and Natural Law Reconsidered". *The Monist* 68 (1985): 364-387.

David O. Brink. "Legal Theory, Legal Interpretation, and Judicial Review." *Philosophy and Public Affairs* 17 (1988): 105-148.

C.D. Broad. "On the Function of False Hypotheses in Ethics" (1916): in: David R. Cheney ed. *Broad's Critical Essays in Moral Philosophy*. London: Allen & Unwin 1971.

John Broome. *Weighing Goods*. Oxford: Blackwell 1991.

P.W. Brouwer. *Samenhang in het recht*. Groningen: Wolters-Noordhoff 1990.

P.W. Brouwer. "Over Coherentie in Recht". *Nederlands Tijdschrift voor Rechtsfilosofie en Rechtstheorie* 21 (1991): 178-192.

Alan Buchanan. "Recognitional Legitimacy and the State System". *Philosophy and Public Affairs* 28 (1999): 46-78.

James Buchanan. *The Limits of Liberty*. Chicago: Univ. of Chicago Press 1975.

James M. Buchanan & Gordon Tullock. *The Calculus of Consent*. Ann Arbor: Univ. of Michigan Press 1962.

W. van der Burg. *Een Andere Visie op Burgerlijke Ongehoorzaamheid*. Dordrecht: Kluwer 1986.

W. van der Burg. "The Myth of Civil Disobedience". *Praxis International* 9 (1989): 287-304.

Bruce Chapman. "Law Games: Defeasible Rules and Revisable Rationality". *Law and Philosophy* 17 (1998): 443-481.

John Charvet. "Political Obligation: Individualism and Communitarianism". In: Paul Harris ed. *On Political Obligation*. London: Routledge and Kegan Paul 1990, 65-88.

H.H. Clark & T.B. Carlson. "Hearers and Speech Acts". *Language* 58 (1982): 382.

H.H. Clark & D. Wilkes-Gibbs. "Referring as a Colloborative Process". *Cognition* 22 (1986): 1-39.

D.S. Clarke Jr. "Exclusionary Reasons". *Mind* 86 (1977): 252-255.

P.B. Cliteur & M.A. Loth. "Een Wereld van Verschil?". In: P.B. Cliteur & M.A. Loth eds. *Rechtsfilosofen van de Twintigste Eeuw*. Arnhem: Gouda Quint 1992, 251-260.

Gerald A. Cohen. *Self-ownership, Freedom and Equality*. Cambridge: Cambridge Univ. Press 1995. Marshall Cohen ed. *Ronal Dworkin and Contemporary Jurisprudence*. London: Duckworth 1984.

Jules L. Coleman. "Negative and Positive Positivism". *Journal of Legal Studies* 11 (1982): 139-164. Repr. in: Cohen 1984, 28-48.

Jules L. Coleman. "On the Relationship between Law and Morality". *Ratio Juris* 2 (1989): 66-78.

Jules L. Coleman. *Risks and Wrongs*. New York: Cambridge Univ. Press 1992.

Jules L. Coleman. "Incorporationism, Conventionality and the Practical Difference Thesis". *Legal Theory* 4 (1998): 381-425.

Jules L. Coleman. "Second Thoughts and Other First Impressions". In: Bix ed. 1998, 257-322.

J.L. Comaroff & S. Roberts. *Rules and Processes*. Chicago: Univ. of Chicago Press 1981.

David Copp. "The Idea of a Legitimate State". *Philosophy and Public Affairs* 28 (1999), 3-45.

S.C. Coval & J.C. Smith. "Rights, Goals, and Hard Cases". *Law and Philosophy* 1 (1982): 451-480.

Robert Cover. *Justice Accused: Antislavery and the Judicial Process*. New Haven: Yale Univ. Press 1975.

Margaret Urban Coyne. "Beyond Rules: Mapping the Normative". *American Philosophical Quarterly* 18 (1981): 331-337.

Ann E. Cudd. "Conventional Foundationalism and the Origins of Norms". *Southern Journal of Philosophy* 28 (1990): 485-503.

Ann E. Cudd. "Game Theory and the History of Ideas about Rationality: An Introductory Survey". *Economics and Philosophy* 9 (1993): 101-134.

J. Dancy. *Moral Reasons*. Oxford: Blackwell 1993.

Donald Davidson. Essays on Actions and Events. Oxford: Clarendon 1980

Lawrence H. Davis. "Prisoners, Paradox, and Rationality". *American Philosophical Quarterly* 14 (1977): 319-327. Repr. in: Richmond Campbell & Lanning Sowden eds. *Paradoxes of Rationality and Cooperation*. Vancouver: Univ. of British Columbia Press 1985, 45-59.

Robyn M. Dawes, Alphons J.C. Van de Kragt, John M. Orbell. "Not Me or Thee but We: The Importance of Group Identity in Eliciting Cooperation in Dilemma Situations: Experimental Manipulations". *Acta Psychologica* 68 (1988): 83-97.

Richard T. DeGeorge. "The Nature and Function of Epistemic Authority". In: R. Baine Harris ed. *Authority: A Philosophical Analysis*. Univ. of Alabama Press 1976, 76-93.

Daniel C. Dennett. *Brainstorms*. Hassocks Suss: Harvester Press 1978.

M.J. Detmold. *The Unity of Law and Morality: a Refutation of Legal Positivism*. London: Routledge & Kegan Paul 1984

Hans van den Doel. *Democracy and Welfare Economics*. Cambridge: Cambridge Univ. Press 1979.

R.S. Downie. *Roles and Values. an Introduction to Social Ethics*. London: Methuen 1971.

R.A. Duff. "Legal Obligation and the Moral Nature of Law". *Juridical Review* 25 (1980): 61-87.

O.D. Duintjer. *Rondom Regels*. Meppel: Boom 1977.

J.M. van Dunné. *Verbintenissenrecht in Ontwikkeling: Op de Grenzen van Geldend en Wordend Recht*. Deventer: Kluwer 1985. Rev. ed. of: *Normatieve Uitleg van Rechtshandelingen* (1971).

Gerald Dworkin. "Review of *In Defense of Anarchism*". *Journal of Philosophy* 68 (1971): 561-567.

Ronald Dworkin. *Taking Rights Seriously*. London: Duckworth 1977.

Ronald Dworkin. "Appendix: A Reply to Critics". In: *Taking Rights Seriously*. (Second ed.) Cambridge: Harvard Univ. Press 1978, 291-368.

Ronald Dworkin. "A Reply". In: Cohen ed. 1984, 247-300.

Ronald Dworkin. *Law's Empire*. London: Fontana 1986.

Ronald Dworkin. "Liberal Community". *California Law Review* 77 (1989): 479. Repr. in: Ronald Dworkin. Sovereign Virtue: The Theory and Practice of Equality. Cambridge Mass.: Harvard Univ. Press 2000, ch. 5.

Ronald Dworkin. "Pragmatism, Right Answers, and True Banality". In: Michael Brint & William Weaver eds. *Pragmatism in Law and Society*. Boulder: Westview Press 1991, 359-388.

David Dyzenhaus. *Hard Cases in Wicked Legal Systems: South African Law in the Perspective of Legal Philosophy*. Oxford: Clarendon 1991.

David Dyzenhaus. "The Legitimacy of Law: A Response to Critics". *Ratio Juris* 7 (1994): 80-94.

David Dyzenhaus. "Hermann Heller and the Legitimacy of Legality". *Oxford Journal of Legal Studies* 16 (1996): 641-666.

D. Easton. "The Perception of Authority and Political Change". In: Friedrich ed. 1958.

William A. Edmundson. "Rethinking Exclusionary Reasons: A Second Edition of Joseph Raz's *Practical Reason and Norms*". *Law and Philosophy* 12 (1993): 329-343.

William A. Edmundson. "Legitimate Authority without Political Obligation". *Law and Philosophy* 17 (1998): 43-60.

Robert C. Ellickson. *Order without Law: How Neighbors Settle Disputes*. Cambridge Mass.: Harvard Univ. Press 1991.

D. Ellsberg. *The Theory and Practice of Blackmail: Formal Theories of Negotiation*. Urbana: Univ. of Illinois Press 1975.

Jon Elster. *Logic and Society*. Chichester: Wiley and Sons 1978.

Jon Elster. *Ulysses and the Sirens*. Cambridge: Cambridge Univ. Press 1979.

Jon Elster. *The Cement of Society*. Cambridge: Cambridge Univ. Press 1989.

Jon Elster. *Nuts and Bolts for the Social Sciences*. Cambridge: Cambridge Univ. Press 1989b.

Jon Elster. "Norms of Revenge". *Ethics* 100 (1990a): 862-885.

Ernst Fehr & Simon Gächter. "How Effective are Trust- and Reciprocity-Based Incentives?" In: Ben-Ner & Putterman eds. 1998, 337-363.

Joel Feinberg. "Civil Disobedience in the Modern World". *Humanities in Society* 2 (1979): 37-59. Repr. in: Joel Feinberg & Hyman Gross eds., *Philosophy of Law*. (5th ed.) Belmont Cal.: Wadsworth 1995, 121-133.

Joel Feinberg. *The Moral Limits of the Criminal Law Vol. 3: Harm to Self*. New York: Oxford Univ. Press 1986.

Louis E. Feldman. "Originalism through Raz-colored Glasses". *Univ. of Pennsylvania Law Review* 140 (1992): 1389-1428.

Chaim Fershtman & Yoram Weiss. "Why Do We Care What Others Think About Us?". In: Ben-Ner & Putterman eds., 133-150.

John Finnis. *Natural Law and Natural Rights*. Oxford: Clarendon 1980.

John Finnis. "The Authority of Law in the Predicament of Contemporary Social Theory". *Notre Dame Journal of Law. Ethics and Public Policy* 1 (1984): 115-137.

John Finnis. "Positivism and the Foundations of Legal Authority: Comment". In: Gavison ed. 1987, 62-75.

John Finnis. "Law as Coordination." *Ratio Juris* 2 (1989): 97-104.

Richard E. Flathman ed. *Concepts in Social & Political Theory*. London: Collier/Macmillan 1973.

Richard E. Flathman. *The Practice of Political Authority*. Chicago: Univ. of Chicago Press 1980.

Richard Foley. "Illegal Behavior". *Law and Philosophy* 1 (1982): 131-158.

Philippa Foot. "Virtues and Vices". In: Philippa Foot. *Virtues and Vices and Other Essays in Moral Philosophy*. Oxford: Blackwell 1978, 1-18.

Robert Frank. *Passions within Reason: the Strategic Role of the Emotions*. New York: Norton & Comp. 1988.

William K. Frankena. *Ethics*. Englewood Cliffs N.J.: Prentice Hall 1963.

H.G. Frankfurt. "The Anarchism of R.P. Wolff". *Political Theory* 1 (1973): 405-414.

Charles Fried. Contract as Promise: A Theory of Contractual Obligation. Cambridge Mass.: Harvard Univ. Press 1981

Richard B. Friedman. "On the Concept of Authority in Political Philosophy". In: Flathman ed. 1973, 121-146.

Carl J. Friedrich ed. *Authority*. NOMOS, Vol. 1. Bobbs-Merrill Co. 1958.

Carl J. Friedrich. *Man and his Government. An Empirical Theory of Politics*. New York: McGraw-Hill 1963.

Carl J. Friedrich. "Authority. Reason. and Discretion". In: Friedrich ed. 1958. Repr. in: Flathman ed. 1973, 167-181.

Lon L. Fuller. *The Law in Quest of Itself: Lectures*. Chicago: The Foundations Press 1940. Repr. New York: AMS Press 1978.

Lon L. Fuller. *The Morality of Law*. New Haven and London: Yale Univ. Press 1964. Rev. ed. 1969.

Lon L. Fuller. *The Principles of Social Order: Selected Essays*. (Ed. Kenneth J. Winston) Durham NC: Duke Univ. Press 1981.

Chaim Gans. "The Normativity of Law and its Co-ordinative Function". *Israel Law Review* 16 (1981): 333-349.

Chaim Gans. "Mandatory Rules and Exclusionary Reasons". *Philosophia* 15 (1985): 373-394.

Chaim Gans. *Philosophical Anarchism and Political Disobedience*. New York: Cambridge Univ. Press 1992.

S. Garrod & A. Anderson. "Saying What You Mean in Dialogue: A Study in Conceptual and Semantic Coordination". *Cognition* 27 (1987): 181-228.

David Gauthier. "Deterrence, Maximization, and Rationality". *Ethics* 94 (1984): 474-495.

David Gauthier. *Morals by Agreement*. Oxford: Clarendon 1986.

David Gauthier. "Assure and Threaten". *Ethics* 104 (1994): 690-721

Ruth Gavison ed. *Issues in Contemporary Legal Philosophy: The Influence of H.L.A. Hart*. Oxford: Clarendon 1987.

Alan Gewirth. "Political Justice". In: R.B. Brandt ed. *Social Justice*. Englewood Cliffs N.J.: Prentice Hall 1962, 119-169.

Allen F. Gibbard. "Rule-Utilitarianism: A Merely Illusory Alternative?" *Australasian Journal of Philosophy* 43 91965), 211.

Alan Gibbard. "Human Evolution and the Sense of Justice". *Midwest Studies in Philosophy* 7 (1982): 31-46.

Alan Gibbard. *Wise Choices, Apt Feelings: A Theory of Normative Judgment.* Cambridge Mass: Harvard Univ. Press 1990.

Otto von Gierke. *Johannes Althusius und die Entwicklung der Naturrechtlichen Staatstheorien.* (Dritte Auflage) Breslau: Marcus 1913. (Erste Auflage 1880)

Margaret Gilbert. *On Social Facts.* London: Routledge & Kegan Paul 1989. Repr. Princeton: Princeton Univ. Press 1992.

Margaret Gilbert. "Agreements, Coercion, and Obligation". *Ethics* 103 (1993): 679-706. Repr. in: Margaret Gilbert. *Living Together: Rationality, Sociality, and Obligation.* Lanham MD: Rowman & Littlefield 1996.

Margaret Gilbert. "Obligation and Joint Commitment". *Utilitas* 11 (1999): 143-163. Repr. in Gilbert 2000.

Margaret Gilbert. "Social Rules: Some Problems for Hart's Account and an Alternative Proposal". *Law and Philosophy* 18 (1999): 141-171. Repr. in Gilbert 2000.

Margaret Gilbert. "Reconsidering the 'Actual Contract' Theory of Political Obligation". *Ethics* 109 (1999): 236-260. Repr. in Gilbert 2000.

Margaret Gilbert. *Sociality and Responsibility: New Essays in Plural Subject Theory.* Lanham MD: Rowman & Littlefield 2000.

William Godwin. *An Enquiry concerning Political Justice.* (1793) Harmondsworth: Penguin Books 1976.

Martin P. Golding. *Philosophy of Law.* Englewood Cliffs N.J.: Prentice Hall 1975

Laurence Goldstein ed. *Precedent in Law.* Oxford: Clarendon 1987.

Jeffrey D. Goldsworthy. "The Self-Destruction of Legal Positivism". *Oxford Journal of Legal Studies* 10 (1990): 449-486.

Trudy Govier. "Distrust as a Practical Problem". *Journal of Social Philosophy* 23 (1992): 52-63.

Alvin W. Gouldner. "The Norm of Reciprocity: A Preliminary Statement". (1960) In: Alvin W. Goulner. *For Sociology.* London: Allen Lane 1973.

Keith Graham. "Democracy and the Autonomous Agent". In: Keith Graham ed. *Contemporary Political Philosoph: Radical Studies.* Cambridge: Cambridge Univ. Press 1982.

Leslie Green. *The Authority of the State.* Oxford: Clarendon 1988.

Leslie Green. "Law, Legitimacy and Consent". *Southern California Law Review* 62 (1989a): 795.

Leslie Green. "Associative Obligations and the State". In: Allan C. Hutchinson & Leslie J.M. Green. *Law and the Community: the End of Individualism?* Toronto: Carswell 1989b, 93-118.

Leslie Green. "The Concept of Law Revisited". *Michigan Law Review* 94 (1996): 1687-1717.

Leslie Green. "Positivism and Conventionalism". *Canadian Journal of Law and Jurisprudence* 12 (1996): 35-52.

Leslie Green. "Who Believes in Political Obligation?" In: Sanders & Narveson eds. 1996, 1-18.

Kent Greenawalt. "The Natural Duty to Obey the Law". *Michigan Law Review* 84 (1985): 1-62.

Kent Greenawalt. "The Obligation to Obey the Law: Comment". In: Gavison ed. 1987a, 156-179.

Kent Greenawalt. *Conflicts of Law and Morality.* Oxford: Clarendon 1987b.

James Griffin. *Well-being: Its Meaning, Measurement and Moral Importance.* Oxford: Clarendon 1986.

John Griffiths. "Legal Reasoning from the External and the Internal Perspectives" . *New York Univ. Law Review* 11 (1978): 1124-1149.

John Griffiths, Alex Bood, Heleen Weyers. *Euthanasia and the Law in the Netherlands*. Amsterdam: Amsterdam Univ. Press 1998.

Germain Grisez, Joseph Boyle, John Finnis. "Practical Principles, Moral Truth, and Ultimate Ends". *American Journal of Jurisprudence* 32 (1987): 99-151.

Raymond D. Gumb. *Rule-Governed Linguistic Behaviour*. The Hague: Mouton 1972.

P.M.S. Hacker. "Hart's Philosophy of Law". In: Hacker & Raz eds. 1977, 1-25.

P.M.S. Hacker & J. Raz eds. *Law, Morality and Society: Essays in Honour of H.L.A. Hart*. Oxford: Clarendon 1977.

J.C. Hage. *Reasoning with Rules*. Dordrecht: Kluwer 1997.

Jean Hampton. *Hobbes and the Social Contract Tradition*. Cambridge: Cambridge Univ. Press 1986.

Jean Hampton. "Free-Rider Problems in the Production of Collective Goods". *Economics and Philosophy* 3 (1987): 245-273.

R.H. Happé. *Drie Beginselen van Fiscale Rechtsbescherming*. Devnter: Kluwer 1996.

Michael O. Hardimon. "Role Obligations". *Journal of Philosophy* 91 (1994): 333-363.

Garrett Hardin. "The Tragedy of the Commons". *Science* 161 (1968): 1243-1248.

Russell Hardin. "Collective Action as an Agreeable n-Prisoner's Dilemma". *Behavioral Science* 16 (1971): 472-481. Repr. In: Brian Barry & Russell Hardin eds. *Rational Man and Irrational Society*. Beverly Hills: Sage Publications 1982, 121-135.

Russell Hardin. *Collective Action*. Baltimore: Johns Hopkins Univ. Press 1982.

Russell Hardin. "Sanction and Obligation". *The Monist* 68 (1985): 403-418.

Howard H. Harriott. "Games, Anarchy, and the Nonnecessity of the State". In: Sanders & Narveson eds. 1996, 119-136.

Paul Harris ed. *On Political Obligation*. London: Routledge & Kegan Paul 1990.

R.F. Harrod. 1936. "Utilitarianism Revised". *Mind* 45 (1936): 137-156.

John Harsanyi. "Rule Utilitarianism and Decision Theory". *Erkenntnis* 11 (1977): 25-53.

J. Harsanyi & R. Selten. *A General Theory of Equilibrium Selection in Games*. Cambridge Mass.: MIT Press 1988.

H.L.A. Hart. "Are there any Natural Rights?". *Philosophical Review* 64 (1955): 175-191. Repr. in: David Lyons ed. *Rights*. Belmont Cal., Wadsworth 1979, 14-25.

H.L.A. Hart. "Legal and Moral Obligation". In: A.I. Melden ed. *Essays in Moral Philosophy*. Seattle: Univ. of Washington Press 1958: 82-107. Repr. in Flathman ed. 1973, 187-200.

H.L.A. Hart. "Positivism and the Separation of Law and Morals". *Harvard Law Review* 71 (1958): 593. Repr. in Hart 1983, 49-87.

H.L.A. Hart. *The Concept of Law*. Oxford: Clarendon 1961.

H.L.A. Hart. *Law, Liberty and Morality*. Stanford: Stanford Univ. Press 1963.

H.L.A. Hart. *Punishment and Responsibility*. Oxford: Oxford Univ. Press 1968.

H.L.A.Hart. *Essays on Bentham*. Oxford: Clarendon 1982.

H.L.A. Hart. *Essays in Jurisprudence and Philosophy*. Oxford: Clarendon 1983.

H.L.A.Hart. "Postscript". In: H.L.A. Hart. *The Concept of Law*, (Second Edition.) Oxford: Clarendon 1994, 238-276.

Govert den Hartogh. "Practical Inference and the Is/Ought Question". *Journal of Value Inquiry* 14 (1980): 129-147.

Govert den Hartogh. *Wederkerige Verwachtingen: Konventie, Norm, Verplichting*. Amsterdam 1985.

Govert den Hartogh. "Burgerschap en Ongehoorzaamheid". *Rechtsgeleerd Magazijn Themis* 151 (1989): 5-33.

Govert den Hartogh. "'Made by Contrivance, and the Consent of Men': Abstract Principle and Historical Fact in Locke's Political Philosophy". *Interpretation*, 17 (1990a): 193-221.

Govert den Hartogh. "Express Consent and Full Membership". *Political Studies* 38 (1990b): 105-115.

Govert den Hartogh. "Coherence as a Legal Virtue: A Conventionalist View". In: P.W. Brouwer e.o. eds. *Coherence and Conflict in Law: Proceedings of the 3rd Benelux-Scandinavian Symposium in Legal Theory*. Dordrecht: Kluwer/Tjeenk Willink 1992, 227-254.

Govert den Hartogh. "Authority and the Balance of Reasons". In: Robert Alexy & Ralf Dreier Hrsg. *Rechtssystem und Praktische Vernunft: Band I,Proceedings 15th World Congress IVR: ARSP-Beiheft* 51. Stuttgart: Franz Steiner Verlag 1993, 136-144.

Govert den Hartogh. "Rehabilitating Legal Conventionalism. A Critical Review of: Eerik Lagerspetz, *A Conventionalist Theory of Institutions*". *Law and Philosophy* 12 (1993): 233-247.

Govert den Hartogh. "The Rationality of Conditional Cooperation". *Erkenntnis* 38 (1993): 405-427.

Govert den Hartogh. "Recht op leven, Recht op de Dood: een Conflict van Plichten?" *Trema, Tijdschrift voor de Rechterlijke Macht*, 1995 nr. 6, 176-182.

Govert den Hartogh. "Soziale und kritische Moral, oder 'Wie sich 'Protestantismus' in der Moralphilosophie und der Moralerziehung vermeiden läszt.'" In: Karl Golser & Robert Heeger Hrsg. *Moralerziehung im Neuen Europa*. Brixen: Verlag A. Weger, 1996, 53-73.

Govert den Hartogh. "A Conventionalist Theory of Obligation". *Law and Philosophy* 17 (1998a): 351-376.

Govert den Hartogh. "The Slippery Slope Argument". In: Peter Singer & Helga Kuhse eds., *Companion to Bioethics*, Blackwell 1998b, 280-290.

Govert den Hartogh. "General and Particular Considerations in Applied Ethics". In: Albert W. Musschenga & Wim J. van der Steen eds. *Reasoning in Ethics and Law: Theory, Principle and Judgement*. Ashgate, Aldershot 1999a, 19-47.

Govert den Hartogh. "The Architectonic of Michael Walzer's Theory of Justice". *Political Theory* 27 (1999b): 491-522.

Govert den Hartogh. "Introduction". To: G.A. den Hartogh ed., *The Good Life as a Public Good*, Dordrecht: Kluwer 2000a, 1-28.

Govert den Hartogh. "Euthanasia: Reflections on the Dutch discussion" . In: Raphael Cohen-Almagor ed., *Medical Ethics at the Dawn of the 21st Century*, New York: Annals of the New York Academy of Sciences, 2000b,174-187.

Govert den Hartogh. "Humanitarian Intervention and the Self-Image of the State". In: Arend Soeteman ed. *Pluralism and Law: Proceedings19th World Congress IVR*. Forthcoming.

Govert den Hartogh. "Intending for Autonomous Reasons". Unpubl. (a).

Govert den Hartogh. "The Authority of Intentions". Unpubl. (b).

Govert den Hartogh. "Games People Play in the State of Nature". Unpubl. (c).

Friedrich A. Hayek. Law, Legislation, and Liberty, Vol. 1: Rules and Order. London: Routledge & Kegan Paul 1973.

Jane Heal. "Common Knowledge". *Philosophical Quarterly* 28 (1978): 116-131.

Anthony Heath. *Rational Choice and Social Exchange*. Cambridge: Cambridge Univ. Press 1976.

Nannerl O. Henry. "Political Obligation and Collective Goods". In: Pennock & Chapman eds. 1970, 263-289.

Don Herzog. *Happy Slaves: A Critique of Consent Theory*. Chicago: Univ. of Chicago Press 1989.

M. Hesselink et al. "Verandering van Omstandigheden en de Uitleg van Overeenkomsten: N.a.v. *Rebus Sic Stantibus* door P. Abas". *Ars Aequi* 39 (1990): 563.

Roscoe E. Hill. "Legal Validity and Legal Obligation". *Yale Law Journal* 80 (1970): 47-74.

Kenneth E. Himma. "Waluchow's Defence of Inclusive Positivism". *Legal Theory* 5 (1999): 101-116.

Fred Hirsch. *Social Limits to Growth.* Cambridge Mass: Harvard Univ. Press 1976.

Norbert Hoerster. "Kants Kategorischer Imperativ als Test unserer Sittlichen Pflichten". In: Manfred Riedel Hrsg.. *Rehabilitierung der Praktischen Philosophie: Vol. II.* Freiburg: Rombach 1974, 455-475.

Barry Hoffmaster. " Professor Hart on Legal Obligation". *Georgia Law Review* 11 (1977): 1303-1324.

Barry Hoffmaster. "Understanding Judicial Discretion". *Law and Philosophy* 1 (1982): 21-55.

Douglas R. Hofstadter. *Metamagical Themes: Questing for the Essence of Mind and Pattern.* New York: Basic Books 1985.

H.J. Hofstra. *Inleiding tot het Nederlands Belastingrecht.* Deventer: Kluwer 1986.

Martin Hollis. "Economic Man and Original Sin". *Political Studies* 29 (1981): 167-180.

Martin Hollis. *The Cunning of Reason.* Cambridge: Cambridge Univ. Press 1987.

Martin Hollis & Robert Sugden. "Rationality in Action". *Mind* 102 (1993): 1-36.

Richard Holton. "Positivism and the Internal Point of View". *Law and Philosophy* 17 (1998): 597-626.

Tony Honoré. *Making Law Bind: Essays Legal and Philosophical.* Oxford: Clarendon 1987.

Tony Honoré. "Must we Obey? Necessity as a Ground of Obligation". Virginia Law Review 67 (1981): 39-62. Rev. repr. ("Nécessité Oblige") in: Honoré 1987.

G.J.H. van Hoof. *Normvervaging en Rechtsbeginsel.* Zwolle: Tjeenk Willink 1987.

Sidney Hook ed.. *Law and Philosophy: a Symposium.* New York: New York Univ. Press 1964.

Brad Hooker. "Compromising with Convention". *American Philosophical Quarterly* 31 (1994): 311-317.

John Horton. *Political Obligation.* London:Macmillan 1992

Heidi Hurd. "Challenging Authority". *Yale Law Journal* 100 (1991): 1611-1677.

Frans Jacobs. *Ten Overstaan van Allen.* Amsterdam 1985.

Rudolf von Jhering. *Der Kampf um's Recht.* (1872) Berlin: Propyläen 1992.

Albert R. Jonsen & Stephen E. Toulmin. *The Abuse of Casuistry: A History of Moral Reasoning.* Berkeley: Univ. of California Press 1988.

M..Z. Kafoglis. *Welfare Economics and Subsidy Programs.* Gainesville Fl: Univ. of Florida Press 1962.

Daniel Kahneman, Jack L. Knetsch, R. Thaler. "Experimental Tests of the Endowment Effect and the Coase Theorem". *Journal of Political Economy* 98 (1990): 1325.

Ehud Kalai & R. Smorodinsky. "Other Solutions to Nash's Bargaining Problem". *Econometrica* 43 (1975): 513.

Immanuel Kant. *Kant's Handschriftlicher Nachlasz, Band VI: Moralphilosophie, Rechtsphilosophie und Religionsphilosophie.* In: *Kant's Gesammelte Schriften,* Hrsg. Von der Preussischen Akademie der Wissenschaften Band XIX. Berlin/Leipzig: Walter de Gruyter & Co 1984. (Erste Auflage 1934).

Gregory S. Kavka. "Rule by Fear". *Noûs* 17 (1983): 601.

Gregory S. Kavka. "Review" (of: Simmons 1979). *Topoi* 2 (1983): 227-230.

Gregory S. Kavka. "The Toxin Puzzle". *Analysis* 43 (1983): 33-36.

Gregory S.Kavka. *Hobbesian Moral and Political Theory.* Princeton: Princeton Univ. Press 1986.

Gregory Kavka. "Why Even Morally Perfect People Would Need Government". *Social Philosophy and Policy* 12 (1995): 1-18. Repr. in: Sanders & Narveson eds. 1996, 41-62.

Hans Kelsen. *Ueber Grenzen zwischen Juristischer und Soziologischer Methode.* Tübingen: Mohr 1911.

Anthony Kenny. *Action, Emotion and Will.* London: Routledge & Kegan Paul 1963.

Hartmut Kliemt. *Antagonistische Kooperation*. Freiburg: Karl Alber 1986.

George Klosko. "The Principle of Fairness and Political Obligation". *Ethics* 97 (1987): 353-362.

George Klosko. *The Principle of Fairness and Political Obligation*. Lanham MD: Rowman & Littlefield 1992.

George Klosko. "Political Obligation and the Natural Duties of Justice." *Philosophy and Public Affairs* 23 (1994): 251-270.

P.C. Kop. *Legisme en Privaatsrechtswetenschap*. Deventer: Kluwer 1982.

Matthew Kramer. "Requirements, Reasons, and Joseph Raz: Legal Positivism and Legal Duties". *Ethics* 109 (1999): 375-407.

Richard Kraut. *Socrates and the State*. Princeton: Princeton Univ. Press 1984.

David M. Kreps. *A Course in Micro-economic Theory*. Princeton: Princeton Univ. Press 1990.

D.M. Kreps & R. Wilson. "Rational Cooperation in Finitely Repeated Prisoner's Dilemma. *Journal of Economic Studies* 27 (1982), 245-282.

Martin Kriele. *Theorie der Rechtsgewinnung: Entwickkelt am Problem der Verfassungsinterpretation*. Berlin: Duncker & Humblott 1976.

Saul A. Kripke. *Wittgenstein on Rules and Private Languages: An Elementary Exposition*. Oxford: Blackwell 1982.

Peter Alekseevic Kropotkin. *Mutual Aid: A Factor of Evolution*. London: William Heinemann 1902.

Timur Kuran. Private Truths, Public Lies: The Social Consequences of Preference Falsification. Cambridge Mass: Harvard Univ. Press 1995.

Will Kymlicka *Liberalism, Community and Culture*. Oxford: Clarendon Press 1989.

Nicola Lacey. "Obligations, Sanctions, and Obedience". In: Neil MacCormick & Peter Birks. *The Legal Mind: Festschrift für Tony Honoré*. Oxford: Clarendon Press 1986, 219-234.

Robert F. Ladenson. "In Defense of a Hobbesian Conception of Law". *Philosophy and Public Affairs* 9 (1980): 134-159.

Eerik Lagerspetz. "Money as a Social Contract". *Theory and Decision* 17 (1984): 1-9.

Eerik Lagerspetz. *The Opposite Mirrors*. Dordrecht: Kluwer 1995.

Eerik Lagerspetz. "Ronald Dworkin on Communities and Obligation". *Ratio Juris* 12 (1999): 108-115.

Olli Lagerspetz. *Trust: The Tacit Demand*. Dordrecht: Kluwer 1998.

Michael Lessnoff. *Social Contract*. London: MacMillan 1986.

Michael Levin. "A Hobbesian Minimal State". *Philosophy and Public Affairs* 11 (1982): 338-353.

David K. Lewis. *Convention: A Philosophical Study*. Cambridge Mass.: Harvard Univ. Press 1969.

David K. Lewis. "Utilitarianism and Truthfulness". *Australasian Journal of Philosophy* 50 (1972): 17-19.

David K. Lewis. "Languages and Language". In: K. Gunderson ed.. *Minnesota Studies in the Philosophy of Science, Vol. VII: Language. Mind and Knowledge*. 1975, 3-35.

J. Leyten. "Sluip- en Dwaalwegen naar de Gerechtigheid". *Tijdschrift voor Privaatrecht* 26 (1989): 445-457.

K. Llewellyn. "Remarks on the Theory of Appellate Decisions and the Rules or Canons about how Statutes are to be Construed". *Vanderbilt Law Review* 3 (1950): 395.

Bjørn Lomborg. "Nucleus and Shield: The Evolution of Social Structure in the Iterated PD". *American Sociological Review* 61 (1996): 278-307.

J.R. Lucas. *The Principles of Politics*. Oxford: Clarendon 1966.

J.R. Lucas. "The Phenomenon of Law" . In: Hacker & Raz eds. 1977, 85-98.

R. Duncan Luce & Howard Raiffa. *Games and Decisions: Introduction and Critical Survey*. New York: John Wiley and Sons 1957.

David Lyons. *Forms and Limits of Utilitarianism*. Oxford: Clarendon 1965.

David Lyons. "Principles, Positivism and Legal Theory". *The Yale Law Journal* 87 (1977): 415-435.

David Lyons. "Need. Necessity. and Political Obligation". *Virginia Law Review* 67 (1981): 63-77.

David Lyons. *Ethics and the Rule of Law*. Cambridge: Cambridge Univ. Press 1984.

David Lyons. "Moral Aspects of Legal Theory". *Midwest Studies in Philosophy* 7 (1982): 223. Repr. in: Cohen 1984, 49-69.

David Lyons. "Derivability, Defensibility. and the Justification of Judicial Decisions". *The Monist* 68 (1985): 326-346.

David Lyons. "Soper's Moral Conception of Law" (Review of Soper 1984): *Ethics* 98 (1987): 158-165.

Neil MacCormick. "Voluntary Obligations and Normative Powers: Part I". *Aristotelian Society. Suppl. Vol.* 46 (1972): 59-78.

Neil MacCormick. *Legal Reasoning and Legal Theory*. Oxford: Clarendon 1978.

Neil MacCormick. *H.L.A. Hart*. London: Edward Arnold 1981.

Neil MacCormick. *Legal Right and Social Democracy: Essays in Legal and Political Philosophy*. Oxford: Clarendon 1982.

Neil MacCormick & Ota Weinberger. *An Institutional Theory of Law: New Approaches to Legal Positivism*. Dordrecht: Reidel 1986.

Neil MacCormick & Zenon Bankowski. "Some Principles of Statutory Interpretation". In: Robert S. Summers, Neil MacCormick, John Bell, Jan van Dunné eds. *Legal Reasoning and Statutory Interpretation*. Arnhem: Gouda Quint 1989, 41-79.

D. Neil MacCormick & Robert S. Summers eds. *Interpreting Statutes: A Comparative Study*. Dartmouth: Aldershot 1991.

D. Neil MacCormick & Robert S. Summers. "Interpretation and Justification". In: MacCormick & Summers 1991, 511-544.

D. Neil MacCormick & Robert S. Summers eds. *Interpreting Precedents. A Comparative Study*. Dartmouth: Aldershot 1996.

D. Neil MacCormick & Robert S. Summers. "Further General Reflections and Conclusions". In: MacCormick. &Summers 1996, 531-550.

Neil MacCormick. "Norms, Institutions, and Institutional Facts". *Law and Philosophy* 17 (1998): 301-345.

Margaret MacDonald. "The Language of Political Theory". In: A.G.N. Flew ed. *Logic and Language· First Series*. Oxford: Blackwell 1963.

Alasdair MacIntyre. *After Virtue: A Study in Moral Theory*. London: Duckworth 1981.

Alasdair MacIntyre. *Is Patriotism a Virtue?* The Lindley Lecture, University of Kansas 1984.

J.L. Mackie. *Ethics: Inventing Right and Wrong*. Harmondsworth: Penguin Books 1977a.

J.L. Mackie. "The Third Theory of Law". *Philosophy and Public Affairs* 7 (1977b): 3. Repr. in: Cohen ed. 1984, 161-170.

J.L. Mackie. "Obligations to Obey the Law". *Virginia Law Review* 67 (1981): 143-158.

Christopher MacMahon. "Autonomy and Authority". *Philosophy and Public Affairs* 16 (1987): 303-328.

Christopher MacMahon. "Promising and Coordination". *American Philosophical Quarterly* 26 (1989): 239-247.

Marco Mariotti. "The Decision-Theoretic Foundations of Game Theory". In: Kenneth J. Arrow, Enesco Colombatto, Mark Perlman, Christian Smith eds. *The Rational Foundations of Economic Behaviour*. Basingstoke: Macmillan 1996, 133-154.

Andrei Marmor. "On Convention". *Synthese* 107 (1996): 349-371.

Andrei Marmor. "Legal Conventionalism". *Legal Theory* 4 (1998): 509-531.

Geoffrey Marshall. "What is Binding in a Precedent?" In: MacCormick & Summers 1996, 503-518.

Edward F. McClennen. *Rationality and Dynamic Choice: Foundational Explorations.* Cambridge: Cambridge Univ. Press 1990.

Edward F. McClennen. "Pragmatic Rationality and Rules". *Philosophy and Public Affairs* 26 (1997): 210-258.

C.G. McClintock & W.B.G. Liebrand. "The Role of Interdependence Structure, Individual Value Orientation and Other's Strategy in Social Decision Making: A Transformational Analysis". *Journal of Personality and Social Psychology* 55 (1988): 396-409.

F.S. McNeilly. "The Enforceability of Law". *Noûs* 2 (1968): 247-264

Thomas McPherson. *Political Obligation.* London: Routledge & Kegan Paul 1967.

Judith Mehta, Chris Starmer, Robert Sugden. "Focal points in Pure Coordination Games: An Experimental Investigation". *Theory and Decision* 36 (1994): 163-185.

A.I. Melden. "Action". *Philosophical Review* 6 (1956): 529-541.

Michael A. Menlowe. "Political Obligation". In: Richard P. Bellamy ed. *Theories and Concepts of Politics.* Manchester: Manchester Univ. Press 1993, 174-196.

Paul T. Menzel. "Wolff's Critics: Confusing the Confusing". *Personalist* 57 (1976):

E.M. Meijers. "Judicia Rusticorum". *Themis Regtskundig Tijdschrift* 77 (1916): 187-226.

Stanley Milgram. *Obedience to Authority: An Experimental View.* New York: Harper and Row 1974

David Miller. *Anarchism.* London: Dent 1984.

Frank Miller & Rolf Sartorius. "Population Policy as Public Goods". *Philosophy and Public Affairs* (1979): 148-174.

Michael Moore. "A Natural Law Theory of Interpretation". *Southern California Law Review* 58 (1985), 277-398.

Michael Moore. "Authority, Law and Razian Reasons". *Southern California Law Review* 62 (1989): 827-912.

A.W.M. Mooij. *Psycho-analyse en Regels.* Meppel: Boom 1982.

Christopher W. Morris. "The Hart-Rawls Principle of Fairness Amended". *Journal of Social Philosophy* 15 (1983): 18-20.

Christopher W. Morris. "Well-Being, Reasons, and the Politics of Law". *Ethics* 106 (1996): 817-833

Christopher W. Morris. *An Essay on the Modern State.* Cambridge: Cambridge Univ. Press 1998.

Stephen Morris & Hyun Song Shin. "Approximate Common Knowledge and Co-ordination: Recent Lessons from Game Theory". *Journal of Logic, Language and Information* 6 (1997): 171-190.

P. Morton. *An Institutional Theory of Law.* Oxford: Clarendon 1998.

Ingo Müller, *Furchtbare Juristen, Die Unbewältigte Vergangenheit unserer Justiz.* Münich: Kindler Verlag 1987. Transl. by Deborah K. Schneider as *Hitler's Justice, The Courts of the Third Reich.* Cambridge Mass.: Harvard Univ. Press 1991.

Jeffrie G. Murphy. "In Defense of Obligation". In: Pennock & Chapman eds. 1970, 36-45.

Mark Murphy. "Acceptance of Authority and the Duty to Comply with Just Institutions: A Comment on Waldron". *Philosophy and Public Affairs* 23 (1994): 271-277.

Mark Murphy. "Philosophical Anarchism and Legal Indifference". *American Philosophical Quarterly* 32 (1995): 195-198.

A.W. Musschenga. *Noodzakelijkheid en Mogelijkheid van Moraal.* Assen: Van Gorcum 1980.

Albert W. Musschenga, Wim J. van der Steen eds. *Reasoning in Ethics and Law: The Role of Theory, Principles and Facts.* Aldershot: Ashgate 2000.

Thomas Nagel. *The Possibility of Altruism.* Oxford: Clarendon 1970.

Jan Narveson. "Utilitarianism, Group Actions, and Coordination". *Noûs* 10 (1976): 173-194.

J.F. Nash Jr. "Two-Person Cooperative Games". *Econometrica* 21 (1953): 128-140.

Onora Nell. *Acting on Principle : An Essay on Kantian Ethics.* New York: Columbia Univ. Press 1975.

John von Neumann & Oskar Morgenstern. *Theory of Games and Economic Behavior.* Princeton 1944, repr. New York: Wiley, 1967.

J.H. Nieuwenhuis. *Drie Beginselen van Contractenrecht.* Deventer: Kluwer 1979.

Robert Nozick. *Anarchy, State, and Utopia.* Oxford: Blackwell 1974.

Robert Nozick. "On Austrian Methodology". *Synthese* 36 (1977): 353-392. Repr. in: *Socratic Puzzles.* Cambridge Mass.: Harvard Univ. Press 1997, 110-141.

Martha C. Nussbaum. *Love's Knowledge: Essays on Philosophy and Literature.* New York: Oxford Univ. Press 1990.

Martha C. Nussbaum. "Human Functioning and Social Justice: In Defence of Aristotelian Essentialism". *Political Theory* 20 (1992): 202-246.

Michael Oakeshott. *On Human Conduct.* Oxford: Clarendon 1975.

Karl Olivecrona. *Law as Fact.* (Second Edition) London: Stevens 1971.

Mancur Olson Jr. *The Logic of Collective Action.* Cambridge Mass.: Harvard Univ. Press 1971. (Second ed. with Appendix; First ed. 1965.)

Helena M. Openshaw. *An Examination of H.L.A. Hart's Theory of Legal Obligation.* Ann Arbor: University Microfilms International 1986.

Martin J. Osborne & Ariel Rubinstein. *Bargaining and Markets.* San Diego: Academic Press 1990.

Walter Ott, Franziska Buob. "Did Legal Positivism Render German Jurists Defenceless During the Third Reich?" Typoscript 1993.

Bruce L. Ottley & Jean G. Zorn. "Criminal Law in Papua New Guinea: Code. Custom and the Courts in Conflict". *American Journal of Comparative Law* 31 (1983): 251-300.

Carole Pateman. *The Problem of Political Obligation.* Chichester: Wiley 1979.

Stanley Paulson. "The Weak Authority in Hans Kelsen's Pure Theory of Law". *Law and Philosophy* 19 (2000), 131-171.

Aleksander Peczenik. *On Law and Reason.* Dordrecht: Kluwer 1989.

J. Roland Pennock & John W. Chapman eds. *Political and Legal Obligation.* NOMOS Vol. XII. New York: Atherton Press 1970.

Stephen R. Perry. "Judicial Obligation, Precedent and the Common Law". *Oxford Journal of Legal Studies* 7 (1987).

Stephen R. Perry. "Second Order Reasons: Uncertainty and Legal Theory". *Southern California Law Review* 62 (1989): 913-994.

Philip Pettit. "Virtus Normativa: Rational Choice Perspectives". *Ethics* 100 (1990): 725-755.

Philip Pettit. *The Common Mind.* New York: Oxford Univ. Press 1993. (Reissue 1996.)

Philip Pettit. "The Cunning of Trust". *Philosophy and Public Affairs* 25 (1996): 202-225.

Hanna Pitkin. "Obligation and Consent, Part I". *American Political Science Review* 5 (1965): 990. Hanna Pitkin. "Obligation and Consent, Part II". *American Political Science Review* 6 (1966): 39. Repr. In Flathman ed. 1973, 201-219. Repr. Pitkin 1972b.

Hanna Pitkin. *Wittgenstein and Justice: On the Significance of Ludwig Wittgenstein for Social and Political Thought.* Berkeley: Univ. of California Press 1972 a.

Hanna Pitkin. "Obligation and Consent". In: Peter Laslett, W.G. Runciman, Quentin Skinner eds. *Philosophy, Politics and Society: Fourth Series*. Oxford: Blackwell 1972b.

John Plamenatz. *Man and Society*. London: Longman 1963.

J.P. Plamenatz. *Consent. Freedom. and Political Obligation* (Second ed. with Postscript, First ed. 1938) Oxford: Clarendon 1968.

Mark Platts. *Ways of Meaning*. London: Routledge & Kegan Paul 1979.

Gerald J. Postema. "Coordination and Convention at the Foundations of the Law". *Journal of Legal Studies* 11 (1982): 165-203.

Gerald J. Postema. *Bentham and the Common Law Tradition*. Oxford: Clarendon 1986.

Gerald J. Postema. "'Protestant' Interpretation and Social Practices". *Law and Philosophy* 6 (1987a): 283-320.

Gerald J. Postema. "Some Roots of our Notion of Precedent". In: Goldstein 1987b, 9-33.

Gerald J. Postema. "The Normativity of Law". In: Gavison ed. 1987c, 81-104.

Gerald J. Postema. "Collective Evils, Harms, and the Law". *Ethics* 97 (1987d): 414-440.

Gerald J. Postema. "Bentham on the Public Character of Law". *Utilitas* 1 (1989): 41-61.

Gerald J. Postema. "On the Moral Presence of Our Past". *McGill Law Journal* 36 (1991a): 1153-1180.

Gerald J. Postema. "Positivism, I Presume?... Comments on Schauer's 'Rules and the Rule of Law'". *Harvard Journal of Law and Public Policy* 14 (1991b): 797-822.

Gerald J. Postema. "Implicit Law". *Law and Philosophy* 13 (1994): 361-387.

Gerald J. Postema. "Morality in the First Person Plural". *Law and Philosophy* 14 (1995a): 35-64.

Gerald J. Postema. "Public Practical Reason: An Archeology". *Social Philosophy and Policy* 12 (1995b): 43-86.

Gerald J. Postema. "Law's Autonomy and Public Practical Reason". In: Robert P. George ed., *The Autonomy of Law, Essays on Legal Positivism*. Oxford: Clarendon 1996.

Gerald J. Postema. "Objectivity Fit for Law". In: Brian Leiter ed., Objectivity in Law and Morals. Cambridge: Cambridge Univ. Press 1997a.

Gerald J. Postema. "Integrity: Justice in Workclothes". *Iowa Law Review* 82 (1997b): 821-856.

H. Prakken. *Logical Tools for Modelling Legal Argument. A Study of Defeasible Reasoning in Law*. Dordrecht: Kluwer 1997.

H.A. Prichard. *Moral Obligation*. Oxford: Clarendon 1968.

Michael S. Pritchard. "Wolff's Anarchism". *Journal of Value Inquiry* 7 (1973): 296-302.

Anthony Quinton ed. *Political Philosophy*. Oxford: Oxford Univ. Press 1967.

Gustav Radbruch. "Gesetzliches Unrecht und übergesetzliches Recht". *Süddeutsche Juristenzeitung* 1 (1946): 105-108. Repr. in: Gustav Radbruch, *Rechtsphilosophie. Achte Auflage*. Stuttgart: Koehler Verlag 1973, 339-350.

D.D. Raphael. *Problems of Political Philosophy*. London: Pall Mall Press 1970. (Revised ed. 1976. London: Macmillan 1976.)

John Rawls. "Two Concepts of Rules". *Philosophical Review* 64 (1955): 3-32. Repr. in: Rawls 1999, ch. 2.

John Rawls. "Justice as Fairness". *Philosophical Review* 67 (1958): 164-194. Repr. in: Rawls 1999, ch. 3.

John Rawls. "Legal Obligation and the Duty of Fair Play". In: Hook ed. 1964, 3-18. Repr. in: Rawls 1999, ch. 6.

John Rawls. *A Theory of Justice*. Cambridge Mass: Harvard Univ. Press 1971.

John Rawls. *Collected Papers*. (Ed. Samuel Freeman). Cambridge Mass.: Harvard Univ. Press 1999.

Joseph Raz. "Normative Powers and Voluntary Obligations". *Proceedings Aristotelian Society, Suppl. Vol.* 46 (1972): 79-102.

Joseph Raz. *Practical Reason and Norms*. London: Hutchinson 1975.

Joseph Raz ed. *Practical Reasoning*. Oxford: Oxford Univ. Press 1978.

Joseph Raz. *The Authority of Law*. Oxford: Clarendon 1979.

Joseph Raz. *The Concept of a Legal System: An Introduction to the Theory of Legal System, Second ed.* Oxford: Clarendon 1980. (First ed. 1970.)

Joseph Raz. "The Morality of Obedience" (Review of Soper 1984). *Michigan Law Review* 83 (1984a): 732-749.

Joseph Raz. "The Obligation to Obey: Revision and Tradition" (Comment on Finnis 1984). *Journal of Law. Ethics and Public Policy* 1 (1984b): 139-155.

Joseph Raz. "Hart on Moral Rights and Legal Duties". *Oxford Journal of Legal Studies* 4 (1984c): 123-131.

Joseph Raz. "Legal Principles and the Limits of Law". (1972) In: Cohen ed. 1984d, 73-87.

Joseph Raz. "Introduction". To: Joseph Raz ed. Authority. Oxford: Blackwell 1984e.

Joseph Raz. "Authority, Law and Morality". *The Monist* 68 (1985): 295-324.

Joseph Raz. *The Morality of Freedom*. Oxford: Clarendon 1986.

Joseph Raz. "Facing Up: A Reply". *Southern California Law Review* 62 (1989): 1153.

Joseph Raz. *Practical Reason and Norms*. (Repr. Raz 1975 with a new Postscript) Princeton: Princeton Univ. Press 1990.

Joseph Raz. "Morality and Interpretation". *Ethics* 101 (1991): 392.

Joseph Raz. *Ethics in the Public Domain: Essays in the Morality of Law and Politics*. Oxford: Clarendon 1994.

Joseph Raz. "Why Interpret?" *Ratio Juris* 9 (1996a): 349-363.

Joseph Raz. "On the Nature of Law". *Archiv für Rechts- und Sozialphilosophie* 82 (1996b): 1-25.

Joseph Raz. "Explaining Normativity: On Rationality and the Justification of Reason". *Ratio* 12 (1999): 354-379. Repr. In: *Engaging Reason: On the Theory of Value and Action*. New York: Oxford Univ. Press 1999.

Donald H. Regan. *Utilitarianism and Cooperation*. Oxford: Clarendon 1980.

Donald Regan. "Law's Halo". *Social Philosophy and Policy* 4 (1986): 15-30.

Donald H. Regan. "Authority and Value: Reflections on Raz's Morality of Freedom". *Southern California Law Review* 62 (1989): 995-1095.

Jeffrey H. Reiman. *In Defense of Political Philosophy: a Reply to Robert Paul Wolff's 'In Defense of Anarchism'* . New York: Harper & Row 1972.

David A.J. Richards. *A Theory of Reasons for Actions*. Oxford: Clarendon 1971.

William H. Riker. "Political Trust as Rational Choice" . In: Leif Lewin & Evert Vedung eds. *Politics as Rational Action*. Dordrecht: Reidel 1980, 1-12.

William H. Riker & Peter C. Ordeshook. *An Introduction to Positive Political Theory*. Prentice Hall: Englewood Cliffs 1973.

Alan Ritter. *Anarchism: a Theoretical Analysis*. Cambridge: Cambridge Univ. Press 1980.

Christopher Roberson. "The State as Political Authority: An Anarchist Justification of Government". *Oxfgord Journal of Legal Studies* 18 (1998): 617-630.

Michael H. Robins. *Promising, Intending, and Moral Autonomy*. Cambridge: Cambridge Univ. Press 1984.

Michael H. Robins. "Is it Rational to Carry out Strategic Intentions?" *Philosophia* 25 (1996): 91-121.

U. Rosenthal. "Politieke Legitimiteit". In: Percy B. Lehning & M.P.C.M. van Schendelen eds. *Actualiteit van Politieke Filosofie*. Amsterdam: Intermediair 1981.

W.D. Ross *The Right and the Good*. Oxford: Clarendon Press 1930.

Alvin Roth ed. *Game-Theoretical Models of Bargaining*. Cambridge: Cambridge Univ. Press 1987.

M.N. Rothbard. *Power and Market: Government and the Economy*. Kansas City: Sheed Andrews & McMeel 1977.

H. Rottleuthner. "Substantieller Dezionismus. Zur Funktion der Rechtsphilosophie im Nationalsozialismus". In: H. Rottleuthner ed.. Recht, Rechtsphilosophie und Nationalsozialismus. *Archiv für Rechts- und Sozialphilosophie Beiheft* 18 (1983): 20.

E.A. van Rouveroy van Nieuwaal-Baerends & E.A.B. van Rouveroy van Nieuwaal. "Het Mogelijke en Onmogelijke in Verzoening bij de Anafóm in Noord-Togo". *Sociologische Gids* 28 (1981): 305-326.

Ariel Rubinstein. "Perfect Equilibrium in a Bargaining Model". *Econometrica* 50 (1982): 97-109.

Dick W.P. Ruiter . *Institutional Legal Facts: Legal Powers and their Effects*. Dordrecht: Kluwer 1993.

W.G. Runciman & Amartya K. Sen. "Games, Justice and the General Will". *Mind* 74 (1965): 554-562.

Bernd Rüthers. *Entartetes Recht. Rechtslehren und Kronjuristen im Dritten Reich*. (Zweite verbesserte Auflage) München: Beck 1989.

John Sabini &Maury Silver. *Moralities of Everyday Life*. Oxford: Oxford Univ. Press 1982.

John T. Sanders & Jan Narveson eds. *For and Against the State*. Lanham MD: Rowman and Littlefield 1996.

Rolf Sartorius. "The Concept of Law". *Archiv für Rechts- und Sozialphilosophie* 52 (1966): 161-193

Rolf Sartorius. "Social Policy and Judicial Legislation". *American Philosophical Quarterly* 8 (1971): 151-160.

Rolf Sartorius. "Political Authority and Political Obligation". *Virginia Law Review* 67 (1981): 3-25

Thomas M. Scanlon. "Promises and Practices". *Philosophy and Public Affairs* 19 (1990): 199-226.

Thomas M. Scanlon. "Value, Desire and Quality of Life". In: Martha C. Nussbaum and Amartya Sen eds. *The Quality of Life*. New York: Oxford Univ. Press 1993.

Frederick F. Schauer. *Playing by the Rules: A Philosophical Examination of Rule-Based Decision-making in Law and Life*. Oxford: Clarendon Press 1991.

Frederick Schauer. "Fuller's Internal Point of View". *Law and Philosophy* 13 (1994): 285-312.

Thomas C. Schelling. *The Strategy of Conflict*. Cambridge Mass: Harvard Univ. Press 1960. (Sixth Ed. 1979.)

Thmas C. Schelling. "Game Theory and the Study of Ethical Systems". *Journal of Conflict Resolution* 12 (1968): 34-44.

Stephen R. Schiffer. *Meaning*. Oxford: Clarendon 1972.

Paul Scholten. *Algemeen Deel*. (First ed. 1931). Third ed. Zwolle: Tjeenk Willink 1974.

H.C.F. Schoordijk. *Oordelen en Vooroordelen*. Deventer: Kluwer 1972.

H.C.F. Schoordijk. "Rebus Sic Stantibus: N.a.v. het Gelijknamige Boek van Prof. mr. P. Abas." *Weekblad voor Privaatrecht, Notariaat en Registratie* 120 (1989): 391-396, 413-417.

Andrew Schotter. *The Economic Theory of Social Institutions*. Cambridge: Cambridge Univ. Press 1981

John R. Searle. "How to Derive "Ought" from "Is"." *Philosophical Review* 73 (1964), 43-58.

John R. Searle. *Speech Acts: An Essay in the Philosophy of Language*. Cambridge: Cambridge Univ. Press 1969.

John R. Searle. *Intentionality: An Essay in the Philosophy of Mind*. New York: Cambridge Univ. Press 1983.

John R. Searle. "Collective Intentions and Actions". In: P. Cohen, J. Morgan, M.E. Pollack eds. *Intentions in Communication*. Cambridge Mass.: Bradford Books/MIT Press 1990.

John R. Searle. *The Construction of Social Reality*. London: Allen Lane 1995.

Amartya K. Sen. "Isolation, Assurance and the Social Rate of Discount". *Quarterly Journal of Economics* 81 (1967): 112-124.

Amartya K. Sen. "Behaviour and the Concept of Preferences". *Econometrica* 40 (1973): 241-259. Repr. in: Sen 1982, 54-73. = Sen 1973, 98, op p. 53?

Amartya K. Sen. "Choice, Orderings and Morality". In: Stephen Körner ed. *Practical Reason.* Oxford: Blackwell 1974, 54-67, with Reply to Comments, 78-82. Repr. in: Sen 1982, 74-83.

Amartya K. Sen. "Rational Fools". *Philosophy and Public Affairs* 6 (1977): 317-344. Repr. in: Sen 1982, 84-106.

Amartya K. Sen. *Choice, Welfare and Measurement.* Oxford: Blackwell 1982.

Amartya K. Sen. *On Ethics and Economics.* Oxford: Blackwell 1987.

Amartya K. Sen. "Foreword". In: Ben-Ner & Putterman eds., vii-xiii.

Thomas D. Senor. 1987. "What if there are no Political Obligations? A Reply to A.J. Simmons". *Philosophy and Public Affairs* 16 (1987): 260-268.

Scott J. Shapiro. "The Difference that Rules Make". In: Bix ed. 1998, 33-62.

George Sher. "Antecedentialism". *Ethics* 94 (1983), 6-17.

George Sher. *Desert.* Princeton: Princeton Univ. Press 1987.

Roger Shiner. *Norm and Nature: the Movements of Legal Thought.* Oxford, Clarendon 1992.

D.S. Shwayder. *The Stratification of Behaviour.* New York: Routledge and Kegan Paul 1965.

F.A. Siegler. "Hart on Rules of Obligation". *Australasian Journal of Philosophy* 45 (1967): 341-355.

A. John Simmons. *Moral Principles and Political Obligations.* Princeton: Princeton Univ. Press 1979.

A. John Simmons. "Consent, Free Choice, and Democratic Government". *Georgia Law Review* 18 (1984): 290.

A.John Simmons. "The Principle of Fair Play". In: Robert M. Stewart ed. *Readings in Social and Political Philosophy.* Oxford: Oxford Univ. Press 1986.

A. John Simmons. "The Anarchist Position: A Reply to Klosko and Senor". *Philosophy and Public Affairs* 16 (1987): 269-279.

A. John Simmons. *On the Edge of Anarchy: Locke, Consent, and the Limits of Society.* Princeton: Princeton Univ. Press 1993.

A. John Simmons. "Associative Political Obligations". *Ethics* 106 (1996a), 247-273.

A. John Simmons. "External Justifications and Institutional Roles". *Journal of Philosophy* 93 (1996b), 28-36. =1996b?

A. John Simmons. "Philosophical Anarchism" In: Sanders & Narveson eds. 1996c, 19-40.

A.John Simmons. "'Denisons' and 'Aliens': Locke's Problem of Political Consent. *Social Theory and Practice* 24 (1998): 161-182.

Peter Singer. *Democracy and Disobedience.* Oxford: Clarendon 1973.

Brian Skyrms. *The Dynamics of Rational Deliberation.* Cambridge Mass.: Harvard Univ. Press 1990.

Brian Skyrms. *Evolution and the Social Contract.* Cambridge: Cambridge Univ. Press 1996.

M.B.E. Smith. "Is there a Prima Facie Obligation to Obey the Law ?". *Yale Law Journal* 82 (1973): 950-976. Repr. in: Wasserstrom ed. 1975, 384-409.

John Maynard Smith. *Evolution and the Theory of Games.* Cambridge: Cambridge Univ. Press 1982.

Elliott Sober & David Sloan Wilson. *Unto Others: Th Evolution and Psyhcology of Unselfish Behavior.* Cambridge Mass: Harvard Univ. Press 1998.

A. Soeteman. *Machtig Recht.* Alphen a.d. Rijn: Samsom/Tjeenk Willink 1986.

Philip Soper. "Legal Theory and the Obligation of a Judge: The Hart/Dworkin Dispute". *Michigan Law Review* 75 (1977): Repr. in: Cohen ed. 1984, 3-27.

Philip Soper. *A Theory of Law.* Cambridge Mass.: Harvard Univ. Press 1984.

Philip Soper. "Legal Theory and the Claim of Authority". *Philosophy and Public Affairs* 18 (1989): 209-237.

D. Sperber & D. Wilson. *Relevance: Communication and Cognition.* Oxford: Blackwell 1986.

H.P. Stein. *The Fiber and the Fabric: An Inquiry into Wittgenstein's Views on Rule-Following and Linguistic Normativity.* Amsterdam: ILLC Diss. Series 1997.

Michael Stokes. "Formalism, Realism, and the Concept of Law". *Law and Philosophy* 13 (1994): 115-159.

Peter F. Strawson. "Social Morality and Individual Ideal". *Philosophy* 36 (1961): 1-17. Repr. in: Peter F. Strawson. *Freedom and Resentment.* London: Methuen 1974.

B. Strümpel. "The Contribution of Survey Research to Public Finance". In: A.T. Peacock ed., *Quantitative Analysis in Public Finance.* New York: Praeger 1969.

Robert Sugden. "Reciprocity: The Supply of Public Goods through Voluntary Contributions". *Economic Journal* 94 (1984): 772-787.

Robert Sugden. *The Economics of Rights, Co-operation and Welfare.* Oxford: Blackwell 1986.

Robert Sugden. "Spontaneous Order". *Journal of Economic Perspectives* 3 (1989), 85-97.

Robert Sugden. "Contractarianism and Norms". *Ethics* 100 (1990): 768-786.

Robert Sugden. "Rational Choice: A Survey of Contributions from Economics and Philosophy". *Economic Journal* 101 (1991): 751-785.

Robert Sugden. "Thinking as a Team: Towards an Explanation of Nonselfish Behavior". *Social Philosophy and Policy* 10 (1993): 69-89.

Robert Sugden. "Normative Expectations: The Simultaneous Evolution of Institutions and Norms". In: Ben-Ner & Putterman eds. 1998, 73-100.

Robert S. Summers. "Statutory Interpretation in the United States". In: MacCormick & Summers 1991, 407-459.

Cass R. Sunstein. "Norms in Surprising Places: The Case of Statutory Interpretation". *Ethics* 100 (1990): 803-820.

Yael Tamir. *Liberal Nationalism.* Princeton: Princeton Univ. Press 1993.

Charles Taylor. "Cross-Purposes: The Liberal-Communitarian Debate. In: Nancy L. Rosenblum ed. *Liberalism and the Moral Life.* Cambridge Mass.: Harvard Univ. Press 1989, 159-182.

Michael Taylor. *Community, Anarchy and Liberty.* Cambridge: Cambridge Univ. Press 1982.

Michael Taylor & Hugh Ward. "Chickens, Whales, and Lumpy Goods: Alternative Models of Pulbic-Goods Provision". *Political Studies* 30 (1982): 350-370.

Michael Taylor. *The Possibility of Cooperation.* Cambridge: Cambridge Univ. Press 1987

C.L. Ten. "The Soundest Theory of Law". *Mind* 88 (1979): 522-537.

Henry David Thoreau. *Civil Disobedience.* Boston Mass.: Tichnor and Fields 1849. Repr. (*Walden and Civil Disobedience*) Harmondsworth: Penguin Books 1983.

Michel Troper, Christophe Grzegorczyk & Jean-Louis Gardies. "Statutory Interpretation in France". In: MacCormick & Summers 1991, 171-211.

Ernst Tugendhat. *Vorlesungen zur Einführung in die Sprachanalytische Philosophie.* Frankfurt a.M.: Suhrkamp 1976.

Raimo Tuomela. *A Theory of Social Action.* Dordrecht: Reidel 1984.

Joseph Tussman. *Obligation and the Body Politic.* Oxford: Clarendon 1960.

Tom R. Tyler. *Why People Obey the Law.* New Haven: Yale Univ. Press 1990.

Edna Ullmann-Margalit. *The Emergence of Norms.* Oxford: Clarendon 1977.

Edna Ullmann-Margalit. "Is Law a Co-ordinative Authority ?" *Israel Law Review* 16 (1981): 350-351.

Ruurd Veldhuis. 1983. "Liberalisme, Anarchisme en het Probleem van de Politieke Verplichting." *Filosofie en Praktijk* 4 (1983): 3-19.

F. Veltman. "Redelijkheid in het Redeneren". In: H. Parret ed., *In Alle Redelijkheid.* Meppel/Amsterdam: Boom 1989, 203-215.

Frank Veltman. "Defaults in Update Semantics". *Journal of Philosophical Logic* 25 (1996): 221-261.

Bruno Verbeek. *The Virtues of Cooperation.* Amsterdam 1998.

C. van Vollenhoven. *Het Adatrecht van Nederlandsch-Indië.* (Eerste Deel) Leiden: Brill 1918.

Frans de Waal. *Good Natured: The Origins of Right and Wrong in Humans and Other Animals.* Cambridge Mass.: Harvard Univ. Press 1996.

Jeremy Waldron. "Special Ties and Natural Duties". *Philosophy and Public Affairs* 22 (1993): 3-30.

Jeremy Waldron. "Kant's Legal Positivism". *Harvard Law Review* 109 (1996a): 1535-1566.

Jeremy Waldron. "Legislation, Authority and Voting". *Georgetown Law Journal* 84 (1996b), 2185-2214.

Jeremy Waldron. "All We Like Sheep". *Canadian Journal of Law and Jurisprudence* 12 (1999): 169-186.

A.D.M. Walker. "Political Obligation and the Argument from Gratitude". *Philosophy and Public Affairs* 17 (1988): 191-211.

W.J. Waluchow. *Inclusive Legal Positivism.* Oxford: Clarendon 1994.

Michael Walzer. *Obligations: Essays on Disobedience. War. and Citizenship.* Cambridge Mass.: Harvard Univ. Press 1970.

Michael Walzer. *Just and Unjust Wars: A Moral Argument with Historical Illustrations.* (1977) Harmonsworth: Penguin Books 1980.

Michael Walzer. *Spheres of Justice.* Oxford: Robertson 1983.

G.J. Warnock. *The Object of Morality.* London: Methuen 1971.

Richard Wasserstrom. "Of Disobeying the Law". *Journal of Philosophy* 58 (1963): 641-652.

Richard Wasserstrom. "The Obligation to Obey the Law". *UCLA Law Review* 10 (1963): 780-807. Repr. in: Flathman ed. 1973, 230-251; Wasserstrom 1975, 358-384.

Richard Wasserstrom ed. *Today's Moral Problems.* New York: Macmillan 1975.

Albert Weale. "Consent". *Political Studies* 26 (1978): 65.

Christopher Wellman. "Liberalism, Samaritanism, and Political Legitimacy". *Philosophy and Public Affairs* 25 (1996): 211-237.

Christopher Wellman. "Associative Allegiances and Political Obligations". *Social Theory and Practice* 23 (1997), 181-204.

Pauline Westerman. *The Disintegration of Natural Law Theory: Aquinas to Finnis.* Leiden: Brill 1998.

Stuart White. "Liberal Equality, Exploitation, and the Case for an Unconditional Basic Income". *Poltical Studies* 45 (1997): 312-325.

G.J. Wiarda. *Drie Typen van Rechtsvinding.* (Third ed.).Zwolle: Tjeenk Willink 1988.

Theo van Willigenburg. "Guidance by Moral Rules, Guidance by Moral Precedents". In: Musschenga & Van der Steen eds. 1999, 49-62.

Peter Winch. *The Idea of a Social Science and its Relation to Philosophy.* London: Routledge and Kegan Paul 1958.

Peter Winch. "Authority". *Proceedings of the Aristetolian Society. Suppl. Vol.* 32 (1958b): 224-240. Repr. in Quinton 1967, 97-111.

E.R. Winkler. "From Kantianism to Contextualism: The Rise and Fall of the Paradigm Theory in Bioethics". In: E.R. Winkler, J.R. Coombs eds., *Applied Ethics: A Reader.* Oxford: Blackwell 1993, 366-389.

John Wisdom. *Philosophy and Psycho-analysis.* (1953) Oxford: Blackwell 1964.

Jonathan Wolff . "What is the Problem of Political Obligation?" *Proceedings of the Aristotelian Society Suppl. Vol.* 91 (1991): 153-169.

Jonathan Wolff. "Political Obligation, Fairness and Independence". *Ratio* 8 (1995), 87-99.

Robert Paul Wolff. "On Violence". *Journal of Philosophy* 66 (1969): 601-616.

Robert Paul Wolff. *In Defense of Anarchism.* New York: Harper & Row 1970.

Robert Paul Wolff. *In Defense of Anarchism*: (Second. Ed. with a Reply to Reiman) New York: Harper & Row 1976.

A.D. Woozley. *Law and Obedience: the Arguments of Plato's Crito.* London: Duckworth 1979.

Dennis Wrong. *Power: its Forms. Bases. and Uses.* New York: Harper & Row 1979.

Dieter Wunderlich . *Studien zur Sprechakttheorie.* Frankfurt am Main: Suhrkamp 1978.

H. Peyton Young. "The Economics of Convention". *Journal of Economic Perspectives* 10 (1996): 105-122.

Zetten. Frans van. "What's Wrong with Social Norms? An Alternative to Elster's Theory". *Canadian Journal of Philosophy* 27 (1997): 339-360.

# INDEX OF AUTHORS

# INDEX OF CONCEPTS

# Law and Philosophy Library

1.  E. Bulygin, J.-L. Gardies and I. Niiniluoto (eds.): *Man, Law and Modern Forms of Life*. With an Introduction by M.D. Bayles. 1985                     ISBN 90-277-1869-5

2.  W. Sadurski: *Giving Desert Its Due*. Social Justice and Legal Theory. 1985
                                                                                ISBN 90-277-1941-1

3.  N. MacCormick and O. Weinberger: *An Institutional Theory of Law*. New Approaches to Legal Positivism. 1986                                                ISBN 90-277-2079-7

4.  A. Aarnio: *The Rational as Reasonable*. A Treatise on Legal Justification. 1987
                                                                                ISBN 90-277-2276-5

5.  M.D. Bayles: *Principles of Law*. A Normative Analysis. 1987
                                                          ISBN 90-277-2412-1; Pb: 90-277-2413-X

6.  A. Soeteman: *Logic in Law*. Remarks on Logic and Rationality in Normative Reasoning, Especially in Law. 1989                                             ISBN 0-7923-0042-4

7.  C.T. Sistare: *Responsibility and Criminal Liability*. 1989              ISBN 0-7923-0396-2

8.  A. Peczenik: *On Law and Reason*. 1989                                   ISBN 0-7923-0444-6

9.  W. Sadurski: *Moral Pluralism and Legal Neutrality*. 1990               ISBN 0-7923-0565-5

10. M.D. Bayles: *Procedural Justice*. Allocating to Individuals. 1990      ISBN 0-7923-0567-1

11. P. Nerhot (ed.): *Law, Interpretation and Reality*. Essays in Epistemology, Hermeneutics and Jurisprudence. 1990                                           ISBN 0-7923-0593-0

12. A.W. Norrie: *Law, Ideology and Punishment*. Retrieval and Critique of the Liberal Ideal of Criminal Justice. 1991                                         ISBN 0-7923-1013-6

13. P. Nerhot (ed.): *Legal Knowledge and Analogy*. Fragments of Legal Epistemology, Hermeneutics and Linguistics. 1991                                      ISBN 0-7923-1065-9

14. O. Weinberger: *Law, Institution and Legal Politics*. Fundamental Problems of Legal Theory and Social Philosophy. 1991                                       ISBN 0-7923-1143-4

15. J. Wróblewski: *The Judicial Application of Law*. Edited by Z. Bańkowski and N. MacCormick. 1992                                                          ISBN 0-7923-1569-3

16. T. Wilhelmsson: *Critical Studies in Private Law*. A Treatise on Need-Rational Principles in Modern Law. 1992                                             ISBN 0-7923-1659-2

17. M.D. Bayles: *Hart's Legal Philosophy*. An Examination. 1992            ISBN 0-7923-1981-8

18. D.W.P. Ruiter: *Institutional Legal Facts*. Legal Powers and their Effects. 1993
                                                                                ISBN 0-7923-2441-2

19. J. Schonsheck: *On Criminalization*. An Essay in the Philosophy of the Criminal Law. 1994
                                                                                ISBN 0-7923-2663-6

20. R.P. Malloy and J. Evensky (eds.): *Adam Smith and the Philosophy of Law and Economics*. 1994                                                             ISBN 0-7923-2796-9

21. Z. Bańkowski, I. White and U. Hahn (eds.): *Informatics and the Foundations of Legal Reasoning*. 1995                                                     ISBN 0-7923-3455-8

# Law and Philosophy Library

22. E. Lagerspetz: *The Opposite Mirrors*. An Essay on the Conventionalist Theory of Institutions. 1995                                    ISBN 0-7923-3325-X

23. M. van Hees: *Rights and Decisions*. Formal Models of Law and Liberalism. 1995
ISBN 0-7923-3754-9

24. B. Anderson: *"Discovery" in Legal Decision-Making*. 1996       ISBN 0-7923-3981-9

25. S. Urbina: *Reason, Democracy, Society*. A Study on the Basis of Legal Thinking. 1996
ISBN 0-7923-4262-3

26. E. Attwooll: *The Tapestry of the Law*. Scotland, Legal Culture and Legal Theory. 1997
ISBN 0-7923-4310-7

27. J.C. Hage: *Reasoning with Rules*. An Essay on Legal Reasoning and Its Underlying Logic. 1997                                    ISBN 0-7923-4325-5

28. R.A. Hillman: *The Richness of Contract Law*. An Analysis and Critique of Contemporary Theories of Contract Law. 1997       ISBN 0-7923-4336-0; 0-7923-5063-4 (Pb)

29. C. Wellman: *An Approach to Rights*. Studies in the Philosophy of Law and Morals. 1997
ISBN 0-7923-4467-7

30. B. van Roermund: *Law, Narrative and Reality*. An Essay in Intercepting Politics. 1997
ISBN 0-7923-4621-1

31. I. Ward: *Kantianism, Postmodernism and Critical Legal Thought*. 1997
ISBN 0-7923-4745-5

32. H. Prakken: *Logical Tools for Modelling Legal Argument*. A Study of Defeasible Reasoning in Law. 1997                                    ISBN 0-7923-4776-5

33. T. May: *Autonomy, Authority and Moral Responsibility*. 1998       ISBN 0-7923-4851-6

34. M. Atienza and J.R. Manero: *A Theory of Legal Sentences*. 1998       ISBN 0-7923-4856-7

35. E.A. Christodoulidis: *Law and Reflexive Politics*. 1998       ISBN 0-7923-4954-7

36. L.M.M. Royakkers: *Extending Deontic Logic for the Formalisation of Legal Rules*. 1998
ISBN 0-7923-4982-2

37. J.J. Moreso: *Legal Indeterminacy and Constitutional Interpretation*. 1998
ISBN 0-7923-5156-8

38. W. Sadurski: *Freedom of Speech and Its Limits*. 1999       ISBN 0-7923-5523-7

39. J. Wolenski (ed.): *Kazimierz Opalek Selected Papers in Legal Philosophy*. 1999
ISBN 0-7923-5732-9

40. H.P. Visser 't Hooft: *Justice to Future Generations and the Environment*. 1999
ISBN 0-7923-5756-6

41. L.J. Wintgens (ed.): *The Law in Philosophical Perspectives*. My Philosophy of Law. 1999
ISBN 0-7923-5796-5

42. A.R. Lodder: *DiaLaw*. On Legal Justification and Dialogical Models of Argumentation. 1999
ISBN 0-7923-5830-9

43. C. Redondo: *Reasons for Action and the Law*. 1999       ISBN 0-7923-5912-7

# Law and Philosophy Library

---

*Volumes 1–55 were published by Kluwer Academic Publishers.*

---